50% OFF Online GED Prep C

Dear Customer,

We consider it an honor and a privilege that you chose our GED Study Guide. As a way of showing our appreciation and to help us better serve you, we have partnered with Mometrix Test Preparation to offer **50% off their online GED Prep Course.** Many GED courses are needlessly expensive and don't deliver enough value. With their course, you get access to the best GED prep material, and **you only pay half price**.

Mometrix has structured their online course to perfectly complement your printed study guide. The GED Prep Course contains **in-depth lessons** that cover all the most important topics, **330+ video reviews** that explain difficult concepts, **over 1,250 practice questions** to ensure you feel prepared, and **300+ digital flashcards**, so you can fit some studying in while you're on the go.

Online GED Prep Course

Topics Covered:

- Reasoning Through Language Arts
  - Reading for Meaning
  - Identifying and Creating Arguments
  - Agreement and Sentence Structure
- Mathematical Reasoning
  - Geometry
  - Statistics and Probability
  - Algebra
- Science
  - Designing and Interpreting Science Experiments
  - Using Numbers and Graphics in Science
  - Science Knowledge Overview
- Social Studies
  - Analyzing Historical Events and Arguments in Social Studies
  - Social Studies Knowledge Overview

Course Features:

- GED Study Guide
  - Get content that complements our best-selling study guide.
- 6 Full-Length Practice Tests
  - With over 1,250 practice questions, you can test yourself again and again.
- Mobile Friendly
  - If you need to study on-the-go, the course is easily accessible from your mobile device.
- GED Flashcards
  - The course includes a flashcard mode consisting of over 300 content cards to help you study.

To receive this discount, simply head to their website: mometrix.com/university/ged or simply scan this QR code with your smartphone. At the checkout page, enter the discount code: **TPBGED50**

If you have any questions or concerns, please contact Mometrix at support@mometrix.com.

Sincerely,

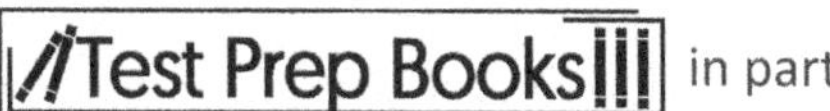

in partnership with Mometrix TEST PREPARATION

FREE Test Taking Tips DVD Offer

To help us better serve you, we have developed a Test Taking Tips DVD that we would like to give you for FREE. **This DVD covers world-class test taking tips that you can use to be even more successful when you are taking your test.**

All that we ask is that you email us your feedback about your study guide. Please let us know what you thought about it – whether that is good, bad or indifferent.

To get your **FREE Test Taking Tips DVD**, email freedvd@studyguideteam.com with "FREE DVD" in the subject line and the following information in the body of the email:

a. The title of your study guide.

b. Your product rating on a scale of 1-5, with 5 being the highest rating.

c. Your feedback about the study guide. What did you think of it?

d. Your full name and shipping address to send your free DVD.

If you have any questions or concerns, please don't hesitate to contact us at freedvd@studyguideteam.com.

Thanks again!

GED Test Prep Study Guide 2023-2024

3 Practice Exams and GED Book for All Subjects [8th Edition]

Joshua Rueda

Written and edited by TPB Publishing.

ISBN 13: 9781637758182
ISBN 10: 1637758189

Table of Contents

Welcome ... *1*

FREE Videos/DVD OFFER ... 1

Quick Overview ... *1*

Test-Taking Strategies ... *2*

Bonus Content ... *6*

Introduction to the GED Exam ... *7*

Study Prep Plan for the GED Exam ... *10*

Math Reference Sheet ... *12*

Mathematical Reasoning ... *13*

Basic Math ... 13

Geometry ... 54

Basic Algebra ... 80

Graphs and Functions ... 106

Practice Quiz ... 124

Answer Explanations ... 125

Reasoning Through Language Arts ... *126*

Reading for Meaning ... 126

Identifying and Creating Arguments ... 141

Grammar and Language ... 152

Practice Quiz ... 171

Answer Explanations ... 173

Science ... *175*

Reading for Meaning in Science ... 175

Designing and Interpreting Science Experiments 182
Using Numbers and Graphics in Science 194
GED Science Questions 206
Practice Quiz 209
Answer Explanations 213
Social Studies 214
Reading for Meaning in Social Studies 214
Analyzing Historical Events and Arguments 229
Using Numbers and Graphics in Social Studies 234
Practice Quiz 239
Answer Explanations 241
GED Practice Test #1 243
Reading Comprehension 243
Extended Response 257
Mathematical Reasoning 258
Science 267
Social Studies 290
Answer Explanations for Practice Test #1 310
Reading Comprehension 310
Mathematical Reasoning 316
Science 324
Social Studies 328
GED Practice Tests #2 & #3 335
Index 336

Welcome

Dear Reader,

Welcome to your new Test Prep Books study guide! We are pleased that you chose us to help you prepare for your exam. There are many study options to choose from, and we appreciate you choosing us. Studying can be a daunting task, but we have designed a smart, effective study guide to help prepare you for what lies ahead.

Whether you're a parent helping your child learn and grow, a high school student working hard to get into your dream college, or a nursing student studying for a complex exam, we want to help give you the tools you need to succeed. We hope this study guide gives you the skills and the confidence to thrive, and we can't thank you enough for allowing us to be part of your journey.

In an effort to continue to improve our products, we welcome feedback from our customers. We look forward to hearing from you. Suggestions, success stories, and criticisms can all be communicated by emailing us at info@studyguideteam.com.

Sincerely,
Test Prep Books Team

FREE Videos/DVD OFFER

Doing well on your exam requires both knowing the test content and understanding how to use that knowledge to do well on the test. We offer completely FREE test taking tip videos. **These videos cover world-class tips that you can use to succeed on your test.**

To get your **FREE videos**, you can use the QR code below or email freevideos@studyguideteam.com with "Free Videos" in the subject line and the following information in the body of the email:

a. The title of your product
b. Your product rating on a scale of 1-5, with 5 being the highest
c. Your feedback about the product

If you have any questions or concerns, please don't hesitate to contact us at info@studyguideteam.com.

Quick Overview

As you draw closer to taking your exam, effective preparation becomes more and more important. Thankfully, you have this study guide to help you get ready. Use this guide to help keep your studying on track and refer to it often.

This study guide contains several key sections that will help you be successful on your exam. The guide contains tips for what you should do the night before and the day of the test. Also included are test-taking tips. Knowing the right information is not always enough. Many well-prepared test takers struggle with exams. These tips will help equip you to accurately read, assess, and answer test questions.

A large part of the guide is devoted to showing you what content to expect on the exam and to helping you better understand that content. In this guide are practice test questions so that you can see how well you have grasped the content. Then, answer explanations are provided so that you can understand why you missed certain questions.

Don't try to cram the night before you take your exam. This is not a wise strategy for a few reasons. First, your retention of the information will be low. Your time would be better used by reviewing information you already know rather than trying to learn a lot of new information. Second, you will likely become stressed as you try to gain a large amount of knowledge in a short amount of time. Third, you will be depriving yourself of sleep. So be sure to go to bed at a reasonable time the night before. Being well-rested helps you focus and remain calm.

Be sure to eat a substantial breakfast the morning of the exam. If you are taking the exam in the afternoon, be sure to have a good lunch as well. Being hungry is distracting and can make it difficult to focus. You have hopefully spent lots of time preparing for the exam. Don't let an empty stomach get in the way of success!

When travelling to the testing center, leave earlier than needed. That way, you have a buffer in case you experience any delays. This will help you remain calm and will keep you from missing your appointment time at the testing center.

Be sure to pace yourself during the exam. Don't try to rush through the exam. There is no need to risk performing poorly on the exam just so you can leave the testing center early. Allow yourself to use all of the allotted time if needed.

Remain positive while taking the exam even if you feel like you are performing poorly. Thinking about the content you should have mastered will not help you perform better on the exam.

Once the exam is complete, take some time to relax. Even if you feel that you need to take the exam again, you will be well served by some down time before you begin studying again. It's often easier to convince yourself to study if you know that it will come with a reward!

Test-Taking Strategies

1. Predicting the Answer

When you feel confident in your preparation for a multiple-choice test, try predicting the answer before reading the answer choices. This is especially useful on questions that test objective factual knowledge. By predicting the answer before reading the available choices, you eliminate the possibility that you will be distracted or led astray by an incorrect answer choice. You will feel more confident in your selection if you read the question, predict the answer, and then find your prediction among the answer choices. After using this strategy, be sure to still read all of the answer choices carefully and completely. If you feel unprepared, you should not attempt to predict the answers. This would be a waste of time and an opportunity for your mind to wander in the wrong direction.

2. Reading the Whole Question

Too often, test takers scan a multiple-choice question, recognize a few familiar words, and immediately jump to the answer choices. Test authors are aware of this common impatience, and they will sometimes prey upon it. For instance, a test author might subtly turn the question into a negative, or he or she might redirect the focus of the question right at the end. The only way to avoid falling into these traps is to read the entirety of the question carefully before reading the answer choices.

3. Looking for Wrong Answers

Long and complicated multiple-choice questions can be intimidating. One way to simplify a difficult multiple-choice question is to eliminate all of the answer choices that are clearly wrong. In most sets of answers, there will be at least one selection that can be dismissed right away. If the test is administered on paper, the test taker could draw a line through it to indicate that it may be ignored; otherwise, the test taker will have to perform this operation mentally or on scratch paper. In either case, once the obviously incorrect answers have been eliminated, the remaining choices may be considered. Sometimes identifying the clearly wrong answers will give the test taker some information about the correct answer. For instance, if one of the remaining answer choices is a direct opposite of one of the eliminated answer choices, it may well be the correct answer. The opposite of obviously wrong is obviously right! Of course, this is not always the case. Some answers are obviously incorrect simply because they are irrelevant to the question being asked. Still, identifying and eliminating some incorrect answer choices is a good way to simplify a multiple-choice question.

4. Don't Overanalyze

Anxious test takers often overanalyze questions. When you are nervous, your brain will often run wild, causing you to make associations and discover clues that don't actually exist. If you feel that this may be a problem for you, do whatever you can to slow down during the test. Try taking a deep breath or counting to ten. As you read and consider the question, restrict yourself to the particular words used by the author. Avoid thought tangents about what the author *really* meant, or what he or she was *trying* to say. The only things that matter on a multiple-choice test are the words that are actually in the question. You must avoid reading too much into a multiple-choice question, or supposing that the writer meant something other than what he or she wrote.

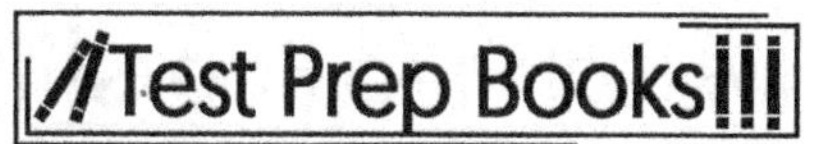

5. No Need for Panic

It is wise to learn as many strategies as possible before taking a multiple-choice test, but it is likely that you will come across a few questions for which you simply don't know the answer. In this situation, avoid panicking. Because most multiple-choice tests include dozens of questions, the relative value of a single wrong answer is small. As much as possible, you should compartmentalize each question on a multiple-choice test. In other words, you should not allow your feelings about one question to affect your success on the others. When you find a question that you either don't understand or don't know how to answer, just take a deep breath and do your best. Read the entire question slowly and carefully. Try rephrasing the question a couple of different ways. Then, read all of the answer choices carefully. After eliminating obviously wrong answers, make a selection and move on to the next question.

6. Confusing Answer Choices

When working on a difficult multiple-choice question, there may be a tendency to focus on the answer choices that are the easiest to understand. Many people, whether consciously or not, gravitate to the answer choices that require the least concentration, knowledge, and memory. This is a mistake. When you come across an answer choice that is confusing, you should give it extra attention. A question might be confusing because you do not know the subject matter to which it refers. If this is the case, don't eliminate the answer before you have affirmatively settled on another. When you come across an answer choice of this type, set it aside as you look at the remaining choices. If you can confidently assert that one of the other choices is correct, you can leave the confusing answer aside. Otherwise, you will need to take a moment to try to better understand the confusing answer choice. Rephrasing is one way to tease out the sense of a confusing answer choice.

7. Your First Instinct

Many people struggle with multiple-choice tests because they overthink the questions. If you have studied sufficiently for the test, you should be prepared to trust your first instinct once you have carefully and completely read the question and all of the answer choices. There is a great deal of research suggesting that the mind can come to the correct conclusion very quickly once it has obtained all of the relevant information. At times, it may seem to you as if your intuition is working faster even than your reasoning mind. This may in fact be true. The knowledge you obtain while studying may be retrieved from your subconscious before you have a chance to work out the associations that support it. Verify your instinct by working out the reasons that it should be trusted.

8. Key Words

Many test takers struggle with multiple-choice questions because they have poor reading comprehension skills. Quickly reading and understanding a multiple-choice question requires a mixture of skill and experience. To help with this, try jotting down a few key words and phrases on a piece of scrap paper. Doing this concentrates the process of reading and forces the mind to weigh the relative importance of the question's parts. In selecting words and phrases to write down, the test taker thinks about the question more deeply and carefully. This is especially true for multiple-choice questions that are preceded by a long prompt.

9. Subtle Negatives

One of the oldest tricks in the multiple-choice test writer's book is to subtly reverse the meaning of a question with a word like *not* or *except*. If you are not paying attention to each word in the question, you can easily be led astray by this trick. For instance, a common question format is, "Which of the following is...?" Obviously, if the question instead is, "Which of the following is not...?," then the answer will be quite different. Even worse, the test makers are aware of the potential for this mistake and will include one answer choice that would be correct if the question were not negated or reversed. A test taker who misses the reversal will find what he or she believes to be a correct answer and will be so confident that he or she will fail to reread the question and discover the original error. The only way to avoid this is to practice a wide variety of multiple-choice questions and to pay close attention to each and every word.

10. Reading Every Answer Choice

It may seem obvious, but you should always read every one of the answer choices! Too many test takers fall into the habit of scanning the question and assuming that they understand the question because they recognize a few key words. From there, they pick the first answer choice that answers the question they believe they have read. Test takers who read all of the answer choices might discover that one of the latter answer choices is actually *more* correct. Moreover, reading all of the answer choices can remind you of facts related to the question that can help you arrive at the correct answer. Sometimes, a misstatement or incorrect detail in one of the latter answer choices will trigger your memory of the subject and will enable you to find the right answer. Failing to read all of the answer choices is like not reading all of the items on a restaurant menu: you might miss out on the perfect choice.

11. Spot the Hedges

One of the keys to success on multiple-choice tests is paying close attention to every word. This is never truer than with words like almost, most, some, and sometimes. These words are called "hedges" because they indicate that a statement is not totally true or not true in every place and time. An absolute statement will contain no hedges, but in many subjects, the answers are not always straightforward or absolute. There are always exceptions to the rules in these subjects. For this reason, you should favor those multiple-choice questions that contain hedging language. The presence of qualifying words indicates that the author is taking special care with their words, which is certainly important when composing the right answer. After all, there are many ways to be wrong, but there is only one way to be right! For this reason, it is wise to avoid answers that are absolute when taking a multiple-choice test. An absolute answer is one that says things are either all one way or all another. They often include words like *every*, *always*, *best*, and *never*. If you are taking a multiple-choice test in a subject that doesn't lend itself to absolute answers, be on your guard if you see any of these words.

12. Long Answers

In many subject areas, the answers are not simple. As already mentioned, the right answer often requires hedges. Another common feature of the answers to a complex or subjective question are qualifying clauses, which are groups of words that subtly modify the meaning of the sentence. If the question or answer choice describes a rule to which there are exceptions or the subject matter is complicated, ambiguous, or confusing, the correct answer will require many words in order to be expressed clearly and accurately. In essence, you should not be deterred by answer choices that seem

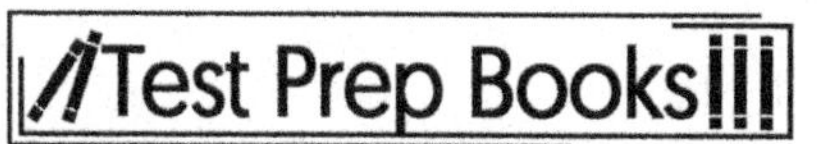

excessively long. Oftentimes, the author of the text will not be able to write the correct answer without offering some qualifications and modifications. Your job is to read the answer choices thoroughly and completely and to select the one that most accurately and precisely answers the question.

13. Restating to Understand

Sometimes, a question on a multiple-choice test is difficult not because of what it asks but because of how it is written. If this is the case, restate the question or answer choice in different words. This process serves a couple of important purposes. First, it forces you to concentrate on the core of the question. In order to rephrase the question accurately, you have to understand it well. Rephrasing the question will concentrate your mind on the key words and ideas. Second, it will present the information to your mind in a fresh way. This process may trigger your memory and render some useful scrap of information picked up while studying.

14. True Statements

Sometimes an answer choice will be true in itself, but it does not answer the question. This is one of the main reasons why it is essential to read the question carefully and completely before proceeding to the answer choices. Too often, test takers skip ahead to the answer choices and look for true statements. Having found one of these, they are content to select it without reference to the question above. Obviously, this provides an easy way for test makers to play tricks. The savvy test taker will always read the entire question before turning to the answer choices. Then, having settled on a correct answer choice, he or she will refer to the original question and ensure that the selected answer is relevant. The mistake of choosing a correct-but-irrelevant answer choice is especially common on questions related to specific pieces of objective knowledge. A prepared test taker will have a wealth of factual knowledge at their disposal, and should not be careless in its application.

15. No Patterns

One of the more dangerous ideas that circulates about multiple-choice tests is that the correct answers tend to fall into patterns. These erroneous ideas range from a belief that B and C are the most common right answers, to the idea that an unprepared test-taker should answer "A-B-A-C-A-D-A-B-A." It cannot be emphasized enough that pattern-seeking of this type is exactly the WRONG way to approach a multiple-choice test. To begin with, it is highly unlikely that the test maker will plot the correct answers according to some predetermined pattern. The questions are scrambled and delivered in a random order. Furthermore, even if the test maker was following a pattern in the assignation of correct answers, there is no reason why the test taker would know which pattern he or she was using. Any attempt to discern a pattern in the answer choices is a waste of time and a distraction from the real work of taking the test. A test taker would be much better served by extra preparation before the test than by reliance on a pattern in the answers.

Bonus Content

We host multiple bonus items online, including all three practice tests in digital format. Scan the QR code or go to this link to access this content:

testprepbooks.com/bonus/ged

The first time you access the page, you will need to register as a "new user" and verify your email address.

If you have any issues, please email support@testprepbooks.com.

Introduction to the GED Exam

Function of the Test

The General Education Development (GED) test is an exam developed and administered by the GED Testing Service, a joint venture of the American Council on Education and Pearson VUE. The GED offers those without a high school diploma the chance to earn a high school equivalency credential by evaluating their knowledge of core high school subjects.

GED test takers represent a wide age group with diverse goals. Generally, the GED is appropriate for people who did not graduate from high school but who wish to pursue advancement in their career and/or education. According to MyGED, approximately 98% of U.S. colleges and universities accept a GED as the equivalent of a high school diploma (other schools may require additional preparation courses in addition to a passing GED score in order to be considered for admission). Over 20 million adults have earned GED credentials, and the latest reported pass rates for the 2014 GED are around 60%.

Test Administration

GED tests are widely offered throughout the United States and Canada, although jurisdictions (state, province, etc.) may vary in terms of things like pricing, scheduling, and test rules. For international students and US military, international testing options are also available. Official GED Testing Centers are often operated by community colleges, adult education centers, and local school boards; GED Testing Service offers a comprehensive search of nearby test centers.

Keeping in mind that rules may vary between jurisdictions, all tests are administered in-person and taken on a computer. Tests are scheduled throughout the year; candidates should refer to their local testing centers for available test times. Candidates may take one of the four subject tests in an administration, or multiple (up to all four). Generally, test takers are able to take any test module three times without any restrictions on retesting. However, after three failed attempts, the candidate must wait a minimum of 60 days to retake the test. GED testing centers can also offer accommodations for students with disabilities, such as additional test time or Braille format tests. Test takers can request these accommodations when they register for an account on GED.com; approvals occur on an individual basis and typically take 30 days to receive.

Test Format

The GED consists of four sections, or modules: Mathematical Reasoning, Science, Social Studies, and Reasoning Through Language Arts. As mentioned, although the complete test is offered together, it is not necessary to take all four modules on one day. Note that for the Mathematical Reasoning section, a formula sheet will be provided. Test subjects vary in length. The following chart provides information about the sections:

Subject	Time	Topics
Mathematical Reasoning	115 minutes	Basic Math, Geometry, Basic Algebra, Graphs and Functions
Science	90 minutes	Reading for Meaning, Designing and Interpreting Science Experiments, Using Numbers and Graphs in Science
Social Studies	70 minutes	Reading for Meaning, Analyzing Historical Events and Arguments, Using Numbers and Graphs in Social Studies
Reasoning Through Language Arts	150 minutes	Reading for Meaning, Identifying and Creating Arguments, Grammar and Language

A ten-minute break is given between each module.

On the testing day, test takers are not permitted to eat, drink, smoke, or use their cell phones during the test. Test takers are permitted to bring a handheld calculator (TI-30XS Multiview Scientific Calculator) to the test; testing centers will not provide handheld calculators, although an on-screen calculator will be available on the computer. Students will also be provided with three erasable note boards to use during the test.

Scoring

Because the GED is now a computer-based test, scores will be available on MyGED within 24 hours of completing the test. The four modules of the GED are scored on a scale of 100–200. In order to earn high school equivalency, it is necessary to achieve a passing score on all of the four modules, and scores cannot be made up between modules—that is, a high score on one subject cannot be used to compensate for a low score on another subject. Scores are divided into four ranges:

1. A score lower than 145 points earns a score of "Not Passing." It is necessary to retake the test to earn high school equivalency.

2. A score at or higher than 145 points earns "GED Passing Score/High School Equivalency."

3. A score of 165-175 is deemed "GED College Ready." This designation advises colleges and universities that the test taker is ready to begin a degree program without further placement testing or preparation courses (policies vary among schools).

4. A score over 175 earns the test taker "GED College Ready + Credit." For some institutions, a score at this level allows the GED graduate to earn college credit for certain courses (policies vary among schools).

Test takers are encouraged to check what scores are required for admission by the colleges they intend to apply to, as some schools may seek scores that differ than the typical requisite 145. In 2017, the average scores of all test takers (including those who did not pass) were 154 for Science, 153 for Social Studies, 152 for Reasoning in Language Arts, and 150 for Math.

Study Prep Plan for the GED Exam

1 **Schedule** - Use one of our study schedules below or come up with one of your own.

2 **Relax** - Test anxiety can hurt even the best students. There are many ways to reduce stress. Find the one that works best for you.

3 **Execute** - Once you have a good plan in place, be sure to stick to it.

One Week Study Schedule

Day	Topic
Day 1	Mathematical Reasoning
Day 2	Basic Algebra
Day 3	Reasoning Through Language Arts
Day 4	Science
Day 5	GED Practice Tests #1 & #3
Day 6	GED Practice Test #2
Day 7	Take Your Exam!

Two Week Study Schedule

Day	Topic	Day	Topic
Day 1	Mathematical Reasoning	Day 8	GED Practice Test #1
Day 2	Geometry	Day 9	Answer Explanations for Practice Test #1
Day 3	Basic Algebra	Day 10	GED Practice Test #2
Day 4	Reasoning Through Language Arts	Day 11	Answer Explanations for Practice Test #2
Day 5	Grammar and Language	Day 12	GED Practice Test #3
Day 6	Science	Day 13	Answer Explanations for Practice Test #3
Day 7	Social Studies	Day 14	Take Your Exam!

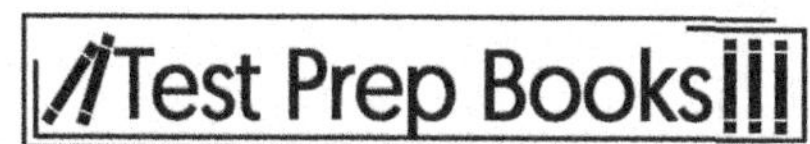

One Month Study Schedule

Day	Topic	Day	Topic	Day	Topic
Day 1	Mathematical Reasoning	Day 11	Practice Quiz	Day 21	Social Studies
Day 2	Division of Whole Numbers	Day 12	Reasoning Through Language Arts	Day 22	Analyzing Historical Events and Arguments
Day 3	Fractions	Day 13	Identifying and Creating Arguments	Day 23	Practice Quiz
Day 4	Percentages	Day 14	Grammar and Language	Day 24	GED Practice Test #1
Day 5	Geometry	Day 15	Transition Words	Day 25	Answer Explanations for Practice Test #1
Day 6	Volume and Surface Area...	Day 16	Practice Quiz	Day 26	GED Practice Test #2
Day 7	Basic Algebra	Day 17	Science	Day 27	Answer Explanations for Practice Test #2
Day 8	Writing an Expression from a Written Description	Day 18	Designing and Interpreting Science Experiments	Day 28	GED Practice Test #3
Day 9	Graphs and Functions	Day 19	Using Numbers and Graphics in Science	Day 29	Answer Explanations for Practice Test #3
Day 10	Equation of a Line from the Slope...	Day 20	Practice Quiz	Day 30	Take Your Exam!

Build your own prep plan by visiting:
testprepbooks.com/prep

Math Reference Sheet

Symbol	Phrase
+	added to, increased by, sum of, more than
-	decreased by, difference between, less than, take away
×	multiplied by, 3 (4, 5 . . .) times as large, product of
÷	divided by, quotient of, half (third, etc.) of
=	is, the same as, results in, as much as
x, t, n, etc.	a variable which is an unknown value or quantity
$<$	is under, is below, smaller than, beneath
$>$	is above, is over, bigger than, exceeds
≤	no more than, at most, maximum; less than or equal to
≥	no less than, at least, minimum; greater than or equal to
√	square root of, exponent divided by 2

Geometry	Description
$P = 2l + 2w$	for perimeter of a rectangle
$P = 4 \times s$	for perimeter of a square
$P = a + b + c$	for perimeter of a triangle
$A = \frac{1}{2} \times b \times h = \frac{bh}{2}$	for area of a triangle
$A = b \times h$	for area of a parallelogram
$A = \frac{1}{2} \times h(b_1 + b_2)$	for area of a trapezoid
$A = \frac{1}{2} \times a \times P$	for area of a regular polygon
$C = 2 \times \pi \times r$	for circumference (perimeter) of a circle
$A = \pi \times r^2$	for area of a circle
$c^2 = a^2 + b^2; c = \sqrt{a^2 + b^2}$	for finding the hypotenuse of a right triangle
$SA = 2xy + 2yz + 2xz$	for finding surface area
$V = \frac{1}{3}xyh$	for finding volume of a rectangular pyramid
$V = \frac{4}{3}\pi r^3;\ \frac{1}{3}\pi r^2 h;\ \pi r^2 h$	for volume of a sphere; a cone; and a cylinder

Radical Expressions	Description
$\sqrt[n]{a} = a^{\frac{1}{n}}, \sqrt[n]{a^m} = (\sqrt[n]{a})^m = a^{\frac{m}{n}}$	a is the radicand, n is the index, m is the exponent
$\sqrt{x^2} = (x^2)^{\frac{1}{2}} = x$	to convert square root to exponent
$a^m \times a^n = a^{m+n}$	multiplying radicands with exponents
$(a^m)^n = a^{m \times n}$	multiplying exponents
$(a \times b)^m = a^m \times b^m$	parentheses with exponents

Property	Addition	Multiplication
Commutative	$a + b = b + a$	$a \times b = b \times a$
Associative	$(a + b) + c = a + (b + c)$	$(a \times b) \times c = a \times (b \times c)$
Identity	$a + 0 = a;\ 0 + a = a$	$a \times 1 = a;\ 1 \times a = a$
Inverse	$a + (-a) = 0$	$a \times \frac{1}{a} = 1;\ a \neq 0$
Distributive	$a(b + c) = ab + ac$	

Data	Description
Mean	equal to the total of the values of a data set, divided by the number of elements in the data set
Median	middle value in an odd number of ordered values of a data set, or the mean of the two middle values in an even number of ordered values in a data set
Mode	the value that appears most often
Range	the difference between the highest and the lowest values in the set

Graphing	Description
(x, y)	ordered pair, plot points in a graph
$y = mx + b$	slope-intercept form; m represents the slope of the line and b represents the y-intercept
$f(x)$	read as f of x, which means it is a function of x
(x_2, y_2) and (x_2, y_2)	two ordered pairs used to determine the slope of a line
$m = \frac{y_2 - y_1}{x_2 - x_1}$	to find the slope of the line, m, for ordered pairs
$Ax + By = C$	standard form of an equation, also for solving a system of equations through the elimination method
$M = (\frac{x_1 + x_2}{2}, \frac{y_1 + y_2}{2})$	for finding the midpoint of an ordered pair
$y = ax^2 + bx + c$	quadratic function for a parabola
$y = a(x - h)^2 + k$	quadratic function for a parabola with vertex
$y = ab^x; y = a \times b^x$	function for exponential curve
$y = ax^2 + bx + c$	standard form of a quadratic function
$x = \frac{-b}{2a}$	for finding axis of symmetry in a parabola; given quadratic formula in standard form
$f = \sqrt{\frac{\Sigma(x - \bar{x})^2}{n - 1}}$	function for standard deviation of the sample; where $\bar{x}$ = sample mean and n = sample size

Proportions and Percentage	Description
$\frac{\text{gallons}}{\text{cost}} = \frac{\text{gallons}}{\text{cost}} : \frac{7 \text{ gallons}}{\$14.70} = \frac{x}{\$20}$	written as equal ratios with a variable representing the missing quantity
$\frac{y_1}{x_1} = \frac{y_2}{x_2}$	for direct proportions
$(y_1)(x_1) = (y_2)(x_2)$	for indirect proportions
$\frac{\text{change}}{\text{original value}} \times 100 = \text{percent change}$	for finding percentage change in value
$\frac{\text{new quantity} - \text{old quantity}}{\text{old quantity}} \times 100$	for calculating the increase or decrease in percentage

Mathematical Reasoning

Basic Math

Numbers usually serve as an adjective representing a quantity of objects. They function as placeholders for a value. Numbers can be better understood by their type and related characteristics.

Definitions

A few definitions:

Whole numbers: describes a set of numbers that does not contain any fractions or decimals. The set of whole numbers includes zero.

Example: 0, 1, 2, 3, 4, 189, 293 are all whole numbers.

Integers: describes whole numbers and their negative counterparts. (Zero does not have a negative counterpart here. Instead, zero is its own negative.)

Example: –1, –2, –3, –4, –5, 0, 1, 2, 3, 4, 5 are all integers.

–1, –2, –3, –4, –5 are considered negative integers, and 1, 2, 3, 4, 5 are considered positive integers.

Absolute value: describes the value of a number regardless of its sign. The symbol for absolute value is | |.

Example: The absolute value of 24 is 24 or |24| = 24.

The absolute value of –693 is 693 or |–693| = 693.

Even numbers: describes any number that can be divided by 2 evenly, meaning the answer has no decimal or remainder portion.

Example: 2, 4, 9082, –2, –16, –504 are all considered even numbers, because they can be divided by 2, without leaving a remainder or forming a decimal. It does not matter whether the number is positive or negative.

Odd numbers: describes any number that does not divide evenly by 2.

Example: 1, 21, 541, 3003, –9, –63, –1257 are all considered odd numbers, because they cannot be divided by 2 without a remainder or a decimal.

Prime numbers: describes a number that is only evenly divisible, resulting in no remainder or decimal, by 1 and itself.

Example: 2, 3, 7, 13, 113 are all considered prime numbers because each can only be evenly divided by 1 and itself.

Composite numbers: describes a positive integer that is formed by multiplying two smaller integers together. Composite numbers can be divided evenly by numbers other than 1 or itself.

> Example: 9, 24, 66, 2348, 1,0002 are all considered composite numbers because they are the result of multiplying two smaller integers together. In particular, these are all divisible by 2.

Decimals: designated by a decimal point which indicates that what follows the point is a value that is less than 1 and is added to the integer number preceding the decimal point. The digit immediately following the decimal point is in the tenths place, the digit following the tenths place is in the hundredths place, and so on.

For example, the decimal number 1.735 has a value greater than 1 but less than 2. The 7 represents seven tenths of the unit 1 (0.7 or $\frac{7}{10}$); the 3 represents three hundredths of 1 (0.03 or $\frac{3}{100}$); and the 5 represents five thousandths of 1 (0.005 or $\frac{5}{1,000}$).

Real numbers: describes rational numbers and irrational numbers.

Rational numbers: describes any number that can be expressed as a fraction, with a non-zero denominator. Since any integer can be written with 1 in the denominator without changing its value, all integers are considered rational numbers. Every rational number has a decimal expression that terminates or repeats. That is, any rational number either will have a countable number of nonzero digits or will end with an ellipsis or a bar (3.6666... or $3.\bar{6}$) to depict repeating decimal digits. Some examples of rational numbers include 12, –3.54, $110.\overline{256}$, $\frac{-35}{10}$, and $4.\overline{7}$.

Irrational numbers: describes numbers that cannot be written as a finite or repeating decimal. Pi (π) is considered to be an irrational number because its decimal portion is unending or a non-repeating decimal. Pi (π) is the most common irrational number, but there are other well-known irrational numbers like *e* and $\sqrt{2}$.

Basic Addition and Subtraction

Addition

Addition is the combination of two numbers so their quantities are added together cumulatively. The sign for an addition operation is the + symbol. For example, 9 + 6 = 15. The 9 and 6 combine to achieve a cumulative value, called a **sum**.

Addition holds the **commutative property**, which means that the order of the numbers in an addition equation can be switched without altering the result. The formula for the commutative property is a + b = b + a. Let's look at a few examples to see how the commutative property works:

$$7 = 3 + 4 = 4 + 3 = 7$$

$$20 = 12 + 8 = 8 + 12 = 20$$

Addition also holds the **associative property**, which means that the grouping of numbers doesn't matter in an addition problem. In other words, the presence or absence of parentheses is irrelevant. The

formula for the associative property is (a + b) + c = a + (b + c). Here are some examples of the associative property at work:

$$30 = (6 + 14) + 10 = 6 + (14 + 10) = 30$$

$$35 = 8 + (2 + 25) = (8 + 2) + 25 = 35$$

There are set columns for addition: ones, tens, hundreds, thousands, ten-thousands, hundred-thousands, millions, and so on. To add how many units there are total, each column needs to be combined, starting from the right, or the ones column.

THOUSANDS	HUNDREDS	TENS	ONES

Every 10 units in the ones column equals one in the tens column, and every 10 units in the tens column equals one in the hundreds column, and so on.

Example: The number 5,432 has 2 ones, 3 tens, 4 hundreds, and 5 thousands. The number 371 has 3 hundreds, 7 tens and 1 one. To combine, or add, these two numbers, simply add up how many units of each column exist. The best way to do this is by lining up the columns:

$$\begin{array}{r} 5\,4\,3\,2 \\ +\quad 3\,7\,1 \\ \hline \end{array}$$

The ones column adds 2 + 1 for a total (sum) of 3.

The tens column adds 3 + 7 for a total of 10; since 10 of that unit was collected, add 1 to the hundreds column to denote the total in the next column:

$$\begin{array}{r} 1\quad\;\; \\ 5\,4\,3\,2 \\ +\quad 3\,7\,1 \\ \hline 0\,3 \end{array}$$

When adding the hundreds column, this extra 1 needs to be combined, so it would be the sum of 4, 3, and 1.

$$4 + 3 + 1 = 8$$

The last, or thousands, column listed would be the sum of 5. Since there are no other numbers in this column, that is the final total.

The answer would look as follows:

$$\begin{array}{r} 5\,4\,3\,2 \\ +\quad 3\,7\,1 \\ \hline 5\,8\,0\,3 \end{array}$$

Example
Find the sum of 9,734 and 895.

Set up the problem:

$$\begin{array}{r} 9\,7\,3\,4 \\ +\quad 8\,9\,5 \\ \hline \end{array}$$

Total the columns:

$$\begin{array}{r} 9\,7\,3\,4 \\ +\quad 8\,9\,5 \\ \hline 1\,0\,6\,2\,9 \end{array}$$

In this example, another column (ten-thousands) is added to the left of the thousands column, to denote a carryover of 10 units in the thousands column. The final sum is 10,629.

When adding using all negative integers, the total is negative. The integers are simply added together and the negative symbol is tacked on.

$$(-12) + (-435) = -447$$

Subtraction

Subtraction is taking away one number from another, so their quantities are reduced. The sign designating a subtraction operation is the – symbol, and the result is called the **difference**. For example, 9 - 6 = 3. The number *6* detracts from the number *9* to reach the difference *3*.

Unlike addition, subtraction follows neither the commutative nor associative properties. The order and grouping in subtraction impact the result.

$$15 = 22 - 7 \neq 7 - 22 = -15$$

$$3 = (10 - 5) - 2 \neq 10 - (5 - 2) = 7$$

When working through subtraction problems involving larger numbers, it's necessary to regroup the numbers. Let's work through a practice problem using regrouping:

$$\begin{array}{r} 3\,2\,5 \\ -\quad 7\,7 \\ \hline \end{array}$$

Here, it is clear that the ones and tens columns for 77 are greater than the ones and tens columns for 325. To subtract this number, borrow from the tens and hundreds columns. When borrowing from a column, subtracting 1 from the lender column will add 10 to the borrower column:

$$\begin{array}{rrr} 3-1 & 10+2-1 & 10+5 \\ - & 7 & 7 \\ \hline \end{array} = \begin{array}{rrr} 2 & 11 & 15 \\ - & 7 & 7 \\ \hline 2 & 4 & 8 \end{array}$$

After ensuring that each digit in the top row is greater than the digit in the corresponding bottom row, subtraction can proceed as normal, and the answer is found to be 248.

Addition and Subtraction with Negative Integers

When adding mixed-sign integers, determine which integer has the larger absolute value. Absolute value is the distance of a number from zero on the number line. Absolute value is indicated by these symbols: | |.

Take this equation for example:

$$12 + (-435)$$

The absolute value of each of the numbers is as follows:

$$|12| = 12$$

$$|-435| = 435$$

Since –435 is the larger integer, the final number will have its sign. In this case, that sign is negative. Now, subtract the smaller integer from the larger one. If this equation is worked out, it will look like this:

$$12 + (-435) = -423$$

Mathematically, the equation looks like the one above, but practically speaking it will be done it like this:

$$435 - 12 = 423$$

(then add the negative sign)

When subtracting with negative integers, every unmarked integer is assumed to have a positive sign. Subtracting an integer is the same as adding a negative integer.

Example:
–3 - 4
–3 + (–4)
–3 + (–4) = –7

Subtracting a negative integer is the same as adding a positive integer.

Example
–3 - (–4)
–3 + 4
–3 + 4 = 1

Multiplication of Whole Numbers

Multiplication involves adding together multiple copies of a number. It is indicated by an × symbol or a number immediately outside of a parenthesis. For example:

$$5(8-2)$$

The two numbers being multiplied together are called **factors**, and their result is called a **product**. For example, $9 \times 6 = 54$. This can be shown alternatively by expansion of either the 9 or the 6:

$$9 \times 6 = 9 + 9 + 9 + 9 + 9 + 9 = 54$$

$$9 \times 6 = 6 + 6 + 6 + 6 + 6 + 6 + 6 + 6 + 6 = 54$$

Like addition, multiplication holds the commutative and associative properties:

$$115 = 23 \times 5 = 5 \times 23 = 115$$

$$84 = 3 \times (7 \times 4) = (3 \times 7) \times 4 = 84$$

Multiplication also follows the **distributive property**, which allows the multiplication to be distributed through parentheses. The formula for distribution is $a \times (b + c) = ab + ac$. This is clear after the examples:

$$45 = 5 \times 9 = 5(3 + 6) = (5 \times 3) + (5 \times 6) = 15 + 30 = 45$$

$$20 = 4 \times 5 = 4(10 - 5) = (4 \times 10) - (4 \times 5) = 40 - 20 = 20$$

For larger-number multiplication, the way the numbers are lined up can make it easier to obtain the product. It is simplest to put the number with the most digits on top and the number with fewer digits on the bottom. If they have the same number of digits, select one for the top and one for the bottom. Line up the problem, and begin by multiplying the far-right column on the top and the far-right column on the bottom. If the answer to a column is more than 9, the ones place digit will be written below that column and the tens place digit will carry to the top of the next column to be added after those digits are multiplied. Write the answer below that column. Move to the next column to the left on the top, and multiply it by the same far-right column on the bottom. Keep moving to the left one column at a time on the top number until the end.

Example
Multiply 37×8

Line up the numbers, placing the one with the most digits on top.

$$\begin{array}{r} 37 \\ \times\ \ 8 \\ \hline \end{array}$$

Multiply the far-right column on the top with the far-right column on the bottom (7 x 8). Write the answer, 56, as below: The ones value, 6, gets recorded, the tens value, 5, is carried.

$$\begin{array}{r} {\scriptstyle +5}\ \ \\ 37 \\ \text{X}\ \ 8 \\ \hline 6 \end{array}$$

Move to the next column left on the top number and multiply with the far-right bottom (3 x 8). Remember to add any carry over after multiplying: 3 x 8 = 24, 24 + 5 = 29. Since there are no more digits on top, write the entire number below.

$$\begin{array}{r} {\scriptstyle +5}\ \ \\ 37 \\ \text{X}\ \ 8 \\ \hline 296 \end{array}$$

The solution is 296.

If there is more than one column to the bottom number, move to the row below the first strand of answers, mark a zero in the far-right column, and then begin the multiplication process again with the far-right column on top and the second column from the right on the bottom. For each digit in the bottom number, there will be a row of answers, each padded with the respective number of zeros on the right. Finally, add up all of the answer rows for one total number.

Example: Multiply 512×36.

Line up the numbers (the one with the most digits on top) to multiply.

Begin with the right column on top and the right column on bottom (2×6).

$$\begin{array}{r} 512 \\ \text{X}\ \ \ 36 \\ \hline \end{array}$$

Move one column left on top and multiply by the far-right column on the bottom (1×6). Add the carry over after multiplying: $1 \times 6 = 6, 6 + 1 = 7$.

$$\begin{array}{r} {\scriptstyle +1} \\ 5\ 1\ 2 \\ \times \quad 3\ 6 \\ \hline 7\ 2 \end{array}$$

Move one column left on top and multiply by the far-right column on the bottom (5×6). Since this is the last digit on top, write the whole answer below.

$$\begin{array}{r} 5\ 1\ 2 \\ \text{X} \quad 3\ 6 \\ \hline 3\ 0\ 7\ 2 \end{array}$$

Now move on to the second column on the bottom number. Starting on the far-right column on the top, repeat this pattern for the next number left on the bottom (2×3). Write the answers below the first line of answers; remember to begin with a zero placeholder on the far right.

$$\begin{array}{r} 5\ 1\ 2 \\ \text{X} \quad 3\ 6 \\ \hline 3\ 0\ 7\ 2 \\ 6\ 0 \end{array}$$

Continue the pattern (1×3).

$$\begin{array}{r} 5\ 1\ 2 \\ \text{X} \quad 3\ 6 \\ \hline 3\ 0\ 7\ 2 \\ 3\ 6\ 0 \end{array}$$

Since this is the last digit on top, write the whole answer below.

$$\begin{array}{r} 5\ 1\ 2 \\ \times \quad 3\ 6 \\ \hline 3\ 0\ 7\ 2 \\ 1\ 5\ 3\ 6\ 0 \end{array}$$

Now add the answer rows together. Pay attention to ensure they are aligned correctly.

$$\begin{array}{r} 5\ 1\ 2 \\ \times \quad 3\ 6 \\ \hline 3\ 0\ 7\ 2 \\ 1\ 5\ 3\ 6\ 0 \\ \hline 1\ 8\ 4\ 3\ 2 \end{array}$$

The solution is 18,432.

Division of Whole Numbers

Division and multiplication are inverses of each other in the same way that addition and subtraction are opposites. The signs designating a division operation are the ÷ and / symbols. In division, the second number divides into the first.

The number before the division sign is called the **dividend** or, if expressed as a fraction, the **numerator**. For example, in $a \div b$, a is the dividend, while in $\frac{a}{b}$, a is the numerator.

The number after the division sign is called the **divisor** or, if expressed as a fraction, the **denominator.** For example, in $a \div b$, b is the divisor, while in $\frac{a}{b}$, b is the denominator.

Like subtraction, division doesn't follow the commutative property, as it matters which number comes before the division sign, and division doesn't follow the associative or distributive properties for the same reason. For example:

$$\frac{3}{2} = 9 \div 6 \neq 6 \div 9 = \frac{2}{3}$$

$$2 = 10 \div 5 = (30 \div 3) \div 5 \neq 30 \div (3 \div 5) = 30 \div \frac{3}{5} = 50$$

$$25 = 20 + 5 = (40 \div 2) + (40 \div 8) \neq 40 \div (2 + 8) = 40 \div 10 = 4$$

The answer to a division problem is called the **quotient.** If a divisor doesn't divide into a dividend evenly, whatever is left over is termed the **remainder**. The remainder can be further divided out into decimal form by using long division; however, this doesn't always give a quotient with a finite number of decimal places, so the remainder can also be expressed as a fraction over the original divisor.

Example

Solve $1050/42$ or $1050 \div 42$.

Set up the problem with the denominator being divided into the numerator.

$$42\overline{)1050}$$

Check for divisibility into the first unit of the numerator, 1.

42 cannot go into 1, so add on the next unit in the denominator, 0.

42 cannot go into 10, so add on the next unit in the denominator, 5.

42 can be divided into 105 two times. Write the 2 over the 5 in 105 and multiply 42 x 2. Write the 84 under 105 for subtraction and note the remainder, 21 is less than 42.

$$\begin{array}{r} 2 \\ 42\overline{)1050} \\ -84 \\ \hline 21 \end{array}$$

Drop the next digit in the numerator down to the remainder (making 21 into 210) to create a number 42 can divide into. 42 divides into 210 five times. Write the 5 over the 0 and multiply 42×5.

$$\begin{array}{r} 25 \\ 42\overline{)1050} \\ -84 \\ \hline 210 \end{array}$$

Write the 210 under 210 for subtraction. The remainder is 0.

$$\begin{array}{r} 25 \\ 42\overline{)1050} \\ -84 \\ \hline 210 \\ -210 \\ \hline 0 \end{array}$$

The solution is 25.

Example

Divide $375/4$ or $375 \div 4$.

Set up the problem.

$$4\overline{)375}$$

4 cannot divide into 3, so add the next unit from the numerator, 7. 4 divides into 37 nine times, so write the 9 above the 7. Multiply $4 \times 9 = 36$. Write the 36 under the 37 for subtraction. The remainder is 1 (1 is less than 4).

$$\begin{array}{r} 9 \\ 4\overline{)375} \\ -36 \\ \hline 1 \end{array}$$

Drop the next digit in the numerator, 5, making the remainder 15. 4 divides into 15, three times, so write the 3 above the 5. Multiply 4×3. Write the 12 under the 15 for subtraction, remainder is 3 (3 is less than 4).

```
   9 3
4|3 7 5
- 3 6
    1 5
  - 1 2
      3
```

The solution is 93 remainder 3 or 93 ¾ (the remainder can be written over the original denominator).

Distance Between Numbers on a Number Line

Aside from zero, numbers can be either positive or negative. The sign for a positive number is the plus sign or the + symbol, while the sign for a negative number is the minus sign or the – symbol. If a number has no designation, then it's assumed to be positive.

Both positive and negative numbers are valued according to their distance from zero. Both +3 and –3 can be considered using the following number line:

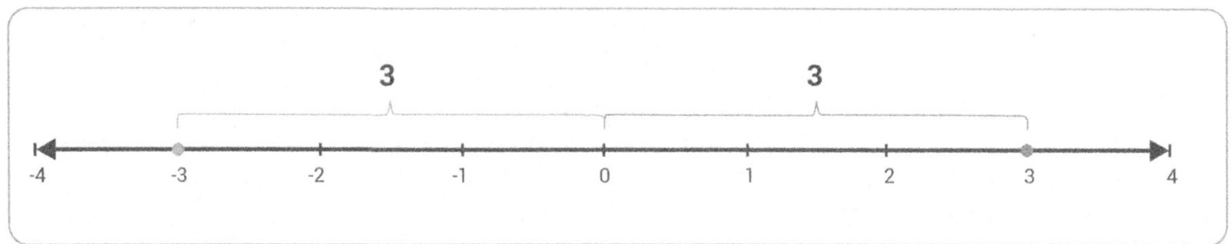

Both 3 and –3 are three spaces from zero. The distance from zero is called its **absolute value**. Thus, both –3 and 3 have an absolute value of 3 since they're both three spaces away from zero.

An absolute number is written by placing | | around the number. So, $|3|$ and $|-3|$ both equal 3, as that's their common absolute value.

Implications for Addition and Subtraction

For addition, if all numbers are either positive or negative, they are simply added together. For example, $4 + 4 = 8$ and $-4 + -4 = -8$. However, things get tricky when some of the numbers are negative, and some are positive.

For example, with $6 + (-4)$, the first step is to take the absolute values of the numbers, which are 6 and 4. Second, the smaller value is subtracted from the larger. The equation becomes $6 - 4 = 2$. Third, the sign of the original larger number is placed on the sum. Here, 6 is the larger number, and it's positive, so the sum is 2.

Here's an example where the negative number has a larger absolute value: $(-6) + 4$. The first two steps are the same as the example above. However, on the third step, the negative sign must be placed on the sum, because the absolute value of (–6) is greater than 4. Thus, $-6 + 4 = -2$.

The absolute value of numbers implies that subtraction can be thought of as flipping the sign of the number following the subtraction sign and simply adding the two numbers. This means that subtracting a negative number will, in fact, be adding the positive absolute value of the negative number.

Here are some examples:

$$-6 - 4 = -6 + -4 = -10$$

$$3 - -6 = 3 + 6 = 9$$

$$-3 - 2 = -3 + -2 = -5$$

Implications for Multiplication and Division

For multiplication and division, if both numbers are positive, then the product or quotient is always positive. If both numbers are negative, then the product or quotient is also positive. However, if the numbers have opposite signs, the product or quotient is always negative.

Simply put, the product in multiplication and quotient in division is always positive, unless the numbers have opposing signs, in which case it's negative. Here are some examples:

$$(-6) \times (-5) = 30$$

$$(-50) \div 10 = -5$$

$$8 \times |-7| = 56$$

$$(-48) \div (-6) = 8$$

If there are more than two numbers in a multiplication or division problem, then whether the product or quotient is positive or negative depends on the number of negative numbers in the problem. If there is an odd number of negatives, then the product or quotient is negative. If there is an even number of negative numbers, then the result is positive.

Here are some examples:

$$(-6) \times 5 \times (-2) \times (-4) = -240$$

$$(-6) \times 5 \times 2 \times (-4) = 240$$

Multiples and Factors

Multiples of a given number are found by taking that number and multiplying it by any other whole number. For example, 3 is a factor of 6, 9, and 12. Therefore, 6, 9, and 12 are multiples of 3. The multiples of any number are an infinite list. For example, the multiples of 5 are 5, 10, 15, 20, and so on. This list continues without end. A list of multiples is used in finding the **least common multiple**, or LCM, for fractions when a common denominator is needed. The denominators are written down and their multiples listed until a common number is found in both lists. This common number is the LCM.

The **factors** of a number are all integers that can be multiplied by another integer to produce the given number. For example, 2 is multiplied by 3 to produce 6. Therefore, 2 and 3 are both factors of 6. Similarly, $1 \times 6 = 6$ and $2 \times 3 = 6$, so 1, 2, 3, and 6 are all factors of 6. Another way to explain a factor

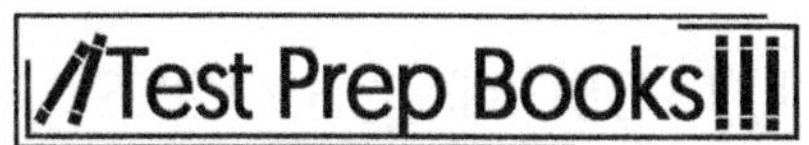

is to say that a given number divides evenly by each of its factors to produce an integer. For example, 6 does not divide evenly by 5. Therefore, 5 is not a factor of 6.

Prime factorization breaks down each factor of a whole number until only prime numbers remain. All composite numbers can be factored into prime numbers. For example, the prime factors of 12 are 2, 2, and:

$$3\ (2 \times 2 \times 3 = 12)$$

To produce the prime factors of a number, the number is factored, and any composite numbers are continuously factored until the result is the product of prime factors only. A **factor tree**, such as the one below, is helpful when exploring this concept.

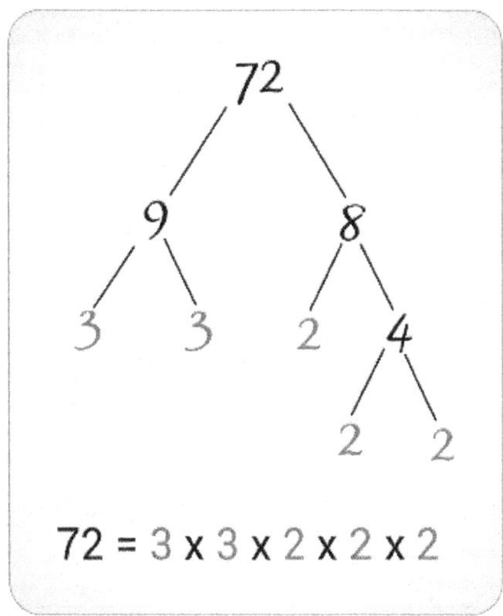

Properties of Operations

Properties of operations exist to make calculations easier and solve problems for missing values. The following table summarizes commonly used properties of real numbers.

Property	Addition	Multiplication
Commutative	$a + b = b + a$	$a \times b = b \times a$
Associative	$(a + b) + c = a + (b + c)$	$(a \times b) \times c = a \times (b \times c)$
Identity	$a + 0 = a;\ 0 + a = a$	$a \times 1 = a;\ 1 \times a = a$
Inverse	$a + (-a) = 0$	$a \times \frac{1}{a} = 1;\ a \neq 0$
Distributive	$a(b + c) = ab + ac$	

The **commutative property of addition** states that the order in which numbers are added does not change the sum. Similarly, the **commutative property of multiplication** states that the order in which numbers are multiplied does not change the product. The **associative property of addition** and **multiplication** state that the grouping of numbers being added or multiplied does not change the sum or product, respectively. The commutative and associative properties are useful for performing calculations. For example, $(47 + 25) + 3$ is equivalent to $(47 + 3) + 25$, which is easier to calculate.

The **identity property of addition** states that adding zero to any number does not change its value. The **identity property of multiplication** states that multiplying a number by one does not change its value. The **inverse property of addition** states that the sum of a number and its opposite equals zero. Opposites are numbers that are the same with different signs (ex. 5 and –5; $-\frac{1}{2}$ and $\frac{1}{2}$). The **inverse property of multiplication** states that the product of a number (other than zero) and its reciprocal equals one. **Reciprocal numbers** have numerators and denominators that are inverted (ex. $\frac{2}{5}$ and $\frac{5}{2}$). Inverse properties are useful for canceling quantities to find missing values (see algebra content). For example, $a + 7 = 12$ is solved by adding the inverse of $7(-7)$ to both sides in order to isolate a.

The **distributive property** states that multiplying a sum (or difference) by a number produces the same result as multiplying each value in the sum (or difference) by the number and adding (or subtracting) the products. Consider the following scenario: You are buying three tickets for a baseball game. Each ticket costs $18. You are also charged a fee of $2 per ticket for purchasing the tickets online. The cost is calculated:

$$3 \times 18 + 3 \times 2$$

Using the distributive property, the cost can also be calculated $3(18 + 2)$.

Prefixes

Moving the decimal place to the left or to the right illustrates multiplying or dividing by factors of 10. The metric system of units for measurement utilizes factors of 10 as displayed in the following table:

kilo	1,000 units
hecto	100 units
deca	10 units
base unit	
deci	0.1 units
centi	0.01 units
milli	0.001 units

It is important to have the ability to quickly manipulate by 10 according to prefixes for units.

Example: How many milliliters are in 5 liters of saline solution?

There are 1,000 milliliters for every 1 liter. If we have 5 liters, it would be $5 \times 1{,}000 = 5000$ mL

You may also count the zeros and which side of the decimal place they are on: 1,000 has three zeroes to the left of the decimal, so insert three zeroes between the 5 and the decimal, or move the decimal place over three places to the right, for your answer of 5000 mL.

Example

How many kilograms are in 4.8 grams?

There is 1 gram for every 0.001 kilograms. Since there is one-thousandth of a kilogram for each gram, that means divide by 1,000, or move the decimal to the left by 3 places – 1 place for each 0. So, the result would be 0.0048 kg.

For quick conversions, move the decimal place the set number of spaces left or right to match the column/slot, as depicted below.

To convert from one prefix to another to the left or right of the base unit (follow the arrow to the left or right), move the decimal place the number of columns/slots as counted.

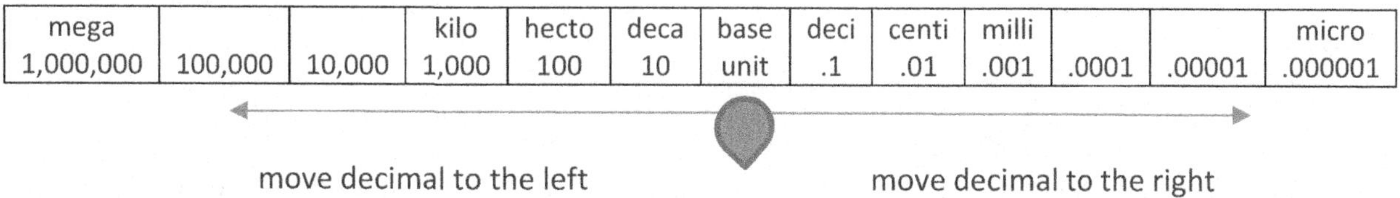

mega			kilo	hecto	deca	base	deci	centi	milli			micro
1,000,000	100,000	10,000	1,000	100	10	unit	.1	.01	.001	.0001	.00001	.000001

Example

How many centiliters are in 4.7 kiloliters?

To convert a number with a unit prefixed as kilo into a unit prefixed as centi, move across five columns to the right, meaning move the decimal place five places to the right.

4.7 kL = 470,000 cL

Example

How many liters are in 30 microliters?

Start with the unit marked micro and count the columns moving to the left until you reach the base unit for liters. Be sure to count the blank columns, as they are important placeholders. There are six columns from micro to the base unit moving to the left, so move the decimal place six places to the left.

30 mL = 0.000030 L

Decimals

Decimals mark the separation between the whole portion and the fractional (or decimal) portion of a number. For example, 3.15 has 3 in the whole portion and 15 in the fractional or decimal portion. A number such as 645 is all whole, but there is still a decimal place. The decimal place in 645 is to the right of the 5, but usually not written, since there is no fractional or decimal portion to this number. The same number can be written as 645.0 or 645.00 or 645.000, etc. The position of the decimal place can change the entire value of a number, and impact a calculation. In the United States, the decimal place is used when representing money. You'll often be asked to round to a certain decimal place. Here is a review of some basic decimal **place value** names:

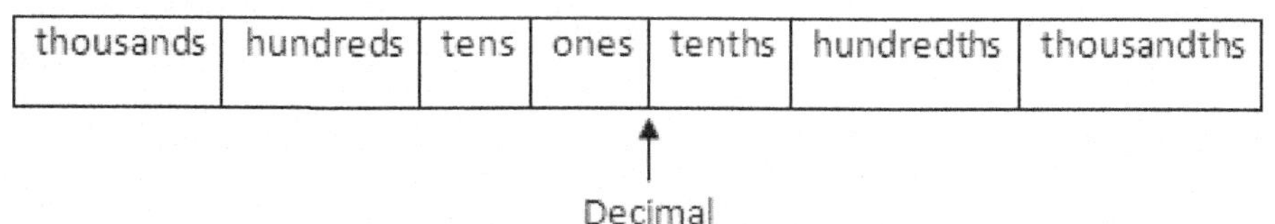

thousands	hundreds	tens	ones	tenths	hundredths	thousandths

The number 12,302.2 would be read as "twelve thousand, three hundred two and two-tenths."

In the United States, a period denotes the decimal place; however, some countries use a comma. The comma is used in the United States to separate thousands, millions, and so on.

To round to the nearest whole number (eliminating the decimal portion), the example would become 12,302. For rounding, go to the number that is one place to the right of what you are rounding to. If the number is 0 through 4, there will be no change. For numbers 5 through 9, round up to the next whole number.

Example

Round 6,423.7 to the ones place.

Since the tenths place is the position to the right of the ones place, we use that number to determine if we round up or not. In this case, the 3 is in the ones place and the 7 is in the tenths place. (6,42$\underline{3}$.7)

The 7 in the tenths place means we round the 3 up, so the final number will be 6,424.0

Example

Round 542.88 to the nearest tens

Since the ones place is the position to the right of the tens, we use that number to determine if we round up or not. In this case, the 4 is in the tens place and the 2 is in the ones place (5$\underline{4}$2.88).

The 2 in the ones place means we do not round the 4 up, so the final number will be 540.00

Note: Everything to the right of the rounded position goes to 0 as a placeholder.

Example: Say you wanted to post an advertisement to sell a used vehicle for $2000.00. However, when typing the price, you accidentally moved the decimal over one place to the left. Now the asking price appears as $200.00. This difference of a factor of 10 is dramatic. As numbers get bigger or smaller, the impact of this mistake becomes more pronounced. If you were looking to sell a condo for $1,000,000.00, but made an error and moved the decimal place to the left one position, the price posts at $100,000.00. A mistake of a factor of 10 cost $900,000.00.

In dividing by 10, you move the decimal one position to the left, making a smaller number than the original. If multiplying by 10, move the decimal one position to the right, making a larger number than the original.

Example

Divide 100 by 10 or 100 ÷ 10.

Move the decimal one place to the left, so the result is a smaller number than the original.

$$100 \div 10 = 10$$

Example

Divide 1.0 by 10 or 1.0 ÷ 10.

Move the decimal one place to the left, so the result is a smaller number than the original.

$$1.0 \div 10 = 0.1$$

Example

Multiply 100 by 10 or 100 x 10.

Move the decimal one place to the right, so the result is a larger number than the original.

$$100 \times 10 = 1{,}000$$

Example

Multiply 0.1 by 10 or 0.1 x 10.

Move the decimal one place to the right, so the result is a larger number than the original.

$$0.1 \times 10 = 1.0$$

Decimal Addition

Addition with decimals is done the same way as regular addition. All numbers could have decimals, but are often removed if the numbers to the right of the decimal are zeros. Line up numbers at the decimal place.

Example: Add $345.89 + 23.54$

Line the numbers up at the decimal place and add.

$$\begin{array}{r} 345.89 \\ +\ \ 23.54 \\ \hline 369.43 \end{array}$$

Decimal Subtraction

Subtraction with decimals is done the same way as regular subtraction.

Example: Subtract $345.89 - 23.54$

Line the numbers up at the decimal place and subtract.

$$\begin{array}{r} 345.89 \\ -\ \ 23.54 \\ \hline 322.35 \end{array}$$

Decimal Multiplication

The simplest way to handle multiplication with decimals is to calculate the multiplication problem pretending the decimals are not there, then count how many decimal places there are in the original problem. Use that total to place the decimal the same number of places over, counting from right to left.

Example: Multiply 42.33×3.3

Line the numbers up and multiply, pretending there are no decimals.

$$\begin{array}{r} 4233 \\ \times \quad 33 \\ \hline 12699 \\ 126990 \\ \hline 139689 \end{array}$$

Now look at the original problem and count how many decimal places were removed. Two decimal places were removed from 42.33 to get 4233, and one decimal place from 3.3 to get 33. Removed were $2 + 1 = 3$ decimal places. Place the decimal three places from the right of the number 139689. The answer is 139.689.

Another way to think of this is that when you move the decimal in the original numbers, it is like multiplying by 10. To put the decimals back, you need to divide the number by 10 the same amount of times you multiplied. It would still be three times for the above solution.

Example: Multiply 0.03×1.22

Line the numbers up and multiply, pretending there are no decimals. The zeroes in front of the 3 are unnecessary, so take them out for now.

$$\begin{array}{r} 122 \\ \times \quad 3 \\ \hline 366 \end{array}$$

Look at the original problem and count how many decimals places were removed, or how many times each number was multiplied by 10. The 1.22 moved two places (or multiplied by 10 twice), as did 0.03. That is $2 + 2 = 4$ decimal places removed. Count that number, from right to left of the number 366, and place the decimal. The result is 0.0366.

Decimal Division

Division with decimals is simplest when you eliminate some of the decimal places. Since you divide the bottom number of a fraction into the top, or divide the denominator into the numerator, the bottom number dictates the movement of the decimals. The goal is to remove the decimals from the denominator and mirror that movement in the numerator. You do not need the numerator to be decimal free, however. Divide as you would normally.

Example

Divide $4.21/0.2$ or $4.21 \div 0.2$

Move the decimal over one place to the right in the denominator, making 0.2 simply 2. Move the decimal in the numerator, 4.21, over the same amount, so it is now 42.1.

$$0.2\overline{)4.21}$$

Becomes

$$2\overline{)42.1}$$

Divide.

$$\begin{array}{r} 21.05 \\ 2\overline{)42.10} \end{array}$$

The answer is 21.05 with the correct decimal placement. In decimal division, move the decimal the same amount for both numerator and denominator. There is no need to adjust anything after the problem is completed.

Fractions

A fraction is an equation that represents a part of a whole but can also be used to present ratios or division problems. An example of a fraction is $\frac{x}{y}$. In this example, x is called the **numerator**, while y is the **denominator**. The numerator represents the number of parts, and the denominator is the total number of parts. They are separated by a line or slash, known as a **fraction bar**. In simple fractions, the numerator and denominator can be nearly any integer. However, the denominator of a fraction can never be zero because dividing by zero is a function that is undefined.

Imagine that an apple pie has been baked for a holiday party, and the full pie has eight slices. After the party, there are five slices left. How could the amount of the pie that remains be expressed as a fraction? The numerator is 5 since there are 5 pieces left, and the denominator is 8 since there were eight total slices in the whole pie. Thus, expressed as a fraction, the leftover pie totals $\frac{5}{8}$ of the original amount.

Fractions come in three different varieties: proper fractions, improper fractions, and mixed numbers. **Proper fractions** have a numerator less than the denominator, such as $\frac{3}{8}$, but **improper fractions** have a numerator greater than the denominator, such as $\frac{7}{2}$. **Mixed numbers** combine a whole number with a proper fraction, such as $3\frac{1}{2}$. Any mixed number can be written as an improper fraction by multiplying the integer by the denominator, adding the product to the value of the numerator, and dividing the sum by the original denominator. For example:

$$3\frac{1}{2} = \frac{3 \times 2 + 1}{2} = \frac{7}{2}$$

Whole numbers can also be converted into fractions by placing the whole number as the numerator and making the denominator 1. For example, $3 = \frac{3}{1}$.

One of the most fundamental concepts of fractions is their ability to be manipulated by multiplication or division. This is possible since $\frac{n}{n} = 1$ for any non-zero integer. As a result, multiplying or dividing by $\frac{n}{n}$ will not alter the original fraction since any number multiplied or divided by 1 doesn't change the value of that number. Fractions of the same value are known as equivalent fractions. For example, $\frac{2}{4}, \frac{4}{8}, \frac{50}{100}$, and $\frac{75}{150}$ are equivalent, as they all equal $\frac{1}{2}$.

Although many equivalent fractions exist, they are easier to compare and interpret when reduced or simplified. The numerator and denominator of a simple fraction will have no factors in common other than 1. When reducing or simplifying fractions, divide the numerator and denominator by the **greatest common factor**. A simple strategy is to divide the numerator and denominator by low numbers, like 2, 3, or 5 until arriving at a simple fraction, but the same thing could be achieved by determining the greatest common factor for both the numerator and denominator and dividing each by it. Using the first method is preferable when both the numerator and denominator are even, end in 5, or are obviously a multiple of another number. However, if no numbers seem to work, it will be necessary to factor the numerator and denominator to find the GCF. For example:

1) Simplify the fraction $\frac{6}{8}$:

Dividing the numerator and denominator by 2 results in $\frac{3}{4}$, which is a simple fraction.

2) Simplify the fraction $\frac{12}{36}$:

Dividing the numerator and denominator by 2 leaves $\frac{6}{18}$. This isn't a simple fraction, as both the numerator and denominator have factors in common. Dividing each by 3 results in $\frac{2}{6}$, but this can be further simplified by dividing by 2 to get $\frac{1}{3}$. This is the simplest fraction, as the numerator is 1. In cases like this, multiple division operations can be avoided by determining the greatest common factor between the numerator and denominator.

3) Simplify the fraction $\frac{18}{54}$ by dividing by the greatest common factor:

First, determine the factors for the numerator and denominator. The factors of 18 are 1, 2, 3, 6, 9, and 18. The factors of 54 are 1, 2, 3, 6, 9, 18, 27, and 54. Thus, the greatest common factor is 18. Dividing both the numerator and denominator by 18 leaves $\frac{1}{3}$, which is the simplest fraction. This method takes slightly more work, but it definitively arrives at the simplest fraction.

Operations with Fractions

Multiplication of Fractions

Of the four basic operations that can be performed on fractions, the one that involves the least amount of work is multiplication. To multiply two fractions, simply multiply the numerators together, multiply the denominators together, and place the products of each as a fraction. Whole numbers and mixed numbers can also be expressed as a fraction, as described above, to multiply with a fraction. Here are a few examples:

1) $\frac{2}{5} \times \frac{3}{4} = \frac{6}{20} = \frac{3}{10}$

2) $\frac{4}{9} \times \frac{7}{11} = \frac{28}{99}$

Division of Fractions

Dividing fractions is similar to multiplication with one key difference. To divide fractions, flip the numerator and denominator of the second fraction, and then proceed as if it were a multiplication problem:

1) $\frac{7}{8} \div \frac{4}{5} = \frac{7}{8} \times \frac{5}{4} = \frac{35}{32}$

2) $\frac{5}{9} \div \frac{1}{3} = \frac{5}{9} \times \frac{3}{1} = \frac{15}{9} = \frac{5}{3}$

Addition and Subtraction of Fractions

Addition and subtraction require more steps than multiplication and division, as these operations require the fractions to have the same denominator, also called a **common denominator**. It is always possible to find a common denominator by multiplying the denominators. However, when the denominators are large numbers, this method is unwieldy, especially if the answer must be provided in its simplest form. Thus, it's beneficial to find the **least common denominator** of the fractions—the least common denominator is incidentally also the least common multiple.

Once equivalent fractions have been found with common denominators, simply add or subtract the numerators to arrive at the answer:

1) $\frac{1}{2} + \frac{3}{4} = \frac{2}{4} + \frac{3}{4} = \frac{5}{4}$

2) $\frac{3}{12} + \frac{11}{20} = \frac{15}{60} + \frac{33}{60} = \frac{48}{60} = \frac{4}{5}$

3) $\frac{7}{9} - \frac{4}{15} = \frac{35}{45} - \frac{12}{45} = \frac{23}{45}$

4) $\frac{5}{6} - \frac{7}{18} = \frac{15}{18} - \frac{7}{18} = \frac{8}{18} = \frac{4}{9}$

Changing Fractions to Decimals

To change a fraction into a decimal, divide the denominator into the numerator until there are no remainders. There may be repeating decimals, so rounding is often acceptable. A straight line above the repeating portion denotes that the decimal repeats.

Example

Express 4/5 as a decimal.

Set up the division problem.

```
5|4
```

5 does not go into 4, so place the decimal and add a zero.

```
5|4 . 0
```

5 goes into 40 eight times. There is no remainder.

```
  0 . 8
5|4 . 0
- 4 . 0
      0
```

The solution is 0.8.

Example

Express 33 1/3 as a decimal.

Since the whole portion of the number is known, set it aside to calculate the decimal from the fraction portion.

Set up the division problem.

```
3|1
```

3 does not go into 1, so place the decimal and add zeros. 3 goes into 10 three times.

```
  0 . 3
3|1 . 0
```

This will repeat with a remainder of 1.

```
  0 . 3 3 3
3|1 . 0 0 0
   - 9
     1 0
     - 9
       1 0
```

So, we will place a line over the 3 to denote the repetition. The solution is written $33.\overline{3}$.

Changing Decimals to Fractions

To change decimals to fractions, place the decimal portion of the number, the numerator, over the respective place value, the denominator, then reduce, if possible.

Example

Express 0.25 as a fraction.

This is read as twenty-five hundredths, so put 25 over 100. Then reduce to find the solution.

$$\frac{25}{100} = \frac{1}{4}$$

Example

Express 0.455 as a fraction

This is read as four hundred fifty-five thousandths, so put 455 over 1,000. Then reduce to find the solution.

$$\frac{455}{1{,}000} = \frac{91}{200}$$

There are two types of problems that commonly involve percentages. The first is to calculate some percentage of a given quantity, where you convert the percentage to a decimal, and multiply the quantity by that decimal. Secondly, you are given a quantity and told it is a fixed percent of an unknown quantity. In this case, convert to a decimal, then divide the given quantity by that decimal.

Example

What is 30% of 760?

Convert the percent into a useable number. "Of" means to multiply.

$$30\% = 0.30$$

Set up the problem based on the givens, and solve.

$$0.30 \times 760 = 228$$

Example

8.4 is 20% of what number?

Convert the percent into a useable number.

$$20\% = 0.20$$

The given number is a percent of the answer needed, so divide the given number by this decimal rather than multiplying it.

$$\frac{8.4}{0.20} = 42$$

Fractions and Decimals in Order

A rational number is any number that can be written as a fraction or ratio. Within the set of rational numbers, several subsets exist that are referenced throughout the mathematics topics. Counting numbers are the first numbers learned as a child. Counting numbers consist of 1,2,3,4, and so on. Whole numbers include all counting numbers and zero (0,1,2,3,4,...). Integers include counting numbers, their opposites, and zero (...,–3,–2,–1,0,1,2,3,...). Rational numbers are inclusive of integers, fractions, and decimals that terminate, or end (1.7, 0.04213) or repeat ($0.136\overline{5}$).

Placing numbers in an order in which they are listed from smallest to largest is known as **ordering**. Ordering numbers properly can help in the comparison of different quantities of items.

When comparing two numbers to determine if they are equal or if one is greater than the other, it is best to look at the digit furthest to the left of the decimal place (or the first value of the decomposed numbers). If this first digit of each number being compared is equal in place value, then move one digit to the right to conduct a similar comparison. Continue this process until it can be determined that both numbers are equal or a difference is found, showing that one number is greater than the other. If a number is greater than the other number it is being compared to, a symbol such as > (greater than) or < (less than) can be utilized to show this comparison. It is important to remember that the "open mouth" of the symbol should be nearest the larger number.

For example:

1,023,100 compared to 1,023,000

First, compare the digit farthest to the left. Both are decomposed to 1,000,000, so this place is equal.

Next, move one place to right on both numbers being compared. This number is zero for both numbers, so move on to the next number to the right. The first number decomposes to 20,000, while the second decomposes to 20,000. These numbers are also equal, so move one more place to the right. The first number decomposes to 3,000, as does the second number, so they are equal again. Moving one place to the right, the first number decomposes to 100, while the second number is zero. Since 100 is greater than zero, the first number is greater than the second. This is expressed using the greater than symbol:

1,023,100 > 1,023,000 because 1,023,100 is greater than 1,023,000 (Note that the "open mouth" of the symbol is nearest to 1,023,100).

Notice the > symbol in the above comparison. When values are the same, the equals sign (=) is used. However, when values are unequal, or an **inequality** exists, the relationship is denoted by various inequality symbols. These symbols describe in what way the values are unequal. A value could be greater than ($>$); less than ($<$); greater than or equal to ($\geq$); or less than or equal to ($\leq$) another value. The statement "five times a number added to forty is more than sixty-five" can be expressed as $5x + 40 > 65$. Common words and phrases that express inequalities are:

Symbol	Phrase
$<$	is under, is below, smaller than, beneath
$>$	is above, is over, bigger than, exceeds
$\leq$	no more than, at most, maximum
$\geq$	no less than, at least, minimum

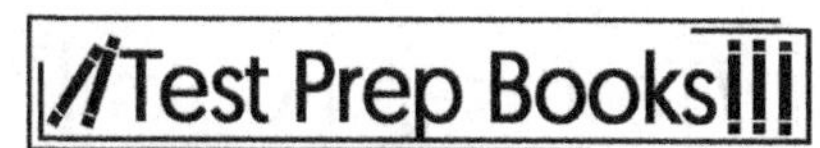

Another way to compare whole numbers with many digits is to use place value. In each number to be compared, it is necessary to find the highest place value in which the numbers differ and to compare the value within that place value. For example, $4{,}523{,}345 < 4{,}532{,}456$ because of the values in the ten thousands place.

Comparing and Ordering Decimals

To compare decimals and order them by their value, utilize a method similar to that of ordering large numbers.

The main difference is where the comparison will start. Assuming that any numbers to left of the decimal point are equal, the next numbers to be compared are those immediately to the right of the decimal point. If those are equal, then move on to compare the values in the next decimal place to the right.

For example:

Which number is greater, 12.35 or 12.38?

Check that the values to the left of the decimal point are equal:

$$12 = 12$$

Next, compare the values of the decimal place to the right of the decimal:

$$12.3 = 12.3$$

Those are also equal in value.

Finally, compare the value of the numbers in the next decimal place to the right on both numbers:

$$12.3\mathbf{5} \text{ and } 12.3\mathbf{8}$$

Here the 5 is less than the 8, so the final way to express this inequality is:

$$12.35 < 12.38$$

Comparing decimals is regularly exemplified with money because the "cents" portion of money ends in the hundredths place. When paying for gasoline or meals in restaurants, and even in bank accounts, if enough errors are made when calculating numbers to the hundredths place, they can add up to dollars and larger amounts of money over time.

Number lines can also be used to compare decimals. Tick marks can be placed within two whole numbers on the number line that represent tenths, hundredths, etc. Each number being compared can then be plotted. The value farthest to the right on the number line is the largest.

Comparing Fractions

To compare fractions with either the same **numerator** (top number) or same **denominator** (bottom number), it is easiest to visualize the fractions with a model.

For example, which is larger, $\frac{1}{3}$ or $\frac{1}{4}$? Both numbers have the same numerator, but a different denominator. In order to demonstrate the difference, shade the amounts on a pie chart split into the number of pieces represented by the denominator.

The first pie chart represents $\frac{1}{3}$, a larger shaded portion, and is therefore a larger fraction than the second pie chart representing $\frac{1}{4}$.

If two fractions have the same denominator (or are split into the same number of pieces), the fraction with the larger numerator is the larger fraction, as seen below in the comparison of $\frac{1}{3}$ and $\frac{2}{3}$:

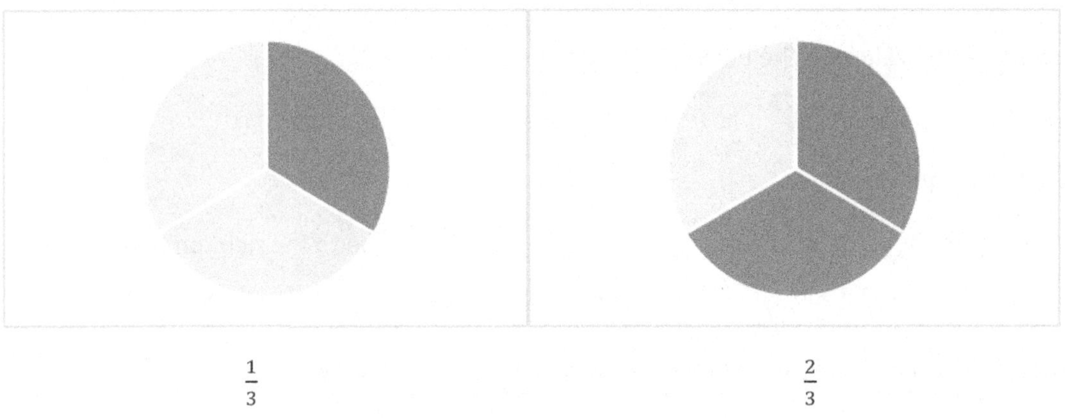

$\frac{1}{3}$ $\frac{2}{3}$

A **unit fraction** is one in which the numerator is 1 ($\frac{1}{2}, \frac{1}{3}, \frac{1}{8}, \frac{1}{20}$, etc.). The denominator indicates the number of equal pieces that the whole is divided into. The greater the number of pieces, the smaller each piece will be. Therefore, the greater the denominator of a unit fraction, the smaller it is in value. Unit fractions can also be compared by converting them to decimals. For example, $\frac{1}{2} = 0.5$, $\frac{1}{3} = 0.\overline{3}$, $\frac{1}{8} = 0.125$, $\frac{1}{20} = 0.05$, etc.

Comparing two fractions with different denominators can be difficult if attempting to guess at how much each represents. Using a number line, blocks, or just finding a common denominator with which to compare the two fractions makes this task easier.

For example, compare the fractions $\frac{3}{4}$ and $\frac{5}{8}$.

The number line method of comparison involves splitting one number line evenly into 4 sections, and the second number line evenly into 8 sections total, as follows:

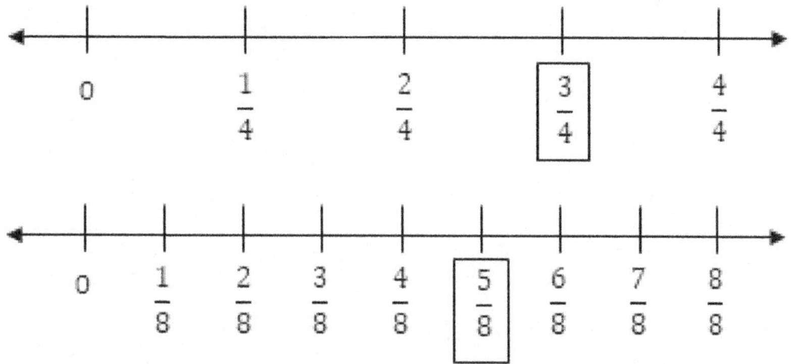

Here it can be observed that $\frac{3}{4}$ is greater than $\frac{5}{8}$, so the comparison is written as $\frac{3}{4} > \frac{5}{8}$.

This could also be shown by finding a common denominator for both fractions, so that they could be compared. First, list out factors of 4: 4, 8, 12, 16.

Then, list out factors of 8: 8, 16, 24.

Both share a common factor of 8, so they can be written in terms of 8 portions. In order for $\frac{3}{4}$ to be written in terms of 8, both the numerator and denominator must be multiplied by 2, thus forming the new fraction $\frac{6}{8}$. Now the two fractions can be compared.

Because both have the same denominator, the numerator will show the comparison.

$$\frac{6}{8} > \frac{5}{8}$$

Ordering Numbers

Whether the question asks to order the numbers from greatest to least or least to greatest, the crux of the question is the same—convert the numbers into a common format. Generally, it's easiest to write the numbers as whole numbers and decimals so they can be placed on a number line. Follow these examples to understand this strategy.

1) Order the following rational numbers from greatest to least:

$$\sqrt{36}, 0.65, 78\%, \frac{3}{4}, 7, 90\%, \frac{5}{2}$$

Of the seven numbers, the whole number (7) and decimal (0.65) are already in an accessible form, so concentrate on the other five.

First, the square root of 36 equals 6. (If the test asks for the root of a non-perfect root, determine which two whole numbers the root lies between.) Next, convert the percentages to decimals. A percentage means "per hundred," so this conversion requires moving the decimal point two places to the left, leaving 0.78 and 0.9. Lastly, evaluate the fractions:

$$\frac{3}{4} = \frac{75}{100} = 0.75$$

$$\frac{5}{2} = 2\frac{1}{2} = 2.5$$

Now, the only step left is to list the numbers in the request order:

$$7, \sqrt{36}, \frac{5}{2}, 90\%, 78\%, \frac{3}{4}, 0.65$$

2) Order the following rational numbers from least to greatest:

$$2.5, \sqrt{9}, -10.5, 0.853, 175\%, \sqrt{4}, \frac{4}{5}$$

$$\sqrt{9} = 3$$

$$175\% = 1.75$$

$$\sqrt{4} = 2$$

$$\frac{4}{5} = 0.8$$

From least to greatest, the answer is: $-10.5, \frac{4}{5}, 0.853, 175\%, \sqrt{4}, 2.5, \sqrt{9}$

It is not possible to give similar relationships between two complex numbers $a + ib$ and $c + id$. This is because the real numbers cannot be identified with the complex numbers, and there is no form of comparison between the two. However, given any polynomial equation, its solutions can be solved in the complex field. If the zeros are real, they can be written as $a + i \times 0$; if they are complex, they can be written as $a + ib$; and if they are imaginary, they can be written as ib.

Ratios and Proportions

Ratios

Ratios are used to show the relationship between two quantities. The ratio of oranges to apples in the grocery store may be 3 to 2. That means that for every 3 oranges, there are 2 apples. This comparison can be expanded to represent the actual number of oranges and apples, such as 36 oranges to 24 apples. Another example may be the number of boys to girls in a math class. If the ratio of boys to girls is given as 2 to 5, that means there are 2 boys to every 5 girls in the class. Ratios can also be compared if the units in each ratio are the same. The ratio of boys to girls in the math class can be compared to the ratio of boys to girls in a science class by stating which ratio is higher and which is lower.

Rates are used to compare two quantities with different units. *Unit rates* are the simplest form of rate. With **unit rates**, the denominator in the comparison of two units is one. For example, if someone can type at a rate of 1,000 words in 5 minutes, then their unit rate for typing is $\frac{1,000}{5} = 200$ words in one minute or 200 words per minute. Any rate can be converted into a unit rate by dividing to make the

denominator one. 1,000 words in 5 minutes has been converted into the unit rate of 200 words per minute.

Ratios and rates can be used together to convert rates into different units. For example, if someone is driving 50 kilometers per hour, that rate can be converted into miles per hour by using a ratio known as the **conversion factor.** Since the given value contains kilometers and the final answer needs to be in miles, the ratio relating miles to kilometers needs to be used. There are 0.62 miles in 1 kilometer. This, written as a ratio and in fraction form, is $\frac{0.62\ miles}{1\ km}$. To convert 50km/hour into miles per hour, the following conversion needs to be set up:

$$\frac{50\ km}{hour} * \frac{0.62\ miles}{1\ km} = 31\ miles\ per\ hour$$

The ratio between two similar geometric figures is called the **scale factor**. For example, a problem may depict two similar triangles, A and B. The scale factor from the smaller triangle A to the larger triangle B is given as 2 because the length of the corresponding side of the larger triangle, 16, is twice the corresponding side on the smaller triangle, 8. This scale factor can also be used to find the value of a missing side, x, in triangle A. Since the scale factor from the smaller triangle (A) to larger one (B) is 2, the larger corresponding side in triangle B (given as 25) can be divided by 2 to find the missing side in A (x = 12.5). The scale factor can also be represented in the equation $2A = B$ because two times the lengths of A gives the corresponding lengths of B. This is the idea behind similar triangles.

Proportions

Much like a scale factor can be written using an equation like $2A = B$, a **relationship** is represented by the equation $Y = kX$. X and Y are proportional because as values of X increase, the values of Y also increase. A relationship that is inversely proportional can be represented by the equation $Y = \frac{k}{X}$, where the value of *Y* decreases as the value of *X* increases and vice versa.

Proportional reasoning can be used to solve problems involving ratios, percentages, and averages. Ratios can be used in setting up proportions and solving them to find unknowns. For example, if a student completes an average of 10 pages of math homework in 3 nights, how long would it take the student to complete 22 pages? Both ratios can be written as fractions. The second ratio would contain the unknown.

The following proportion represents this problem, where x is the unknown number of nights:

$$\frac{10\ pages}{3\ nights} = \frac{22\ pages}{x\ nights}$$

Solving this proportion entails cross-multiplying (multiplying both sets of numbers that are diagonally across and setting them equal to each other) and results in the following equation: $10x = 22 * 3$. Simplifying and solving for x results in the exact solution: $x = 6.6\ nights$. The result would be rounded up to 7 because the homework would actually be completed on the 7th night.

The following problem uses ratios involving percentages:

If 20% of the class is girls and 30 students are in the class, how many girls are in the class?

To set up this problem, it is helpful to use the common proportion: $\frac{\%}{100} = \frac{is}{of}$. Within the proportion, % is the percentage of girls, 100 is the total percentage of the class, *is* is the number of girls, and *of* is the total number of students in the class. Most percentage problems can be written using this language. To solve this problem, the proportion should be set up as $\frac{20}{100} = \frac{x}{30}$ and then solved for x. Cross-multiplying results in the equation $20 * 30 = 100x$, which results in the solution $x = 6$. There are 6 girls in the class.

Ratios can be used to solve problems that concern length, volume, and other units. For example, A problem may ask for the volume of a cone that has a radius, $r = 7m$ and a height, $h = 16m$. Referring to the formulas provided on the test, the volume of a cone is given as: $V = \pi r^2 \frac{h}{3}$, where r is the radius, and h is the height. Plugging $r = 7$ and $h = 16$ into the formula, the following is obtained:

$$V = \pi(7^2)\frac{16}{3}$$

Therefore, the volume of the cone is found to be approximately 821m^3. Sometimes, answers in different units are sought. If this problem wanted the answer in liters, 821m^3 would need to be converted.

Using the equivalence statement 1m^3 = 1,000L, the following ratio would be used to solve for liters:

$$821\text{m}^3 * \frac{1{,}000L}{1m^3}$$

Cubic meters in the numerator and denominator cancel each other out, and the answer is converted to 821,000 liters, or $8.21 * 10^5$ L.

Other conversions can also be made between different given and final units. If the temperature in a pool is 30°C, what is the temperature of the pool in degrees Fahrenheit? To convert these units, an equation is used relating Celsius to Fahrenheit. The following equation is used:

$$T_{°F} = 1.8T_{°C} + 32$$

Plugging in the given temperature and solving the equation for T yields the result:

$$T_{°F} = 1.8(30) + 32 = 86°F$$

Both units in the metric system and U.S. customary system are widely used.

Here are some more examples of how to solve for proportions:

1) $\frac{75\%}{90\%} = \frac{25\%}{x}$

To solve for x, the fractions must be cross multiplied: ($75\%x = 90\% \times 25\%$). To make things easier, let's convert the percentages to decimals: ($0.9 \times 0.25 = 0.225 = 0.75x$). To get rid of x's coefficient,

each side must be divided by that same coefficient to get the answer $x = 0.3$. The question could ask for the answer as a percentage or fraction in lowest terms, which are 30% and $\frac{3}{10}$, respectively.

2) $\frac{x}{12} = \frac{30}{96}$

Cross-multiply: $96x = 30 \times 12$

Multiply: $96x = 360$

Divide: $x = 360 \div 96$

Answer: $x = 3.75$

3) $\frac{0.5}{3} = \frac{x}{6}$

Cross-multiply: $3x = 0.5 \times 6$

Multiply: $3x = 3$

Divide: $x = 3 \div 3$

Answer: $x = 1$

You may have noticed there's a faster way to arrive at the answer. If there is an obvious operation being performed on the proportion, the same operation can be used on the other side of the proportion to solve for x. For example, in the first practice problem, 75% became 25% when divided by 3, and upon doing the same to 90%, the correct answer of 30% would have been found with much less legwork. However, these questions aren't always so intuitive, so it's a good idea to work through the steps, even if the answer seems apparent from the outset.

Percentages

Think of percentages as fractions with a denominator of 100. In fact, **percentage** means "per hundred." Problems often require converting numbers from percentages, fractions, and decimals. The following explains how to work through those conversions.

Conversions

Decimals and Percentages: Since a percentage is based on "per hundred," decimals and percentages can be converted by multiplying or dividing by 100. Practically speaking, this always amounts to moving the decimal point two places to the right or left, depending on the conversion. To convert a percentage to a decimal, move the decimal point two places to the left and remove the % sign. To convert a decimal to a percentage, move the decimal point two places to the right and add a % sign. Here are some examples:

65% = 0.65
0.33 = 33%
0.215 = 21.5%
99.99% = 0.9999
500% = 5.00
7.55 = 755%

Fractions and Percentages: Remember that a percentage is a number per one hundred. So, a percentage can be converted to a fraction by making the number in the percentage the numerator and putting 100 as the denominator:

$$43\% = \frac{43}{100}$$

$$97\% = \frac{97}{100}$$

$$4.7\% = \frac{47}{1{,}000}$$

Note in the last example, that the decimal can be removed by going from 100 to 1,000, because it's accomplished by multiplying the numerator and denominator by 10.

Note that the percent symbol (%) kind of looks like a 0, a 1, and another 0. So, think of a percentage like 54% as 54 over 100. Note that it's often good to simplify a fraction into the smallest possible numbers. So, 54/100 would then become 27/50:

$$\frac{54}{100} \div \frac{2}{2} = \frac{27}{50}$$

To convert a fraction to a percent, follow the same logic. If the fraction happens to have 100 in the denominator, you're in luck. Just take the numerator and add a percent symbol:

$$\frac{28}{100} = 28\%$$

Another option is to make the denominator equal to 100. Be sure to multiply the numerator and the denominator by the same number. For example:

$$\frac{3}{20} \times \frac{5}{5} = \frac{15}{100}$$

$$\frac{15}{100} = 15\%$$

If neither of those strategies work, divide the numerator by the denominator to get a decimal:

$$\frac{9}{12} = 0.75$$

Then convert the decimal to a percentage:

$$0.75 = 75\%$$

Percent Formula

The percent formula looks like this:

$$\frac{\boldsymbol{part}}{\boldsymbol{whole}} = \frac{\%}{\mathbf{100}}$$

After numbers are plugged in, multiply the diagonal numbers and then divide by the remaining one. It works every time.

So, when a question asks what percent 5 is of 10, plug the numbers in like this:

$$\frac{\mathbf{5}}{\mathbf{10}} = \frac{\%}{\mathbf{100}}$$

Multiply the diagonal numbers:

$$5 \times 100 \ = 500$$

Divide by the remaining number:

$$\frac{500}{10} = 50\%$$

The percent formula can be applied in a number of different circumstances by plugging in the numbers appropriately.

Unit Rates

Unit rate word problems will ask you to calculate the rate or quantity of something in a different value. For example, a problem might say that a car drove a certain number of miles in a certain number of minutes and then ask how many miles per hour the car was traveling. These questions involve solving proportions. Consider the following examples:

1) Alexandra made $96 during the first 3 hours of her shift as a temporary worker at a law office. She will continue to earn money at this rate until she finishes in 5 more hours. How much does Alexandra make per hour? How much will Alexandra have made at the end of the day?

This problem can be solved in two ways. The first is to set up a proportion, as the rate of pay is constant. The second is to determine her hourly rate, multiply the 5 hours by that rate, and then add the $96.

To set up a proportion, put the money already earned over the hours already worked on one side of an equation. The other side has x over 8 hours (the total hours worked in the day). It looks like this:

$$\frac{96}{3} = \frac{x}{8}$$

Now, cross-multiply to get $768 = 3x$. To get x, divide by 3, which leaves $x \ = \ 256$. Alternatively, as x is the numerator of one of the proportions, multiplying by its denominator will reduce the solution by one step. Thus, Alexandra will make \$256 at the end of the day. To calculate her hourly rate, divide the total by 8, giving \$32 per hour.

Alternatively, it is possible to figure out the hourly rate by dividing \$96 by 3 hours to get \$32 per hour. Now her total pay can be figured by multiplying \$32 per hour by 8 hours, which comes out to \$256.

2) Jonathan is reading a novel. So far, he has read 215 of the 335 total pages. It takes Jonathan 25 minutes to read 10 pages, and the rate is constant. How long does it take Jonathan to read one page? How much longer will it take him to finish the novel? Express the answer in time.

To calculate how long it takes Jonathan to read one page, divide the 25 minutes by 10 pages to determine the page per minute rate. Thus, it takes 2.5 minutes to read one page.

Jonathan must read 120 more pages to complete the novel. (This is calculated by subtracting the pages already read from the total.) Now, multiply his rate per page by the number of pages. Thus:

$$12 \times 2.5 = 300$$

Expressed in time, 300 minutes is equal to 5 hours.

3) At a hotel, $\frac{4}{5}$ of the 120 rooms are booked for Saturday. On Sunday, $\frac{3}{4}$ of the rooms are booked. On which day are more of the rooms booked, and by how many more?

The first step is to calculate the number of rooms booked for each day. Do this by multiplying the fraction of the rooms booked by the total number of rooms.

Saturday: $\frac{4}{5} \times 120 = \frac{4}{5} \times \frac{120}{1} = \frac{480}{5} = 96$ rooms

Sunday: $\frac{3}{4} \times 120 = \frac{3}{4} \times \frac{120}{1} = \frac{360}{4} = 90$ rooms

Thus, more rooms were booked on Saturday by 6 rooms.

4) In a veterinary hospital, the veterinarian-to-pet ratio is 1:9. The ratio is always constant. If there are 45 pets in the hospital, how many veterinarians are currently in the veterinary hospital?

Set up a proportion to solve for the number of veterinarians: $\frac{1}{9} = \frac{x}{45}$

Cross-multiplying results in $9x = 45$, which works out to 5 veterinarians.

Alternatively, as there are always 9 times as many pets as veterinarians, it is possible to divide the number of pets (45) by 9. This also arrives at the correct answer of 5 veterinarians.

5) At a general practice law firm, 30% of the lawyers work solely on tort cases. If 9 lawyers work solely on tort cases, how many lawyers work at the firm?

First, solve for the total number of lawyers working at the firm, which will be represented here with x. The problem states that 9 lawyers work solely on torts cases, and they make up 30% of the total lawyers at the firm. Thus, 30% multiplied by the total, x, will equal 9. Written as equation, this is: $30\% \times x = 9$.

It's easier to deal with the equation after converting the percentage to a decimal, leaving $0.3x = 9$. Thus:

$$x = \frac{9}{0.3} = 30$$

lawyers working at the firm.

6) Xavier was hospitalized with pneumonia. He was originally given 35mg of antibiotics. Later, after his condition continued to worsen, Xavier's dosage was increased to 60mg. What was the percent increase of the antibiotics? Round the percentage to the nearest tenth.

An increase or decrease in percentage can be calculated by dividing the difference in amounts by the original amount and multiplying by 100. Written as an equation, the formula is:

$$\frac{new\ quantity\ -\ old\ quantity}{old\ quantity} \times 100$$

Here, the question states that the dosage was increased from 35mg to 60mg, so these are plugged into the formula to find the percentage increase.

$$\frac{60\ -\ 35}{35} \times\ 100\ =\ \frac{25}{35} \times 100 =\ .7142\ \times 100\ = 71.4\%$$

Multiple-Step Problems that Use Ratios, Proportions, and Percentages

Solving Real-World Problems Involving Ratios and Rates of Change

Ratios are used to show the relationship between two quantities. The ratio of oranges to apples in the grocery store may be 3 to 2. That means that for every 3 oranges, there are 2 apples. This comparison can be expanded to represent the actual number of oranges and apples, such as 36 oranges to 24 apples. Another example may be the number of boys to girls in a math class. If the ratio of boys to girls is given as 2 to 5, that means there are 2 boys to every 5 girls in the class. Ratios can also be compared if the units in each ratio are the same. The ratio of boys to girls in the math class can be compared to the ratio of boys to girls in a science class by stating which ratio is higher and which is lower.

Rates are used to compare two quantities with different units. **Unit rates** are the simplest form of rate. With unit rates, the denominator in the comparison of two units is one. For example, if someone can type at a rate of 1,000 words in 5 minutes, then their unit rate for typing is $\frac{1,000}{5} = 200$ words in one minute or 200 words per minute. Any rate can be converted into a unit rate by dividing to make the denominator one. 1,000 words in 5 minutes has been converted into the unit rate of 200 words per minute.

Ratios and rates can be used together to convert rates into different units. For example, if someone is driving 50 kilometers per hour, that rate can be converted into miles per hour by using a ratio known as the **conversion factor**. Since the given value contains kilometers and the final answer needs to be in miles, the ratio relating miles to kilometers needs to be used. There are 0.62 miles in 1 kilometer. This, written as a ratio and in fraction form, is $\frac{0.62 \, miles}{1 \, km}$. To convert 50km/hour into miles per hour, the following conversion needs to be set up:

$$\frac{50 \, km}{hour} \times \frac{0.62 \, miles}{1 \, km} = 31 \, miles \, per \, hour$$

When dealing with word problems, there is no fixed series of steps to follow, but there are some general guidelines to use. It is important that the quantity to be found is identified. Then, it can be determined how the given values can be used and manipulated to find the final answer.

Example: Jana wants to travel to visit Alice, who lives one hundred and fifty miles away. If she can drive at fifty miles per hour, how long will her trip take?

The quantity to find is the *time* of the trip. The time of a trip is given by the distance to travel divided by the speed to be traveled. The problem determines that the distance is one hundred and fifty miles, while the speed is fifty miles per hour. Thus, 150 divided by 50 is $150 \div 50 = 3$. Because *miles* and *miles per hour* are the units being divided, the miles cancel out. The result is 3 hours.

Example: Bernard wishes to paint a wall that measures twenty feet wide by eight feet high. It costs ten cents to paint one square foot. How much money will Bernard need for paint?

The final quantity to compute is the *cost* to paint the wall. This will be ten cents ($0.10) for each square foot of area needed to paint. The area to be painted is unknown, but the dimensions of the wall are given; thus, it can be calculated.

The dimensions of the wall are 20 feet wide and 8 feet high. Since the area of a rectangle is length multiplied by width, the area of the wall is:

$8 \times 20 = 160 \, square \, feet$

Multiplying 0.1×160 yields $16 as the cost of the paint.

Solving Real-World Problems Involving Proportions

Much like a scale factor can be written using an equation like $2A = B$, a **relationship** is represented by the equation $Y = kX$. X and Y are proportional because as values of X increase, the values of Y also increase. A relationship that is inversely proportional can be represented by the equation $Y = \frac{k}{X}$, where the value of Y decreases as the value of X increases and vice versa.

Proportional reasoning can be used to solve problems involving ratios, percentages, and averages. Ratios can be used in setting up proportions and solving them to find unknowns. For example, if a student completes an average of 10 pages of math homework in 3 nights, how long would it take the student to complete 22 pages? Both ratios can be written as fractions. The second ratio would contain the unknown.

The following proportion represents this problem, where x is the unknown number of nights:

$$\frac{10 \, pages}{3 \, nights} = \frac{22 \, pages}{x \, nights}$$

Solving this proportion entails cross-multiplying and results in the following equation: $10x = 22 \times 3$. Simplifying and solving for x results in the exact solution: $x = 6.6\ nights$. The result would be rounded up to 7 because the homework would actually be completed on the 7th night.

The following problem uses ratios involving percentages:

If 20% of the class is girls and 30 students are in the class, how many girls are in the class?

To set up this problem, it is helpful to use the common proportion: $\frac{\%}{100} = \frac{is}{of}$. Within the proportion, % is the percentage of girls, 100 is the total percentage of the class, *is* is the number of girls, and *of* is the total number of students in the class. Most percentage problems can be written using this language. To solve this problem, the proportion should be set up as $\frac{20}{100} = \frac{x}{30}$, and then solved for x. Cross-multiplying results in the equation $20 \times 30 = 100x$, which results in the solution $x = 6$. There are 6 girls in the class.

Problems involving volume, length, and other units can also be solved using ratios. For example, a problem may ask for the volume of a cone to be found that has a radius:

$$r = 7m$$

and a height:

$$h = 16m$$

Referring to the formulas provided on the test, the volume of a cone is given as:

$$V = \pi r^2 \frac{h}{3}$$

where r is the radius, and h is the height. Plugging $r = 7$ and $h = 16$ into the formula, the following is obtained:

$$V = \pi(7^2)\frac{16}{3}$$

Therefore, volume of the cone is found to be $821m^3$. Sometimes, answers in different units are sought. If this problem wanted the answer in liters, $821m^3$ would need to be converted. Using the equivalence statement $1m^3 = 1{,}000L$, the following ratio would be used to solve for liters:

$$821\text{m}^3 \times \frac{1{,}000L}{1m^3}$$

Cubic meters in the numerator and denominator cancel each other out, and the answer is converted to 821,000 liters, or 8.21×10^5 L.

Other conversions can also be made between different given and final units. If the temperature in a pool is 30°C, what is the temperature of the pool in degrees Fahrenheit? To convert these units, an equation is used relating Celsius to Fahrenheit. The following equation is used:

$$T_{°F} = 1.8T_{°C} + 32$$

Plugging in the given temperature and solving the equation for T yields the result:

$$T_{°F} = 1.8(30) + 32 = 86°F$$

Units in both the metric system and U.S. customary system are widely used.

Here are some more examples of how to solve for proportions:

1) $\frac{75\%}{90\%} = \frac{25\%}{x}$

To solve for x, the fractions must be cross multiplied:

$$(75\%x = 90\% \times 25\%)$$

To make things easier, let's convert the percentages to decimals:

$$(0.9 \times 0.25 = 0.225 = 0.75x)$$

To get rid of x's coefficient, each side must be divided by that same coefficient to get the answer $x = 0.3$. The question could ask for the answer as a percentage or fraction in lowest terms, which are 30% and $\frac{3}{10}$, respectively.

2) $\frac{x}{12} = \frac{30}{96}$

Cross-multiply: $96x = 30 \times 12$

Multiply: $96x = 360$

Divide: $x = 360 \div 96$

Answer: $x = 3.75$

3) $\frac{0.5}{3} = \frac{x}{6}$

Cross-multiply: $3x = 0.5 \times 6$

Multiply: $3x = 3$

Divide: $x = 3 \div 3$

Answer: $x = 1$

You may have noticed there's a faster way to arrive at the answer. If there is an obvious operation being performed on the proportion, the same operation can be used on the other side of the proportion to solve for x. For example, in the first practice problem, 75% became 25% when divided by 3, and upon doing the same to 90%, the correct answer of 30% would have been found with much less legwork. However, these questions aren't always so intuitive, so it's a good idea to work through the steps, even if the answer seems apparent from the outset.

Solving Real-World Problems Involving Percentages

Questions dealing with percentages can be difficult when they are phrased as word problems. These word problems almost always come in three varieties. The first type will ask to find what percentage of some number will equal another number. The second asks to determine what number is some percentage of another given number. The third will ask what number another number is a given percentage of.

One of the most important parts of correctly answering percentage word problems is to identify the numerator and the denominator. This fraction can then be converted into a percentage, as described above.

The following word problem shows how to make this conversion:

A department store carries several different types of footwear. The store is currently selling 8 athletic shoes, 7 dress shoes, and 5 sandals. What percentage of the store's footwear are sandals?

First, calculate what serves as the **whole**, as this will be the denominator. How many total pieces of footwear does the store sell? The store sells 20 different types ($8\ athletic + 7\ dress + 5\ sandals$).

Second, what footwear type is the question specifically asking about? Sandals. Thus, 5 is the numerator.

Third, the resultant fraction must be expressed as a percentage. The first two steps indicate that $\frac{5}{20}$ of the footwear pieces are sandals. This fraction must now be converted into a percentage:

$$\frac{5}{20} \times \frac{5}{5} = \frac{25}{100} = 25\%$$

Simplifying Exponents

Exponents are used in mathematics to express a number or variable multiplied by itself a certain number of times. For example, x^3 means x is multiplied by itself three times. In this expression, x is called the **base,** and 3 is the **exponent.** Exponents can be used in more complex problems when they contain fractions and negative numbers.

Fractional exponents can be explained by looking first at the inverse of exponents, which are **roots**. Given the expression x^2, the square root can be taken, $\sqrt{x^2}$, cancelling out the 2 and leaving *x* by itself, if *x* is positive. Cancellation occurs because $\sqrt{x}$ can be written with exponents, instead of roots, as $x^{\frac{1}{2}}$. The numerator of 1 is the exponent, and the denominator of 2 is called the root (which is why it's referred to as **square root**). Taking the square root of x^2 is the same as raising it to the $\frac{1}{2}$ power. Written out in mathematical form, it takes the following progression:

$$\sqrt{x^2} = (x^2)^{\frac{1}{2}} = x$$

From properties of exponents:

$$2 \times \frac{1}{2} = 1$$

is the actual exponent of *x*. Another example can be seen with $x^{\frac{4}{7}}$. The variable *x,* raised to four-sevenths, is equal to the seventh root of *x* to the fourth power: $\sqrt[7]{x^4}$. In general,

$$x^{\frac{1}{n}} = \sqrt[n]{x}$$

and

$$x^{\frac{m}{n}} = \sqrt[n]{x^m}$$

Negative exponents also involve fractions. Whereas y^3 can also be rewritten as $\frac{y^3}{1}$, y^{-3} can be rewritten as $\frac{1}{y^3}$. A negative exponent means the exponential expression must be moved to the opposite spot in a fraction to make the exponent positive. If the negative appears in the numerator, it moves to the denominator. If the negative appears in the denominator, it is moved to the numerator. In general, $a^{-n} = \frac{1}{a^n}$, and a^{-n} and a^n are reciprocals.

Take, for example, the following expression:

$$\frac{a^{-4}b^2}{c^{-5}}$$

Since *a* is raised to the negative fourth power, it can be moved to the denominator. Since *c* is raised to the negative fifth power, it can be moved to the numerator. The *b* variable is raised to the positive second power, so it does not move.

The simplified expression is as follows:

$$\frac{b^2c^5}{a^4}$$

In mathematical expressions containing exponents and other operations, the order of operations must be followed. **PEMDAS** states that exponents are calculated after any parentheses and grouping symbols but before any multiplication, division, addition, and subtraction.

There are a few rules for working with exponents. For any numbers $a, b, m, n,$ the following hold true:

$$a^1 = a$$

$$1^a = 1$$

$$a^0 = 1$$

$$a^m \times a^n = a^{m+n}$$

$$a^m \div a^n = a^{m-n}$$

$$(a^m)^n = a^{m \times n}$$

$$(a \times b)^m = a^m \times b^m$$

$$(a \div b)^m = a^m \div b^m$$

Any number, including a fraction, can be an exponent. The same rules apply.

Squares, Square Roots, Cubes, and Cube Roots

A **root** is a different way to write an exponent when the exponent is the reciprocal of a whole number. We use the **radical** symbol to write this in the following way:

$$\sqrt[n]{a} = a^{\frac{1}{n}}$$

This quantity is called the *n-th* **root** of *a*. The *n* is called the **index** of the radical.

Note that if the *n*-th root of *a* is multiplied by itself *n* times, the result will just be *a*. If no number *n* is written by the radical, it is assumed that *n* is 2: $\sqrt{5} = 5^{\frac{1}{2}}$. The special case of the 2nd root is called the **square root,** and the third root is called the **cube root**.

A **perfect square** is a whole number that is the square of another whole number. For example, 16 and 64 are perfect squares because 16 is the square of 4, and 64 is the square of 8.

Undefined Expressions

Expressions can be undefined when they involve dividing by zero or having a zero denominator. In simple fractions, the numerator and denominator can be nearly any integer. However, the denominator of a fraction can never be zero because dividing by zero is a function that is undefined. Trying to take the square root of a negative number also yields an undefined result.

Objects at Scale

Scale drawings are used in designs to model the actual measurements of a real-world object. For example, the blueprint of a house might indicate that it is drawn at a scale of 3 inches to 8 feet. Given one value and asked to determine the width of the house, a proportion should be set up to solve the problem. Given the scale of 3in:8ft and a blueprint width of 1 ft (12 in.), to find the actual width of the building, the proportion $\frac{3}{8} = \frac{12}{x}$ should be used. This results in an actual width of 32 ft.

The ratio between two similar geometric figures is called the **scale factor**. For example, a problem may depict two similar triangles, A and B. The scale factor from the smaller triangle A to the larger triangle B is given as 2 because the length of the corresponding side of the larger triangle, 16, is twice the corresponding side on the smaller triangle, 8. This scale factor can also be used to find the value of a missing side, x, in triangle A. Since the scale factor from the smaller triangle (A) to larger one (B) is 2, the larger corresponding side in triangle B (given as 25) can be divided by 2 to find the missing side in A (x = 12.5). The scale factor can also be represented in the equation $2A = B$ because two times the lengths of A gives the corresponding lengths of B. This is the idea behind similar triangles.

Geometry

Side Lengths of Shapes When Given the Area or Perimeter

The **perimeter** of a polygon is the distance around the outside of the two-dimensional figure or the sum of the lengths of all the sides. Perimeter is a one-dimensional measurement and is therefore expressed in linear units such as centimeters (*cm*), feet (*ft*), and miles (*mi*). The perimeter (*P*) of a figure can be calculated by adding together each of the sides.

Properties of certain polygons allow that the perimeter may be obtained by using formulas. A regular polygon is one in which all sides have equal length and all interior angles have equal measures, such as a square and an equilateral triangle. To find the perimeter of a regular polygon, the length of one side is multiplied by the number of sides.

A rectangle consists of two sides called the length (*l*), which have equal measures, and two sides called the width (*w*), which have equal measures. Therefore, the perimeter (*P*) of a rectangle can be expressed as:

$$P = l + l + w + w$$

This can be simplified to produce the following formula to find the perimeter of a rectangle:

$$P = 2l + 2w \text{ or } P = 2(l + w)$$

Consider the following problem:

The total perimeter of a rectangular garden is 36m. If the length of each side is 12m, what is the width?

The formula for the perimeter of a rectangle is $P = 2L + 2W$, where P is the perimeter, L is the length, and W is the width. The first step is to substitute all of the data into the formula:

$$36 = 2(12) + 2W$$

Simplify by multiplying 2×12:

$$36 = 24 + 2W$$

Simplifying this further by subtracting 24 on each side gives:

$$36 - 24 = 24 - 24 + 2W$$

$$12 = 2W$$

Divide by 2:

$$6 = W$$

The width is 6 cm. Remember to test this answer by substituting this value into the original formula:

$$36 = 2(12) + 2(6)$$

The perimeter of a square is measured by adding together all of the sides. Since a square has four equal sides, its perimeter can be calculated by multiplying the length of one side by 4. Thus, the formula is $P = 4 \times s$, where s equals one side. For example, the following square has side lengths of 5 meters:

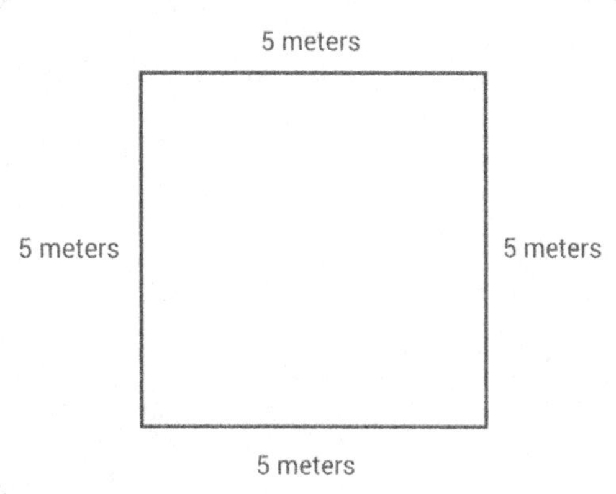

The perimeter is 20 meters because 4 times 5 is 20.

A triangle's perimeter is measured by adding together the three sides, so the formula is $P = a + b + c$, where a, b, and c are the values of the three sides. The area is calculated by multiplying the length of the base times the height times ½, so the formula is:

$$A = \frac{1}{2} \times b \times h = \frac{bh}{2}$$

The base is the bottom of the triangle, and the height is the distance from the base to the peak. If a problem asks to calculate the area of a triangle, it will provide the base and height.

Missing side lengths can be determined using subtraction. For example, if you are told that a triangle has a perimeter of 34 inches and that one side is 12 inches, another side is 16 inches, and the third side is unknown, you can calculate the length of that unknown side by setting up the following subtraction problem:

$$34\ inches = 12\ inches + 16\ inches + x$$

$$34\ inches = 28\ inches + x$$

$$6\ inches = x$$

Therefore, the missing side length is 6 inches.

Area and Perimeter of Two-Dimensional Shapes

As mentioned, the **perimeter** of a polygon is the distance around the outside of the two-dimensional figure. Perimeter is a one-dimensional measurement and is therefore expressed in linear units such as centimeters (*cm*), feet (*ft*), and miles (*mi*). The perimeter (*P*) of a figure can be calculated by adding together each of the sides.

The **area** of a polygon is the number of square units needed to cover the interior region of the figure. Area is a two-dimensional measurement. Therefore, area is expressed in square units, such as square centimeters (cm^2), square feet (ft^2), or square miles (mi^2). Regarding the area of a rectangle with sides of length x and y, the area is given by xy. For a triangle with a base of length b and a height of length h, the area is $\frac{1}{2}bh$. To find the area (A) of a parallelogram, the length of the base (b) is multiplied by the length of the height:

$$(h) \rightarrow A = b \times h$$

Similar to triangles, the height of the parallelogram is measured from one base to the other at a 90° angle (or perpendicular).

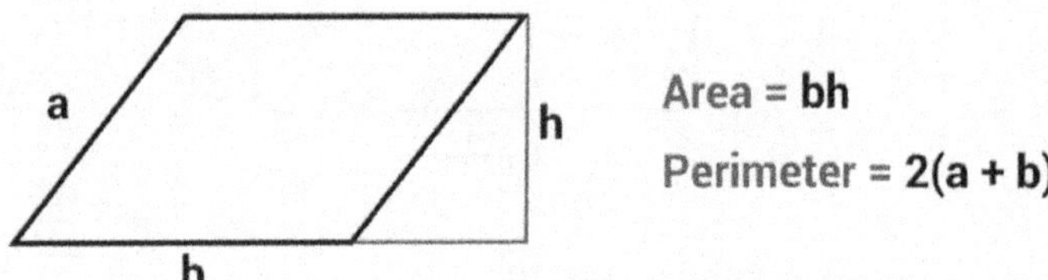

The area of a trapezoid can be calculated using the formula:

$$A = \frac{1}{2} \times h(b_1 + b_2)$$

where h is the height, and b_1 and b_2 are the parallel bases of the trapezoid.

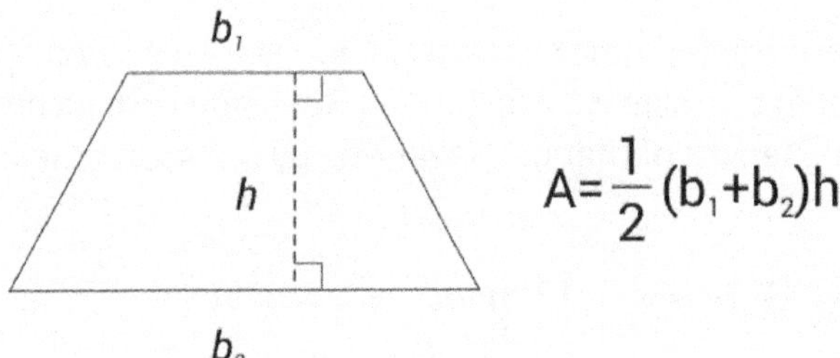

The area of a regular polygon can be determined by using its perimeter and the length of the **apothem**. The apothem is a line from the center of the regular polygon to any of its sides at a right angle. (Note

that the perimeter of a regular polygon can be determined given the length of only one side.) The formula for the area (A) of a regular polygon is

$$A = \frac{1}{2} \times a \times P$$

where a is the length of the apothem, and P is the perimeter of the figure. Consider the following regular pentagon:

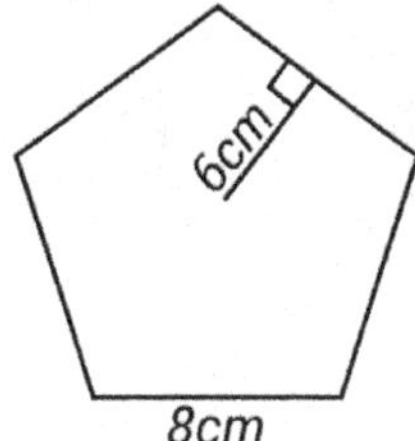

To find the area, the perimeter (P) is calculated first:

$$8cm \times 5 \rightarrow P = 40cm$$

Then the perimeter and the apothem are used to find the area (A):

$$A = \frac{1}{2} \times a \times P$$

$$A = \frac{1}{2} \times (6cm) \times (40cm)$$

$$A = 120cm^2$$

Note that the unit is:

$$cm^2 \rightarrow cm \times cm = cm^2$$

The area of irregular polygons is found by decomposing, or breaking apart, the figure into smaller shapes. When the area of the smaller shapes is determined, the area of the smaller shapes will produce the area of the original figure when added together. Consider the example below:

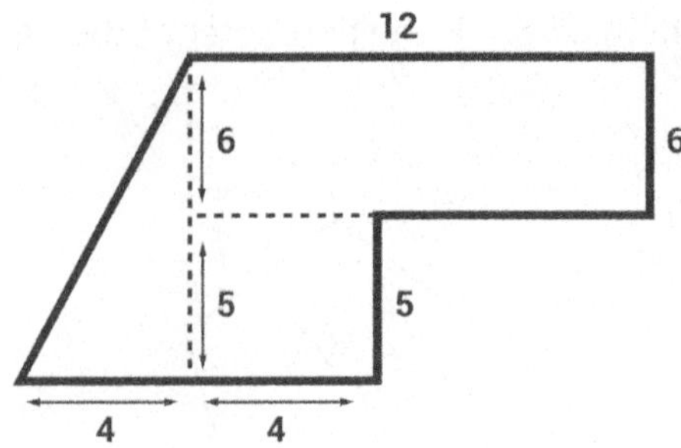

The irregular polygon is decomposed into two rectangles and a triangle. The area of the large rectangle:

$$(A = l \times w \rightarrow A = 12 \times 6)$$

is 72 square units. The area of the small rectangle is 20 square units:

$$A = 4 \times 5$$

The area of the triangle:

$$A = \frac{1}{2} \times b \times h$$

$$A = \frac{1}{2} \times 4 \times 11$$

22 square units

The sum of the areas of these figures produces the total area of the original polygon:

$$A = 72 + 20 + 22$$

A = 114 square units

The perimeter (*P*) of the figure below is calculated by:

$$P = 9m + 5m + 4m + 6m + 8m \rightarrow P = 32\ m$$

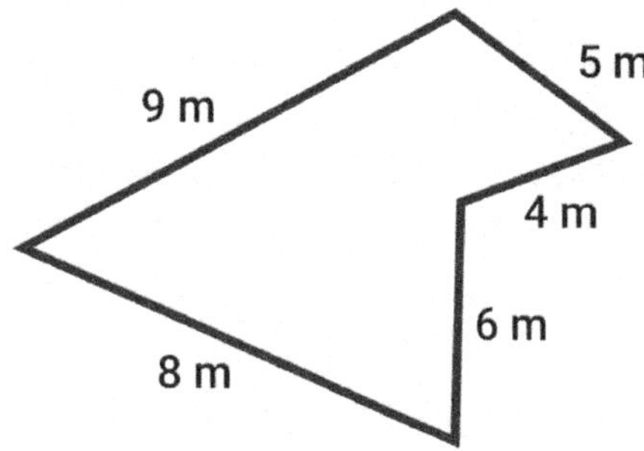

Area, Circumference, Radius, and Diameter of a Circle

A **circle** can be defined as the set of all points that are the same distance (known as the **radius**, *r*) from a single point (known as the **center** of the circle). The center has coordinates (h, k), and any point on the circle can be labelled with coordinates (x, y).

A circle's perimeter—also known as its circumference—is measured by multiplying the diameter (the straight line measured from one end to the direct opposite end of the circle) by π, so the formula is $\pi \times d$. This is sometimes expressed by the formula $C = 2 \times \pi \times r$, where r is the radius of the circle. These formulas are equivalent, as the radius equals half of the diameter.

The area of a circle is calculated through the formula $A = \pi \times r^2$. The test will indicate either to leave the answer with π attached or to calculate to the nearest decimal place, which means multiplying by 3.14 for π.

Given two points on the circumference of a circle, the path along the circle between those points is called an **arc** of the circle. For example, the arc between *B* and *C* is denoted by a thinner line:

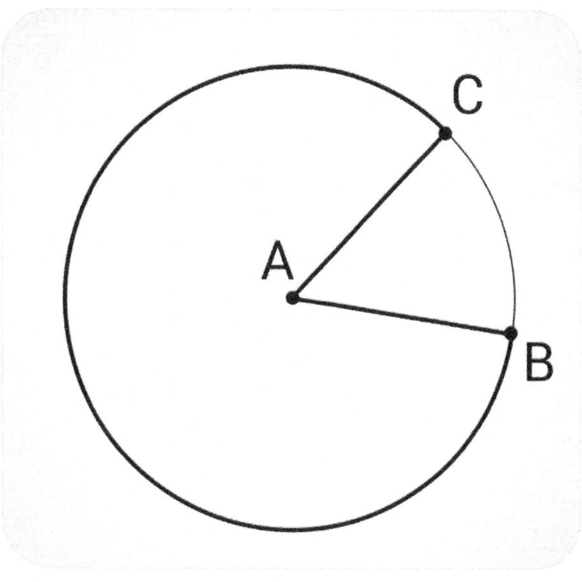

The length of the path along an arc is called the **arc length**. If the circle has radius *r*, then the arc length is given by multiplying the measure of the angle in radians by the radius of the circle.

Pythagorean Theorem

The Pythagorean theorem is an important concept in geometry. It states that for right triangles, the sum of the squares of the two shorter sides will be equal to the square of the longest side (also called the **hypotenuse**). The longest side will always be the side opposite to the 90° angle. If this side is called *c*, and the other two sides are *a* and *b*, then the Pythagorean theorem states that:

$$c^2 = a^2 + b^2$$

Since lengths are always positive, this also can be written as:

$$c = \sqrt{a^2 + b^2}$$

A diagram to show the parts of a triangle using the Pythagorean theorem is below.

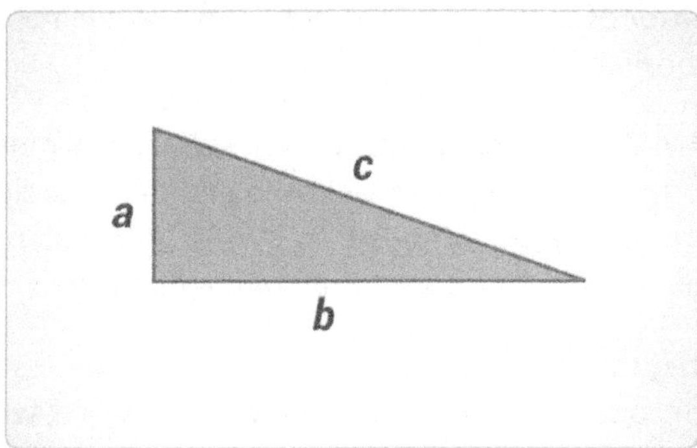

As an example of the theorem, suppose that Shirley has a rectangular field that is 5 feet wide and 12 feet long, and she wants to split it in half using a fence that goes from one corner to the opposite corner. How long will this fence need to be? To figure this out, note that this makes the field into two right triangles, whose hypotenuse will be the fence dividing it in half. Therefore, the fence length will be given by

$$\sqrt{5^2 + 12^2} = \sqrt{169} = 13 \text{ feet long}$$

Graphical Data Including Graphs, Tables, and More

A set of data can be visually displayed in various forms allowing for quick identification of characteristics of the set. **Histograms**, such as the one shown below, display the number of data points (vertical axis) that fall into given intervals (horizontal axis) across the range of the set. The histogram below displays the heights of black cherry trees in a certain city park. Each rectangle represents the number of trees with heights between a given five-point span. For example, the furthest bar to the right indicates that

two trees are between 85 and 90 feet. Histograms can describe the center, spread, shape, and any unusual characteristics of a data set.

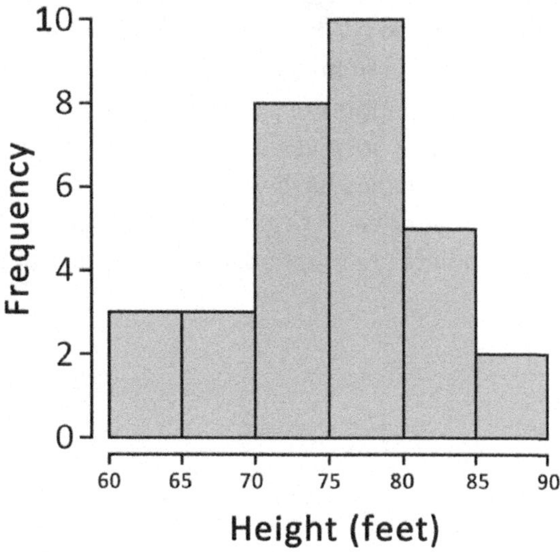

A **box plot**, also called a **box-and-whisker plot**, divides the data points into four groups and displays the five-number summary for the set as well as any outliers. The five-number summary consists of:

- The lower extreme: the lowest value that is not an outlier
- The higher extreme: the highest value that is not an outlier
- The median of the set: also referred to as the second quartile or Q_2
- The first quartile or Q_1: the median of values below Q_2
- The third quartile or Q_3: the median of values above Q_2

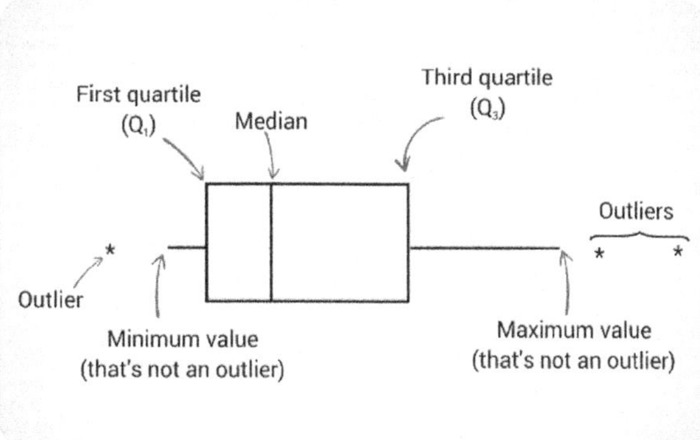

Suppose the box plot displays IQ scores for 12th grade students at a given school. The five-number summary of the data consists of: lower extreme (67); upper extreme (127); Q_2or median (100); Q_1 (91); Q_3 (108); and outliers (135 and 140). Although all data points are not known from the plot, the points are divided into four quartiles each, including 25% of the data points. Therefore, 25% of students scored between 67 and 91, 25% scored between 91 and 100, 25% scored between 100 and 108, and 25%

scored between 108 and 127. These percentages include the normal values for the set and exclude the outliers. This information is useful when comparing a given score with the rest of the scores in the set.

A **scatter plot** is a mathematical diagram that visually displays the relationship or connection between two variables. The independent variable is placed on the *x*-axis, or horizontal axis, and the dependent variable is placed on the *y*-axis, or vertical axis. When visually examining the points on the graph, if the points model a linear relationship, or if a line of best-fit can be drawn through the points with the points relatively close on either side, then a correlation exists. If the line of best-fit has a positive slope (rises from left to right), then the variables have a positive correlation. If the line of best-fit has a negative slope (falls from left to right), then the variables have a negative correlation. If a line of best-fit cannot be drawn, then no correlation exists. A positive or negative correlation can be categorized as strong or weak, depending on how closely the points are graphed around the line of best-fit.

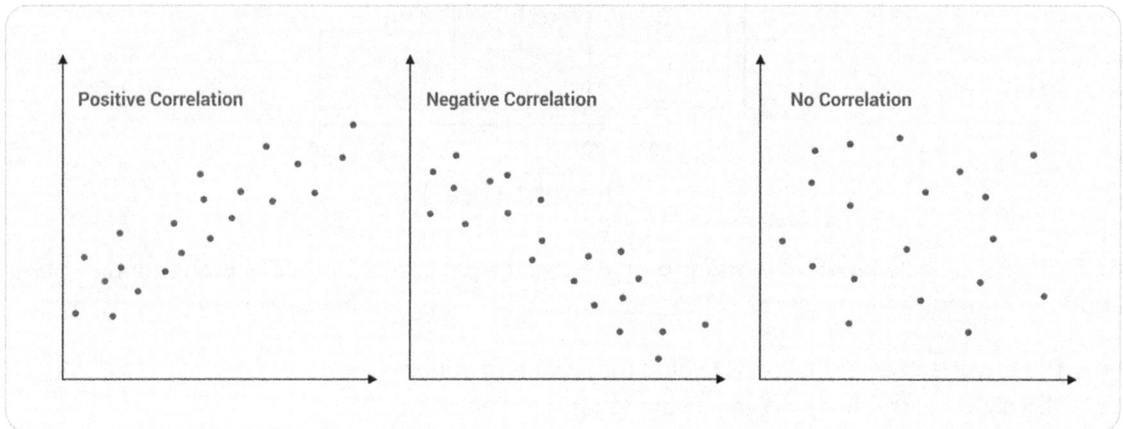

Like a scatter plot, a **line graph** compares variables that change continuously, typically over time. Paired data values (ordered pair) are plotted on a coordinate grid with the *x*- and *y*-axis representing the variables. A line is drawn from each point to the next, going from left to right. The line graph below displays cell phone use for given years (two variables) for men, women, and both sexes (three data sets).

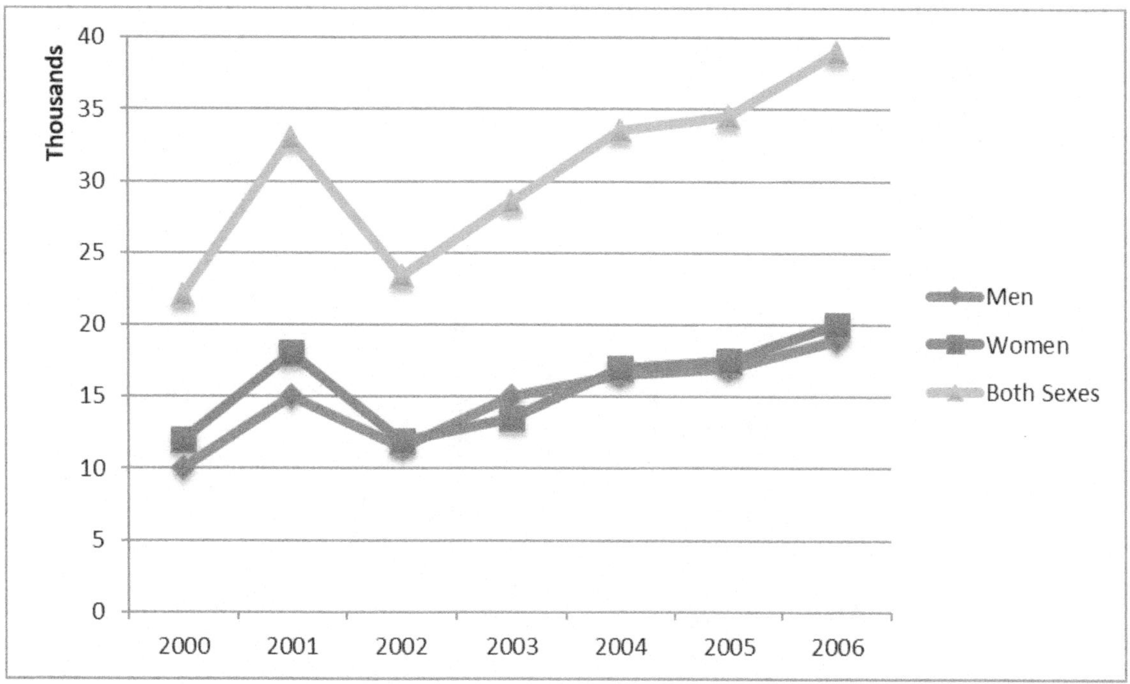

A **line plot**, also called **dot plot**, displays the frequency of data (numerical values) on a number line. To construct a line plot, a number line is used that includes all unique data values. It is marked with x's or dots above the value the number of times that the value occurs in the data set.

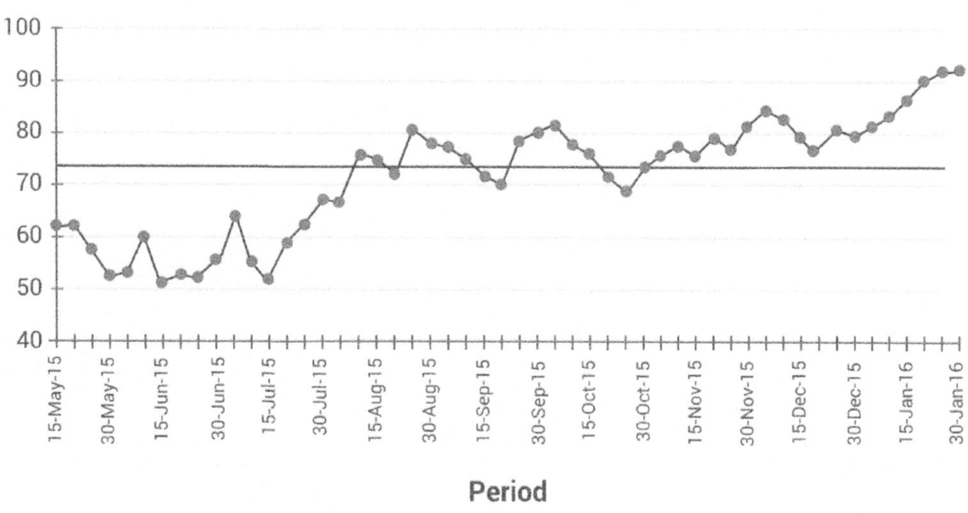

A **bar graph** is a diagram in which the quantity of items within a specific classification is represented by the height of a rectangle. Each type of classification is represented by a rectangle of equal width. Here is an example of a bar graph:

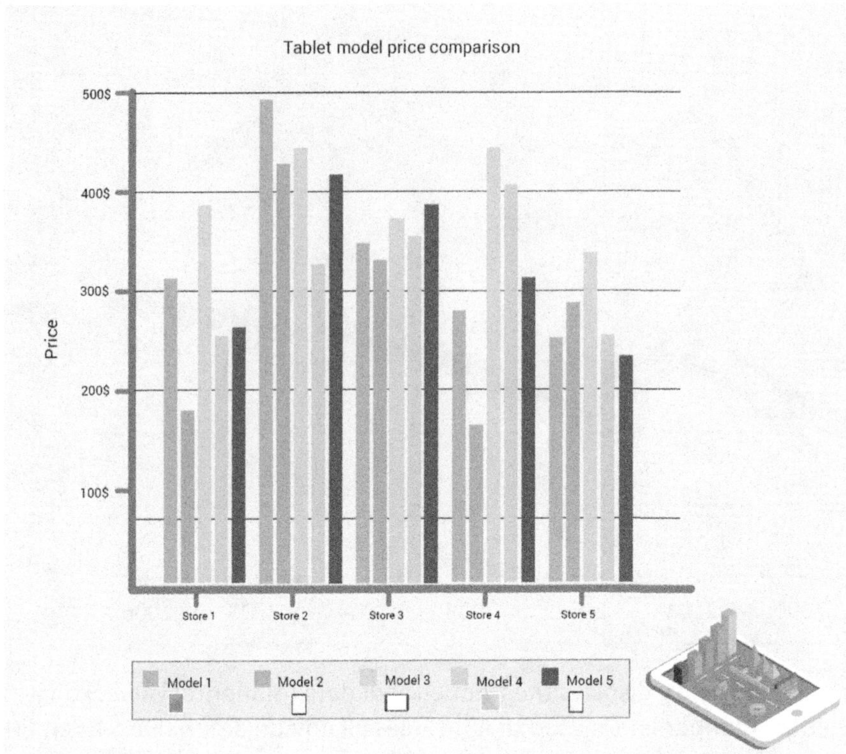

A **circle graph**, also called a **pie chart**, shows categorical data with each category representing a percentage of the whole data set. To make a circle graph, the percent of the data set for each category must be determined. To do so, the frequency of the category is divided by the total number of data points and converted to a percent. For example, if 80 people were asked what their favorite sport is and 20 responded basketball, basketball makes up 25% of the data ($\frac{20}{80} = 0.25 = 25\%$). Each category in a data set is represented by a slice of the circle proportionate to its percentage of the whole.

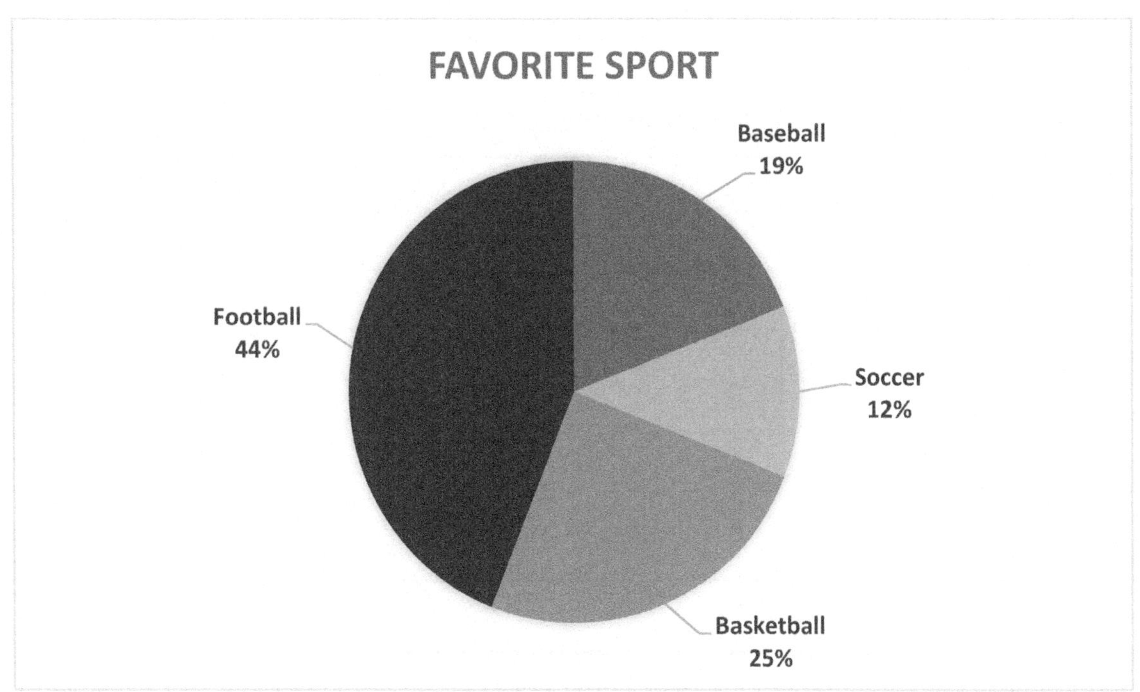

A **stem-and-leaf plot** is a method of displaying sets of data by organizing numbers by their stems (usually the tens digit) and different leaf values (usually the ones digit).

For example, to organize a number of movie critic's ratings, as listed below, a stem-and-leaf plot could be utilized to display the information in a more condensed manner.

Movie critic scores: 47, 52, 56, 59, 61, 64, 66, 68, 68, 70, 73, 75, 79, 81, 83, 85, 86, 88, 88, 89, 90, 90, 91, 93, 94, 96, 96, 99.

	Movie Ratings
4	7
5	2 6 9
6	1 4 6 8 8
7	0 3 5 9
8	1 3 5 6 8 8 9
9	0 0 1 3 4 6 6 9
Key	6 | 1 represents 61

Looking at this stem and leaf plot, it is easy to ascertain key features of the data set. For example, what is the range of the data in the stem-and-leaf plot?

Using this method, it is easier to visualize the distribution of the scores and answer the question pertaining to the range of scores, which is $99 - 47 = 52$.

A **tally chart** is a diagram in which tally marks are utilized to represent data. Tally marks are a means of showing a quantity of objects within a specific classification. Here is an example of a tally chart:

Number of days with rain	Number of weeks
0	II
1	卌
2	卌
3	卌
4	卌 卌 卌 IIII
5	卌 I
6	卌 I
7	IIII

Data is often recorded using fractions, such as half a mile, and understanding fractions is critical because of their popular use in real-world applications. Also, it is extremely important to label values with their units when using data. For example, regarding length, the number 2 is meaningless unless it is attached to a unit. Writing 2 cm shows that the number refers to the length of an object.

Volume and Surface Area of Three-Dimensional Shapes

Geometry in three dimensions is similar to geometry in two dimensions. The main new feature is that three points now define a unique **plane** that passes through each of them. Three-dimensional objects can be made by putting together two-dimensional figures in different surfaces. Below, some of the possible three-dimensional figures will be provided, along with formulas for their volumes and surface areas.

Volume is the measurement of how much space an object occupies, like how much space is in the cube. Volume questions will ask how much of something is needed to completely fill the object. The most common surface area and volume questions deal with spheres, cubes, and rectangular prisms.

Surface area of a three-dimensional figure refers to the number of square units needed to cover the entire surface of the figure. This concept is similar to using wrapping paper to completely cover the outside of a box. For example, if a triangular pyramid has a surface area of 17 square inches (written $17in^2$), it will take 17 squares, each with sides one inch in length, to cover the entire surface of the pyramid. Surface area is also measured in square units.

A **rectangular prism** is a box whose sides are all rectangles meeting at 90° angles. Such a box has three dimensions: length, width, and height. If the length is *x*, the width is *y*, and the height is *z*, then the volume is given by $V = xyz$.

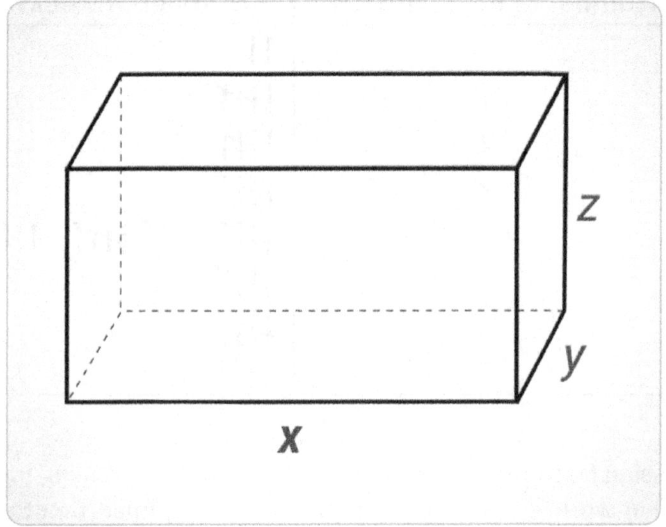

The **surface area** will be given by computing the surface area of each rectangle and adding them together. There is a total of six rectangles. Two of them have sides of length *x* and *y*, two have sides of length *y* and *z*, and two have sides of length *x* and *z*. Therefore, the total surface area will be given by:

$$SA = 2xy + 2yz + 2xz$$

A **cube** is a special type of rectangular solid in which its length, width, and height are the same. If this length is *s*, then the formula for the volume of a cube is $V = s \times s \times s$. The surface area of a cube is $SA = 6s^2$.

A **rectangular pyramid** is a figure with a rectangular base and four triangular sides that meet at a single vertex. If the rectangle has sides of length *x* and *y*, then the volume will be given by $V = \frac{1}{3}xyh$.

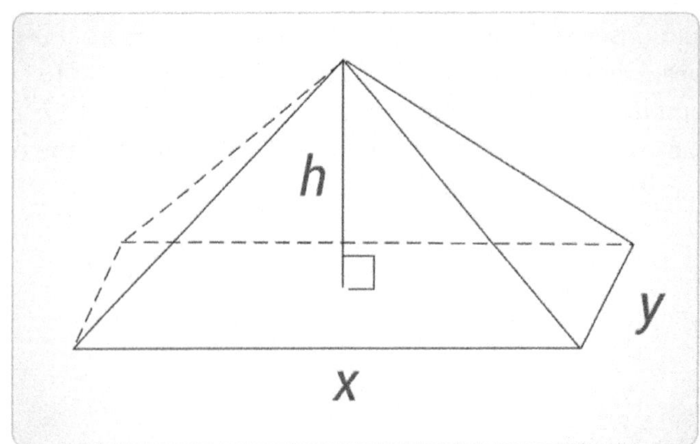

Many three-dimensional figures (solid figures) can be represented by nets consisting of rectangles and triangles. The surface area of such solids can be determined by adding the areas of each of its faces and bases. Finding the surface area using this method requires calculating the areas of rectangles and triangles.

Consider the following triangular prism, which is represented by a net consisting of two triangles and three rectangles.

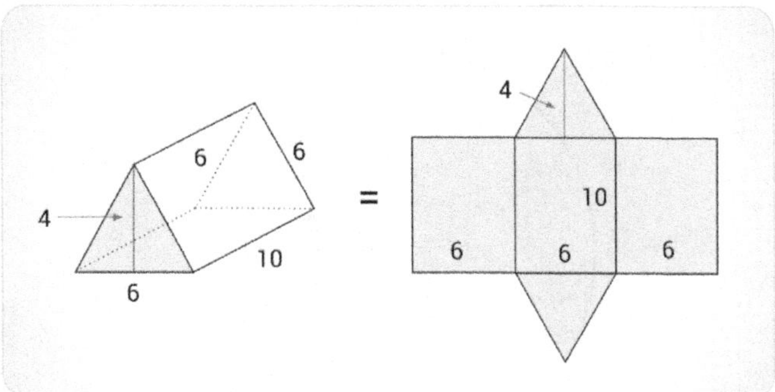

The surface area of the prism can be determined by adding the areas of each of its faces and bases. The surface area (*SA*) = area of triangle + area of triangle + area of rectangle + area of rectangle + area of rectangle.

$$SA = \left(\frac{1}{2} \times b \times h\right) + \left(\frac{1}{2} \times b \times h\right) + (l \times w) + (l \times w) + (l \times w)$$

$$SA = \left(\frac{1}{2} \times 6 \times 4\right) + \left(\frac{1}{2} \times 6 \times 4\right) + (6 \times 10) + (6 \times 10) + (6 \times 10)$$

$$SA = (12) + (12) + (60) + (60) + (60)$$

$$SA = 204 \; square \; units$$

A **sphere** is a set of points all of which are equidistant from some central point. It is like a circle, but in three dimensions. The volume of a sphere of radius *r* is given by:

$$V = \frac{4}{3}\pi r^3$$

The surface area is given by $A = 4\pi r^2$.

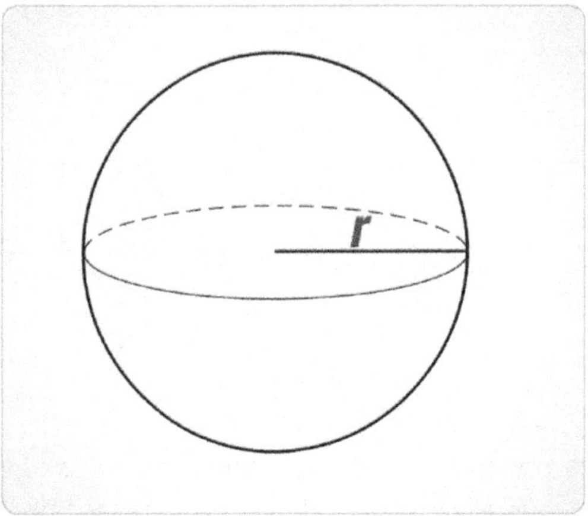

The volume of a **cylinder** is then found by adding a third dimension onto the circle. Volume of a cylinder is calculated by multiplying the area of the base (which is a circle) by the height of the cylinder. Doing so results in the equation $V = \pi r^2 h$. The volume of a **cone** is $\frac{1}{3}$ of the volume of a cylinder. Therefore, the formula for the volume of a **cone** is:

$$\frac{1}{3}\pi r^2 h$$

Solving Three-Dimensional Problems

Three-dimensional objects can be simplified into related two-dimensional shapes to solve problems. This simplification can make problem-solving a much easier experience. An isometric representation of a three-dimensional object can be completed so that important properties (e.g., shape, relationships of faces and surfaces) are noted. Edges and vertices can be translated into two-dimensional objects as well.

For example, below is a three-dimensional object that's been partitioned into two-dimensional representations of its faces:

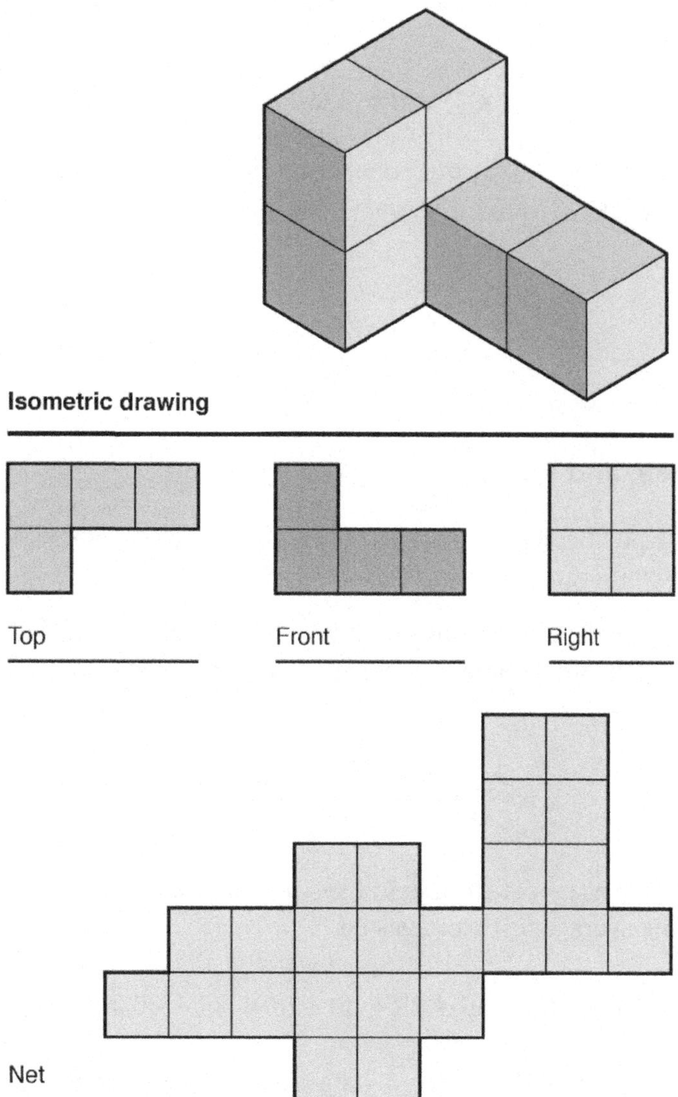

The net represents the sum of the three different faces. Depending on the problem, using a smaller portion of the given shape may be helpful, by simplifying the steps necessary to solve.

Many objects in the real world consist of three-dimensional shapes such as prisms, cylinders, and spheres. Surface area problems involve quantifying the outside area of such a three-dimensional object, and volume problems involve quantifying how much space the object takes up. Surface area of a prism is the sum of the areas, which is simplified into $SA = 2A + Bh$, where A is the area of the base, B is the perimeter of the base, and h is the height of the prism. The volume of the same prism is $V = Ah$. The surface area of a cylinder is equal to the sum of the areas of each end and the side, which is:

$$SA = 2\pi rh + 2\pi r^2$$

An example when one of these formulas should be used would be when calculating how much paint is needed for the outside of a house. In this scenario, surface area must be used. The sum of all individual areas of each side of the house must be found. Also, when calculating how much water a cylindrical tank can hold, a volume formula is used. Therefore, the amount of water that a cylindrical tank that is 8 feet tall with a radius of 3 feet is:

$$\pi \times 3^2 \times 8 = 226.1 \text{ cubic feet}$$

The formula used to calculate the volume of a cone is $\frac{1}{3}\pi r^2 h$. In a real-life example where the radius of a cone is 2 meters and the height of a cone is 5 meters, the volume of the cone is calculated by utilizing the formula:

$$\frac{1}{3}\pi 2^2 \times 5$$

After substituting 3.14 for π, the volume is $20.9\ m^3$.

Mean, Median, Mode, and Range

Suppose that *X* is a set of data points $(x_1, x_2, x_3, \ldots x_n)$ and some description of the general properties of this data need to be found.

The first property that can be defined for this set of data is the **mean**. To find the mean, add up all the data points, then divide by the total number of data points. This can be expressed using **summation notation** as:

$$\bar{X} = \frac{x_1 + x_2 + x_3 + \ldots + x_n}{n} = \frac{1}{n}\sum_{i=1}^{n} x_i$$

For example, suppose that in a class of 10 students, the scores on a test were 50, 60, 65, 65, 75, 80, 85, 85, 90, 100. Therefore, the average test score will be:

$$\frac{1}{10}(50 + 60 + 65 + 65 + 75 + 80 + 85 + 85 + 90 + 100) = 75.5$$

The mean is a useful number if the distribution of data is normal (more on this later), which roughly means that the frequency of different outcomes has a single peak and is roughly equally distributed on both sides of that peak. However, it is less useful in some cases where the data might be split or where there are some outliers. **Outliers** are data points that are far from the rest of the data. For example, suppose there are 10 executives and 90 employees at a company. The executives make \$1,000 per hour, and the employees make \$10 per hour.

Therefore, the average pay rate will be:

$$\frac{\$1{,}000 \times 10 + \$10 \times 90}{100} = \$109 \text{ per hour}$$

In this case, this average is not very descriptive since it's not close to the actual pay of the executives or the employees.

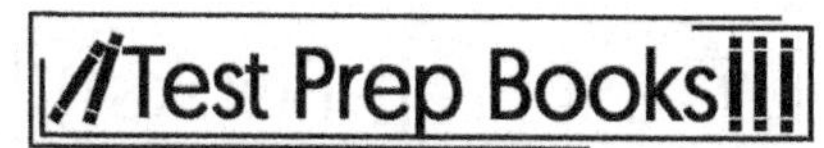

Another useful measurement is the **median**. In a data set *X* consisting of data points $x_1, x_2, x_3, \ldots x_n$, the median is the point in the middle. The middle refers to the point where half the data comes before it and half comes after, when the data is recorded in numerical order. If *n* is odd, then the median is:

$$x_{\frac{n+1}{2}}$$

If *n* is even, it is defined as $\frac{1}{2}\left(x_{\frac{n}{2}} + x_{\frac{n}{2}+1}\right)$, the mean of the two data points closest to the middle of the data points. In the previous example of test scores, the two middle points are 75 and 80. Since there is no single point, the average of these two scores needs to be found. The average is:

$$\frac{75 + 80}{2} = 77.5$$

The median is generally a good value to use if there are a few outliers in the data. It prevents those outliers from affecting the "middle" value as much as when using the mean.

One additional measure to define for *X* is the **mode**. This is the data point that appears more frequently. If two or more data points all tie for the most frequent appearance, then each of them is considered a mode. In the case of the test scores, where the numbers were 50, 60, 65, 65, 75, 80, 85, 85, 90, 100, there are two modes: 65 and 85.

Since an outlier is a data point that is far from most of the other data points in a data set, this means an outlier also is any point that is far from the median of the data set. The outliers can have a substantial effect on the mean of a data set but usually do not change the median or mode, or do not change them by a large quantity. For example, consider the data set (3, 5, 6, 6, 6, 8). This has a median of 6 and a mode of 6, with a mean of $\frac{34}{6} \approx 5.67$. Now, suppose a new data point of 1,000 is added so that the data set is now (3, 5, 6, 6, 6, 8, 1,000). The median and mode, which are both still 6, remain unchanged. However, the average is now $\frac{1034}{7}$, which is approximately 147.7. In this case, the median and mode will be better descriptions for most of the data points.

Outliers in a given data set are sometimes the result of an error by the experimenter, but oftentimes, they are perfectly valid data points that must be taken into consideration.

The **first quartile** of a set of data *X* refers to the largest value from the first ¼ of the data points. In practice, there are sometimes slightly different definitions that can be used, such as the median of the first half of the data points (excluding the median itself if there are an odd number of data points). The term also has a slightly different use: when it is said that a data point lies in the first quartile, it means it is less than or equal to the median of the first half of the data points. Conversely, if it lies *at* the first quartile, then it is equal to the first quartile.

When it is said that a data point lies in the **second quartile**, it means it is between the first quartile and the median.

The **third quartile** refers to data that lies between ½ and ¾ of the way through the data set. Again, there are various methods for defining this precisely, but the simplest way is to include all of the data that lie between the median and the median of the top half of the data.

Data that lies in the **fourth quartile** refers to all of the data above the third quartile.

Percentiles may be defined in a similar manner to quartiles. Generally, this is defined in the following manner:

If a data point lies **in the nth percentile**, this means it lies in the range of the first *n%* of the data.

If a data point lies **at the nth percentile**, then it means that *n%* of the data lies below this data point.

Given a data set *X* consisting of data points $(x_1, x_2, x_3, \ldots x_n)$, the **variance of X** is defined to be:

$$\frac{\sum_{i=1}^{n}(x_i - \bar{X})^2}{n}$$

This means that the variance of *X* is the average of the squares of the differences between each data point and the mean of *X*. In the formula, $\bar{X}$ is the mean of the values in the data set, and x_i represents each individual value in the data set. The sigma notation indicates that the sum should be found with n being the number of values to add together. $i = 1$ means that the values should begin with the first value.

Given a data set *X* consisting of data points $(x_1, x_2, x_3, \ldots x_n)$, the **standard deviation of X** is defined to be

$$=$$

In other words, the standard deviation is the square root of the variance.

Both the variance and the standard deviation are measures of how much the data tend to be spread out. When the standard deviation is low, the data points are mostly clustered around the mean. When the standard deviation is high, this generally indicates that the data are quite spread out, or else that there are a few substantial outliers.

As a simple example, compute the standard deviation for the data set (1, 3, 3, 5). First, compute the mean, which will be:

$$\frac{1+3+3+5}{4} = \frac{12}{4} = 3$$

Now, find the variance of *X* with the formula:

$$\sum_{i=1}^{4}(x_i - \bar{X})^2 = (1-3)^2 + (3-3)^2 + (3-3)^2 + (5-3)^2$$

$$-2^2 + 0^2 + 0^2 + 2^2 = 8$$

Therefore, the variance is $\frac{8}{4} = 2$. Taking the square root, the standard deviation will be $\sqrt{2}$.

Note that the standard deviation only depends upon the mean, not upon the median or mode(s). Generally, if there are multiple modes that are far apart from one another, the standard deviation will be high. A high standard deviation does not always mean there are multiple modes, however.

Describing a Set of Data

A set of data can be described in terms of its center, spread, shape and any unusual features. The center of a data set can be measured by its mean, median, or mode. The spread of a data set refers to how far the data points are from the center (mean or median). The spread can be measured by the range or the quartiles and interquartile range. A data set with all its data points clustered around the center will have a small spread. A data set covering a wide range of values will have a large spread.

When a data set is displayed as a **histogram** or frequency distribution plot, the shape indicates if a sample is normally distributed, symmetrical, or has measures of skewness or kurtosis. When graphed, a data set with a **normal distribution** will resemble a bell curve.

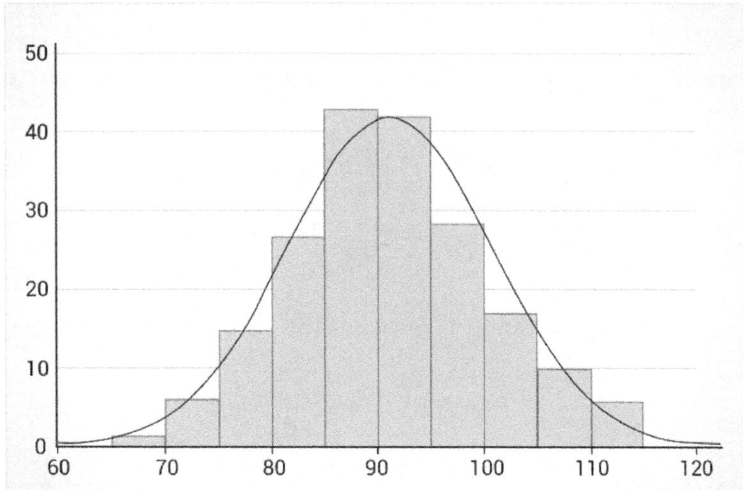

If the data set is symmetrical, each half of the graph when divided at the center is a mirror image of the other. If the graph has fewer data points to the right, the data is **skewed right**. If it has fewer data points to the left, the data is **skewed left**.

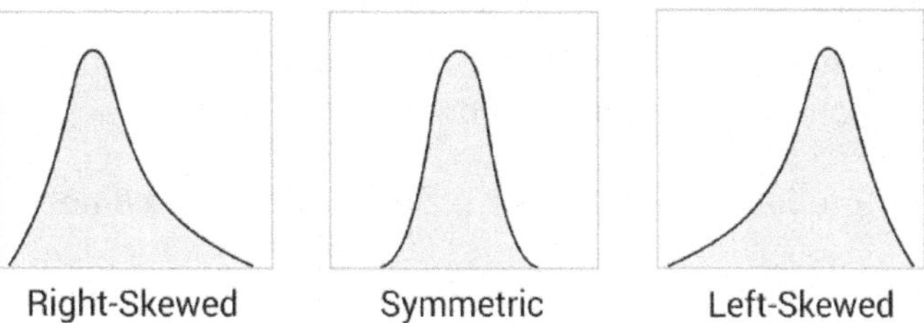

Kurtosis is a measure of whether the data is heavy-tailed with a high number of outliers, or light-tailed with a low number of outliers.

A description of a data set should include any unusual features such as gaps or outliers. A **gap** is a span within the range of the data set containing no data points. An **outlier** is a data point with a value either extremely large or extremely small when compared to the other values in the set.

Counting Techniques

The **addition rule** for probabilities states that the probability of *A* or *B* happening is:

$$P(A \cup B) = P(A) + P(B) - P(A \cap B)$$

Note that the subtraction of $P(A \cap B)$ must be performed, or else it would result in double counting any outcomes that lie in both *A* and in *B*. For example, suppose that a 20-sided die is being rolled. Fred bets that the outcome will be greater than 10, while Helen bets that it will be greater than 4 but less than 15. What is the probability that at least one of them is correct?

We apply the rule:

$$P(A \cup B) = P(A) + P(B) - P(A \cap B)$$

where *A* is that outcome *x* is in the range $x > 10$, and *B* is that outcome *x* is in the range $4 < x < 15$.

$$P(A) = 10 \times \frac{1}{20} = \frac{1}{2}$$

$$P(B) = 10 \times \frac{1}{20} = \frac{1}{2}$$

$P(A \cap B)$ can be computed by noting that $A \cap B$ means the outcome *x* is in the range $10 < x < 15$, so

$$P(A \cap B) = 4 \times \frac{1}{20} = \frac{1}{5}$$

Therefore:

$$P(A \cup B) = P(A) + P(B) - P(A \cap B)$$

$$\frac{1}{2} + \frac{1}{2} - \frac{1}{5} = \frac{4}{5}$$

Note that in this particular example, we could also have directly reasoned about the set of possible outcomes $A \cup B$, by noting that this would mean that *x* must be in the range $5 \leq x$. However, this is not always the case, depending on the given information.

The **multiplication rule** for probabilities states the probability of *A* and *B* both happening is:

$$P(A \cap B) = P(A)P(B|A)$$

As an example, suppose that when Jamie wears black pants, there is a ½ probability that she wears a black shirt as well, and that she wears black pants ¾ of the time. What is the probability that she is wearing both a black shirt and black pants?

To figure this, use the above formula, where *A* will be "Jamie is wearing black pants," while *B* will be "Jamie is wearing a black shirt." It is known that $P(A)$ is ¾. It is also known that $P(B|A) = \frac{1}{2}$. Multiplying the two, the probability that she is wearing both black pants and a black shirt is:

$$P(A)P(B|A) = \frac{3}{4} \times \frac{1}{2} = \frac{3}{8}$$

Probability of an Event

Given a set of possible outcomes *X*, a **probability distribution** of *X* is a function that assigns a probability to each possible outcome. If the outcomes are $(x_1, x_2, x_3, \ldots x_n)$, and the probability distribution is *p*, then the following rules are applied.

- $0 \leq p(x_i) \leq 1$, for any i.
- $\sum_{i=1}^{n} p(x_i) = 1$.

In other words, the probability of a given outcome must be between zero and 1, while the total probability must be 1.

If $p(x_i)$ is constant, then this is called a **uniform probability distribution**, and $p(x_i) = \frac{1}{n}$. For example, on a six-sided die, the probability of each of the six outcomes will be $\frac{1}{6}$.

If seeking the probability of an outcome occurring in some specific range *A* of possible outcomes, written $P(A)$, add up the probabilities for each outcome in that range. For example, consider a six-sided die, and figure the probability of getting a 3 or lower when it is rolled. The possible rolls are 1, 2, 3, 4, 5, and 6. So, to get a 3 or lower, a roll of 1, 2, or 3 must be completed. The probabilities of each of these is $\frac{1}{6}$, so add these to get:

$$p(1) + p(2) + p(3) = \frac{1}{6} + \frac{1}{6} + \frac{1}{6} = \frac{1}{2}$$

An outcome occasionally lies within some range of possibilities *B*, and the probability that the outcomes also lie within some set of possibilities *A* needs to be figured. This is called a **conditional probability**. It is written as $P(A|B)$, which is read "the probability of *A* given *B*." The general formula for computing conditional probabilities is:

$$P(A|B) = \frac{P(A \cap B)}{P(B)}$$

However, when dealing with uniform probability distributions, simplify this a bit. Write $|A|$ to indicate the number of outcomes in *A*. Then, for uniform probability distributions, write:

$$P(A|B) = \frac{|A \cap B|}{|B|}$$

(recall that $A \cap B$ means "*A* intersect *B*," and consists of all of the outcomes that lie in both *A* and *B*)

This means that all possible outcomes do not need to be known. To see why this formula works, suppose that the set of outcomes *X* is $(x_1, x_2, x_3, \ldots x_n)$, so that $|X| = n$. Then, for a uniform probability distribution:

$$P(A) = \frac{|A|}{n}$$

However, this means:

$$(A|B) = \frac{P(A \cap B)}{P(B)} = \frac{\frac{|A \cap B|}{n}}{\frac{|B|}{n}} = \frac{|A \cap B|}{|B|}$$

since the *n*'s cancel out.

For example, suppose a die is rolled, and it is known that it will land between 1 and 4. However, how many sides the die has is unknown. Figure the probability that the die is rolled higher than 2. To figure this, $P(3)$ or $P(4)$ does not need to be determined, or any of the other probabilities, since it is known that a fair die has a uniform probability distribution. Therefore, apply the formula $\frac{|A \cap B|}{|B|}$. So, in this case *B* is (1, 2, 3, 4) and $A \cap B$ is (3, 4). Therefore:

$$\frac{|A \cap B|}{|B|} = \frac{2}{4} = \frac{1}{2}$$

Conditional probability is an important concept because, in many situations, the likelihood of one outcome can differ radically depending on how something else comes out. The probability of passing a test given that one has studied all of the material is generally much higher than the probability of passing a test given that one has not studied at all. The probability of a person having heart trouble is much lower if that person exercises regularly. The probability that a college student will graduate is higher when their SAT scores are higher, and so on. For this reason, there are many people who are interested in conditional probabilities.

Note that in some practical situations, changing the order of the conditional probabilities can make the outcome very different. For example, the probability that a person with heart trouble has exercised regularly is quite different than the probability that a person who exercises regularly will have heart trouble. The probability of a person receiving a military-only award, given that he or she is or was a soldier, is generally not very high, but the probability that a person being or having been a soldier, given that he or she received a military-only award, is 1.

However, in some cases, the outcomes do not influence one another this way. If the probability of *A* is the same regardless of whether *B* is given; that is, if $P(A|B) = P(A)$, then *A* and *B* are considered **independent**. In this case:

$$P(A|B) = \frac{P(A \cap B)}{P(B)} = P(A)$$

So:

$$P(A \cap B) = P(A)P(B)$$

In fact, if $P(A \cap B) = P(A)P(B)$, it can be determined that $P(A|B) = P(A)$ and $P(A|B) = P(B)$ by working backward. Therefore, *B* is also independent of *A*.

An example of something being independent can be seen in rolling dice. In this case, consider a red die and a green die. It is expected that when the dice are rolled, the outcome of the green die should not depend in any way on the outcome of the red die. Or, to take another example, if the same die is rolled repeatedly, then the next number rolled should not depend on which numbers have been rolled previously. Similarly, if a coin is flipped, then the next flip's outcome does not depend on the outcomes of previous flips.

This can sometimes be counter-intuitive, since when rolling a die or flipping a coin, there can be a streak of surprising results. If, however, it is known that the die or coin is fair, then these results are just the result of the fact that over long periods of time, it is very likely that some unlikely streaks of outcomes will occur. Therefore, avoid making the mistake of thinking that when considering a series of independent outcomes, a particular outcome is "due to happen" simply because a surprising series of outcomes has already been seen.

There is a second type of common mistake that people tend to make when reasoning about statistical outcomes: the idea that when something of low probability happens, this is surprising. It would be surprising that something with low probability happened after just one attempt. However, with so much happening all at once, it is easy to see at least something happen in a way that seems to have a very low probability. In fact, a lottery is a good example. The odds of winning a lottery are very small, but the odds that somebody wins the lottery each week are actually fairly high. Therefore, no one should be surprised when some low probability things happen.

A **simple event** consists of only one outcome. The most popular simple event is flipping a coin, which results in either heads or tails. A **compound event** results in more than one outcome and consists of more than one simple event. An example of a compound event is flipping a coin while tossing a die. The result is either heads or tails on the coin and a number from one to six on the die. The probability of a simple event is calculated by dividing the number of possible outcomes by the total number of outcomes. Therefore, the probability of obtaining heads on a coin is $\frac{1}{2}$, and the probability of rolling a 6 on a die is $\frac{1}{6}$. The probability of compound events is calculated using the basic idea of the probability of simple events. If the two events are independent, the probability of one outcome is equal to the product of the probabilities of each simple event. For example, the probability of obtaining heads on a coin and rolling a 6 is equal to:

$$\frac{1}{2} \times \frac{1}{6} = \frac{1}{12}$$

The probability of either A or B occurring is equal to the sum of the probabilities minus the probability that both A and B will occur. Therefore, the probability of obtaining either heads on a coin or rolling a 6 on a die is:

$$\frac{1}{2} + \frac{1}{6} - \frac{1}{12} = \frac{7}{12}$$

The two events aren't mutually exclusive because they can happen at the same time. If two events are mutually exclusive, and the probability of both events occurring at the same time is zero, the probability of event A or B occurring equals the sum of both probabilities. An example of calculating the probability of two mutually exclusive events is determining the probability of pulling a king or a queen from a deck of cards. The two events cannot occur at the same time.

Basic Algebra

Adding, Subtracting, Multiplying, and Factoring Linear Expressions

Algebraic expressions look similar to equations, but they do not include the equal sign. Algebraic expressions are comprised of numbers, variables, and mathematical operations. Some examples of algebraic expressions are:

$$8x + 7y - 12z$$

$$3a^2$$

$$5x^3 - 4y^4$$

Algebraic expressions consist of variables, numbers, and operations. A term of an expression is any combination of numbers and/or variables, and terms are separated by addition and subtraction. For example, the expression:

$$5x^2 - 3xy + 4y - 2$$

consists of 4 terms: $5x^2$, $-3xy$, $4y$, and -2. Note that each term includes it's given sign (+ or −). The variable part of a term is a letter that represents an unknown quantity. The coefficient of a term is the number by which the variable is multiplied. For the term $4y$, the variable is y, and the coefficient is 4. Terms are identified by the power (or exponent) of its variable.

A number without a variable is referred to as a constant. If the variable is to the first power (x^1 or simply x), it is referred to as a linear term. A term with a variable to the second power (x^2) is quadratic, and a term to the third power (x^3) is cubic. Consider the expression:

$$x^3 + 3x - 1$$

The constant is −1. The linear term is $3x$. There is no quadratic term. The cubic term is x^3.

An algebraic expression can also be classified by how many terms exist in the expression. Any like terms should be combined before classifying. A monomial is an expression consisting of only one term. Examples of monomials are: 17, $2x$, and $-5ab^2$. A binomial is an expression consisting of two terms separated by addition or subtraction. Examples include $2x - 4$ and $-3y^2 + 2y$. A trinomial consists of 3 terms. For example:

$$5x^2 - 2x + 1$$

is a trinomial.

Algebraic expressions and equations can be used to represent real-life situations and model the behavior of different variables. For example, $2x + 5$ could represent the cost to play games at an arcade. In this case, 5 represents the price of admission to the arcade, and 2 represents the cost of each

game played. To calculate the total cost, use the number of games played for x, multiply it by 2, and add 5.

Adding and Subtracting Linear Algebraic Expressions

An algebraic expression is simplified by combining like terms. A term is a number, variable, or product of a number and variables separated by addition and subtraction. For the algebraic expression:

$$3x^2 - 4x + 5 - 5x^2 + x - 3$$

the terms are $3x^2$, $-4x$, 5, $-5x^2$, x, and -3. Like terms have the same variables raised to the same powers (exponents). The like terms for the previous example are $3x^2$ and $-5x^2$, $-4x$ and x, 5 and -3. To combine like terms, the coefficients (numerical factor of the term including sign) are added, and the variables and their powers are kept the same. Note that if a coefficient is not written, it is an implied coefficient of 1 ($x = 1x$). The previous example will simplify to:

$$-2x^2 - 3x + 2$$

When adding or subtracting algebraic expressions, each expression is written in parentheses. The negative sign is distributed when necessary, and like terms are combined. Consider the following:

$$\text{add } 2a + 5b - 2 \text{ to } a - 2b + 8c - 4$$

The sum is set as follows:

$$(a - 2b + 8c - 4) + (2a + 5b - 2)$$

In front of each set of parentheses is an implied positive one, which, when distributed, does not change any of the terms. Therefore, the parentheses are dropped and like terms are combined:

$$a - 2b + 8c - 4 + 2a + 5b - 2$$

$$3a + 3b + 8c - 6$$

Consider the following problem:

$$\text{Subtract } 2a + 5b - 2 \text{ from } a - 2b + 8c - 4$$

The difference is set as follows:

$$(a - 2b + 8c - 4) - (2a + 5b - 2)$$

The implied one in front of the first set of parentheses will not change those four terms. However, distributing the implied –1 in front of the second set of parentheses will change the sign of each of those three terms:

$$a - 2b + 8c - 4 - 2a - 5b + 2$$

Combining like terms yields the simplified expression:

$$-a - 7b + 8c - 2$$

Distributive Property

The **distributive property** states that multiplying a sum (or difference) by a number produces the same result as multiplying each value in the sum (or difference) by the number and adding (or subtracting) the products. Using mathematical symbols, the distributive property states:

$$a(b + c) = ab + ac$$

The expression $4(3 + 2)$ is simplified using the order of operations. Simplifying inside the parentheses first produces 4×5, which equals 20. The expression $4(3 + 2)$ can also be simplified using the distributive property:

$$4(3 + 2)$$

$$4 \times 3 + 4 \times 2$$

$$12 + 8$$

$$20$$

Consider the following example: $4(3x - 2)$. The expression cannot be simplified inside the parentheses because $3x$ and -2 are not like terms and therefore cannot be combined. However, the expression can be simplified by using the distributive property and multiplying each term inside of the parentheses by the term outside of the parentheses: $12x - 8$. The resulting equivalent expression contains no like terms, so it cannot be further simplified.

Consider the expression:

$$(3x + 2y + 1) - (5x - 3) + 2(3y + 4)$$

Again, there are no like terms, but the distributive property is used to simplify the expression. Note there is an implied one in front of the first set of parentheses and an implied -1 in front of the second set of parentheses. Distributing the 1, -1, and 2 produces:

$$1(3x) + 1(2y) + 1(1) - 1(5x) - 1(-3) + 2(3y) + 2(4)$$

$$3x + 2y + 1 - 5x + 3 + 6y + 8$$

This expression contains like terms that are combined to produce the simplified expression:

$$-2x + 8y + 12$$

Algebraic expressions are tested to be equivalent by choosing values for the variables and evaluating both expressions. For example, $4(3x - 2)$ and $12x - 8$ are tested by substituting 3 for the variable x and calculating to determine if equivalent values result.

Evaluating Algebraic Expressions

To evaluate the expression, the given values for the variables are substituted (or replaced), and the expression is simplified using the order of operations. Parentheses should be used when substituting.

Consider the following: Evaluate $a - 2b + ab$ for $a = 3$ and $b = -1$. To evaluate, any variable *a* is replaced with 3 and any variable *b* with –1, producing:

$$(3) - 2(-1) + (3)(-1)$$

Next, the order of operations is used to calculate the value of the expression, which is 2.

Let's try two more.

Evaluate:

$$\frac{1}{2}x^2 - 3$$

$$x = 4$$

The first step is to substitute in 4 for *x* in the expression:

$$\frac{1}{2}(4)^2 - 3$$

Then, the order of operations is used to simplify.

The exponent comes first, $\frac{1}{2}(16) - 3$, then the multiplication 8 – 3, and then, after subtraction, the solution is 5.

Evaluate:

$$4|5 - x| + 2y$$

$$x = 4$$

$$y = -3$$

The first step is to substitute 4 in for *x* and –3 in for *y* in the expression:

$$4|5 - 4| + 2(-3)$$

Then, the absolute value expression is simplified, which is:

$$|5 - 4| = |1| = 1$$

The expression is:

$$4(1) + 2(-3)$$

which can be simplified using the order of operations.

First is the multiplication, $4 + (-6)$; then addition yields an answer of –2.

Creating Algebraic Expressions

A linear expression is a statement about an unknown quantity expressed in mathematical symbols. The statement "five times a number added to forty" can be expressed as $5x + 40$. A linear equation is a statement in which two expressions (at least one containing a variable) are equal to each other. The statement "five times a number added to forty is equal to ten" can be expressed as:

$$5x + 40 = 10$$

Real world scenarios can also be expressed mathematically. Suppose a job pays its employees $300 per week and $40 for each sale made. The weekly pay is represented by the expression $40x + 300$ where *x* is the number of sales made during the week.

Consider the following scenario: Bob had $20 and Tom had $4. After selling 4 ice cream cones to Bob, Tom has as much money as Bob. The cost of an ice cream cone is an unknown quantity and can be represented by a variable (*x*). The amount of money Bob has after his purchase is four times the cost of an ice cream cone subtracted from his original:

$$\$20 \rightarrow 20 - 4x$$

The amount of money Tom has after his sale is four times the cost of an ice cream cone added to his original:

$$\$4 \rightarrow 4x + 4$$

After the sale, the amount of money that Bob and Tom have is equal:

$$20 - 4x = 4x + 4$$

Adding, Subtracting, Multiplying, Dividing, and Factoring Polynomials

An expression of the form ax^n, where n is a non-negative integer, is called a **monomial** because it contains one term. A sum of monomials is called a **polynomial**. For example, $-4x^3 + x$ is a polynomial, while $5x^7$ is a monomial. A function equal to a polynomial is called a **polynomial function**.

The monomials in a polynomial are also called the **terms** of the polynomial.

The constants that precede the variables are called **coefficients**.

The highest value of the exponent of x in a polynomial is called the **degree** of the polynomial. So, $-4x^3 + x$ has a degree of 3, while:

$$-2x^5 + x^3 + 4x + 1$$

has a degree of 5. When multiplying polynomials, the degree of the result will be the sum of the degrees of the two polynomials being multiplied.

Addition and subtraction operations can be performed on polynomials with like terms. **Like terms** refers to terms that have the same variable and exponent. The two following polynomials can be added together by collecting like terms:

$$(x^2 + 3x - 4) + (4x^2 - 7x + 8)$$

The x^2 terms can be added as:

$$x^2 + 4x^2 = 5x^2$$

The x terms can be added as:

$$3x + -7x = -4x$$

and the constants can be added as $-4 + 8 = 4$.

The following expression is the result of the addition:

$$5x^2 - 4x + 4$$

Let's try another:

$$(-2x^5 + x^3 + 4x + 1) + (-4x^3 + x)$$

$$-2x^5 + (1 - 4)x^3 + (4 + 1)x + 1$$

$$-2x^5 - 3x^3 + 5x + 1$$

Likewise, subtraction of polynomials is performed by subtracting coefficients of like powers of x. So:

$$(-2x^5 + x^3 + 4x + 1) - (-4x^3 + x)$$

$$-2x^5 + (1 + 4)x^3 + (4 - 1)x + 1$$

$$-2x^5 + 5x^3 + 3x + 1$$

To multiply two polynomials, multiply each term of the first polynomial by each term of the second polynomial and add the results. For example:

$$(4x^2 + x)(-x^3 + x)$$

$$4x^2(-x^3) + 4x^2(x) + x(-x^3) + x(x)$$

$$-4x^5 + 4x^3 - x^4 + x^2$$

In the case where each polynomial has two terms, like in this example, some students find it helpful to remember this as multiplying the First terms, then the Outer terms, then the Inner terms, and finally the Last terms, with the mnemonic FOIL. For longer polynomials, the multiplication process is the same, but there will be, of course, more terms, and there is no common mnemonic to remember each combination.

Factors for polynomials are similar to factors for integers—they are numbers, variables, or polynomials that, when multiplied together, give a product equal to the polynomial in question. One polynomial is a factor of a second polynomial if the second polynomial can be obtained from the first by multiplying by a third polynomial.

$$6x^6 + 13x^4 + 6x^2$$

can be obtained by multiplying together:

$$(3x^4 + 2x^2)(2x^2 + 3)$$

This means:

$$2x^2 + 3$$

and

$$3x^4 + 2x^2$$

are factors of:

$$6x^6 + 13x^4 + 6x^2$$

In general, finding the factors of a polynomial can be tricky. However, there are a few types of polynomials that can be factored in a straightforward way.

If a certain monomial is in each term of a polynomial, it can be factored out. There are several common forms polynomials take, which if you recognize, you can solve. The first example is a perfect square trinomial. To factor this polynomial, first expand the middle term of the expression:

$$x^2 + 2xy + y^2$$

$$x^2 + xy + xy + y^2$$

Factor out a common term in each half of the expression (in this case x from the left and y from the right):

$$x(x + y) + y(x + y)$$

Then the same can be done again, treating $(x + y)$ as the common factor:

$$(x + y)(x + y) = (x + y)^2$$

Therefore, the formula for this polynomial is:

$$x^2 + 2xy + y^2 = (x + y)^2$$

Next is another example of a perfect square trinomial. The process is the similar, but notice the difference in sign:

$$x^2 - 2xy + y^2$$

$$x^2 - xy - xy + y^2$$

Factor out the common term on each side:

$$x(x-y)-y(x-y)$$

Factoring out the common term again:

$$(x-y)(x-y)=(x-y)^2$$

Thus:

$$x^2-2xy+y^2=(x-y)^2$$

The next is known as a difference of squares. This process is effectively the reverse of binomial multiplication:

$$x^2-y^2$$

$$x^2-xy+xy-y^2$$

$$x(x-y)+y(x-y)$$

$$(x+y)(x-y)$$

Therefore:

$$x^2-y^2=(x+y)(x-y)$$

The following two polynomials are known as the sum or difference of cubes. These are special polynomials that take the form of x^3+y^3 or x^3-y^3. The following formula factors the sum of cubes:

$$x^3+y^3=(x+y)(x^2-xy+y^2)$$

Next is the difference of cubes, but note the change in sign. The formulas for both are similar, but the order of signs for factoring the sum or difference of cubes can be remembered by using the acronym SOAP, which stands for "same, opposite, always positive." The first sign is the same as the sign in the first expression, the second is opposite, and the third is always positive. The next formula factors the difference of cubes:

$$x^3-y^3=(x-y)(x^2+xy+y^2)$$

The following two examples are expansions of cubed binomials. Similarly, these polynomials always follow a pattern:

$$x^3+3x^2y+3xy^2+y^3=(x+y)^3$$

$$x^3-3x^2y+3xy^2-y^3=(x-y)^3$$

These rules can be used in many combinations with one another. For example, the expression $3x^3-24$ has a common factor of 3, which becomes:

$$3(x^3-8)$$

A difference of cubes still remains which can then be factored out:

$$3(x-2)(x^2+2x+4)$$

There are no other terms to be pulled out, so this expression is completely factored.

When factoring polynomials, a good strategy is to multiply the factors to check the result. Let's try another example:

$$4x^3+16x^2$$

Both sides of the expression can be divided by 4, and both contain x^2, because $4x^3$ can be thought of as $4x^2(x)$, so the common term can simply be factored out:

$$4x^2(x+4)$$

It sometimes can be necessary to rewrite the polynomial in some clever way before applying the above rules. Consider the problem of factoring x^4-1. This does not immediately look like any of the previous polynomials. However, it's possible to think of this polynomial as:

$$x^4-1=(x^2)^2-(1^2)^2$$

and now it can be treated as a difference of squares to simplify this:

$$(x^2)^2-(1^2)^2$$

$$(x^2)^2-x^21^2+x^21^2-(1^2)^2$$

$$x^2(x^2-1^2)+1^2(x^2-1^2)$$

$$(x^2+1^2)(x^2-1^2)$$

$$(x^2+1)(x^2-1)$$

Creating Polynomials from Written Descriptions

Polynomials that represent mathematical or real-world problems can also be created from written descriptions, much like algebraic expressions. For example, polynomials might be created when working with formulas. Formulas are mathematical expressions that define the value of one quantity, given the value of one or more different quantities. Formulas look like equations because they contain variables, numbers, operators, and an equal sign. All formulas are equations, but not all equations are formulas. A formula must have more than one variable. For example, $2x+7=y$ is an equation and a formula (it relates the unknown quantities *x* and *y*). However, $2x+7=3$ is an equation but not a formula (it only expresses the value of the unknown quantity *x*).

Formulas are typically written with one variable alone (or isolated) on one side of the equal sign. This variable can be thought of as the **subject** in that the formula is stating the value of the subject in terms of the relationship between the other variables. Consider the distance formula:

$$distance = rate \times time$$

or

$$d = rt$$

The value of the subject variable *d* (distance) is the product of the variable *r* and *t* (rate and time). Given the rate and time, the distance traveled can easily be determined by substituting the values into the formula and evaluating.

The formula $P = 2l + 2w$ expresses how to calculate the perimeter of a rectangle (*P*) given its length (*l*) and width (*w*). To find the perimeter of a rectangle with a length of 3ft and a width of 2ft, these values are substituted into the formula for *l* and *w*:

$$P = 2(3ft) + 2(2ft)$$

Following the order of operations, the perimeter is determined to be 10ft. When working with formulas such as these, including units is an important step.

Given a formula expressed in terms of one variable, the formula can be manipulated to express the relationship in terms of any other variable. In other words, the formula can be rearranged to change which variable is the *subject*. To solve for a variable of interest by manipulating a formula, the equation may be solved as if all other variables were numbers. The same steps for solving are followed, leaving operations in terms of the variables instead of calculating numerical values. For the formula $P = 2l + 2w$, the perimeter is the subject expressed in terms of the length and width. To write a formula to calculate the width of a rectangle, given its length and perimeter, the previous formula relating the three variables is solved for the variable *w*. If *P* and *l* were numerical values, this is a two-step linear equation solved by subtraction and division. To solve the equation $P = 2l + 2w$ for *w*, 2*l* is first subtracted from both sides:

$$P - 2l = 2w$$

Then both sides are divided by 2:

$$\frac{P - 2l}{2} = w$$

Test questions may involve creating a polynomial based on a formula. For example, using the perimeter of a rectangle formula, a problem may ask for the perimeter of a rectangle with a length of $2x + 12$ and a width of $x + 1$. Using the formula $P = 2l + 2w$, the perimeter would then be:

$$P = 2(2x + 12) + 2(x + 1)$$

This equals:

$$4x + 24 + 2x + 2 = 6x + 26$$

The area of the same rectangle, which uses the formula $A = l \times w,$ would be:

$$A = (2x + 12)(x + 1)$$

$$2x^2 + 2x + 12x + 12$$

$$2x^2 + 14x + 12$$

Adding, Subtracting, Multiplying, Dividing Rational Expressions

A fraction, or ratio, wherein each part is a polynomial, defines **rational expressions**. Some examples include:

$$\frac{2x + 6}{x}$$

$$\frac{1}{x^2 - 4x + 8}$$

and

$$\frac{z^2}{x + 5}$$

Exponents on the variables are restricted to whole numbers, which means roots and negative exponents are not included in rational expressions.

Rational expressions can be transformed by factoring. For example, the expression:

$$\frac{x^2 - 5x + 6}{(x - 3)}$$

can be rewritten by factoring the numerator to obtain:

$$\frac{(x - 3)(x - 2)}{(x - 3)}$$

Therefore, the common binomial $(x - 3)$ can cancel so that the simplified expression is:

$$\frac{(x - 2)}{1} = (x - 2)$$

Additionally, other rational expressions can be rewritten to take on different forms. Some may be factorable in themselves, while others can be transformed through arithmetic operations. Rational expressions are closed under addition, subtraction, multiplication, and division by a nonzero expression. **Closed** means that if any one of these operations is performed on a rational expression, the result will still be a rational expression. The set of all real numbers is another example of a set closed under all four operations.

Adding and subtracting rational expressions is based on the same concepts as adding and subtracting simple fractions. For both concepts, the denominators must be the same for the operation to take place. For example, here are two rational expressions:

$$\frac{x^3-4}{(x-3)}+\frac{x+8}{(x-3)}$$

Since the denominators are both $(x-3)$, the numerators can be combined by collecting like terms to form:

$$\frac{x^3+x+4}{(x-3)}$$

If the denominators are different, they need to be made common (the same) by using the **Least Common Denominator (LCD)**. Each denominator needs to be factored, and the LCD contains each factor that appears in any one denominator the greatest number of times it appears in any denominator. The original expressions need to be multiplied by a form of 1 such as $\frac{5}{5}$ or $\frac{x-2}{x-2}$, which will turn each denominator into the LCD. This process is like adding fractions with unlike denominators. It is also important when working with rational expressions to define what value of the variable makes the denominator zero. For this particular value, the expression is undefined.

Multiplication of rational expressions is performed like multiplication of fractions. The numerators are multiplied; then, the denominators are multiplied. The final fraction is then simplified. The expressions are simplified by factoring and cancelling out common terms. In the following example, the numerator of the second expression can be factored first to simplify the expression before multiplying:

$$\frac{x^2}{(x-4)}\times\frac{x^2-x-12}{2}$$

$$\frac{x^2}{(x-4)}\times\frac{(x-4)(x+3)}{2}$$

The $(x-4)$ on the top and bottom cancel out:

$$\frac{x^2}{1}\times\frac{(x+3)}{2}$$

Then multiplication is performed, resulting in:

$$\frac{x^3+3x^2}{2}$$

Dividing rational expressions is similar to the division of fractions, where division turns into multiplying by a reciprocal. Thus, the following expression can be rewritten as a multiplication problem:

$$\frac{x^2 - 3x + 7}{x - 4} \div \frac{x^2 - 5x + 3}{x - 4}$$

$$\frac{x^2 - 3x + 7}{x - 4} \times \frac{x - 4}{x^2 - 5x + 3}$$

The $x - 4$ cancels out, leaving:

$$\frac{x^2 - 3x + 7}{x^2 - 5x + 3}$$

The final answers should always be completely simplified. If a function is composed of a rational expression, the zeros of the graph can be found from setting the polynomial in the numerator as equal to zero and solving. The values that make the denominator equal to zero will either exist on the graph as a **hole** or a **vertical asymptote**.

A **complex fraction** is a fraction in which the numerator and denominator are themselves fractions, of the form:

$$\frac{(\frac{a}{b})}{(\frac{c}{d})}$$

These can be simplified by following the usual rules for the order of operations, or by remembering that dividing one fraction by another is the same as multiplying by the reciprocal of the divisor. This means that any complex fraction can be rewritten using the following form:

$$\frac{(\frac{a}{b})}{(\frac{c}{d})} = \frac{a}{b} \times \frac{d}{c}$$

The following problem is an example of solving a complex fraction:

$$\frac{(\frac{5}{4})}{(\frac{3}{8})} = \frac{5}{4} \times \frac{8}{3} = \frac{40}{12} = \frac{10}{3}$$

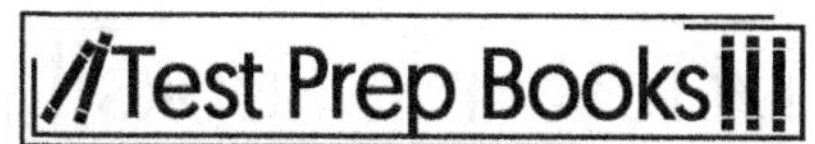

Writing an Expression from a Written Description

When expressing a verbal or written statement mathematically, it is vital to understand words or phrases that can be represented with symbols. The following are examples:

Symbol	Phrase
+	Added to; increased by; sum of; more than
−	Decreased by; difference between; less than; take away
×	Multiplied by; 3(4,5...) times as large; product of
÷	Divided by; quotient of; half (third, etc.) of
=	Is; the same as; results in; as much as; equal to
x,t,n, etc.	A number; unknown quantity; value of; variable

Addition and subtraction are **inverse operations**. Adding a number and then subtracting the same number will cancel each other out, resulting in the original number, and vice versa. For example:

$$8 + 7 - 7 = 8$$

and

$$137 - 100 + 100 = 137$$

Similarly, multiplication and division are inverse operations. Therefore, multiplying by a number and then dividing by the same number results in the original number, and vice versa. For example:

$$8 \times 2 \div 2 = 8$$

and

$$12 \div 4 \times 4 = 12$$

Inverse operations are used to work backwards to solve problems. In the case that 7 and a number add to 18, the inverse operation of subtraction is used to find the unknown value ($18 - 7 = 11$). If a school's entire 4th grade was divided evenly into 3 classes each with 22 students, the inverse operation of multiplication is used to determine the total students in the grade ($22 \times 3 = 66$).

Recall that a rational expression is a fraction where the numerator and denominator are both polynomials.

Some examples of rational expressions include the following:

$$\frac{4x^3y^5}{3z^4}$$

$$\frac{4x^3 + 3x}{x^2}$$

and

$$\frac{x^2 + 7x + 10}{x + 2}$$

Since these refer to expressions and not equations, they can be simplified but not solved. Using the rules of exponents and roots, some rational expressions with monomials can be simplified. Other rational expressions such as the last example:

$$\frac{x^2 + 7x + 10}{x + 2}$$

take more steps to be simplified. First, the polynomial on top can be factored from:

$$x^2 + 7x + 10$$

into

$$(x + 5)(x + 2)$$

Then the common factors can be canceled, and the expression can be simplified to $(x + 5)$.

Consider this problem as an example of using rational expressions. Reggie wants to lay sod in his rectangular backyard. The length of the yard is given by the expression $4x + 2$, and the width is unknown. The area of the yard is $20x + 10$. Reggie needs to find the width of the yard. Knowing that the area of a rectangle is length multiplied by width, an expression can be written to find the width:

$$\frac{20x + 10}{4x + 2}$$

area divided by length. Simplifying this expression by factoring out 10 on the top and 2 on the bottom leads to this expression:

$$\frac{10(2x + 1)}{2(2x + 1)}$$

By cancelling out the $2x + 1$, that results in $\frac{10}{2} = 5$. The width of the yard is found to be 5 by simplifying a rational expression.

Using Linear Equations to Solve Real-World Problems

Linear relationships describe the way two quantities change with respect to each other. The relationship is defined as linear because a line is produced if all the sets of corresponding values are graphed on a

coordinate grid. When expressing the linear relationship as an equation, the equation is often written in the form $y = mx + b$ (slope-intercept form) where *m* and *b* are numerical values and *x* and *y* are variables (for example, $y = 5x + 10$). Given a linear equation and the value of either variable (*x* or *y*), the value of the other variable can be determined.

Imagine the following problem: The sum of a number and 5 is equal to –8 times the number.

To find this unknown number, a simple equation can be written to represent the problem. Key words such as difference, equal, and times are used to form the following equation with one variable:

$$n + 5 = -8n$$

When solving for n, opposite operations are used. First, n is subtracted from $-8n$ across the equals sign, resulting in $5 = -9n$. Then, –9 is divided on both sides, leaving $n = -\frac{5}{9}$. This solution can be graphed on the number line with a dot as shown below:

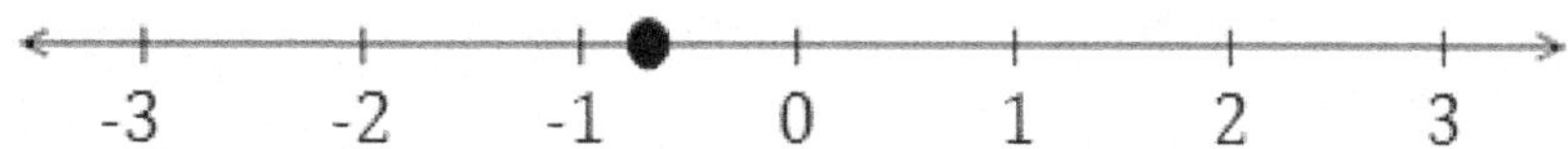

Suppose a teacher is grading a test containing 20 questions with 5 points given for each correct answer, adding a curve of 10 points to each test. This linear relationship can be expressed as the equation:

$$y = 5x + 10$$

where *x* represents the number of correct answers, and *y* represents the test score. To determine the score of a test with a given number of correct answers, the number of correct answers is substituted into the equation for *x* and evaluated. For example, for 10 correct answers, 10 is substituted for *x*:

$$y = 5(10) + 10 \rightarrow y = 60$$

Therefore, 10 correct answers will result in a score of 60. The number of correct answers needed to obtain a certain score can also be determined. To determine the number of correct answers needed to score a 90, 90 is substituted for *y* in the equation (*y* represents the test score) and solved:

$$90 = 5x + 10 \rightarrow 80 = 5x \rightarrow 16 = x$$

Therefore, 16 correct answers are needed to score a 90.

Linear relationships may be represented by a table of 2 corresponding values. Certain tables may determine the relationship between the values and predict other corresponding sets. Consider the table below, which displays the money in a checking account that charges a monthly fee:

Month	0	1	2	3	4
Balance	\$210	\$195	\$180	\$165	\$150

An examination of the values reveals that the account loses \$15 every month (the month increases by one and the balance decreases by 15). This information can be used to predict future values. To determine what the value will be in month 6, the pattern can be continued, and it can be concluded that the balance will be \$120. To determine which month the balance will be \$0, \$210 is divided by \$15 (since the balance decreases \$15 every month), resulting in month 14.

Solving a System of Two Linear Equations

A **system of equations** is a group of equations that have the same variables or unknowns. These equations can be linear, but they are not always so. Finding a solution to a system of equations means finding the values of the variables that satisfy each equation. For a linear system of two equations and two variables, there could be a single solution, no solution, or infinitely many solutions.

A single solution occurs when there is one value for x and y that satisfies the system. This would be shown on the graph where the lines cross at exactly one point. When there is no solution, the lines are parallel and do not ever cross. With infinitely many solutions, the equations may look different, but they are the same line. One equation will be a multiple of the other, and on the graph, they lie on top of each other.

The process of elimination can be used to solve a system of equations. For example, the following equations make up a system:

$$x + 3y = 10 \text{ and } 2x - 5y = 9$$

Immediately adding these equations does not eliminate a variable, but it is possible to change the first equation by multiplying the whole equation by -2. This changes the first equation to

$$-2x - 6y = -20$$

The equations can be then added to obtain $-11y = -11$. Solving for y yields $y = 1$. To find the rest of the solution, 1 can be substituted in for y in either original equation to find the value of $x = 7$. The solution to the system is (7, 1) because it makes both equations true, and it is the point in which the lines intersect. If the system is **dependent**—having infinitely many solutions—then both variables will cancel out when the elimination method is used, resulting in an equation that is true for many values of x and y. Since the system is dependent, both equations can be simplified to the same equation or line.

A system can also be solved using **substitution.** This involves solving one equation for a variable and then plugging that solved equation into the other equation in the system. For example:

$$x - y = -2$$

and

$$3x + 2y = 9$$

can be solved using substitution. The first equation can be solved for x, where $x = -2 + y$. Then it can be plugged into the other equation:

$$3(-2 + y) + 2y = 9$$

Solving for y yields:

$$-6 + 3y + 2y = 9$$

That shows that $y = 3$. If $y = 3$, then $x = 1$.

This solution can be checked by plugging in these values for the variables in each equation to see if it makes a true statement.

Finally, a solution to a system of equations can be found graphically. The solution to a linear system is the point or points where the lines cross. The values of x and y represent the coordinates (x, y) where the lines intersect. Using the same system of equations as above, they can be solved for y to put them in slope-intercept form, $y = mx + b$.

These equations become:

$$y = x + 2$$

and

$$y = -\frac{3}{2}x + 4.5$$

The slope is the coefficient of x, and the y-intercept is the constant value.

This system with the solution is shown below:

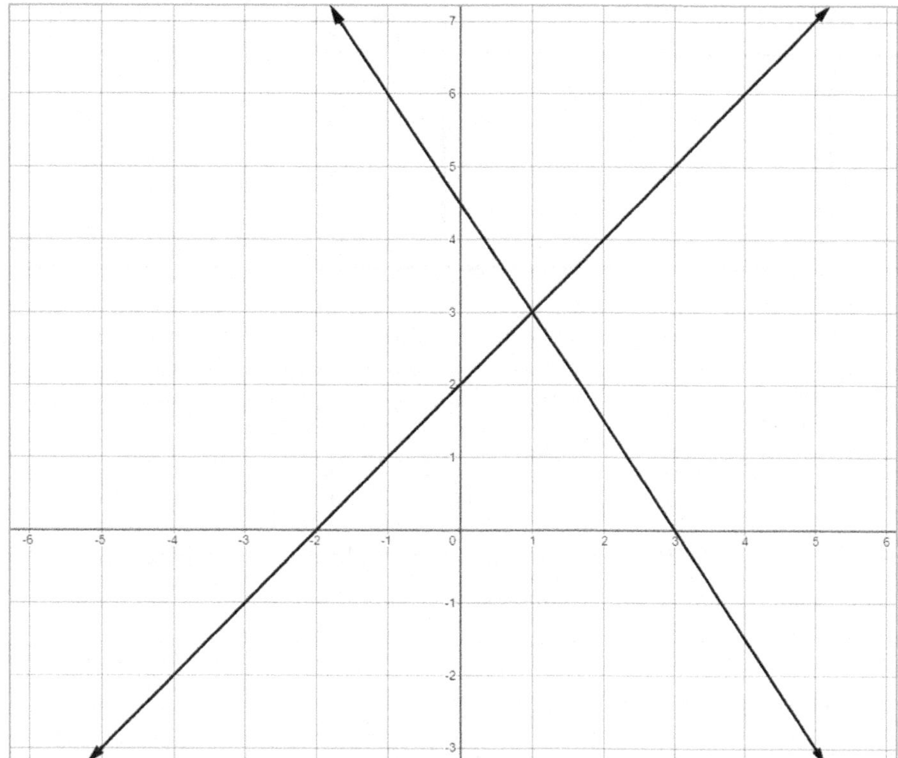

If the lines intersect, the point of intersection is the solution to the system. Every point on a line represents an ordered pair that makes its equation true. The ordered pair represented by this point of intersection lies on both lines and therefore makes both equations true. This ordered pair should be checked by substituting its values into both of the original equations of the system. Note that given a system of equations and an ordered pair, the ordered pair can be determined to be a solution or not by checking it in both equations.

If, when graphed, the lines representing the equations of a system do not intersect, then the two lines are parallel to each other or they are the same exact line. Parallel lines extend in the same direction without ever meeting. A system consisting of parallel lines has no solution. If the equations for a system represent the same exact line, then every point on the line is a solution to the system. In this case, there would be an infinite number of solutions. A system consisting of intersecting lines is referred to as independent; a system consisting of parallel lines is referred to as inconsistent; and a system consisting of coinciding lines is referred to as dependent.

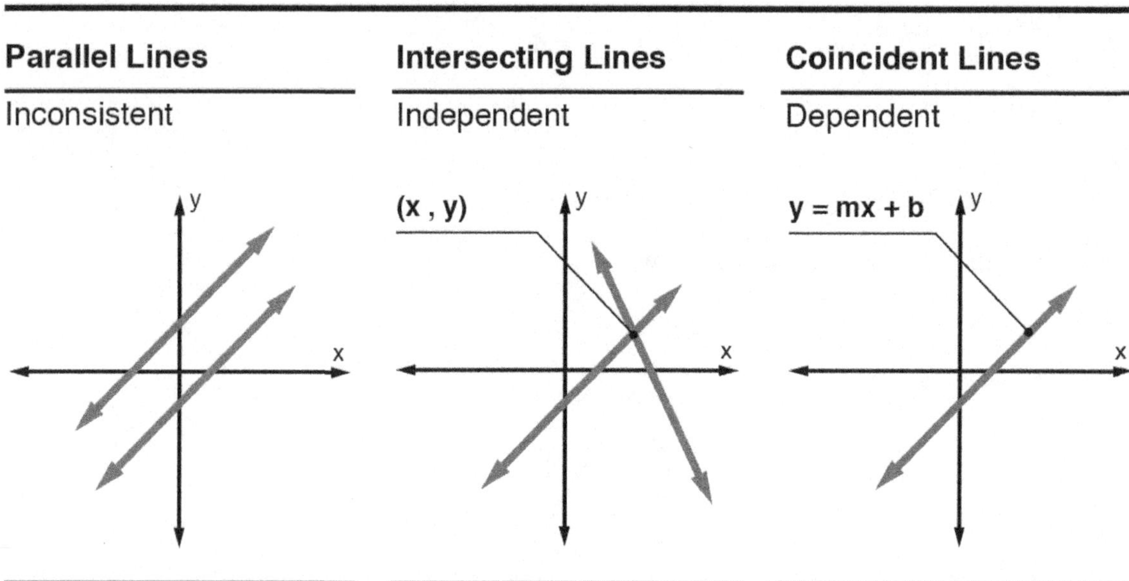

Matrices can also be used to solve systems of linear equations. Specifically, for systems, the coefficients of the linear equations in standard form are the entries in the matrix. Using the same system of linear equations as above, $x - y = -2$ and $3x + 2y = 9$, the matrix to represent the system is:

$$\begin{bmatrix} 1 & -1 \\ 3 & 2 \end{bmatrix} \begin{bmatrix} x \\ y \end{bmatrix} = \begin{bmatrix} -2 \\ 9 \end{bmatrix}$$

To solve this system using matrices, the inverse matrix must be found. For a general 2×2 matrix:

$$\begin{bmatrix} a & b \\ c & d \end{bmatrix}$$

The inverse matrix is found by the expression:

$$\frac{1}{ad - bc} \begin{bmatrix} d & -b \\ -c & a \end{bmatrix}$$

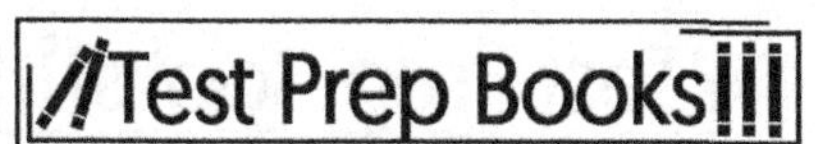

The inverse matrix for the system given above is:

$$\frac{1}{2 - -3}\begin{bmatrix} 2 & 1 \\ -3 & 1 \end{bmatrix} = \frac{1}{5}\begin{bmatrix} 2 & 1 \\ -3 & 1 \end{bmatrix}$$

The next step in solving is to multiply this identity matrix by the system matrix above. This is given by the following equation:

$$\frac{1}{5}\begin{bmatrix} 2 & 1 \\ -3 & 1 \end{bmatrix}\begin{bmatrix} 1 & -1 \\ 3 & 2 \end{bmatrix}\begin{bmatrix} x \\ y \end{bmatrix} = \begin{bmatrix} 2 & 1 \\ -3 & 1 \end{bmatrix}\begin{bmatrix} -2 \\ 9 \end{bmatrix}\frac{1}{5}$$

which simplifies to

$$\frac{1}{5}\begin{bmatrix} 5 & 0 \\ 0 & 5 \end{bmatrix}\begin{bmatrix} x \\ y \end{bmatrix} = \frac{1}{5}\begin{bmatrix} 5 \\ 15 \end{bmatrix}$$

Solving for the solution matrix, the answer is:

$$\begin{bmatrix} 1 & 0 \\ 0 & 1 \end{bmatrix}\begin{bmatrix} x \\ y \end{bmatrix} = \begin{bmatrix} 1 \\ 3 \end{bmatrix}$$

Since the first matrix is the identity matrix, the solution is $x = 1$ and $y = 3$.

Finding solutions to systems of equations is essentially finding what values of the variables make both equations true. It is finding the input value that yields the same output value in both equations. For functions $g(x)$ and $f(x)$, the equation $g(x) = f(x)$ means the output values are being set equal to each other. Solving for the value of x means finding the x-coordinate that gives the same output in both functions.

For example:

$$f(x) = x + 2$$

and

$$g(x) = -3x + 10$$

is a system of equations. Setting $f(x) = g(x)$ yields the equation:

$$x + 2 = -3x + 10$$

Solving for x, gives the x-coordinate $x = 2$ where the two lines cross. This value can also be found by using a table or a graph. On a table, both equations can be given the same inputs, and the outputs can be recorded to find the point(s) where the lines cross. Any method of solving finds the same solution, but some methods are more appropriate for some systems of equations than others.

Solving Inequalities and Graphing the Answer on a Number Line

Linear inequalities and linear equations are both comparisons of two algebraic expressions. However, unlike equations in which the expressions are equal to each other, linear inequalities compare expressions that are unequal. Linear equations typically have one value for the variable that makes the statement true. Linear inequalities generally have an infinite number of values that make the statement true.

If a problem were to say, "The sum of a number and 5 is greater than –8 times the number," then an inequality would be used instead of an equation. Using key words again, *greater than* is represented by the symbol >. The inequality"

$$n + 5 > -8n$$

can be solved using the same techniques, resulting in:

$$n < -\frac{5}{9}$$

The only time solving an inequality differs from solving an equation is when a negative number is either multiplied by or divided by each side of the inequality. The sign must be switched in this case. For this example, the graph of the solution changes to the following graph because the solution represents all real numbers less than $-\frac{5}{9}$. Not included in this solution is $-\frac{5}{9}$ because it is a *less than* symbol, not *equal to*.

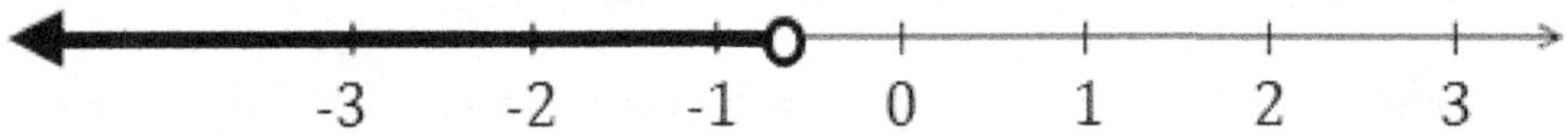

When solving a linear inequality, the solution is the set of all numbers that makes the statement true. The inequality $x + 2 \geq 6$ has a solution set of 4 and every number greater than 4 (4.0001, 5, 12, 107, etc.). Adding 2 to 4 or any number greater than 4 would result in a value that is greater than or equal to 6. Therefore, $x \geq 4$ would be the solution set.

Solution sets for linear inequalities often will be displayed using a number line. If a value is included in the set (≥ or ≤), there is a shaded dot placed on that value and an arrow extending in the direction of the solutions. For a variable > or ≥ a number, the arrow would point right on the number line (the direction where the numbers increase); and if a variable is < or ≤ a number, the arrow would point left (where the numbers decrease). If the value is not included in the set (> or <), an open circle on that value would be used with an arrow in the appropriate direction.

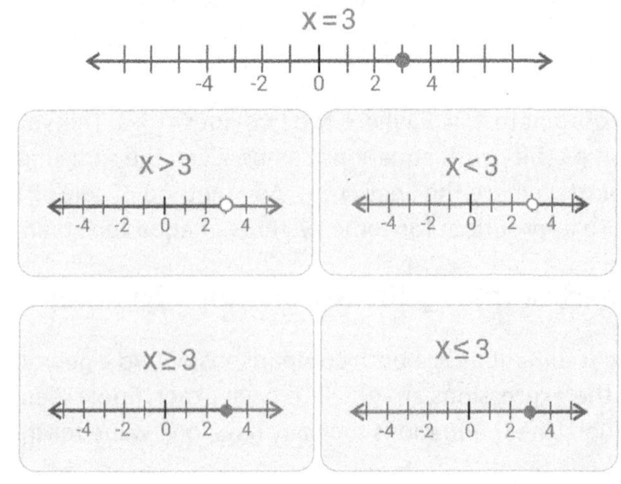

Students may be asked to write a linear inequality given a graph of its solution set. To do so, they should identify whether the value is included (shaded dot or open circle) and the direction in which the arrow is pointing.

In order to algebraically solve a linear inequality, the same steps should be followed as in solving a linear equation. The inequality symbol stays the same for all operations EXCEPT when multiplying or dividing by a negative number. If multiplying or dividing by a negative number while solving an inequality, the relationship reverses (the sign flips). Multiplying or dividing by a positive does not change the relationship, so the sign stays the same. In other words, $>$ switches to $<$ and vice versa. An example is shown below:

Solve $-2(x + 4) \leq 22$ for the value of x.

First, distribute –2 to the binomial by multiplying:

$$-2x - 8 \leq 22$$

Next, add 8 to both sides to isolate the variable:

$$-2x \leq 30$$

Divide both sides by –2 to solve for x:

$$x \geq -15$$

With a single equation in two variables, the solutions are limited only by the situation the equation represents. When two equations or inequalities are used, more constraints are added. For example, in a system of linear equations, there is often—although not always—only one answer. The point of intersection of two lines is the solution. For a system of inequalities, there are infinitely many answers.

The intersection of two solution sets gives the solution set of the system of inequalities. In the following graph, the darker shaded region is where two inequalities overlap. Any set of x and y found in that region satisfies both inequalities. The line with the positive slope is solid, meaning the values on that line are included in the solution.

The line with the negative slope is dotted, so the coordinates on that line are not included.

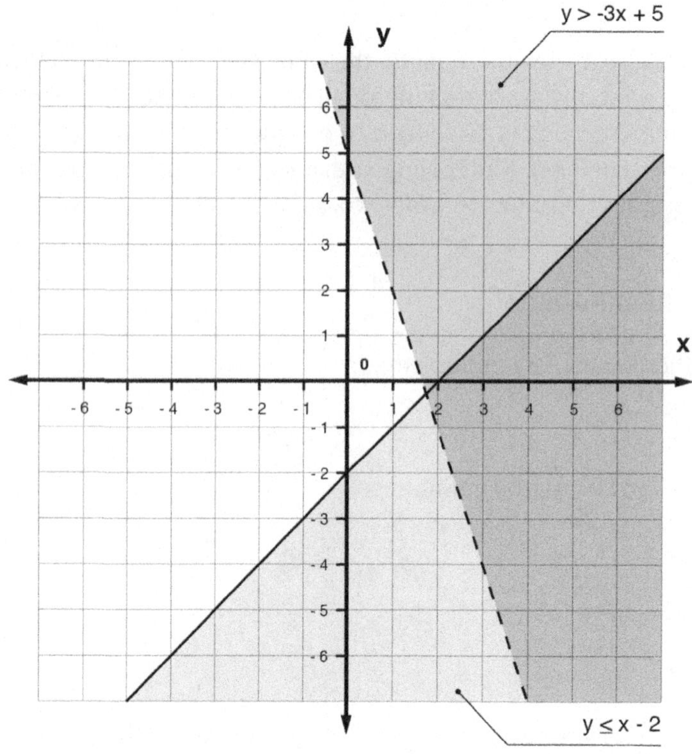

Quadratic Equations with One Variable

A **quadratic equation** can be written in the form:

$$y = ax^2 + bx + c$$

The u-shaped graph of a quadratic equation is called a **parabola**. The graph can either open up or open down (upside down u). The graph is symmetric about a vertical line, called the **axis of symmetry**. Corresponding points on the parabola are directly across from each other (same *y*-value) and are the same distance from the axis of symmetry (on either side). The axis of symmetry intersects the parabola at its **vertex**. The *y*-value of the vertex represents the minimum or maximum value of the function. If the graph opens up, the value of *a* in its equation is positive, and the vertex represents the minimum of the function. If the graph opens down, the value of *a* in its equation is negative, and the vertex represents the maximum of the function.

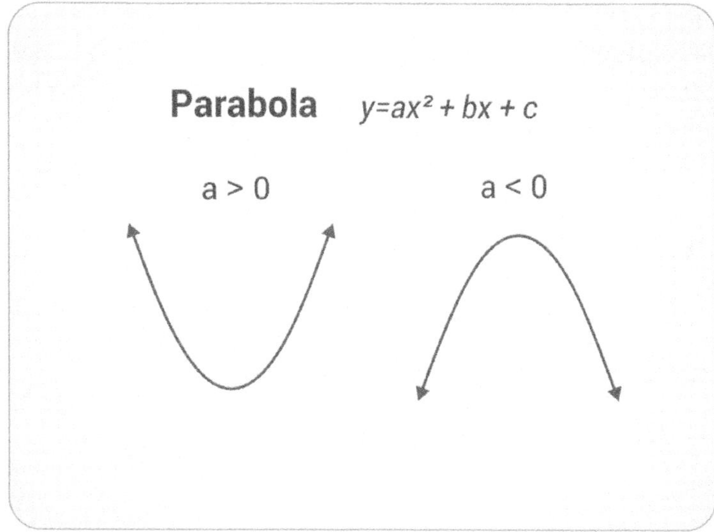

For a quadratic equation where the value of *a* is positive, as the inputs increase, the outputs increase until a certain value (maximum of the function) is reached. As inputs increase past the value that corresponds with the maximum output, the relationship reverses, and the outputs decrease. For a quadratic equation where *a* is negative, as the inputs increase, the outputs (1) decrease, (2) reach a maximum, and (3) then increase.

Consider a ball thrown straight up into the air. As time passes, the height of the ball increases until it reaches its maximum height. After reaching the maximum height, as time increases, the height of the ball decreases (it is falling toward the ground). This relationship can be expressed as a quadratic equation where time is the input (x), and the height of the ball is the output (y).

Equations with one variable (linear equations) can be solved using the addition principle and multiplication principle. If $a = b$, then $a + c = b + c$, and $ac = bc$. Given the equation"

$$2x - 3 = 5x + 7$$

the first step is to combine the variable terms and the constant terms. Using the principles, expressions can be added and subtracted onto and off both sides of the equals sign, so the equation turns into $-10 = 3x$. Dividing by 3 on both sides through the multiplication principle with $c = \frac{1}{3}$ results in the final answer of $x = \frac{-10}{3}$.

However, this same process cannot be used to solve nonlinear equations, including quadratic equations. Quadratic equations have a higher degree than linear ones (2 versus 1) and are not solved by simply using opposite operations. When an equation has a degree of 2, completing the square is an option. For example, the quadratic equation:

$$x^2 - 6x + 2 = 0$$

can be rewritten by completing the square. The goal of completing the square is to get the equation into the form:

$$(x-p)^2 = q$$

Using the example, the constant term 2 first needs to be moved over to the opposite side by subtracting. Then, the square can be completed by adding 9 to both sides, which is the square of half of the coefficient of the middle term $-6x$. The current equation is:

$$x^2 - 6x + 9 = 7$$

The left side can be factored into a square of a binomial, resulting in:

$$(x-3)^2 = 7$$

To solve for x, the square root of both sides should be taken, resulting in:

$$(x-3) = \pm\sqrt{7}$$

and

$$x = 3 \pm \sqrt{7}$$

Other ways of solving quadratic equations include graphing, factoring, and using the quadratic formula. The equation:

$$y = x^2 - 4x + 3$$

can be graphed on the coordinate plane, and the solutions can be observed where it crosses the x-axis. The graph will be a parabola that opens up with two solutions at 1 and 3.

If quadratic equations take the form $ax^2 - b = 0$, then the equation can be solved by adding *b* to both sides and dividing by *a* to get:

$$x^2 = \frac{b}{a} \text{ or } x = \pm\sqrt{\frac{b}{a}}$$

Note that this is actually two separate solutions, unless *b* happens to be 0.

If a quadratic equation has no constant—so that it takes the form:

$$ax^2 + bx = 0$$

then the *x* can be factored out to get

$$x(ax + b) = 0$$

Then, the solutions are $x = 0$, together with the solutions to

$$ax + b = 0$$

Both factors x and $(ax + b)$ can be set equal to zero to solve for x because one of those values must be zero for their product to equal zero. For an equation $ab = 0$ to be true, either $a = 0$, or $b = 0$.

A given quadratic equation:

$$x^2 + bx + c$$

can be factored into:

$$(x + A)(x + B)$$

where $A + B = b$, and $AB = c$. Finding the values of A and B can take time, but such a pair of numbers can be found by guessing and checking. Looking at the positive and negative factors for *c* offers a good starting point.

For example, in:

$$x^2 - 5x + 6$$

the factors of 6 are 1, 2, and 3. Now,$(-2)(-3) = 6$, and $-2 - 3 = -5$. In general, however, this may not work, in which case another approach may need to be used.

A quadratic equation of the form:

$$x^2 + 2xb + b^2 = 0$$

can be factored into $(x + b)^2 = 0$. Similarly

$$x^2 - 2xy + y^2 = 0$$

factors into $(x - y)^2 = 0$.

The first method of completing the square can be used in finding the second method, the quadratic formula. It can be used to solve any quadratic equation. This formula may be the longest method for solving quadratic equations and is commonly used as a last resort after other methods are ruled out.

It can be helpful in memorizing the formula to see where it comes from, so here are the steps involved.

The most general form for a quadratic equation is:

$$ax^2 + bx + c = 0$$

First, dividing both sides by *a* leaves us with:

$$x^2 + \frac{b}{a}x + \frac{c}{a} = 0$$

To complete the square on the left-hand side, c/a can be subtracted on both sides to get:

$$x^2 + \frac{b}{a}x = -\frac{c}{a}$$

$(\frac{b}{2a})^2$ is then added to both sides.

This gives:

$$x^2 + \frac{b}{a}x + (\frac{b}{2a})^2 = (\frac{b}{2a})^2 - \frac{c}{a}$$

The left can now be factored and the right-hand side simplified to give:

$$(x + \frac{b}{2a})^2 = \frac{b^2 - 4ac}{4a}$$

Taking the square roots gives:

$$x + \frac{b}{2a} = \pm\frac{\sqrt{b^2 - 4ac}}{2a}$$

Solving for x yields the quadratic formula:

$$x = \frac{-b \pm \sqrt{b^2 - 4ac}}{2a}$$

It isn't necessary to remember how to get this formula but memorizing the formula itself is the goal.

If an equation involves taking a root, then the first step is to move the root to one side of the equation and everything else to the other side. That way, both sides can be raised to the index of the radical in order to remove it, and solving the equation can continue.

Graphs and Functions

Locating Points and Graphing Equations

The coordinate plane, sometimes referred to as the Cartesian plane, is a two-dimensional surface consisting of a horizontal and a vertical number line. The horizontal number line is referred to as the *x*-axis, and the vertical number line is referred to as the *y*-axis. The *x*-axis and *y*-axis intersect (or cross) at a point called the origin. At the origin, the value of the *x*-axis is zero, and the value of the *y*-axis is zero. The coordinate plane identifies the exact location of a point that is plotted on the two-dimensional surface. Like a map, the location of all points on the plane are in relation to the origin. Along the *x*-axis (horizontal line), numbers to the right of the origin are positive and increasing in value (1,2,3, ...) and to the left of the origin numbers are negative and decreasing in value (–1,–2,–3, ...). Along the *y*-axis (vertical line), numbers above the origin are positive and increasing in value and numbers below the origin are negative and decreasing in value.

The *x*- and *y*-axis divide the coordinate plane into four sections. These sections are referred to as quadrant one, quadrant two, quadrant three, and quadrant four, and are often written with Roman numerals I, II, III, and IV.

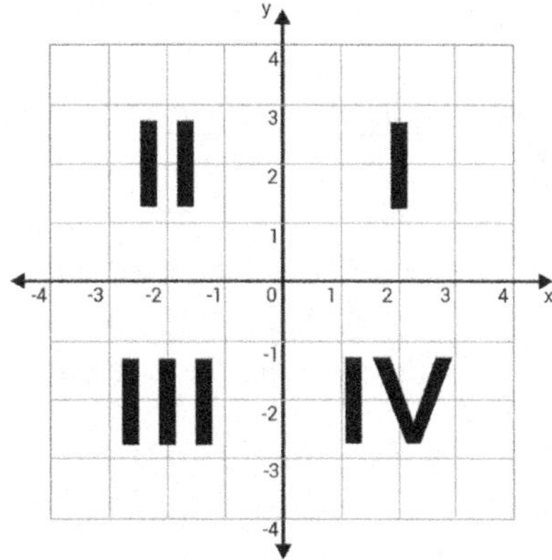

The upper right section is Quadrant I and consists of points with positive *x*-values and positive *y*-values. The upper left section is Quadrant II and consists of points with negative *x*-values and positive *y*-values. The bottom left section is Quadrant III and consists of points with negative *x*-values and negative *y*-values. The bottom right section is Quadrant IV and consists of points with positive *x*-values and negative *y*-values.

Graphing in the Coordinate Plane

The coordinate plane represents a representation of real-world space, and any point within the plane can be defined by a set of **coordinates** (x, y). The coordinates consist of two numbers, x and y, which represent a position on each number line. The coordinates can also be referred to as an **ordered pair,** and $(0,0)$ is the ordered pair known as the **vertex**, or the origin, the point in which the axes intersect.

Here is an example of the coordinate plane with a point plotted:

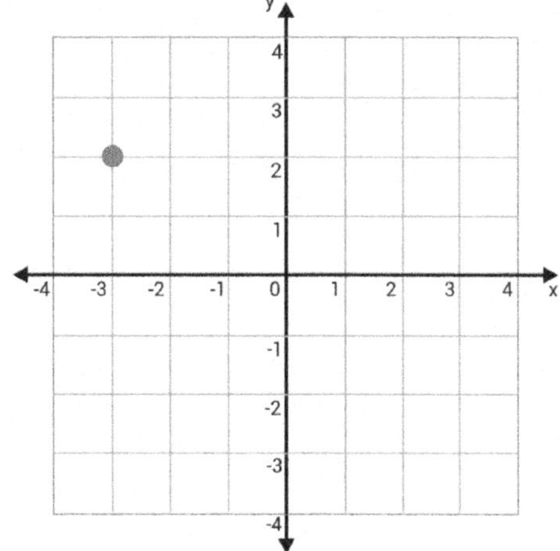

In order to plot a point on the coordinate plane, each coordinate must be considered individually. The value of x represents how many units away from the vertex the point lies on the x-axis. The value of y represents the number of units away from the vertex that the point lies on the y-axis.

For example, given the ordered pair (5, 4), the x-coordinate, 5, is the distance from the origin along the x-axis, and the y-coordinate, 4, is the distance from the origin along the y-axis. This is determined by counting 5 units to the right from (0, 0) along the x-axis and then counting 4 units up from that point, to reach the point where $x = 5$ and $y = 4$. In order to graph the single point, the point should be marked there with a dot and labeled as (5, 4). Every point on the plane has its own ordered pair.

Graphing on the Coordinate Plane Using Mathematical Problems, Tables, and Patterns

Data can be recorded using a coordinate plane. Graphs are utilized frequently in real-world applications and can be seen in many facets of everyday life. A relationship can exist between the *x*- and *y*-coordinates that are plotted on a graph, and those values can represent a set of data that can be listed in a table. Going back and forth between the table and the graph is an important concept and defining the relationship between the variables is the key that links the data to a real-life application.

For example, temperature increases during a summer day. The *x*-coordinate can be used to represent hours in the day, and the *y*-coordinate can be used to represent the temperature in degrees. The graph would show the temperature at each hour of the day. Time is almost always plotted on the *x*-axis, and utilizing different units on each axis, if necessary, is important. Labeling the axes with units is also important.

Within the first quadrant of the coordinate plane, both the x and y values are positive. Most real-world problems can be plotted in this quadrant because most real-world quantities, such as time and distance, are positive. Consider the following table of values:

X	Y
1	2
2	4
3	6
4	8

Each row gives a coordinate pair. For example, the first row gives the coordinates (1,2). Each *x*-value tells you how far to move from the origin, the point (0,0), to the right, and each *y*-value tells you how far to move up from the origin.

Here is the graph of the points listed above in the table in addition to the origin:

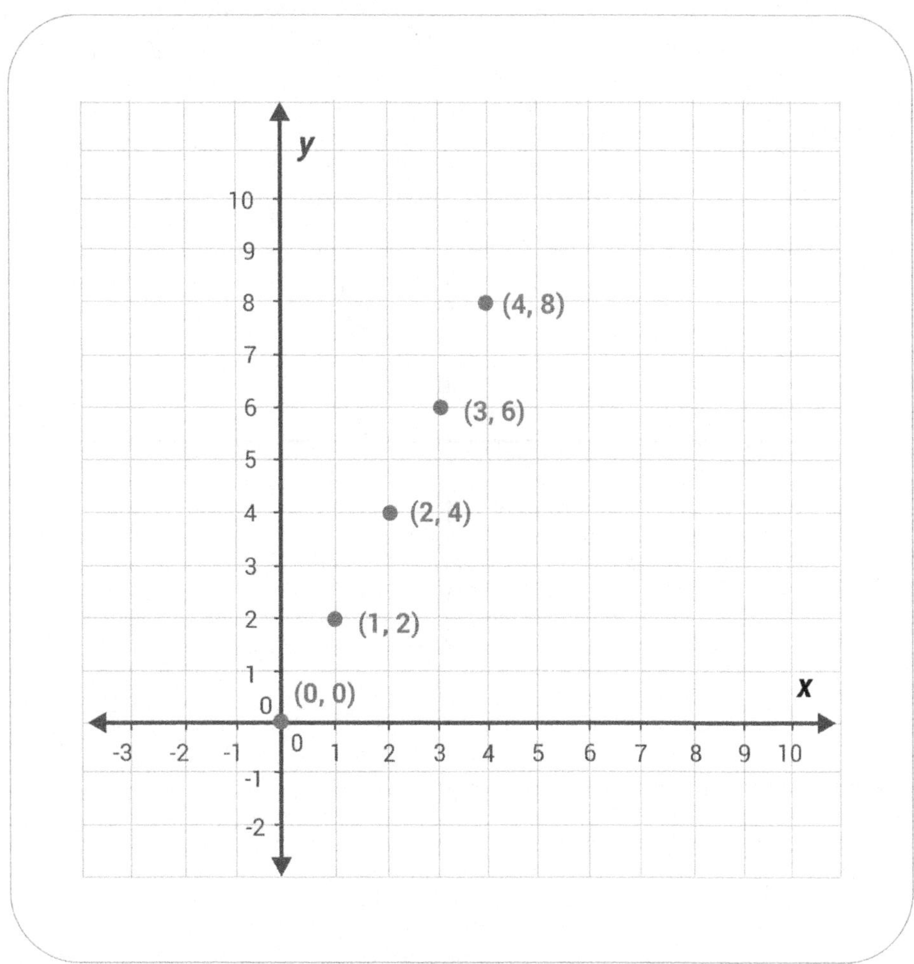

Notice that each *y*-value is found by doubling the *x*-value that forms the other portion of its coordinate pair.

Determining the Slope of a Line from a Graph, Equation, or Table

Rate of change for any line calculates the steepness of the line over a given interval. Rate of change is also known as the **slope** or rise/run. The slope of a linear function is given by the change in *y* divided by the change in *x*. So, the formula looks like this:

$$slope = \frac{y_2 - y_1}{x_2 - x_1}$$

In the graph below, two points are plotted. The first has the coordinates of (0, 1), and the second point is (2, 3). Remember that the x coordinate is always placed first in coordinate pairs. Work from left to right when identifying coordinates. Thus, the point on the left is point 1 (0, 1), and the point on the right is point 2 (2, 3).

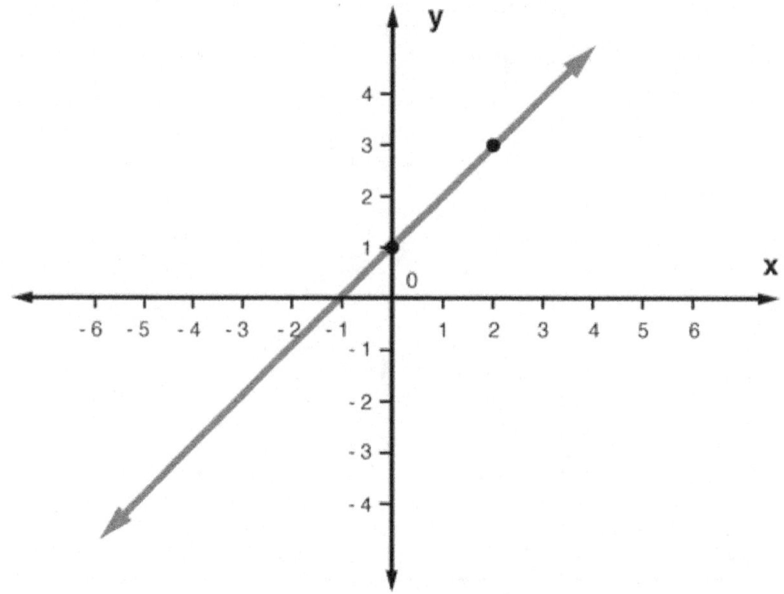

Now we need to just plug those numbers into the equation:

$$slope = \frac{3-1}{2-0}$$

$$slope = \frac{2}{2}$$

$$slope = 1$$

This means that for every increase of 1 for x, y also increased by 1. You can see this in the line. When x equaled 0, y equaled 1, and when x was increased to 1, y equaled 2.

Slope can be thought of as determining the rise over run:

$$slope = \frac{rise}{run}$$

The rise being the change vertically on the y axis and the run being the change horizontally on the x axis.

Proportional Relationships for Equations and Graphs

The rate of change for a linear function is constant and can be determined based on a few representations. One method is to place the equation in slope-intercept form: $y = mx + b$. Thus, m is the slope, and b is the y-intercept. In the graph below, the equation is $y = x + 1$, where the slope is 1 and the y-intercept is 1. For every vertical change of 1 unit, there is a horizontal change of 1 unit.

The x-intercept is -1, which is the point where the line crosses the x-axis:

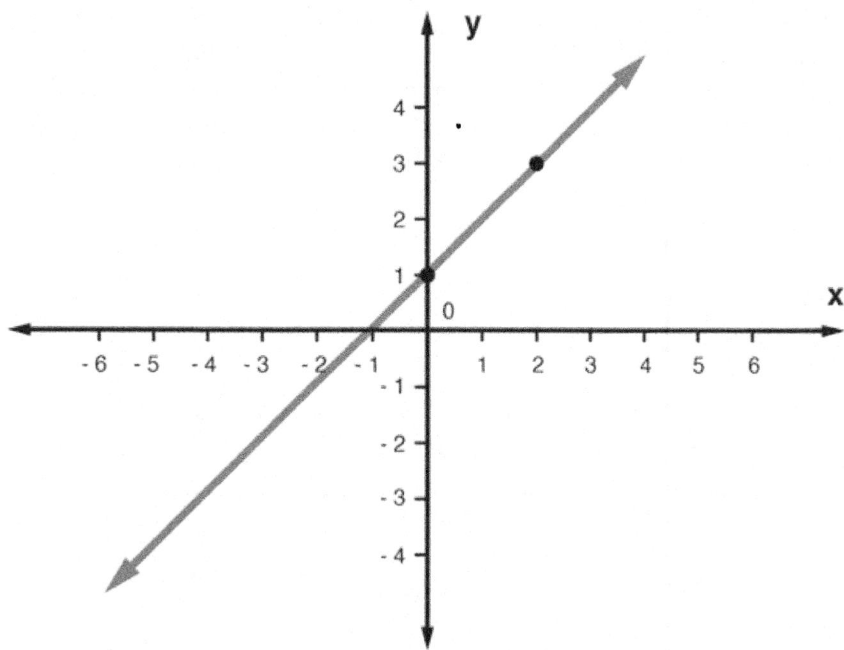

Let's look at an example of a proportional, or linear relationship, seen in the real world.

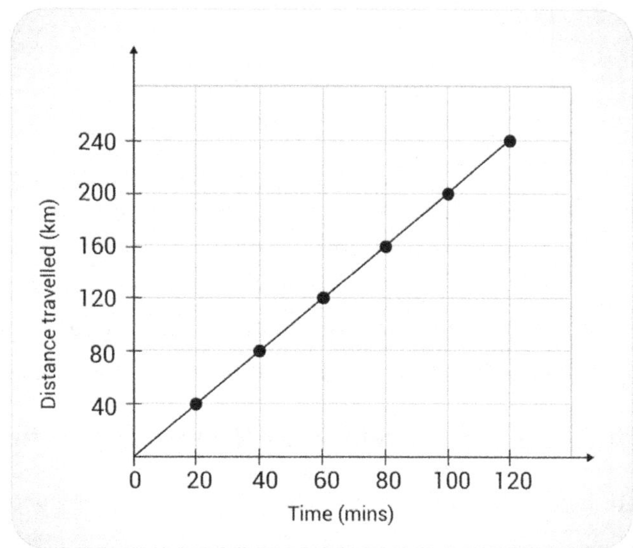

The graph above represents the relationship between distance traveled and time. To find the distance traveled in 80 minutes, the mark for 80 minutes is located at the bottom of the graph. By following this mark directly up on the graph, the corresponding point for 80 minutes is directly across from the 160 kilometer mark. This information indicates that the distance travelled in 80 minutes is 160 kilometers. To predict information not displayed on the graph, the way in which the variables change with respect to one another is determined. In this case, distance increases by 40 kilometers as time increases by 20 minutes. This information can be used to continue the data in the graph or convert the values to a table.

Let's try another example. Jim owns a car wash and charges \$40 per car. The rent for the facility is \$350 per month. An equation can be written to relate the number of cars Jim cleans to the money he makes per month. Let x represent the number of cars and y represent the profit Jim makes each month from the car wash. The equation $y = 40x - 350$ can be used to show Jim's profit or loss. Since this equation has two variables, the coordinate plane can be used to show the relationship and predict profit or loss for Jim. The following graph shows that Jim must wash at least nine cars to pay the rent, where $x = 9$. Anything nine cars and above yield a profit shown in the value on the y-axis.

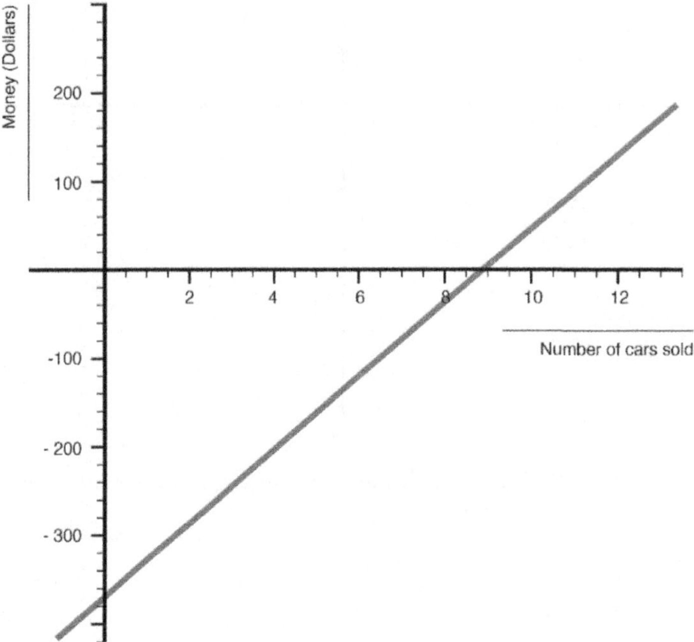

Formulas with two variables are equations used to represent a specific relationship. For example, the formula $d = rt$ represents the relationship between distance, rate, and time. If Bob travels at a rate of 35 miles per hour on his road trip from Westminster to Seneca, the formula $d = 35t$ can be used to represent his distance traveled in a specific length of time. Formulas can also be used to show different roles of the variables, transformed without any given numbers. Solving for r, the formula becomes $\frac{d}{t} = r$. The t is moved over by division so that **rate** is a function of distance and time.

Features of Graphs and Tables for Linear and Nonlinear Relationships

As mentioned, linear relationships describe the way two quantities change with respect to each other. The relationship is defined as linear because a line is produced if all the sets of corresponding values are graphed on a coordinate grid. When expressing the linear relationship as an equation, the equation is often written in the form $y = mx + b$ (**slope-intercept form**) where *m* and *b* are numerical values and *x* and *y* are variables (for example, $y = 5x + 10$). The slope is the coefficient of x, and the y-intercept is the constant value. The slope of the line containing the same two points is:

$$m = \frac{y_2 - y_1}{x_2 - x_1}$$

and is also equal to rise/run. Given a linear equation and the value of either variable (*x* or *y*), the value of the other variable can be determined.

With polynomial functions such as quadratics, the x-intercepts represent zeros of the function. Finding the **zeros of polynomial functions** is the same process as finding the solutions of polynomial equations. These are the points at which the graph of the function crosses the x-axis. In the following quadratic equation, factoring the binomial leads to finding the zeros of the function:

$$x^2 - 5x + 6 = y$$

This equation factors into

$$(x - 3)(x - 2) = y$$

where 2 and 3 are found to be the zeros of the function when y is set equal to zero. The zeros of any function are the x-values where the graph of the function on the coordinate plane crosses the x-axis, which is the same as an x-intercept.

Selecting an Equation that Best Represents a Graph

Three common functions used to model different relationships between quantities are linear, quadratic, and exponential functions. **Linear functions** are the simplest of the three, and the independent variable x has an exponent of 1. Written in the most common form:

$$y = mx + b$$

the coefficient of *x* indicates how fast the function grows at a constant rate, and the *b*-value denotes the starting point. A **quadratic function** has an exponent of 2 on the independent variable x. Standard form for this type of function is:

$$y = ax^2 + bx + c$$

and the graph is a parabola. These type functions grow at a changing rate. An **exponential function** has an independent variable in the exponent $y = ab^x$. The graph of these types of functions is described as **growth** or **decay**, based on whether the **base**, b, is greater than or less than 1. These functions are different from quadratic functions because the base stays constant. A common base is base *e*.

The following three functions model a linear, quadratic, and exponential function respectively: $y = 2x$, $y = x^2$, and $y = 2^x$. Their graphs are shown below. The first graph, modeling the linear function, shows that the growth is constant over each interval. With a horizontal change of 1, the vertical change is 2. It models constant positive growth. The second graph shows the quadratic function, which is a curve that is symmetric across the y-axis. The growth is not constant, but the change is mirrored over the axis. The last graph models the exponential function, where the horizontal change of 1 yields a vertical change that increases more and more with each iteration of horizontal change. The exponential graph gets very close to the x-axis, but never touches it, meaning there is an asymptote there. The y-value can never be zero because the base of 2 can never be raised to an input value that yields an output of zero.

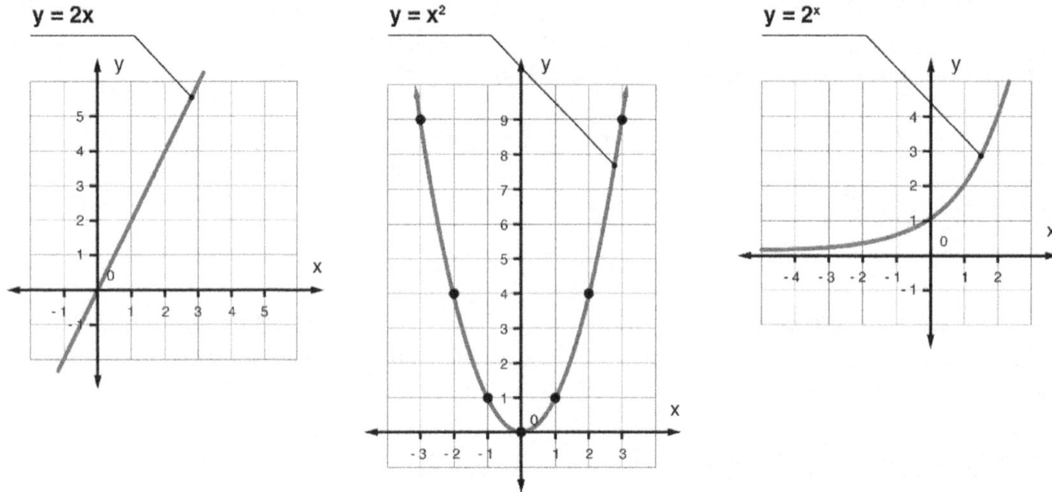

Determining the Graphical Properties and Sketch a Graph Given an Equation

Graphing a Linear Function

The process for graphing a line depends on the form in which its equation is written: slope-intercept form or standard form.

When an equation is written in slope-intercept form, $y = mx + b$, m represents the slope of the line and b represents the y-intercept. The y-intercept is the value of y when $x = 0$ and the point at which the graph of the line crosses the y-axis. The slope is the rate of change between the variables, expressed as a fraction. The fraction expresses the change in y compared to the change in x. If the slope is an integer, it should be written as a fraction with a denominator of 1. For example, 5 would be written as $\frac{5}{1}$.

To graph a line given an equation in slope-intercept form, the y-intercept should first be plotted. For example, to graph:

$$y = -\frac{2}{3}x + 7$$

the y-intercept of 7 would be plotted on the y-axis (vertical axis) at the point (0, 7). Next, the slope would be used to determine a second point for the line. Note that all that is necessary to graph a line is two points on that line. The slope will indicate how to get from one point on the line to another. The slope expresses vertical change (y) compared to horizontal change (x) and therefore is sometimes referred to as $\frac{rise}{run}$. The numerator indicates the change in the y value (move up for positive integers and move down for negative integers), and the denominator indicates the change in the x value. For the previous example, using the slope of $-\frac{2}{3}$, from the first point at the y-intercept, the second point should be found by counting down 2 and to the right 3. This point would be located at (3, 5).

When an equation is written in standard form, $Ax + By = C$, it is easy to identify the *x*- and *y*-intercepts for the graph of the line. Just as the *y*-intercept is the point at which the line intercepts the *y*-axis, the *x*-intercept is the point at which the line intercepts the *x*-axis. At the *y*-intercept, $x = 0$; and at the *x*-intercept, $y = 0$. Given an equation in standard form, $x = 0$ should be used to find the *y*-intercept. Likewise, $y = 0$ should be used to find the *x*-intercept. For example, to graph $3x + 2y = 6$, 0 for *y* results in $3x + 2(0) = 6$. Solving for *y* yields $x = 2$; therefore, an ordered pair for the line is (2, 0). Substituting 0 for *x* results in $3(0) + 2y = 6$. Solving for *y* yields $y = 3$; therefore, an ordered pair for the line is (0, 3). The two ordered pairs (the *x*- and *y*-intercepts) can be plotted, and a straight line through them can be constructed.

T - chart

x	y
0	3
2	0

Intercepts

x - intercept : (2,0)

y - intercept : (0,3)

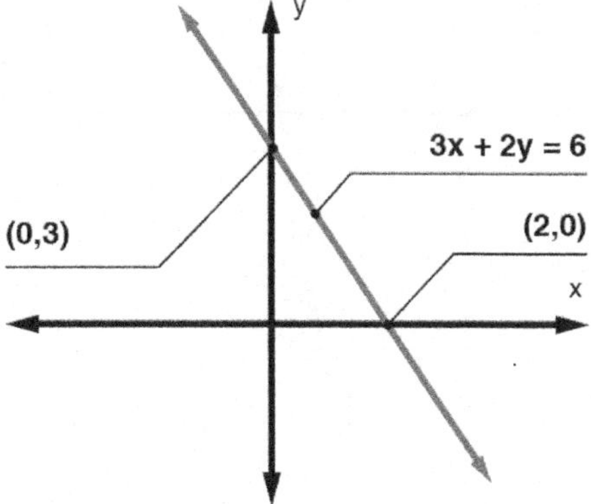

Graphing a Quadratic Function

The standard form of a quadratic function is:

$$y = ax^2 + bx + c$$

The graph of a quadratic function is a u-shaped (or upside-down u) curve, called a parabola, which is symmetric about a vertical line (axis of symmetry). To graph a parabola, its vertex (high or low point for the curve) and at least two points on each side of the axis of symmetry need to be determined.

Given a quadratic function in standard form, the axis of symmetry for its graph is the line $x = -\frac{b}{2a}$. The vertex for the parabola has an x-coordinate of $-\frac{b}{2a}$. To find the y-coordinate for the vertex, the calculated x-coordinate needs to be substituted. To complete the graph, two different x-values need to be selected and substituted into the quadratic function to obtain the corresponding y-values. This will give two points on the parabola. These two points and the axis of symmetry are used to determine the two points corresponding to these. The corresponding points are the same distance from the axis of symmetry (on the other side) and contain the same y-coordinate. Plotting the vertex and four other points on the parabola allows for constructing the curve.

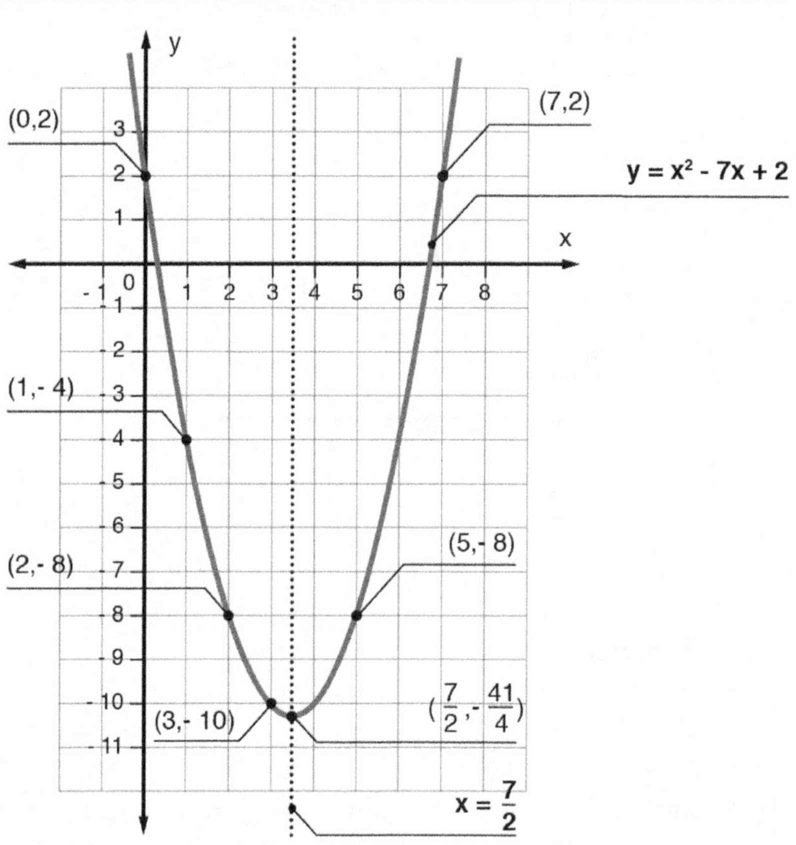

Graphing an Exponential Function

Exponential functions have a general form of:

$$y = a \times b^x$$

The graph of an exponential function is a curve that slopes upward or downward from left to right. The graph approaches a line, called an asymptote, as x or y increases or decreases. To graph the curve for an exponential function, x-values are selected and then substituted into the function to obtain the corresponding y-values. A general rule of thumb is to select three negative values, zero, and three positive values. Plotting the seven points on the graph for an exponential function should allow for constructing a smooth curve through them.

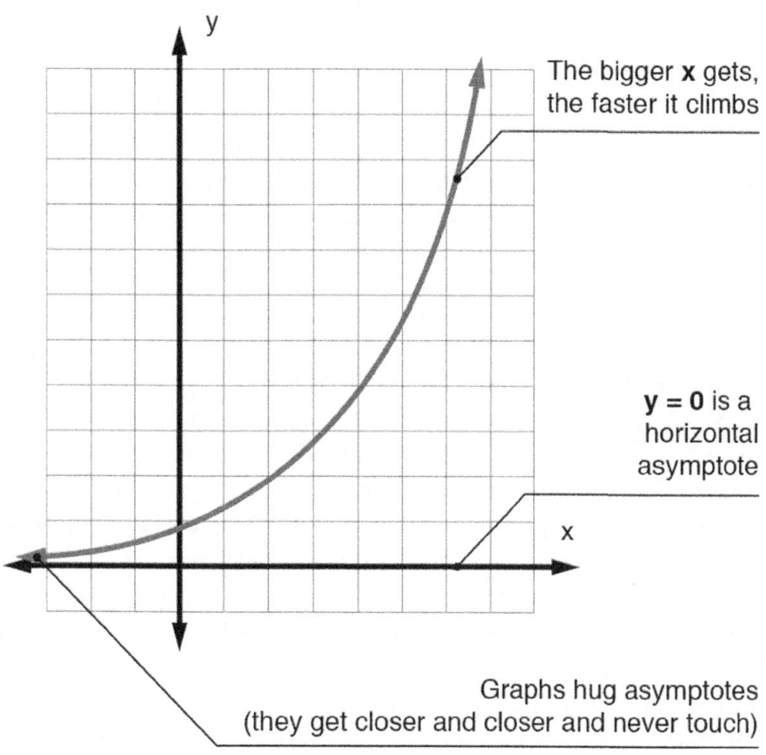

Equation of a Line from the Slope and a Point on a Line

The point-slope form of a line:

$$y - y_1 = m(x - x_1)$$

is used to write an equation when given an ordered pair (point on the equation's graph) for the function and its rate of change (slope of the line). The values for the slope, m, and the point (x_1, y_1) are substituted into the point-slope form to obtain the equation of the line. A line with a slope of 3 and an ordered pair (4, –2) would have an equation:

$$y - (-2) = 3(x - 4)$$

If a question specifies that the equation be written in slope-intercept form, the equation should be manipulated to isolate y:

Solve: $y - (-2) = 3(x - 4)$

Distribute: $y + 2 = 3x - 12$

Subtract 2 from both sides: $y = 3x - 14$

Equation of a Line from Two Points

Given two ordered pairs for a function, (x_1, y_1) and (x_2, y_2), it is possible to determine the rate of change between the variables (slope of the line). To calculate the slope of the line, m, the values for the ordered pairs should be substituted into the formula:

$$m = \frac{y_2 - y_1}{x_2 - x_1}$$

The expression is substituted to obtain a whole number or fraction for the slope. Once the slope is calculated, the slope and either of the ordered pairs should be substituted into the point-slope form to obtain the equation of the line.

Using Slope of a Line

Two lines are parallel if they have the same slope and a different intercept. Two lines are **perpendicular** if the product of their slope equals −1. Parallel lines never intersect unless they are the same line, and perpendicular lines intersect at a right angle. If two lines aren't parallel, they must intersect at one point. If lines do cross, they're labeled as **intersecting lines** because they "intersect" at one point. If they intersect at more than one point, they're the same line. Determining equations of lines based on properties of parallel and perpendicular lines appears in word problems. To find an equation of a line, both the slope and a point the line goes through are necessary. Therefore, if an equation of a line is needed that's parallel to a given line and runs through a specified point, the slope of the given line and the point are plugged into the point-slope form of an equation of a line. Secondly, if an equation of a line is needed that's perpendicular to a given line running through a specified point, the negative reciprocal of the slope of the given line and the point are plugged into the **point-slope form**. Also, if the point of intersection of two lines is known, that point will be used to solve the set of equations. Therefore, to solve a system of equations, the point of intersection must be found. If a set of two equations with two unknown variables has no solution, the lines are parallel.

The **Parallel Postulate** states that if two parallel lines are cut by a transversal, then the corresponding angles are equal. Here is a picture that highlights this postulate:

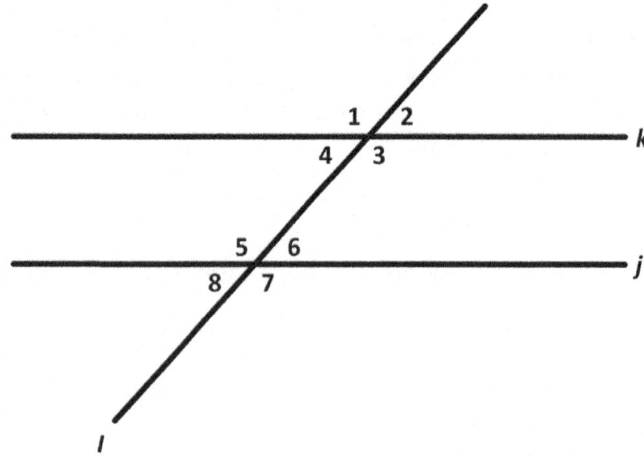

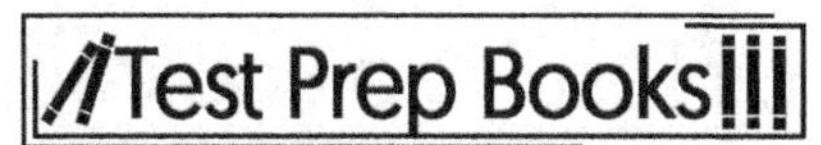

Because lines *k* and *i* are parallel, when cut by transversal *l*, angles 1 and 5 are equal, angles 2 and 6 are equal, angles 4 and 8 are equal, and angles 3 and 7 are equal. Note that angles 1 and 2, 3 and 4, 5 and 6, and 7 and 8 add up to 180 degrees.

This statement is equivalent to the **Alternate Interior Angle Theorem**, which states that when two parallel lines are cut by a transversal, the resultant interior angles are congruent. In the picture above, angles 3 and 5 are congruent, and angles 4 and 6 are congruent.

The Parallel Postulate or the Alternate Interior Angle Theorem can be used to find the missing angles in the following picture:

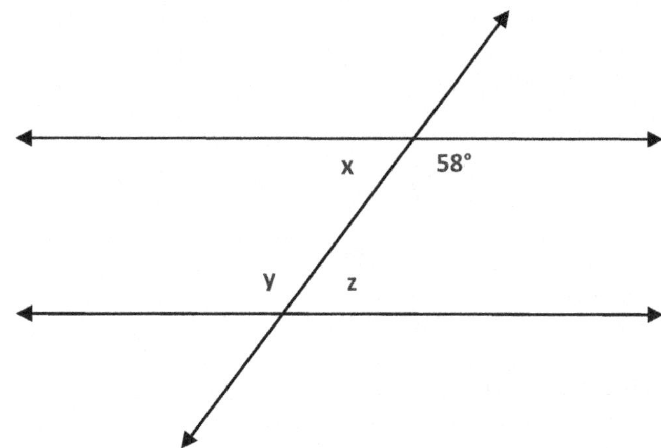

Assuming that the lines are parallel, angle x is found to be 122 degrees. Angle x and the 58-degree angle add up to 180 degrees. The Alternate Interior Angle Theorem states that angle y is equal to 58 degrees. Also, angles y and z add up to 180 degrees, so angle z is 122 degrees. Note that angles x and z are also alternate interior angles, so their equivalence can be used to find angle z as well.

An equivalent statement to the Parallel Postulate is that the sum of all angles in a triangle is 180 degrees. Therefore, given any triangle, if two angles are known, the third can be found accordingly.

Functions Shown in Different Ways

First, it's important to understand the definition of a **relation**. Given two variables, *x* and *y*, which stand for unknown numbers, a **relation** between *x* and *y* is an object that splits all of the pairs (*x*, *y*) into those for which the relation is true and those for which it is false. For example, consider the relation of $x^2 = y^2$. This relationship is true for the pair (1, 1) and for the pair (–2, 2), but false for (2, 3). Another example of a relation is $x \leq y$. This is true whenever *x* is less than or equal to *y*.

A **function** is a special kind of relation where, for each value of *x*, there is only a single value of *y* that satisfies the relation. So, $x^2 = y^2$ is *not* a function because in this case, if *x* is 1, *y* can be either 1 or –1: the pair (1, 1) and (1, –1) both satisfy the relation. More generally, for this relation, any pair of the form $(a, \pm a)$ will satisfy it. On the other hand, consider the following relation:

$$y = x^2 + 1$$

This is a function because for each value of *x*, there is a unique value of *y* that satisfies the relation. Notice, however, there are multiple values of *x* that give us the same value of *y*. This is perfectly acceptable for a function. Therefore, *y* is a function of *x*.

To determine if a relation is a function, check to see if every *x* value has a unique corresponding *y* value.

A function can be viewed as an object that has *x* as its input and outputs a unique *y*-value. It is sometimes convenient to express this using **function notation**, where the function itself is given a name, often *f*. To emphasize that *f* takes *x* as its input, the function is written as $f(x)$. In the above example, the equation could be rewritten as:

$$f(x) = x^2 + 1$$

To write the value that a function yields for some specific value of *x*, that value is put in place of *x* in the function notation. For example, $f(3)$ means the value that the function outputs when the input value is 3. If:

$$f(x) = x^2 + 1$$

then:

$$f(3) = 3^2 + 1 = 10$$

Another example of a function would be:

$$f(x) = 4x + 4$$

read "*f* of *x* is equal to four times *x* plus four." In this example, the input would be *x* and the output would be f(*x*). Ordered pairs would be represented as (*x*, f(*x*)). To find the output for an input value of 3, 3 would be substituted for *x* into the function as follows:

$$f(3) = 4(3) + 4$$

resulting in $f(3) = 16$. Therefore, the ordered pair:

$$(3, f(3)) = (3, 16)$$

Note f(*x*) is a function of *x* denoted by *f*. Functions of *x* could be named *g*(*x*), read "*g* of *x*"; *p*(*x*), read "*p* of *x*"; etc.

As an example, the following function is in function notation:

$$f(x) = 3x - 4$$

The $f(x)$ represents the output value for an input of x. If $x = 2$, the equation becomes:

$$f(2) = 3(2) - 4 = 6 - 4 = 2$$

The input of 2 yields an output of 2, forming the ordered pair $(2, 2)$. The following set of ordered pairs corresponds to the given function: $(2, 2), (0, -4), (-2, -10)$. The set of all possible inputs of a function is its **domain**, and all possible outputs is called the **range**. By definition, each member of the domain is paired with only one member of the range.

Functions can also be defined recursively. In this form, they are not defined explicitly in terms of variables. Instead, they are defined using previously-evaluated function outputs, starting with either $f(0)$ or $f(1)$. An example of a recursively-defined function is:

$$f(1) = 2, f(n) = 2f(n-1) + 2n, n > 1$$

The domain of this function is the set of all integers.

A function can also be viewed as a table of pairs (*x*, *y*), which lists the value for *y* for each possible value of *x*.

Functions in Tables and Graphs

The domain and range of a function can be found by observing a table. The table below shows the input values $x = -2$ to $x = 2$ for the function:

$$f(x) = x^2 - 3$$

The range, or output, for these inputs results in a minimum of -3. On each side of $x = 0$, the numbers increase, showing that the range is all real numbers greater than or equal to -3.

x (domain/input)	y (range/output)
−2	1
−1	−2
0	−3
−1	−2
2	1

Determining the Domain and Range from a Given Graph of a Function

The domain and range of a function can also be found visually by its plot on the coordinate plane. In the function:

$$f(x) = x^2 - 3$$

for example, the domain is all real numbers because the parabola can stretch infinitely far left and right with no restrictions. This means that any input value from the real number system will yield an output in the real number system. For the range, the inequality $y \geq -3$ would be used to describe the possible output values because the parabola has a minimum at $y = -3$. This means there will not be any real output values less than -3 because -3 is the lowest value the function reaches on the y-axis.

Determining the Domain and Range of a Given Function

The set of all possible values for *x* in $f(x)$ is called the **domain** of the function, and the set of all possible outputs is called the **range** of the function. Note that usually the domain is assumed to be all real numbers, except those for which the expression for $f(x)$ is not defined, unless the problem specifies otherwise. An example of how a function might not be defined is in the case of:

$$f(x) = \frac{1}{x+1}$$

which is not defined when $x = -1$ (which would require dividing by zero). Therefore, in this case the domain would be all real numbers except $x = -1$.

Interpreting Domain and Range in Real-World Settings

A function can be built from the information given in a situation. For example, the relationship between the money paid for a gym membership and the number of months that someone has been a member can be described through a function. If the one-time membership fee is $40 and the monthly fee is $30, then the function can be written:

$$f(x) = 30x + 40$$

The x-value represents the number of months the person has been part of the gym, while the output is the total money paid for the membership. The table below shows this relationship. It is a representation of the function because the initial cost is $40 and the cost increases each month by $30.

x (months)	f(x) (money paid to gym)
0	40
1	70
2	100
3	130

In this situation, the domain of the function is real numbers greater than or equal to zero because it represents the number of months that a membership is held. We aren't told if the gym prorates memberships for partial months (if you join 10 days into a month, for example). If not, the domain would only be whole numbers plus zero, since there's a meaningful data point of $40, as a fee for joining. The range is real numbers greater than or equal to 40, because the range represents the total cost of the gym membership. Because there is a one-time fee of $40, the cost of carrying a membership will never be less than $40, so this is the minimum value.

When working through any word problem, the domain and range of the function should be considered in terms of the real-world context that the function models. For example, considering the above function for the cost of a gym membership, it would be nonsensical to include negative numbers in either the domain or range because there can't be negative months that someone holds a membership and similarly, the gym isn't going to pay a person for months prior to becoming a member. Therefore, while the function to model the situation (defined as $f(x) = 30x + 40$) theoretically could result in a true mathematical statement if negative values of are inputted, this would not make sense in the real-world context for which the function applies. Therefore, defining the domain as whole numbers and the range as all real numbers greater than or equal to 40 is important.

Evaluating Functions

To evaluate functions, plug in the given value everywhere the variable appears in the expression for the function. For example, find $f(-2)$ where:

$$f(x) = 2x^2 - \frac{4}{x}$$

To complete the problem, plug in –2 in the following way:

$$f(-2) = 2(-2)^2 - \frac{4}{-2}$$

$$2 \times 4 + 2$$

$$8 + 2 = 10$$

Practice Quiz

1. The graph of which function has an x-intercept of -2?
   a. $y = 2x - 3$
   b. $y = 4x + 2$
   c. $y = x^2 + 5x + 6$
   d. $y = 2x^2 + 3x - 1$

2. The table below displays the number of three-year-olds at Kids First Daycare who are potty-trained and those who still wear diapers.

	Potty-trained	**Wear diapers**	
Boys	26	22	48
Girls	34	18	52
	60	40	

What is the probability of a three-year-old girl from the school being potty-trained?
   a. 52%
   b. 34%
   c. 65%
   d. 57%

3. A rectangle was formed out of pipe cleaner. Its length was $\frac{1}{2}$ foot and its width was $\frac{11}{2}$ inches. What is its area in square inches?
   a. $\frac{11}{4}$ inches^2
   b. $\frac{11}{2}$ inches^2
   c. 22 inches^2
   d. 33 inches^2

4. You measure the width of your door to be 36 inches. The true width of the door is 35.75 inches. What is the relative error in your measurement?
   a. 0.7%
   b. 0.007%
   c. 0.99%
   d. 0.1%

5. A couple buys a house for $150,000. They sell it for $165,000. By what percentage did the house's value increase?
   a. 10%
   b. 13%
   c. 15%
   d. 17%

Answer Explanations

1. C: An x-intercept is the point where the graph crosses the x-axis. At this point, the value of y is 0. To determine if an equation has an x-intercept of –2, substitute –2 for x, and calculate the value of y. If the value of –2 for x corresponds with a y-value of 0, then the equation has an x-intercept of –2. The only answer choice that produces this result is Choice *C*.

$$0 = (-2)^2 + 5(-2) + 6$$

2. C: There are 34 girls who are potty-trained out of a total of 52 girls:

$$34 \div 52 = 0.65 = 65\%$$

3. D: Recall the formula for area of a rectangle, area $=$ length $\times$ width. The answer must be in square inches, so all values must be converted to inches. Half of a foot is equal to 6 inches. Therefore, the area of the rectangle is equal to:

$$6 \text{ in} \times \frac{11}{2} \text{in} = \frac{66}{2} \text{in}^2 = 33 \text{ in}^2$$

4. A: The relative error can be found by finding the absolute error and making it a percent of the true value. The absolute error is $36 - 35.75 = 0.25$. This error is then divided by 35.75—the true value—to find 0.7%.

5. A: The value went up by:

$$\$165,000 - \$150,000 = \$15,000$$

Out of \$150,000, this is $\frac{15,000}{150,000} = \frac{1}{10}$. Convert this to having a denominator of 100, the result is $\frac{10}{100}$, or 10%.

Reading for Meaning

Events, Plots, Characters, Settings, and Ideas

Putting Events in Order

One of the most crucial skills for conquering the GED's Reasoning Through Language Arts questions is the ability to recognize the sequences of events for each passage and place them in the correct order. Every passage has a plot, whether it is from a short story, a manual, a newspaper article or editorial, or a history text. And each plot has a logical order, which is also known as a sequence. Some of the most straightforward sequences can be found in technology directions, science experiments, instructional materials, and recipes. These forms of writing list actions that must occur in a proper sequence in order to get sufficient results. Other forms of writing, however, use style and ideas in ways that completely change the sequence of events. Poetry, for instance, may introduce repetitions that make the events seem cyclical. Postmodern writers are famous for experimenting with different concepts of place and time, creating "cut scenes" that distort straightforward sequences and abruptly transport the audience to different contexts or times. Even everyday newspaper articles, editorials, and historical sources may experiment with different sequential forms for stylistic effect.

Most questions that call for test takers to apply their sequential knowledge use key words such as **sequence**, **sequence of events**, or **sequential order** to cue the test taker in to the task at hand. In social studies or history passages, the test questions might employ key words such as **chronology** or **chronological order** to cue the test taker. In some cases, sequence can be found through comprehension techniques. These literal passages number the sequences, or they use key words such as *firstly*, *secondly*, *finally*, *next*, or *then*. The sequences of these stories can be found by rereading the passage and charting these numbers or key words. In most cases, however, readers have to correctly order events through inferential and evaluative reading techniques; they have to place events in a logical order without explicit cues.

Making Inferences

Predictions

Some texts use suspense and foreshadowing to captivate readers. For example, an intriguing aspect of murder mysteries is that the reader is never sure of the culprit until the author reveals the individual's identity. Authors often build suspense and add depth and meaning to a work by leaving clues to provide hints or predict future events in the story; this is called foreshadowing. While some instances of foreshadowing are subtle, others are quite obvious.

Inferences

Another way to read actively is to identify examples of inference within text. Making an inference requires the reader to read between the lines and look for what is implied rather than what is explicitly stated. That is, using information that is known from the text, the reader is able to make a logical assumption about information that is not explicitly stated but is probably true.

Authors employ literary devices such as tone, characterization, and theme to engage the audience by showing details of the story instead of merely telling them. For example, if an author said *Bob is selfish*,

there's little left to infer. If the author said, *Bob cheated on his test, ignored his mom's calls, and parked illegally*, the reader can infer Bob is selfish. Authors also make implications through character dialogue, thoughts, effects on others, actions, and looks. Like in life, readers must assemble all the clues to form a complete picture.

Read the following passage:

> "Hey, do you wanna meet my new puppy?" Jonathan asked.
>
> "Oh, I'm sorry but please don't—" Jacinta began to protest, but before she could finish, Jonathan had already opened the passenger side door of his car and a perfect white ball of fur came bouncing towards Jacinta.
>
> "Isn't he the cutest?" beamed Jonathan.
>
> "Yes—achoo!—he's pretty—aaaachooo!!—adora—aaa—aaaachoo!" Jacinta managed to say in between sneezes. "But if you don't mind, I—I—achoo!—need to go inside."

Which of the following can be inferred from Jacinta's reaction to the puppy?

a. She hates animals.
b. She is allergic to dogs.
c. She prefers cats to dogs.
d. She is angry at Jonathan.

An inference requires the reader to consider the information presented and then form their own idea about what is probably true. Based on the details in the passage, what is the best answer to the question? Important details to pay attention to include the tone of Jacinta's dialogue, which is overall polite and apologetic, as well as her reaction itself, which is a long string of sneezes. Answer choices (a) and (d) both express strong emotions ("hates" and "angry") that are not evident in Jacinta's speech or actions. Answer choice (c) mentions cats, but there is nothing in the passage to indicate Jacinta's feelings about cats. Answer choice (b), "she is allergic to dogs," is the most logical choice. Based on the fact that she began sneezing as soon as a fluffy dog approached her, it makes sense to guess that Jacinta might be allergic to dogs. Using the clues in the passage, it is reasonable to guess that this is true even though Jacinta never directly states, "Sorry, I'm allergic to dogs!"

Making inferences is crucial for readers of literature because literary texts often avoid presenting complete and direct information to readers about characters' thoughts or feelings, or they present this information in an unclear way, leaving it up to the reader to interpret clues given in the text. In order to make inferences while reading, readers should ask themselves:

- What details are being presented in the text?
- Is there any important information that seems to be missing?
- Based on the information that the author *does* include, what else is probably true?
- Is this inference reasonable based on what is already known?

Conclusions

Active readers should also draw conclusions. When doing so, the reader should ask the following questions: What is this piece about? What does the author believe? Does this piece have merit? Do I believe the author? Would this piece support my argument? The reader should first determine the author's intent. Identify the author's viewpoint and connect relevant evidence to support it. Readers may then move to the most important step: deciding whether to agree and determining whether they are correct. Always read cautiously and critically. Interact with text, and record reactions in the margins. These active reading skills help determine not only what the author thinks, but what you think as the reader.

Analyzing Relationships within Passages

Inferences are useful in gaining a deeper understanding of how people, events, and ideas are connected in a passage. Readers can use the same strategies used with general inferences and analyzing texts—paying attention to details and using them to make reasonable guesses about the text—to read between the lines and get a more complete picture of how (and why) characters are thinking, feeling, and acting. Read the following passage from O. Henry's story "The Gift of the Magi":

> One dollar and eighty-seven cents. That was all. And sixty cents of it was in pennies. Pennies saved one and two at a time by bulldozing the grocer and the vegetable man and the butcher until one's cheeks burned with the silent imputation of parsimony that such close dealing implied. Three times Della counted it. One dollar and eighty-seven cents. And the next day would be Christmas.
>
> There was clearly nothing to do but flop down on the shabby little couch and howl. So Della did it.

These paragraphs introduce the reader to the character Della. Even though the author doesn't include a direct description of Della, the reader can already form a general impression of her personality and emotions. One detail that should stick out to the reader is repetition: "one dollar and eighty-seven cents." This amount is repeated twice in the first paragraph, along with other descriptions of money: "sixty cents of it was in pennies," "pennies saved one and two at a time." The story's preoccupation with money parallels how Della herself is constantly thinking about her finances—"three times Della counted" her meager savings. Already the reader can guess that Della is having money problems. Next, think about her emotions. The first paragraph describes haggling over groceries "until one's cheeks burned"—another way to describe blushing. People tend to blush when they are embarrassed or ashamed, so readers can infer that Della is ashamed by her financial situation. This inference is also supported by the second paragraph, when she flops down and howls on her "shabby little couch." Clearly, she's in distress. Without saying, "Della has no money and is embarrassed to be poor," O. Henry is able to communicate the same impression to readers through his careful inclusion of details.

A character's **motive** is their reason for acting a certain way. Usually, characters are motivated by something that they want. In the passage, above, why is Della upset about not having enough money? There's an important detail at the end of the first paragraph: "the next day would be Christmas." Why is money especially important around Christmas? Christmas is a holiday when people exchange gifts. If Della is struggling with money, she's probably also struggling to buy gifts. So a shrewd reader should be able to guess that Della's motivation is wanting to buy a gift for someone—but she's currently unable to afford it, leading to feelings of shame and frustration.

In order to understand characters in a text, readers should keep the following questions in mind:

- What words does the author use to describe the character? Are these words related to any specific emotions or personality traits (for example, characteristics like rude, friendly, unapproachable, or innocent)?
- What does the character say? Does their dialogue seem to be straightforward, or are they hiding some thoughts or emotions?
- What actions can be observed from this character? How do their actions reflect their feelings?
- What does the character want? What do they do to get it?

Understanding Main Ideas and Details

Determining the Relationship Between Ideas

It is very important to know the difference between the topic and the main idea of the text. Even though these two are similar because they both present the central point of a text, they have distinctive differences. A **topic** is the subject of the text; This can usually be described in a concise one- to two-word phrase. On the other hand, the **main idea** is more detailed and provides the author's central point of the text. It can be expressed through a complete sentence and is often found in the beginning, the middle, or at the end of a paragraph.. In most nonfiction books, the first sentence of the passage usually (but not always) states the main idea.

Review the passage below to explore the topic versus the main idea:

> Cheetahs are one of the fastest mammals on the land, reaching up to 70 miles an hour over short distances. Even though cheetahs can run as fast as 70 miles an hour, they usually only have to run half that speed to catch up with their choice of prey. Cheetahs cannot maintain a fast pace over long periods of time because their bodies will overheat. After a chase, cheetahs need to rest for approximately 30 minutes prior to eating or returning to any other activity.

In the example above, the topic of the passage is "Cheetahs" simply because that is the subject of the text. The main idea of the text is "Cheetahs are one of the fastest mammals on the land but can only maintain a fast pace for shorter distances." While it covers the topic, it is more detailed and refers to the text in its entirety. The text continues to provide additional details called **supporting details**, which will be discussed in the next section.

How Details Develop the Main Idea

Supporting details help readers better develop and understand the main idea. Supporting details answer questions like *who, what, where, when, why,* and *how*. Different types of supporting details include examples, facts and statistics, anecdotes, and sensory details.

Persuasive and informative texts often use supporting details. In persuasive texts, authors attempt to make readers agree with their points of view, and supporting details are often used as "selling points." If authors make a statement, they need to support the statement with evidence in order to adequately persuade readers. Informative texts use supporting details such as examples and facts to inform readers. Review the previous "Cheetahs" passage to find examples of supporting details.

> Cheetahs are one of the fastest mammals on the land, reaching up to 70 miles an hour over short distances. Even though cheetahs can run as fast as 70 miles an hour, they usually only have to run half that speed to catch up with their choice of prey. Cheetahs cannot maintain a fast pace over long periods of time because their bodies will overheat. After a chase, cheetahs need to rest for approximately 30 minutes prior to eating or returning to any other activity.

In the example, supporting details include:

- Cheetahs reach up to 70 miles per hour over short distances.
- They usually only have to run half that speed to catch up with their prey.
- Cheetahs will overheat if they exert a high speed over longer distances.
- Cheetahs need to rest for 30 minutes after a chase.

Look at the diagram below (applying the cheetah example) to help determine the hierarchy of topic, main idea, and supporting details.

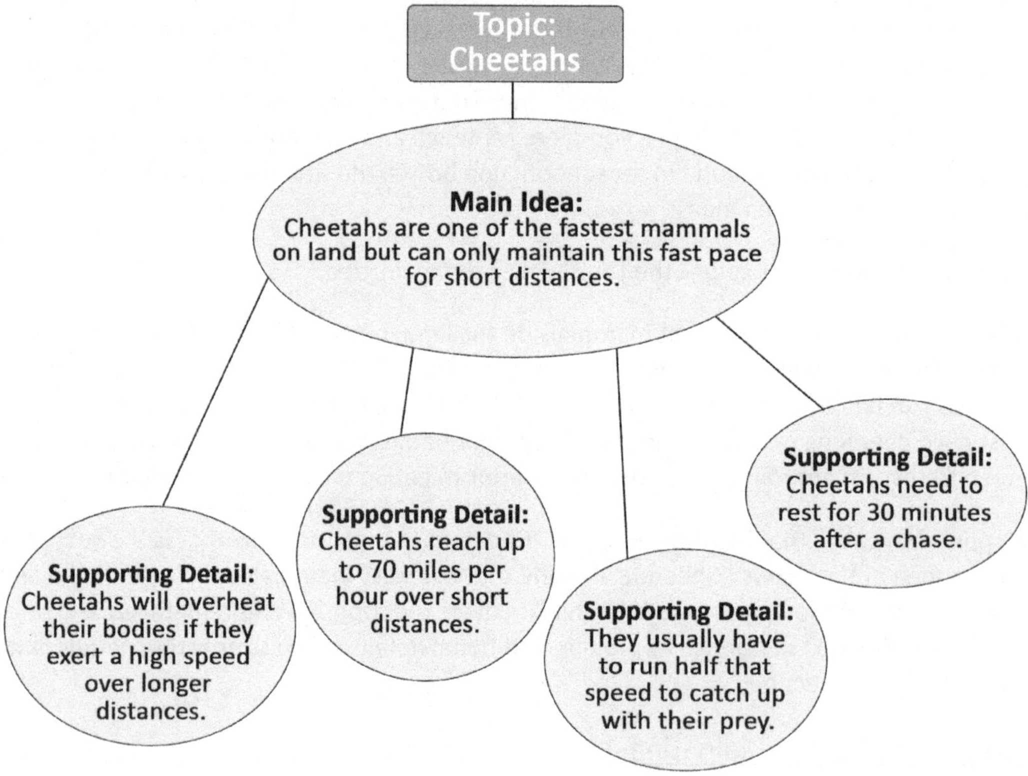

Point of View and Purpose

Author's Point of View and Purpose

When it comes to an author's writing, readers should always identify a **position** or **stance**. No matter how objective a text may seem, readers should assume the author has preconceived beliefs. One can reduce the likelihood of accepting an invalid argument by looking for multiple articles on the topic, including those with varying opinions. If several opinions point in the same direction and are backed by reputable peer-reviewed sources, it's more likely that the author has a valid argument. Positions that

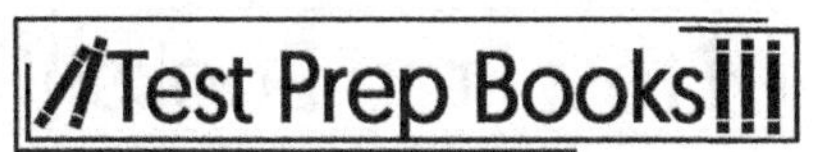

run contrary to widely held beliefs and existing data should invite scrutiny. There are exceptions to the rule, so readers should be careful consumers of information.

While themes, symbols, and motifs are buried deep within the text and can sometimes be difficult to infer, an author's **purpose** is usually obvious from the beginning. There are four purposes of writing: to inform, to persuade, to describe, and to entertain. **Informative** writing presents facts in an accessible way. **Persuasive** writing appeals to emotions and logic to inspire the reader to adopt a specific stance. Readers should be wary of this type of writing, as it can mask a lack of objectivity with powerful emotion. **Descriptive** writing is designed to paint a picture in the reader's mind, while texts that **entertain** are often narratives designed to engage and delight the reader.

The various writing styles are usually blended, with one purpose dominating the rest. A persuasive text, for example, might begin with a humorous tale to make readers more receptive to the persuasive message, or a recipe in a cookbook designed to inform might be preceded by an entertaining anecdote that makes the recipes more appealing.

Author's Position and Response to Different Viewpoints

If an author presents a differing opinion or a counterargument in order to refute it, the reader should consider how and why the information is being presented. It is meant to strengthen the original argument and shouldn't be confused with the author's intended conclusion, but it should also be considered in the reader's final evaluation.

Authors can also use bias if they ignore the opposing viewpoint or present their side in an unbalanced way. A strong argument considers the opposition and finds a way to refute it. Critical readers should look for an unfair or one-sided presentation of the argument and be skeptical, as a bias may be present. Even if this bias is unintentional, if it exists in the writing, the reader should be wary of the validity of the argument. Readers should also look for the use of stereotypes, which refer to specific groups. Stereotypes are often negative connotations about a person or place and should always be avoided. When a critical reader finds stereotypes in a piece of writing, they should be critical of the argument, and consider the validity of anything the author presents. Stereotypes reveal a flaw in the writer's thinking and may suggest a lack of knowledge or understanding about the subject.

Inferring the Author's Purpose in the Passage

In nonfiction writing, authors employ argumentative techniques to present their opinion to readers in the most convincing way. Persuasive writing usually includes at least one type of appeal: an appeal to logic (**logos**), emotion (**pathos**), or credibility and trustworthiness (**ethos**). When a writer appeals to logic, they are asking readers to agree with them based on research, evidence, and an established line of reasoning. An author's argument might also appeal to readers' emotions, perhaps by including personal stories and anecdotes (a short narrative of a specific event). A final type of appeal—appeal to authority—asks the reader to agree with the author's argument on the basis of their expertise or credentials. Consider three different approaches to arguing the same opinion:

Logic (Logos)

Below is an example of an appeal to logic. The author uses evidence to disprove the logic of the school's rule (the rule was supposed to reduce discipline problems, but the number of problems has not been reduced; therefore, the rule is not working) and he or she calls for its repeal.

> Our school should abolish its current ban on campus cell phone use. The ban was adopted last year as an attempt to reduce class disruptions and help students focus more on their lessons. However, since the rule was enacted, there has been no change in the number of disciplinary problems in class. Therefore, the rule is ineffective and should be done away with.

Emotion (Pathos)

An author's argument might also appeal to readers' emotions, perhaps by including personal stories and anecdotes. The next example presents an appeal to emotion. By sharing the personal anecdote of one student and speaking about emotional topics like family relationships, the author invokes the reader's empathy in asking them to reconsider the school rule.

> Our school should abolish its current ban on campus cell phone use. If students aren't able to use their phones during the school day, many of them feel isolated from their loved ones. For example, last semester, one student's grandmother had a heart attack in the morning. However, because he couldn't use his cell phone, the student didn't know about his grandmother's condition until the end of the day—when she had already passed away, and it was too late to say goodbye. By preventing students from contacting their friends and family, our school is placing undue stress and anxiety on students.

Credibility (Ethos)

Finally, an appeal to authority includes a statement from a relevant expert. In this case, the author uses a doctor in the field of education to support the argument. All three examples begin from the same opinion—the school's phone ban needs to change—but rely on different argumentative styles to persuade the reader.

> Our school should abolish its current ban on campus cell phone use. According to Dr. Bartholomew Everett, a leading educational expert, "Research studies show that cell phone usage has no real impact on student attentiveness. Rather, phones provide a valuable technological resource for learning. Schools need to learn how to integrate this new technology into their curriculum." Rather than banning phones altogether, our school should follow the advice of experts and allow students to use phones as part of their learning.

Rhetorical Questions

Another commonly used argumentative technique is asking **rhetorical questions**, questions that do not actually require an answer but that push the reader to consider the topic further.

> I wholly disagree with the proposal to ban restaurants from serving foods with high sugar and sodium contents. Do we really want to live in a world where the government can control what we eat? I prefer to make my own food choices.

Here, the author's rhetorical question prompts readers to put themselves in a hypothetical situation and imagine how they would feel about it.

Tone and Figurative Language

How Words Affect Tone

Tone refers to the writer's attitude toward the subject matter. For example, the tone conveys how the writer feels about the topic he or she is writing about. A lot of nonfiction writing has a neutral tone,

which is an important tone for the writer to take. A neutral tone demonstrates that the writer is presenting a topic impartially and letting the information speak for itself. On the other hand, nonfiction writing can be just as effective and appropriate if the tone isn't neutral. For instance, consider this example:

> Seat belts save more lives than any other automobile safety feature. Many studies show that airbags save lives as well; however, not all cars have airbags. For instance, some older cars don't. Furthermore, air bags aren't entirely reliable. For example, studies show that in 15% of accidents, airbags don't deploy as designed; but, on the other hand, seat belt malfunctions are extremely rare. The number of highway fatalities has plummeted since laws requiring seat belt usage were enacted.

In this passage, the writer mostly chooses to retain a neutral tone when presenting information. If the writer would instead include their own personal experience of losing a friend or family member in a car accident, the tone would change dramatically. The tone would no longer be neutral and would show that the writer has a personal stake in the content, allowing them to interpret the information in a different way. When analyzing tone, consider what the writer is trying to achieve in the text and how they *create* the tone using style.

An author's choice of words—also referred to as **diction**—helps to convey their meaning in a particular way. Through diction, an author can convey a particular tone—e.g., a humorous tone, a serious tone—in order to support the thesis in a meaningful way to the reader.

Connotation and Denotation

Connotation is when an author chooses words or phrases that invoke ideas or feelings other than their literal meaning. An example of the use of connotation is the word *cheap*, which suggests something is poor in value or negatively describes a person as reluctant to spend money. When something or someone is described this way, the reader is more inclined to have a particular image or feeling about it or him/her. Thus, connotation can be a very effective language tool in creating emotion and swaying opinion. However, connotations are sometimes hard to pin down because varying emotions can be associated with a word. Generally, though, connotative meanings tend to be fairly consistent within a specific cultural group.

Denotation refers to words or phrases that mean exactly what they say. It is helpful when a writer wants to present hard facts or vocabulary terms with which readers may be unfamiliar. Some examples of denotation are the words *inexpensive* and *frugal*. *Inexpensive* refers to the cost of something, not its value, and *frugal* indicates that a person is conscientiously watching their spending. These terms do not elicit the same emotions that *cheap* does.

Authors sometimes choose to use both, but what they choose and when they use it is what critical readers need to differentiate. One method isn't inherently better than the other; however, one may create a better effect, depending upon an author's intent. If, for example, an author's purpose is to inform, to instruct, and to familiarize readers with a difficult subject, their use of connotation may be helpful. However, it may also undermine credibility and confuse readers. An author who wants to create a credible, scholarly effect in their text would most likely use denotation, which emphasizes literal, factual meaning and examples.

How Figurative Language Affects the Meaning of Words

It's important to be able to recognize and interpret **figurative,** or non-literal, language. Literal statements rely directly on the denotations of words and express exactly what's happening in reality. Figurative language uses non-literal expressions to present information in a creative way. Consider the following sentences:

a. His pillow was very soft, and he fell asleep quickly.

b. His pillow was a fluffy cloud, and he floated away on it to the dream world.

Sentence *A* is literal, employing only the real meanings of each word. Sentence *B* is figurative. It employs a metaphor by stating that his pillow was a cloud. Of course, he isn't actually sleeping on a cloud, but the reader can draw on images of clouds as light, soft, fluffy, and relaxing to get a sense of how the character felt as he fell asleep. Also, in sentence *B*, the pillow becomes a vehicle that transports him to a magical dream world. The character isn't literally floating through the air—he's simply falling asleep! But by utilizing figurative language, the author creates a scene of peace, comfort, and relaxation that conveys stronger emotions and more creative imagery than the purely literal sentence. While there are countless types of figurative language, there are a few common ones that any reader should recognize.

Simile and **metaphor** are comparisons between two things, but their formats differ slightly. A simile says that two things are *similar* and makes a comparison using "like" or "as"—*A* is like *B*, or *A* is as [some characteristic] as *B*—whereas a metaphor states that two things are exactly the same—*A* is *B*. In both cases, simile and metaphor invite the reader to think more deeply about the characteristics of the two subjects and consider where they overlap. An example of metaphor can be found in the above sentence about the sleeper ("His pillow was a fluffy cloud"). For an example of simile, look at the first line of Robert Burns' famous poem:

My love is like a red, red rose

This is comparison using "like," and the two things being compared are love and a rose. Some characteristics of a rose are that it's fragrant, beautiful, blossoming, colorful, vibrant—by comparing his love to a rose, Burns asks the reader to apply these qualities to his love. In this way, he implies that his love is also fresh, blossoming, and brilliant.

Similes can also compare things that appear dissimilar. Here's a song lyric from Florence and the Machine:

Happiness hit her like a bullet in the back

"Happiness" has a very positive connotation, but getting "a bullet in the back" seems violent and aggressive, not at all related to happiness. By using an unexpected comparison, the writer forces readers to think more deeply about the comparison and ask themselves how could getting shot be similar to feeling happy. "A bullet in the back" is something that she doesn't see coming; it's sudden and forceful; and presumably, it has a strong impact on her life. So, in this way, the author seems to be saying that unexpected happiness made a sudden and powerful change in her life.

Another common form of figurative language is **personification,** when a non-human object is given human characteristics. William Blake uses personification here:

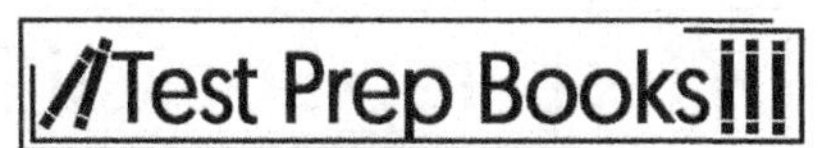

> ... the stars threw down their spears,
>
> And watered heaven with their tears

He imagines the stars as combatants in a heavenly battle, giving them both action (throwing down their spears) and emotion (the sadness and disappointment of their tears). Personification helps to add emotion or develop relationships between characters and non-human objects. In fact, most people use personification in their everyday lives:

> My alarm clock betrayed me! It didn't go off this morning!
>
> The last piece of chocolate cake was staring at me from the refrigerator.

Next is **hyperbole,** a type of figurative language that uses extreme exaggeration. Sentences like, "I love you to the Moon and back," or "I will love you for a million years," are examples of hyperbole. They aren't literally true—unfortunately, people cannot jump to outer space or live for a million years—but they're creative expressions that communicate the depth of feeling of the author.

Another way that writers add deeper meaning to their work is through **allusions.** An allusion is a reference to something from history, literature, or another cultural source. When the text is from a different culture or a time period, readers may not be familiar with every allusion. However, allusions tend to be well-known because the author wants the reader to make a connection between what's happening in the text and what's being referenced.

> I can't believe my best friend told our professor that I was skipping class to finish my final project! What a Judas!

This sentence contains a Biblical allusion to Judas, a friend and follower of Jesus who betrayed Jesus to the Romans. In this case, the allusion to Judas is used to give a deeper impression of betrayal and disloyalty from a trusted friend. Commonly used allusions in Western texts may come from the Bible, Greek or Roman mythology, or well-known literature such as Shakespeare. By familiarizing themselves with these touchstones of history and culture, readers can be more prepared to recognize allusions.

How Figurative Language Influences the Author's Purpose

A **rhetorical strategy**—also referred to as a **rhetorical mode**—is the structural way an author chooses to present their argument. Though the terms noted below are similar to the organizational structures noted earlier, these strategies do not imply that the entire text follows the approach. For example, a cause and effect organizational structure is solely that, nothing more. A persuasive text may use cause and effect as a strategy to convey a singular point. Thus, an argument may include several of the strategies as the author strives to convince their audience to take action or accept a different point of view. It's important that readers are able to identify an author's thesis and position on the topic in order to be able to identify the careful construction through which the author speaks to the reader.

The following are some of the more common rhetorical strategies:

- **Cause and effect**—establishing a logical correlation or causation between two ideas
- **Classification/division**—the grouping of similar items together or division of something into parts
- **Comparison/contrast**—the distinguishing of similarities/differences to expand on an idea

- **Definition**—used to clarify abstract ideas, unfamiliar concepts, or to distinguish one idea from another
- **Description**—use of vivid imagery, active verbs, and clear adjectives to explain ideas
- **Exemplification**—the use of examples to explain an idea
- **Narration**—using anecdotes or personal experience to present or expand on a concept
- **Problem/Solution**—presentation of a problem or problems, followed by proposed solution(s)

How Rhetorical Language Conveys Meaning, Emotion, or Persuades Readers

A **rhetorical device** is the phrasing and presentation of an idea that reinforces and emphasizes a point in an argument. A rhetorical device is often quite memorable. One of the more famous uses of a rhetorical device is in John F. Kennedy's 1961 inaugural address: "Ask not what your country can do for you, ask what you can do for your country." The contrast of ideas presented in the phrasing is an example of the rhetorical device of antimetabole. Some other common examples are provided below, but test takers should be aware that this is not a complete list.

Device	Definition	Example
Allusion	A reference to a famous person, event, or significant literary text as a form of significant comparison	"We are apt to shut our eyes against a painful truth, and listen to the song of that siren till she transforms us into beasts." Patrick Henry
Anaphora	The repetition of the same words at the beginning of successive words, phrases, or clauses, designed to emphasize an idea	"We shall not flag or fail. We shall go on to the end. We shall fight in France, we shall fight on the seas and oceans, we shall fight with growing confidence ... we shall fight in the fields and in the streets, we shall fight in the hills. We shall never surrender." Winston Churchill
Understatement	A statement meant to portray a situation as less important than it actually is to create an ironic effect	"The war in the Pacific has not necessarily developed in Japan's favor." Emperor Hirohito, surrendering Japan in World War II
Parallelism	A syntactical similarity in a structure or series of structures used for impact of an idea, making it memorable	"A penny saved is a penny earned." Ben Franklin

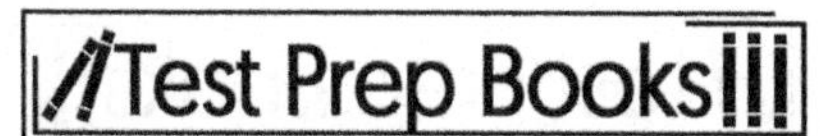

Device	Definition	Example
Rhetorical question	A question posed that is not answered by the writer though there is a desired response, most often designed to emphasize a point	"Can anyone look at our reduced standing in the world today and say, 'Let's have four more years of this?'" Ronald Reagan

Organizing Ideas

How a Section Fits into a Passage and Helps Develop the Ideas

Being able to determine what is most important while reading is critical to synthesis. It is the difference between being able to tell what is necessary to full comprehension and that which is interesting but not necessary.

When determining the importance of an author's ideas, consider the following:

- Ask how critical an author's particular idea, assertion, or concept is to the overall message.
- Ask "is this an interesting fact or is this information essential to understanding the author's main idea?"
- Make a simple chart. On one side, list all of the important, essential points an author makes and on the other, list all of the interesting yet non-critical ideas.
- Highlight, circle, or underline any dates or data in non-fiction passages. Pay attention to headings, captions, and any graphs or diagrams.
- When reading a fictional passage, delineate important information such as theme, character, setting, conflict (what the problem is), and resolution (how the problem is fixed). Most often, these are the most important aspects contained in fictional text.
- If a non-fiction passage is instructional in nature, take physical note of any steps in the order of their importance as presented by the author. Look for words such as *first*, *next*, *then*, and *last*.

Determining the importance of an author's ideas is critical to synthesis in that it requires the test taker to parse out any unnecessary information and demonstrate they have the ability to make sound determination on what is important to the author, and what is merely a supporting or less critical detail.

Analyzing How a Text is Organized

Depending on what the author is attempting to accomplish, certain formats or text structures work better than others. For example, a sequence structure might work for narration but not for identifying similarities and differences between concepts. Similarly, a comparison-contrast structure is not useful for narration. It's the author's job to put the right information in the correct format.

Readers should be familiar with the five main literary structures:

Sequence Structure

Sequence structure (sometimes referred to as the order structure) is when the order of events proceeds in a predictable order. In many cases, this means the text goes through the plot elements: exposition, rising action, climax, falling action, and resolution. Readers are introduced to characters, setting, and conflict in the **exposition**. In the **rising action**, there's an increase in tension and suspense. The **climax** is the height of tension and the point of no return. **Tension** decreases during the falling action. In the **resolution**, any conflicts presented in the exposition are resolved, and the story concludes. An informative text that is structured sequentially will often go in order from one step to the next.

Problem-Solution

In the **problem-solution structure**, authors identify a potential problem and suggest a solution. This form of writing is usually divided into two parts (the problem and the solution) and can be found in informational texts. For example, cell phone, cable, and satellite providers use this structure in manuals to help customers troubleshoot or identify problems with services or products.

Comparison-Contrast

When authors want to discuss similarities and differences between separate concepts, they arrange thoughts in a **comparison-contrast paragraph structure**. **Venn diagrams** are an effective graphic organizer for comparison-contrast structures because they feature two overlapping circles that can be used to organize similarities and differences. A comparison-contrast essay organizes one paragraph based on similarities and another based on differences. A comparison-contrast essay can also be arranged with the similarities and differences of individual traits addressed within individual paragraphs. Words such as *however*, *but*, and *nevertheless* help signal a contrast in ideas.

Descriptive

Descriptive writing is designed to appeal to your senses. Much like an artist who constructs a painting, good descriptive writing builds an image in the reader's mind by appealing to the five senses: *sight, hearing, taste, touch,* and *smell.* However, overly descriptive writing can become tedious; likewise, sparse descriptions can make settings and characters seem flat. Good authors strike a balance by applying descriptions only to facts that are integral to the passage.

Cause and Effect

Passages that use the **cause and effect structure** are simply asking *why* by demonstrating some type of connection between ideas. Words such as *if*, *since*, *because*, *then*, or *consequently* indicate a relationship. By switching the order of a complex sentence, the writer can rearrange the emphasis on different clauses. Saying, *If Sheryl is late, we'll miss the dance*, is different from saying *We'll miss the dance if Sheryl is late*. One emphasizes Sheryl's tardiness while the other emphasizes missing the dance. Paragraphs can also be arranged in a cause and effect format. Cause-and-effect writing discusses the impact of decisions that have been made or could be made. Researchers often apply this paragraph structure to the scientific method.

Understanding the Meaning and Purpose of Transition Words

The writer should act as a guide, showing the reader how all the sentences fit together. Consider this example:

> Seat belts save more lives than any other automobile safety feature. Many studies show that airbags save lives as well. Not all cars have airbags. Many older cars don't. Air bags aren't entirely reliable. Studies show that in 15% of accidents, airbags don't deploy as designed. Seat belt malfunctions are extremely rare.

There's nothing wrong with any of these sentences individually, but together they're disjointed and difficult to follow. The best way for the writer to communicate information is through the use of

transition words. Here are examples of transition words and phrases that tie sentences together, enabling a more natural flow:

- To show causality: *as a result*, *therefore*, and *consequently*
- To compare and contrast: *however*, *but*, and *on the other hand*
- To introduce examples*: for instance*, *namely*, and *including*
- To show order of importance: *foremost*, *primarily*, *secondly*, and *lastly*

Note: This is not a complete list of transitions. There are many more that can be used; however, most fit into these or similar categories. The point is that the words should clearly show the relationship between sentences, supporting information, and the main idea.

Here is an update to the previous example using transition words. These changes make it easier to read and bring clarity to the writer's points:

> Seat belts save more lives than any other automobile safety feature. Many studies show that airbags save lives as well; however, not all cars have airbags. For instance, some older cars don't. Furthermore, air bags aren't entirely reliable. For example, studies show that in 15% of accidents, airbags don't deploy as designed; but, on the other hand, seat belt malfunctions are extremely rare.

Also, be prepared to analyze whether the writer is using the best transition word or phrase for the situation. Take this sentence for example: "As a result, seat belt malfunctions are extremely rare." This sentence doesn't make sense in the context above because the writer is trying to show the contrast between seat belts and airbags, not the causality.

How the Passage Organization Supports the Author's Ideas

Even if the writer includes plenty of information to support their point, the writing is only coherent when the information is in a logical order. **Logical sequencing** is really just common sense, but it's also an important writing technique. First, the writer should introduce the main idea, whether for a paragraph, a section, or the entire piece. Second, they should present evidence to support the main idea by using transitional language. This shows the reader how the information relates to the main idea and the sentences around it. The writer should then take time to interpret the information, making sure necessary connections are obvious to the reader. Finally, the writer can summarize the information in a closing section.

Note: Though most writing follows this pattern, it isn't a set rule. Sometimes writers change the order for effect. For example, the writer can begin with a surprising piece of supporting information to grab the reader's attention, and then transition to the main idea. Thus, if a passage doesn't follow the logical order, don't immediately assume it's wrong. However, most writing usually settles into a logical sequence after a nontraditional beginning.

Introductions and Conclusions

Examining the writer's strategies for introductions and conclusions puts the reader in the right mindset to interpret the rest of the text. Look for methods the writer might use for **introductions** such as:

- Stating the main point immediately, followed by outlining how the rest of the piece supports this claim.

- Establishing important, smaller pieces of the main idea first, and then grouping these points into a case for the main idea.
- Opening with a quotation, anecdote, question, seeming paradox, or other piece of interesting information, and then using it to lead to the main point.
- Whatever method the writer chooses, the introduction should make their intention clear, establish their voice as a credible one, and encourage a person to continue reading.

Conclusions tend to follow a similar pattern. In them, the writer restates their main idea a final time, often after summarizing the smaller pieces of that idea. If the introduction uses a quote or anecdote to grab the reader's attention, the conclusion often makes reference to it again. Whatever way the writer chooses to arrange the conclusion, the final restatement of the main idea should be clear and simple for the reader to interpret. Finally, conclusions shouldn't introduce any new information.

Comparing Different Ways of Presenting Ideas

Evaluating Two Different Texts

Every passage offered in the GED Reasoning Through Language Arts section has its own unique scope, purpose, and emphasis, or what it covers, why it is written, and what its specific focus is centered upon. Additionally, each passage is written with a particular audience in mind, and each passage affects its audience differently. The scope, purpose, and emphasis of each passage can be found by comparing the parts of the piece with the whole framework of the piece. Word choices, grammatical choices, and syntactical choices can help the reader figure out the scope, purpose, and emphasis. These choices are embedded in the words and sentences of the passage (the parts).

They help show the intentions and goals of the author (the "whole"). For example, if an author uses strong language like *enrage*, *ignite*, *infuriate*, and *antagonize*, then they may be cueing the reader in to their own rage, or they may be trying to incite anger in others. Likewise, if an author continually uses short, simple sentences, he or she might be trying to incite excitement or nervousness. These different choices and styles affect the overall message, or purpose. Sometimes the subject matter or audience is discussed explicitly, but often, on GED tests, test takers have to break a passage down, also known as decoding the passage. In this way, test takers can find the passage's target audience and intentions. Meanwhile, the impact of the article can be personal or historical, depending upon the passage—it can either speak to the test taker personally or capture a historical era.

When two passages are analyzed in juxtaposition—or side-by-side—it can help the audience have a clearer picture of the scope, purpose, emphasis, audience, and impact. Evaluating and comparing passages side-by-side helps shed light on similarities and differences that are helpful for test takers. The key is to figure out both the parts and the "wholes" of each passage. Compare the word choices, grammatical choices, and syntactical choices of each passage, and then compare the big picture of each passage. As a result, test takers will have a stronger basis for understanding the intricate details and broader frameworks of all passages they encounter.

Evaluating Two Different Passages

Every passage offered in the GED Reasoning Through Language Arts section has its own view, tone, style, organization, purpose, or impact. It is extremely important to compare the parts to the "wholes" of each passage. Additionally, these parts and "wholes" are better understood through **intertextual analysis** (for

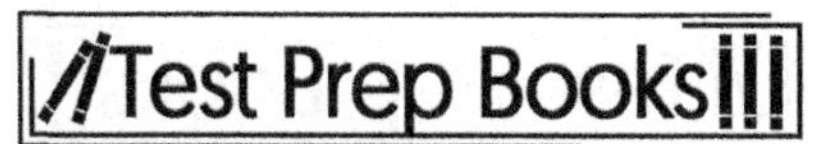

example, comparing the texts as if they were side by side). The viewpoint of the text can be found through a close analysis of the author's biases, or personal opinions or perceptions. All biases are embedded in the word choices, grammatical choices, and syntactical choices of each passage. For example, if an author continually uses negative words like *dislike, hate, despise, detrimental*, or *loathe*, they are trying to illustrate their own hatred of something or convey a character's hatred of something. These negative terms inevitably affect the view and tone of a passage. Comparing terminologies and biases can help a test taker better understand the similarities and differences of two or more passages. Similarly, the purposes of each can be better highlighted with a closer examination of word choices, grammatical choices, and syntactical choices.

Organization, on the other hand, is more easily understood by studying the passage on its own. Organizational differences on the page are likely to jump out at the test taker. A poetry passage, for instance, is traditionally organized differently than a prose passage. Test takers can see the differences in structures: one uses paragraphs, while the other uses stanzas. If organizational differences cannot be deduced through visual analysis, test takers should try to take a closer look at the sequence of events or the content of each paragraph. Organization, nevertheless, is not something that is separate from view, tone, purpose, style, and impact. It can skew or connect a viewpoint, shift or solidify tone, reinforce or undermine purpose, express or conceal a particular style, or establish or disestablish the impact of passage. Organization is the backbone of every form of written expression—it unifies all the parts and sets the parameters for the wholes. Thus, organization should be analyzed strategically when comparing passages.

Identifying and Creating Arguments

The Relationship Between Evidence and Main Ideas and Details

Summarizing Information from a Passage

Summarizing is an effective way to draw a conclusion from a passage. A summary is a shortened version of the original text, written by the reader in their own words. Focusing on the main points of the original text and including only the relevant details can help readers reach a conclusion. It's important to retain the original meaning of the passage.

Like summarizing, **paraphrasing** can also help a reader fully understand different parts of a text. Paraphrasing calls for the reader to take a small part of the passage and list or describe its main points. Paraphrasing is more than rewording the original passage, though. It should be written in the reader's own words, while still retaining the meaning of the original source. This will indicate an understanding of the original source, yet still help the reader expand on their interpretation.

Readers should pay attention to the **sequence**, or the order in which details are laid out in the text, as this can be important to understanding its meaning as a whole. Writers will often use transitional words to help the reader understand the order of events and to stay on track. Words like *next, then, after*, and *finally* show that the order of events is important to the author. In some cases, the author omits these transitional words, and the sequence is implied. Authors may even purposely present the information out of order to make an impact or have an effect on the reader. An example might be when a narrative writer uses **flashback** to reveal information.

Relationship Between the Main Idea and Details of a Passage

In order to understand any text, readers first must determine the **topic**, or what the text is about. In non-fiction writing, the topic can generally be expressed in a few words. For example, a passage might be about college education, moving to a new neighborhood, or dog breeds. Slightly more specific information is found in the **main idea**, or what the writer wants readers to know about the topic. An article might be about the history of popular dog breeds; another article might tell how certain dog breeds are unfairly stereotyped. In both cases, the topic is the same—dog breeds—but the main ideas are quite different. Each writer has a distinct purpose for writing and a different set of details for what they want us to know about dog breeds. When a writer expresses their main idea in one sentence, this is known as a **thesis statement**. If a writer uses a thesis statement, it can generally be found at the beginning of the passage. Finally, the most specific information in a text is in the **supporting details**. An article about dog breed stereotyping might discuss a case study of pit bulls and provide statistics about how many dog attacks are caused by pit bulls versus other breeds.

Main Idea of a Passage

Topics and main ideas are critical parts of writing. The **topic** is the subject matter of the piece. An example of a topic would be *the use of cell phones in a classroom*.

The **main idea** is what the writer wants to say about that topic. A writer may make the point that the use of cell phones in a classroom is a serious problem that must be addressed in order for students to learn better. Therefore, the topic is cell phone usage in a classroom, and the main idea is that it's *a serious problem needing to be addressed.* The topic can be expressed in a word or two, but the main idea should be a complete thought.

An author will likely identify the topic immediately within the title or the first sentence of the passage. The main idea is usually presented in the introduction. In a single passage, the main idea may be identified in the first or last sentence, but it will most likely be directly stated and easily recognized by the reader. Because it is not always stated immediately in a passage, it's important that readers carefully read the entire passage to identify the main idea.

The main idea should not be confused with the thesis statement. A **thesis statement** is a clear statement of the writer's specific stance and can often be found in the introduction of a nonfiction piece. The thesis is a specific sentence (or two) that offers the direction and focus of the discussion.

In order to illustrate the main idea, a writer will use **supporting details**, which provide evidence or examples to help make a point. Supporting details are typically found in nonfiction pieces that seek to inform or persuade the reader.

Determining Which Details Support a Main Idea

An important skill is the ability to determine which details in a passage support the main idea. In the example of cell phone usage in the classroom, where the author's main idea is to show the seriousness of this problem and the need to "unplug", supporting details would be critical for effectively making that point. Supporting details used here might include statistics on a decline in student focus and studies showing the impact of digital technology usage on students' attention spans. The author could also include testimonies from teachers surveyed on the topic.

It's important that readers evaluate the author's supporting details to be sure that they are credible, provide evidence of the author's point, and directly support the main idea. Although shocking statistics

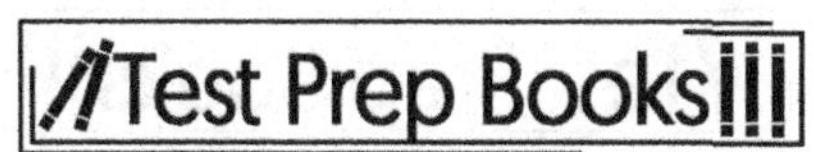

grab readers' attention, their use may provide ineffective information in the piece. Details like this are crucial to understanding the passage and evaluating how well the author presents their argument and evidence.

Drawing Conclusions, Making Inferences, and Evaluating Evidence

Making Generalizations Based on Evidence

One way to make generalizations is to look for main topics. When doing so, pay particular attention to any titles, headlines, or opening statements made by the author. Topic sentences or repetitive ideas can be clues in gleaning inferred ideas. For example, if a passage contains the phrase *While some consider DNA testing to be infallible, it is an inherently flawed technique,* the test taker can infer the rest of the passage will contain information that points to problems with DNA testing.

The test taker may be asked to make a generalization based on prior knowledge but may also be asked to make predictions based on new ideas. For example, the test taker may have no prior knowledge of DNA other than its genetic property to replicate. However, if the reader is given passages on the flaws of DNA testing with enough factual evidence, the test taker may arrive at the inferred conclusion or generalization that the author does not support the infallibility of DNA testing in all identification cases.

When making generalizations, it is important to remember that the critical thinking process involved must be fluid and open to change. While a reader may infer an idea from a main topic, general statement, or other clues, they must be open to receiving new information within a particular passage. New ideas presented by an author may require the test taker to alter a generalization. Similarly, when asked questions that require making an inference, it's important to read the entire test passage and all of the answer options. Often, a test taker will need to refine a generalization based on new ideas that may be presented within the text itself.

Using Main Ideas to Draw Conclusions

Determining conclusions requires being an active reader, as a reader must make a prediction and analyze facts to identify a conclusion. There are a few ways to determine a logical conclusion, but careful reading is the most important. It's helpful to read a passage a few times, noting details that seem important to the text. A reader should also identify key words in a passage to determine the logical conclusion or determination that flows from the information presented.

Textual evidence within the details helps readers draw a conclusion about a passage. **Textual evidence** refers to information—facts and examples that support the main point; it will likely come from outside sources and can be in the form of quoted or paraphrased material. In order to draw a conclusion from evidence, it's important to examine the credibility and validity of that evidence as well as how (and if) it relates to the main idea.

If an author presents a differing opinion or a **counterargument** in order to refute it, the reader should consider how and why the information is being presented. It is meant to strengthen the original argument and shouldn't be confused with the author's intended conclusion, but it should also be considered in the reader's final evaluation.

Sometimes, authors explicitly state the conclusion they want readers to understand. Alternatively, a conclusion may not be directly stated. In that case, readers must rely on the implications to form a logical conclusion:

> On the way to the bus stop, Michael realized his homework wasn't in his backpack. He ran back to the house to get it and made it back to the bus just in time.

In this example, though it's never explicitly stated, it can be inferred that Michael is a student on his way to school in the morning. When forming a conclusion from implied information, it's important to read the text carefully to find several pieces of evidence to support the conclusion.

Describing the Steps of an Argument

Strong arguments tend to follow a fairly defined format. In the introduction, background information regarding the problem is shared, the implications of the issue are stated, and the author's thesis or claims are given. Supporting evidence is then presented in the body paragraphs, along with the counterargument, which then gets refuted with specific evidence. Lastly, in the conclusion, the author summarizes the points and claims again.

Evidence Used to Support a Claim or Conclusion

Premises are the why, and **conclusions** are the what. Stated differently, premises are the evidence or facts supporting why the conclusion is logical and valid. GED Reasoning Through Language Arts questions do not require evaluation of the factual accuracy of the arguments; instead, the questions evaluate the test taker's ability to assess an argument's logical strength. For example, John eats all red food. Apples are red. Therefore, John eats apples. This argument is logically sound, despite having no factual basis in reality. Below is an example of a practice argument.

> Julie is an American track athlete. She's the star of the number one collegiate team in the country. Her times are consistently at the top of national rankings. Julie is extremely likely to represent the United States at the upcoming Olympics.

In this example, the conclusion, or the *what*, is that she will likely be on the American Olympic team. The author supports this conclusion with two premises. First, Julie is the star of an elite track team. Second, she runs some of the best times of the country. This is the *why* behind the conclusion. The following builds off this basic argument:

> Julie is an American track athlete. She's the star of the number one collegiate team in the country. Her times are consistently at the top of national rankings. Julie is extremely likely to represent the United States at the upcoming Olympics. Julie will continue to develop after the Olympic trials. She will be a frontrunner for the gold. Julie is likely to become a world-famous track star.

These additions to the argument make the conclusion different. Now, the conclusion is that Julie is likely to become a world-famous track star. The previous conclusion, Julie will likely be on the Olympic team, functions as a **sub-conclusion** in this argument. Like conclusions, premises must adequately support sub-conclusions. However, sub-conclusions function like premises, since sub-conclusions also support the overall conclusion.

Determining Whether Evidence is Relevant and Sufficient

A **hasty generalization** involves an argument relying on insufficient statistical data or inaccurately generalizing. One common generalization occurs when a group of individuals under observation have some quality or attribute that is asserted to be universal or true for a much larger number of people than actually documented. Here's an example of a hasty generalization:

> A man smokes a lot of cigarettes, but so did his grandfather. The grandfather smoked nearly two packs per day since his World War II service until he died at ninety years of age. Continuing to smoke cigarettes will clearly not impact the grandson's long-term health.

This argument is a hasty generalization because it assumes that one person's addiction and lack of consequences will naturally be reflected in a different individual. There is no reasonable justification for such extrapolation. It is common knowledge that any smoking is detrimental to everyone's health. The fact that the man's grandfather smoked two packs per day and lived a long life has no logical connection with the grandson engaging in similar behavior. The hasty generalization doesn't take into account other reasons behind the grandfather's longevity. Nor does the author offer evidence that might support the idea that the man would share a similar lifetime if he smokes. It might be different if the author stated that the man's family shares some genetic trait rendering them immune to the effects of tar and chemicals on the lungs. If this were in the argument, we would assume it as truth and find the generalization to be valid rather than hasty. Of course, this is not the case in our example.

Determining Whether a Statement Is or Is Not Supported

The basic tenet of reading comprehension is the ability to read and understand a text. One way to understand a text is to look for information that supports the author's main idea, topic, or position statement. This information may be factual, or it may be based on the author's opinion. This section will focus on the test taker's ability to identify factual information, as opposed to opinionated bias. The GED will ask test takers to read passages containing factual information, and then logically relate those passages by drawing conclusions based on evidence.

In order to identify factual information within one or more text passages, begin by looking for statements of fact. Factual statements can be either true or false. Identifying factual statements as opposed to opinion statements is important in demonstrating full command of evidence in reading. For example, the statement *The temperature outside was unbearably hot* may seem like a fact; however, it's not. While anyone can point to a temperature gauge as factual evidence, the statement itself reflects only an opinion. Some people may find the temperature unbearably hot. Others may find it comfortably warm. Thus, the sentence, *The temperature outside was unbearably hot,* reflects the opinion of the author who found it unbearable. If the text passage followed up the sentence with atmospheric conditions indicating heat indices above 140 degrees Fahrenheit, then the reader knows there is factual information that supports the author's assertion of *unbearably hot*.

In looking for information that can be proven or disproven, it's helpful to scan for dates, numbers, timelines, equations, statistics, and other similar data within any given text passage. These types of indicators will point to proven particulars. For example, the statement, *The temperature outside was unbearably hot on that summer day, July 10, 1913,* most likely indicates factual information, even if the reader is unaware that this is the hottest day on record in the United States. Be careful when reading biased words from an author. Biased words indicate opinion, as opposed to fact. The following list contains a sampling of common biased words:

- Good/bad
- Great/greatest
- Better/best/worst
- Amazing
- Terrible/bad/awful
- Beautiful/handsome/ugly
- More/most
- Exciting/dull/boring
- Favorite
- Very
- Probably/should/seem/possibly

Remember, most of what is written is actually opinion or carefully worded information that seems like fact when it isn't. To say, *duplicating DNA results is not cost-effective* sounds like it could be a scientific fact, but it isn't. Factual information can be verified through independent sources.

The simplest type of test question may provide a text passage, then ask the test taker to distinguish the correct factual supporting statement that best answers the corresponding question on the test. However, be aware that most questions may ask the test taker to read more than one text passage and identify which answer best supports an author's topic. While the ability to identify factual information is critical, these types of questions require the test taker to identify chunks of details, and then relate them to one another.

Assessing Whether an Argument is Valid

Although different from conditions and If/Then Statements, **reasonableness** is another important foundational concept. Evaluating an argument for reasonableness and validity entails evaluating the evidence presented by the author to justify their conclusions. Everything contained in the argument should be considered, but remember to ignore outside biases, judgments, and knowledge. For the purposes of this test, the test taker is a one-person jury at a criminal trial using a standard of reasonableness under the circumstances presented by the argument.

These arguments are encountered on a daily basis through social media, entertainment, and cable news. An example is:

> Although many believe it to be a natural occurrence, some believe that the red tide that occurs in Florida each year may actually be a result of human sewage and agricultural runoff. However, it is arguable that both natural and human factors contribute to this annual phenomenon. On one hand, the red tide has been occurring every year since the time of explorers like Cabeza de Vaca in the 1500's. On the other hand, the red tide seems to be getting worse each year, and scientists from the Florida Fish & Wildlife Conservation say the bacteria found inside the tide feed off of nutrients found in fertilizer runoff.

The author's conclusion is that both natural phenomena and human activity contribute to the red tide that happens annually in Florida. The author backs this information up by historical data to prove the natural occurrence of the red tide, and then again with scientific data to back up the human contribution to the red tide. Both of these statements are examples of the premises in the argument. Evaluating the strength of the logical connection between the premises and conclusion is how reasonableness is determined. Another example is:

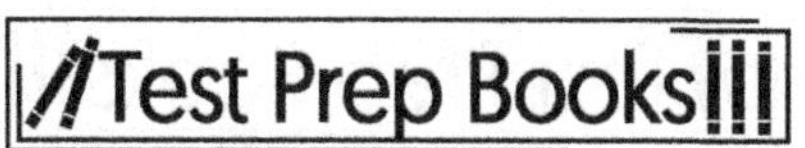

> The local railroad is a disaster. Tickets are exorbitantly priced, bathrooms leak, and the floor is sticky.

The author is clearly unhappy with the railroad service. They cite three examples of why they believe the railroad to be a disaster. An argument more familiar to everyday life is:

> Alexandra said the movie she just saw was amazing. We should go see it tonight.

Although not immediately apparent, this is an argument. The author is making the argument that they should go see the movie. This conclusion is based on the premise that Alexandra said the movie was amazing. There's an inferred note that Alexandra is knowledgeable on the subject, and she's credible enough to prompt her friends to go see the movie. This seems like a reasonable argument. A less reasonable argument is:

> Alexandra is a film student, and she's written the perfect romantic comedy script. We should put our life savings toward its production as an investment in our future.

The author's conclusion is that they should invest their life savings into the production of a movie, and it is justified by referencing Alexandra's credibility and current work. However, the premises are entirely too weak to support the conclusion. Alexandra is only a film *student*, and the script is seemingly her first work. This is not enough evidence to justify investing one's life savings in the film's success.

Assumptions in an Argument

Think of assumptions as unwritten premises. Although they never explicitly appear in the argument, the author is relying on it to defend the argument, just like a premise. Assumptions are the most important part of an argument that will never appear in an argument.

An argument in the abstract is: The author concludes Z based on W and X premises. But the W and X premises actually depend on the unmentioned assumption of Y. Therefore, what the author is really saying is that, X, W, and Y make Z correct, but Y is assumed.

People assume all of the time. Assumptions and inferences allow the human mind to process the constant flow of information. Many assumptions underlie even the most basic arguments. However, in the world of Legal Reasoning arguments, assumptions must be avoided. An argument must be fully presented to be valid; relying on an assumption is considered weak. The test requires that test takers identify these underlying assumptions. One example is:

> Peyton Manning is the most over-rated quarterback of all time. He lost more big games than anyone else. Plus, he allegedly assaulted his female trainer in college. Peyton clearly shouldn't make the Hall of Fame.

The author certainly relies on a lot of assumptions. A few assumptions are:

- Peyton Manning plays quarterback.
- He is considered to be a great quarterback by at least some people.
- He played in many big games.

- Allegations and past settlements without any admission of guilt from over a decade ago can be relied upon as evidence against Hall of Fame acceptance.
- The Hall of Fame voters factor in off-the-field incidents, even if true.
- The best players should make the Hall of Fame.
- Losing big games negates, at least in part, the achievement of making it to those big games
- Peyton Manning is retired, and people will vote on whether he makes the Hall of Fame at some point in the future.

The author is relying on all of these assumptions. Some are clearly more important to his argument than others. In fact, disproving a necessary assumption can destroy a premise and possibly an entire conclusion. For example, what if the Hall of Fame did not factor in any of the off-the-field incidents? Then the alleged assault no longer factors into the argument. Even worse, what if making the big games actually was more important than losing those games in the eyes of the Hall of Fame voters? Then the whole conclusion falls apart and is no longer justified if that premise is disproven.

Assumption questions test this exact point by asking the test taker to identify which assumption the argument relies upon. If the author is making numerous assumptions, then the most important assumption must be chosen.

If the author truly relies on an assumption, then the argument will completely fall apart if the assumption isn't true. **Negating** a necessary assumption will *always* make the argument fall apart. This is a universal rule of logic and should be the first thing done in testing answer choices.

Here are some ways that underlying assumptions will appear as questions:

- Which of the following is a hidden assumption that the author makes to advance his argument?
- Which assumption, if true, would support the argument's conclusion (make it more logical)?
- The strength of the argument depends on which of the following?
- Upon which of the following assumptions does the author rely?
- Which assumption does the argument presuppose?

An example is:

> Frank Underwood is a terrible president. The man is a typical spend, spend, spend liberal. His employment program would exponentially increase the annual deficit and pile on the national debt. Not to mention, Underwood is also on the verge of starting a war with Russia.

Upon which of the following assumptions does the author's argument most rely?

a. Frank Underwood is a terrible president.
b. The United States cannot afford Frank Underwood's policy plans without spending more than the country raises in revenue.
c. No spend, spend, spend liberal has ever succeeded as president.
d. Starting a war with Russia is beneficial to the United States.

Use the negation rule to find the correct answer in the choices below.

Choice *A* is not an assumption—it is the author's conclusion. This type of restatement will never be the correct answer, but test it anyway. After negating the choice, what remains is: *Frank Underwood is a fantastic president.* Does this make the argument fall apart? No, it just becomes the new conclusion. The argument is certainly worse since it does not seem reasonable for someone to praise a president for being a spend, spend, spend liberal or raising the national debt; however, the argument still makes *logical* sense. Eliminate this choice.

Choice *B* is certainly an assumption. It underlies the premises that the country cannot afford Underwood's economic plans. When reversed to: *The United States can afford Frank Underwood's policy plans without spending more than the country raises in revenue,* this destroys the argument. If the United States can afford his plans, then the annual deficit and national debt won't increase; therefore, Underwood being a terrible president would only be based on the final premise. The argument is much weaker without the two sentences involving the financials. Keep it as a benchmark while working through the remaining choices.

Choice *C* is irrelevant. The author is not necessarily claiming that all loose-pocket liberals make for bad presidents. His argument specifically pertains to Underwood. Negate it— *Some spend, spend, spend liberals have succeeded as president.* This does not destroy the argument. Some other candidate could have succeeded as president. However, the author is pointing out that those policies would be disastrous considering the rising budget and debt. The author is not making an appeal to historical precedent. Although not a terrible choice, it is certainly weaker than Choice *B*. Eliminate this choice.

Choice *D* is definitely not an assumption made by the author. The author is assuming that a war with Russia is disastrous. Negate it anyway—*Starting a war with Russia is not beneficial for the United States.* This does not destroy the argument; it makes it stronger. Eliminate this choice.

Analyzing Two Arguments and Evaluating the Types of Evidence Used to Support Each Claim

Arguments use evidence and reasoning to support a position or prove a point. Claims are typically controversial and may be faced with some degree of contention. Thus, authors support claims with evidence. Two arguments might present different types of evidence that readers will need to evaluate for merit, worthiness, accuracy, relevance, and impact. Evidence can take on many forms such as numbers (statistics, measurements, numerical data, etc.), expert opinions or quotes, testimonies, anecdotal evidence or stories from individuals, and textual evidence, such as that obtained from documents like diaries, newspapers, and laws.

Data, Graphs, or Pictures as Evidence

Some writing in the test contains **infographics** such as charts, tables, or graphs. In these cases, interpret the information presented and determine how well it supports the claims made in the text. For example, if the writer makes a case that seat belts save more lives than other automobile safety measures, they might want to include a graph (like the one below) showing the number of lives saved by seat belts versus those saved by air bags.

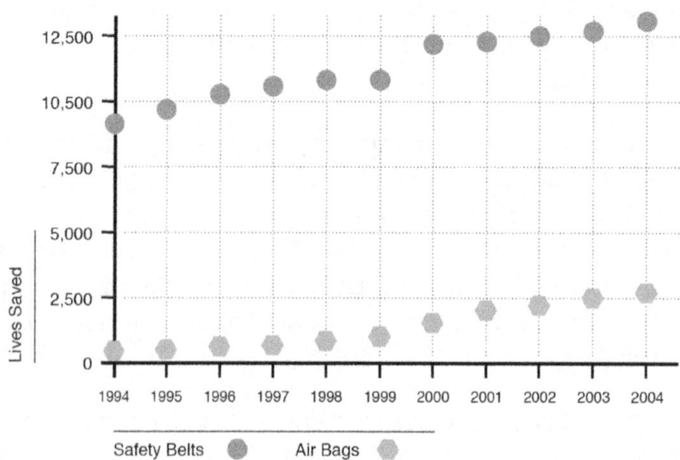

Based on data from the National Highway Traffic Safety Administration

If the graph clearly shows a higher number of lives are saved by seat belts, then it's effective. However, if the graph shows air bags save more lives than seat belts, then it doesn't support the writer's case.

Finally, graphs should be easy to understand. Their information should immediately be clear to the reader at a glance. Here are some basic things to keep in mind when interpreting infographics:

- In a **bar graph**, higher bars represent larger numbers. Lower bars represent smaller numbers.
- **Line graphs** often show trends over time. Points that are higher represent larger numbers than points that are lower. A line that consistently ascends from left to right shows a steady increase over time. A line that consistently descends from left to right shows a steady decrease over time. A line that bounces up and down represents instability or inconsistency in the trend. When interpreting a line graph, determine the point the writer is trying to make, and then see if the graph supports that point.
- **Pie charts** are used to show proportions or percentages of a whole but are less effective in showing change over time.
- **Tables** present information in numerical form, not as graphics. When interpreting a table, make sure to look for patterns in the numbers.

There can also be timelines, illustrations, or maps on the test. When interpreting these, keep in mind the writer's intentions and determine whether or not the graphic supports the case.

Extending Your Understanding to New Situations

Combining Information from Different Sources

Synthesizing, or combining, ideas and information from different sources is a skill that helps test takers pass the GED and also thrive in the workforce. The theories and concepts offered in different passages cannot just haphazardly be tossed together. Every test taker has to come up with their own recipe for success when it comes to synthesizing separate sources.

One way for test takers to think about synthesizing sources is to imagine their written responses as empty homes that need to be decorated. They can then imagine the words, concepts, and theories in the different sources as their desired décor. At times, two different sources combine to create perfectly matched décor—the words, concepts, and theories blend seamlessly upon the walls of the test taker's literary home, creating a balance. At other times, two different sources clash, forcing test takers to sort and separate the ideas into different rooms (for example, different paragraphs or sentences). At still other times, the two sources are incomplete, so test takers need to combine materials with their own interests and statements. If sources contradict one another, it is best to highlight these contradictions. A test taker should take note of the contradictions and use their best judgment in choosing which source is more aligned with their own theories. At times, the test taker may even disagree with information in both articles. It is perfectly acceptable to make the audience aware of all contradictions and disagreements.

Writers, like interior designers, must hone their craft through experience. The best way to begin synthesizing sources is to *practice*. There are four practical ways test takers can start practicing synthesis. Firstly, they need to learn how to properly identify and cite captivating quotations. Secondly, they need to learn how to summarize ideas succinctly in their own words. Thirdly, they need to create unique sentences that are part quotation and part summary. And, lastly, they need to ensure that all of the above is backed by sound grammar, syntax, and organization. The best way to ensure quality is to read other high-quality works and enlist a group of friends or colleagues to edit.

Transferring Information to New Situations

A natural extension of being able to make an inference from a given set of information is also being able to apply that information to a new context. This is especially useful in non-fiction or informative writing. Considering the facts and details presented in the text, readers should consider how the same information might be relevant in a different situation. The following is an example of applying an inferential conclusion to a different context:

> Often, individuals behave differently in large groups than they do as individuals. One example of this is the psychological phenomenon known as the bystander effect. According to the bystander effect, the more people who witness an accident or crime occur, the less likely each individual bystander is to respond or offer assistance to the victim. A classic example of this is the murder of Kitty Genovese in New York City in the 1960s. Although there were over thirty witnesses to her killing by a stabber, none of them intervened to help Kitty or contact the police.

Considering the phenomenon of the bystander effect, what would probably happen if somebody tripped on the stairs in a crowded subway station?

a. Everybody would stop to help the person who tripped
b. Bystanders would point and laugh at the person who tripped
c. Someone would call the police after walking away from the station
d. Few if any bystanders would offer assistance to the person who tripped

This question asks readers to apply the information they learned from the passage, which is an informative paragraph about the bystander effect. According to the passage, this is a concept in psychology that describes the way people in groups respond to an accident—the more people are present, the less likely any one person is to intervene. While the passage illustrates this effect with the example of a woman's murder, the question asks readers to apply it to a different context—in this case, someone falling down the stairs in front of many subway passengers. Although this specific situation is not discussed in the passage, readers should be able to apply the general concepts described in the paragraph. The definition of the bystander effect includes any instance of an accident or crime in front of a large group of people. The question asks about a situation that falls within the same definition, so the general concept should still hold true: in the midst of a large crowd, few individuals are likely to actually respond to an accident. In this case, Choice *D* is the best response.

Grammar and Language

Word Usage

Correcting Errors with Frequently Confused Words

The English language is interesting because many of its words sound so similar or identical that they confuse readers and writers alike. Errors involving these words are hard to spot because they *sound* right even when they're wrong. Also, because these mistakes are so pervasive, many people think they're correct. Here are a few examples that may be encountered on the test:

They're vs. Their vs. There

This set of words is probably the all-time winner of misuse. The word *they're* is a contraction of "they are." Remember that contractions combine two words, using an apostrophe to replace any eliminated letters. If a question asks whether the writer is using the word *they're* correctly, change the word to "they are" and reread the sentence. Look at the following example:

> Legislators can be proud of they're work on this issue.

This sentence *sounds* correct, but replace the contraction *they're* with "they are" to see what happens:

> Legislators can be proud of they are work on this issue.

The result doesn't make sense, which shows that it's an incorrect use of the word *they're*. Did the writer mean to use the word *their* instead? The word *their* indicates possession because it shows that something *belongs* to something else. Now put the word *their* into the sentence:

> Legislators can be proud of their work on this issue.

To check the answer, find the word that comes right after the word *their* (which in this case is *work*). Pose this question: whose *work* is it? If the question can be answered in the sentence, then the word signifies possession. In the sentence above, it's the legislators' work. Therefore, the writer is using the word *their* correctly.

If the words *they're* and *their* don't make sense in the sentence, then the correct word is almost always *there*. The word *there* can be used in many different ways, so it's easy to remember to use it when *they're* and *their* don't work. Now test these methods with the following sentences:

> Their going to have a hard time passing these laws.
>
> Enforcement officials will have there hands full.
>
> They're are many issues to consider when discussing car safety.

In the first sentence, asking the question "Whose going is it?" doesn't make sense. Thus the word *their* is incorrect. However, when replaced with the conjunction *they're* (or *they are*), the sentence works. Thus, the correct word for the first sentence should be *they're.*

In the second sentence, ask this question: "Whose hands are full?" The answer (*enforcement officials*) is correct in the sentence. Therefore, the word *their* should replace *there* in this sentence.

In the third sentence, changing the word *they're* to "they are" ("They are are many issues") doesn't make sense. Ask this question: "Whose are is it?" This makes even less sense, since neither of the words *they're* or *their* makes sense. Therefore, the correct word must be *there*.

Who's vs. Whose

Who's is a contraction of "who is" while the word *whose* indicates possession. Look at the following sentence:

> Who's job is it to protect America's drivers?

The easiest way to check for correct usage is to replace the word *who's* with "who is" and see if the sentence makes sense:

> Who is job is it to protect America's drivers?

By changing the contraction to "Who is" the sentence no longer makes sense. Therefore, the correct word must be *whose*.

Your vs. You're

The word *your* indicates possession, while *you're* is a contraction for "you are." Look at the following example:

> Your going to have to write your congressman if you want to see action.

Again, the easiest way to check correct usage is to replace the word *Your* with "You are" and see if the sentence still makes sense.

> You are going to have to write your congressman if you want to see action.

By replacing Your with "You are," the sentence still makes sense. Thus, in this case, the writer should have used "You're."

Its vs. It's

Its is a word that indicates possession, while the word *it's* is a contraction of "it is." Once again, the easiest way to check for correct usage is to replace the word with "it is" and see if the sentence makes sense. Look at the following sentence:

> It's going to take a lot of work to pass this law.

Replacing *it's* with "it is" results in this: "It is going to take a lot of work to pass this law." This makes sense, so the contraction (*it's*) is correct. Now look at another example:

> The car company will have to redesign it's vehicles.

Replacing *it's* with "it is" results in this: "The car company will have to redesign it is vehicles." This sentence doesn't make sense, so the contraction (*it's*) is incorrect.

Than vs. Then

Than is used in sentences that involve comparisons, while *then* is used to indicate an order of events. Consider the following sentence:

> Japan has more traffic fatalities than the U.S.

The use of the word *than* is correct because it compares Japan to the U.S. Now look at another example:

> Laws must be passed, and then we'll see a change in behavior.

Here the use of the word *then* is correct because one thing happens after the other.

Affect vs. Effect

Affect is a verb that means to change something, while *effect* is a noun that indicates such a change. Look at the following sentence:

> There are thousands of people affected by the new law.

This sentence is correct because *affected* is a verb that tells what's happening. Now look at this sentence:

> The law will have a dramatic effect.

This sentence is also correct because *effect* is a noun and the thing that happens.

Note that a noun version of *affect* is occasionally used. It means "emotion" or "desire," usually in a psychological sense.

Two vs. Too vs. To

Two is the number (2). *Too* refers to an amount of something, or it can mean *also*. *To* is used for everything else. Look at the following sentence:

> Two senators still haven't signed the bill.

This is correct because there are *two* (2) senators. Here's another example:

> There are too many questions about this issue.

In this sentence, the word *too* refers to an amount ("too many questions"). Now here's another example:

> Senator Wilson is supporting this legislation, too.

In this sentence, the word *also* can be substituted for the word *too*, so it's also correct. Finally, one last example:

> I look forward to signing this bill into law.

In this sentence, the tests for *two* and *too* don't work. Thus, the word *to* fits the bill!

Other Common Writing Confusions

In addition to all of the above, there are other words that writers often misuse. This doesn't happen because the words sound alike, but because the writer is not aware of the proper way to use them.

Correcting Subject-Verb Agreement Errors

In English, verbs must agree with the subject. The form of a verb may change depending on whether the subject is singular or plural, or whether it is first, second, or third person. For example, the verb *to be* has various forms:

> I am a student.
>
> You are a student.
>
> She is a student.
>
> We are students.
>
> They are students.

Errors occur when a verb does not agree with its subject. Sometimes, the error is readily apparent:

> We is hungry.

Is is not the appropriate form of *to be* when used with the third person plural *we*.

> We are hungry.

This sentence now has correct subject-verb agreement.

However, some cases are trickier, particularly when the subject consists of a lengthy noun phrase with many modifiers:

> Students who are hoping to accompany the anthropology department on its annual summer trip to Ecuador needs to sign up by March 31st.

The verb in this sentence is *needs*. However, its subject is not the noun adjacent to it—Ecuador. The subject is the noun at the beginning of the sentence—students. Because *students* is plural, *needs* is the incorrect verb form.

> *Students* who are hoping to accompany the anthropology department on its annual summer trip to Ecuador *need* to sign up by March 31st.

This sentence now uses correct agreement between *students* and *need*.

Another case to be aware of is a **collective noun**. A collective noun refers to a group of many things or people but can be singular in itself—e.g., *family, committee, army, pair team, council, jury*. Whether or not a collective noun uses a singular or plural verb depends on how the noun is being used. If the noun refers to the group performing a collective action as one unit, it should use a singular verb conjugation:

> The family is moving to a new neighborhood.

The whole family is moving together in unison, so the singular verb form *is* is appropriate here.

> The committee has made its decision.

The verb *has* and the possessive pronoun *its* both reflect the word *committee* as a singular noun in the sentence above; however, when a collective noun refers to the group as individuals, it can take a plural verb:

> The newlywed pair spend every moment together.

This sentence emphasizes the love between two people in a pair, so it can use the plural verb *spend*.

> The council are all newly elected members.

The sentence refers to the council in terms of its individual members and uses the plural verb *are*.

Overall, though, American English is more likely to pair a collective noun with a singular verb, while British English is more likely to pair a collective noun with a plural verb.

Which of the following sentences is correct?

> A large crowd of protesters was on hand.

> A large crowd of protesters were on hand.

Many people would say the second sentence is correct, but they'd be wrong. However, they probably wouldn't be alone. Most people just look at two words: *protesters were*. Together they make sense. They sound right. The problem is that the verb *were* doesn't refer to the word *protesters*. Here, the word *protesters* is part of a prepositional phrase that clarifies the actual subject of the sentence (*crowd*).

Take the phrase "of protesters" away and re-examine the sentences:

> A large crowd was on hand.

> A large crowd were on hand.

Without the prepositional phrase to separate the subject and verb, the answer is obvious. The first sentence is correct. On the test, look for confusing prepositional phrases when answering questions about subject-verb agreement. Take the phrase away, and then recheck the sentence.

Correcting Pronoun Errors

Pronoun Person

Pronoun person refers to the narrative voice the writer uses in a piece of writing. A great deal of nonfiction is written in third person, which uses pronouns like *he, she, it,* and *they* to convey meaning. Occasionally a writer uses first person (*I, me, we,* etc.) or second person (*you*). Any choice of pronoun person can be appropriate for a particular situation, but the writer must remain consistent and logical.

Test questions may cover examining samples that should stay in a single pronoun person, be it first, second, or third. Look out for shifts between words like *you* and *I* or *he* and *they.*

Pronoun Clarity

Pronouns always refer back to a noun. However, as the writer composes longer, more complicated sentences, the reader may be unsure which noun the pronoun should replace. For example:

> An amendment was made to the bill, but now it has been voted down.

Was the amendment voted down or the entire bill? It's impossible to tell from this sentence. To correct this error, the writer needs to restate the appropriate noun rather than using a pronoun:

> An amendment was made to the bill, but now the bill has been voted down.

Pronouns in Combination

Writers often make mistakes when choosing pronouns to use in combination with other nouns. The most common mistakes are found in sentences like this:

> Please join Senator Wilson and I at the event tomorrow.

Notice anything wrong? Though many people think the sentence sounds perfectly fine, the use of the pronoun *I* is actually incorrect. To double-check this, take the other person out of the sentence:

> Please join I at the event tomorrow.

Now the sentence is obviously incorrect, as it should read, "Please join *me* at the event tomorrow." Thus, the first sentence should replace *I* with *me*:

> Please join Senator Wilson and me at the event tomorrow.

For many people, this sounds wrong because they're used to hearing and saying it incorrectly. Take extra care when answering this kind of question and follow the double-checking procedure.

Eliminating Non-Standard English Words or Phrases

Non-standard English words and phrases, such as slang, should be eliminated, as it not only reduces the professionalism and formality of a text, but it also opens the door for confusion. Slang tends to evolve quickly, and it is less universally-understood than standard English. Therefore, unless working on a narrative fiction piece that purposely includes non-standard English as part of the dialogue, writers should make every effort to eliminate this type of language from their writing.

Sentence Structure

Eliminating Dangling or Misplaced Modifiers

Modifiers are words or phrases (often adjectives or nouns) that add detail to, explain, or limit the meaning of other parts of a sentence. Look at the following example:

A big pine tree is in the yard.

In the sentence, the words *big* (an adjective) and *pine* (a noun) modify *tree* (the head noun).

All related parts of a sentence must be placed together correctly. **Misplaced** and **dangling modifiers** are common writing mistakes. In fact, they're so common that many people are accustomed to seeing them and can decipher an incorrect sentence without much difficulty. On the test, expect to be asked to identify and correct this kind of error.

Misplaced Modifiers

Since modifiers refer to something else in the sentence (*big* and *pine* refer to *tree* in the example above), they need to be placed close to what they modify. If a modifier is so far away that the reader isn't sure what it's describing, it becomes a **misplaced modifier**. For example:

Seat belts almost saved 5,000 lives in 2009.

It's likely that the writer means that the total number of lives saved by seat belts in 2009 is close to 5,000. However, due to the misplaced modifier (*almost*), the sentence actually says there are 5,000 instances when seat belts *almost saved lives.* In this case, the position of the modifier is actually the difference between life and death (at least in the meaning of the sentence). A clearer way to write the sentence is:

Seat belts saved almost 5,000 lives in 2009.

Now that the modifier is close to the 5,000 lives it references, the sentence's meaning is clearer.

Another common example of a misplaced modifier occurs when the writer uses the modifier to begin a sentence. For example:

Having saved 5,000 lives in 2009, Senator Wilson praised the seat belt legislation.

It seems unlikely that Senator Wilson saved 5,000 lives on her own, but that's what the writer is saying in this sentence. To correct this error, the writer should move the modifier closer to the intended object it modifies. Here are two possible solutions:

Having saved 5,000 lives in 2009, the seat belt legislation was praised by Senator Wilson.

Senator Wilson praised the seat belt legislation, which saved 5,000 lives in 2009.

When choosing a solution for a misplaced modifier, look for an option that places the modifier close to the object or idea it describes.

Dangling Modifiers

A modifier must have a target word or phrase that it's modifying. Without this, it's a **dangling modifier**. Dangling modifiers are usually found at the beginning of sentences:

After passing the new law, there is sure to be an improvement in highway safety.

This sentence doesn't say anything about who is passing the law. Therefore, "After passing the new law" is a dangling modifier because it doesn't modify anything in the sentence. To correct this type of error, determine what the writer intended the modifier to point to:

After passing the new law, legislators are sure to see an improvement in highway safety.

"After passing the new law" now points to *legislators*, which makes the sentence clearer and eliminates the dangling modifier.

Editing Sentences for Parallel Structure and Correct Use of Conjunctions

Parallel Structure

Parallel structure occurs when phrases or clauses within a sentence contain the same structure. Parallelism increases readability and comprehensibility because it is easy to tell which sentence elements are paired with each other in meaning.

Jennifer enjoys cooking, knitting, and to spend time with her cat.

This sentence is not parallel because the items in the list appear in two different forms. Some are **gerunds**, which is the verb + ing: *cooking, knitting*. The other item uses the **infinitive** form, which is to + verb: *to spend*. To create parallelism, all items in the list may reflect the same form:

Jennifer enjoys cooking, knitting, and spending time with her cat.

All of the items in the list are now in gerund forms, so this sentence exhibits parallel structure. Here's another example:

The company is looking for employees who are responsible and with a lot of experience.

Again, the items that are listed in this sentence are not parallel. "Responsible" is an adjective, yet "with a lot of experience" is a prepositional phrase. The sentence elements do not utilize parallel parts of speech.

The company is looking for employees who are responsible and experienced.

"Responsible" and "experienced" are both adjectives, so this sentence now has parallel structure.

Conjunctions

Conjunctions join words, phrases, clauses, or sentences together, indicating the type of connection between these elements.

I like pizza, *and* I enjoy spaghetti.

I like to play baseball, *but* I'm allergic to mitts.

Some conjunctions are **coordinating**, meaning they give equal emphasis to two main clauses. Coordinating conjunctions are short, simple words that can be remembered using the mnemonic FANBOYS: for, and, nor, but, or, yet, so. Other conjunctions are subordinating. **Subordinating conjunctions** introduce dependent clauses and include words such as *because*, *since*, *before*, *after*, *if*, and *while*.

Conjunctions can also be classified as follows:

- **Cumulative conjunctions** add one statement to another.
    - Examples: *and, both, also, as well as, not only*
    - E.g. The juice is sweet *and* sour.
- **Adversative conjunctions** are used to contrast two clauses.
    - Examples: *but, while, still, yet, nevertheless*
    - E.g. She was tired, *but* she was happy.
- **Alternative conjunctions** express two alternatives.
    - Examples: *or, either, neither, nor, else, otherwise*
    - E.g. He must eat, *or* he will die.

Editing for Subject-Verb and Pronoun-Antecedent Agreement

Subject-Verb Agreement

The subject of a sentence and its verb must agree. The cornerstone rule of subject-verb agreement is that subject and verb must agree in number. Whether the subject is singular or plural, the verb must follow suit.

Incorrect: The houses is new.

Correct: The houses are new.

Also Correct: The house is new.

In other words, a singular subject requires a singular verb; a plural subject requires a plural verb.

The words or phrases that come between the subject and verb do not alter this rule.

Incorrect: The houses built of brick is new.

Correct: The houses built of brick are new.

Incorrect: The houses with the sturdy porches is new.

Correct: The houses with the sturdy porches are new.

The subject will always follow the verb when a sentence begins with *here* or *there.* Identify these with care.

Incorrect: Here *is* the *houses* with sturdy porches.

Correct: Here *are* the *houses* with sturdy porches.

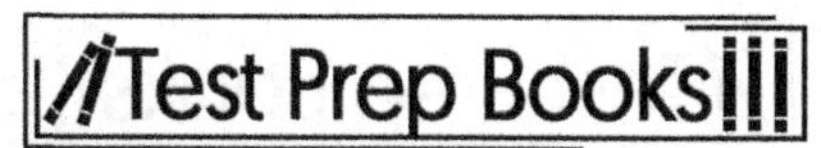

The subject in the sentences above is not *here*, it is *houses*. Remember, *here* and *there* are never subjects. Be careful that contractions such as *here's* or *there're* do not cause confusion!

Two subjects joined by *and* require a plural verb form, except when the two combine to make one thing:

Incorrect: Garrett and Jonathan is over there.

Correct: Garrett and Jonathan are over there.

Incorrect: Spaghetti and meatballs are a delicious meal!

Correct: Spaghetti and meatballs is a delicious meal!

In the example above, *spaghetti and meatballs* is a compound noun. However, *Garrett and Jonathan* is not a compound noun.

Two singular subjects joined by *or, either/or,* or *neither/nor* call for a singular verb form.

Incorrect: Butter or syrup are acceptable.

Correct: Butter or syrup is acceptable.

Plural subjects joined by *or*, *either/or*, or *neither/nor* are, indeed, plural.

The chairs or the boxes are being moved next.

If one subject is singular and the other is plural, the verb should agree with the closest noun.

Correct: The chair or the boxes are being moved next.

Correct: The chairs or the box is being moved next.

Some plurals of money, distance, and time call for a singular verb.

Incorrect: Three dollars *are* enough to buy that.

Correct: Three dollars *is* enough to buy that.

For words declaring degrees of quantity such as *many of, some of,* or *most of,* let the noun that follows *of* be the guide:

Incorrect: Many of the books is in the shelf.

Correct: Many of the books are in the shelf.

Incorrect: Most of the pie *are* on the table.

Correct: Most of the pie *is* on the table.

For indefinite pronouns like anybody or everybody, use singular verbs.

Everybody *is* going to the store.

However, the pronouns *few, many, several, all, some,* and *both* have their own rules and use plural forms.

> Some *are* ready.

Some nouns like *crowd* and *congress* are called **collective nouns** and they require a singular verb form.

> Congress *is* in session.
>
> The news *is* over.

Books and movie titles, though, including plural nouns such as *Great Expectations*, also require a singular verb. Remember that only the subject affects the verb. While writing tricky subject-verb arrangements, say them aloud. Listen to them. Once the rules have been learned, one's ear will become sensitive to them, making it easier to pick out what's right and what's wrong.

Pronoun-Antecedent Agreement

An **antecedent** is the noun to which a pronoun refers; it needs to be written or spoken before the pronoun is used. For many pronouns, antecedents are imperative for clarity. In particular, a lot of the personal, possessive, and demonstrative pronouns need antecedents. Otherwise, it would be unclear who or what someone is referring to when they use a pronoun like *he* or *this*.

Pronoun reference means that the pronoun should refer clearly to one, clear, unmistakable noun (the antecedent).

Pronoun-antecedent agreement refers to the need for the antecedent and the corresponding pronoun to agree in gender, person, and number. Here are some examples:

> The *kidneys* (plural antecedent) are part of the urinary system. *They* (plural pronoun) serve several roles.
>
> The kidneys are part of the *urinary system* (singular antecedent). *It* (singular pronoun) is also known as the renal system.

Eliminating Wordiness or Awkward Sentence Structure

A great Facebook or Twitter post is witty, to the point, and even moving. Good writing is like a good social media post—it needs to be seamless, succinct, and sound in its organization. Alternatively, there are also social media rants so jumbled that they do not make sense or are so endless that readers lose interest. The most captivating social media entries are the ones that meet a high standard of organization. Likewise, the most captivating essays follow these same standards.

Wordiness and awkward sentence structure can happen as a result of many factors. Firstly, they can result from poor grammar or run-on sentences. In order to avoid this, test takers should try using punctuation with fidelity and breaking up independent and dependent clauses into simpler, bite-size nuggets of knowledge. Secondly, wordiness and awkward sentence structure can stem from the overuse of adjectives and adverbs. Test takers should try to limit adverbs and adjectives to ensure clarity. Lastly, wordiness and awkward sentence structure can be the product of flawed organization. Not only should sentences be succinct, but paragraphs and pages should also be succinct—they should use space efficiently and effectively. Test takers should try conveying a message using the fewest words possible.

Below are examples of ways to rectify wordiness and awkward sentences in writing.

WORDINESS:

BEFORE: Science is an important subject of study, and it is important for all students to learn because it focuses on the way the world works and it has important subfields like biology, physics, and chemistry.	AFTER: Science—which is composed of important subfields like biology, physics, and chemistry—helps students understand the way the world works.
BEFORE: History is about important people, places, events, movements, and eras in the past it is a really, really interesting field with lots of different lenses of study such as economic history, political history, and cultural history to name a few types of history.	AFTER: History can be studied through many lenses: economics, politics, and culture. However, all types of history focus on interesting people, places, events, movements, and eras in the past.

AWKWARDNESS:

BEFORE: The administrative expertise of George Washington's presidential administration was known for its powerfully powerful administrators.	AFTER: George Washington's presidential administration was known for its powerful leadership and expertise.
BEFORE: I want to study history, working hard, and becoming a historian.	AFTER: I want to study history, work hard, and become a historian.

Eliminating Run-On Sentences and Sentence Fragments

A **sentence fragment** is a failed attempt to create a complete sentence because it's missing a required noun or verb. Fragments don't function properly because there isn't enough information to understand the writer's intended meaning. For example:

> Seat belt use corresponds to a lower rate of hospital visits, reducing strain on an already overburdened healthcare system. Insurance claims as well.

Look at the last sentence: *Insurance claims as well.* What does this mean? This is a fragment because it has a noun but no verb, and it leaves the reader guessing what the writer means about insurance claims. Many readers can probably infer what the writer means, but this distracts them from the flow of the writer's argument. Choosing a suitable replacement for a sentence fragment may be one of the questions on the test. The fragment is probably related to the surrounding content, so look at the overall point the writer is trying to make and choose the answer that best fits that idea.

Remember that sometimes a fragment can *look* like a complete sentence or have all the nouns and verbs it needs to make sense. Consider the following two examples:

> Seat belt use corresponds to a lower rate of hospital visits.
>
> Although seat belt use corresponds to a lower rate of hospital visits.

Both examples above have nouns and verbs, but only the first sentence is correct. The second sentence is a fragment, even though it's actually longer. The key is the writer's use of the word *although*. Starting a sentence with *although* turns that part into a *subordinate clause* (more on that next). Keep in mind that one doesn't have to remember that it's called a subordinate clause on the test. Just be able to recognize that the words form an incomplete thought and identify the problem as a sentence fragment.

A **run-on sentence** is, in some ways, the opposite of a fragment. It contains two or more sentences that have been improperly forced together into one. An example of a run-on sentence looks something like this:

> Seat belt use corresponds to a lower rate of hospital visits it also leads to fewer insurance claims.

Here, there are two separate ideas in one sentence. It's difficult for the reader to follow the writer's thinking because there is no transition from one idea to the next. On the test, choose the best way to correct the run-on sentence.

Here are two possibilities for the sentence above:

> Seat belt use corresponds to a lower rate of hospital visits. It also leads to fewer insurance claims.
>
> Seat belt use corresponds to a lower rate of hospital visits, but it also leads to fewer insurance claims.

Both solutions are grammatically correct, so which one is the best choice? That depends on the point that the writer is trying to make. Always read the surrounding text to determine what the writer wants to demonstrate, and choose the option that best supports that thought.

Transition Words

Transitions are the glue that helps put ideas together seamlessly, within sentences and paragraphs, between them, and (in longer documents) even between sections. Transitions may be single words, sentences, or whole paragraphs (as in the prior example). Transitions help readers to digest and understand what to feel about what has gone on and clue readers in on what is going on, what will be, and how they might react to all these factors. Transitions are like good clues left at a crime scene.

Recall this list of some common transition words and phrases:

- To show causality: *as a result, therefore*, and *consequently*
- To compare and contrast: *however, but*, and *on the other hand*
- To introduce examples: *for instance, namely*, and *including*
- To show order of importance: *foremost, primarily, secondly*, and *lastly*

Capitalization, Punctuation, and Apostrophes

Correct Capitalization

Here's a non-exhaustive list of things that should be capitalized:

- The first word of every sentence
- The first word of every line of poetry
- The first letter of proper nouns (World War II)
- Holidays (Valentine's Day)
- The days of the week and months of the year (Tuesday, March)
- The first word, last word, and all major words in the titles of books, movies, songs, and other creative works (In the novel, *To Kill a Mockingbird*, note that *a* is lowercase since it's not a major word, but *to* is capitalized since it's the first word of the title.)
- Titles when preceding a proper noun (President Roberto Gonzales, Aunt Judy)

When simply using a word such as president or secretary, though, the word is not capitalized.

> Officers of the new business must include a *president* and *treasurer*.

Seasons—spring, fall, etc.—are not capitalized.

North, *south*, *east*, and *west* are capitalized when referring to regions but are not when being used for directions. In general, if it's preceded by *the* it should be capitalized.

> I'm from the South.

> I drove south.

Using Apostrophes with Possessive Nouns Correctly

Possessives

In grammar, **possessive nouns** and possessive pronouns show ownership.

Singular nouns are generally made possessive with an apostrophe and an *s* (*'s*).

> My *uncle's* new car is silver.

> The *dog's* bowl is empty.

> *James's* ties are becoming outdated.

Plural nouns ending in *s* are generally made possessive by just adding an apostrophe ('):

> The pistachio nuts' saltiness is added during roasting. (The saltiness of pistachio nuts is added during roasting.)

> The students' achievement tests are difficult. (The achievement tests of the students are difficult.)

If the plural noun does not end in an *s* such as *women,* then it is made possessive by adding an **apostrophe** *s* (*'s*)—*women's.*

"Possessive pronouns can be first person (mine), second person (yours), or third person (theirs).

Indefinite possessive pronouns such as *nobody* or *someone* become possessive by adding an apostrophe *s* to become *nobody's* or *someone's*."

Using Correct Punctuation

Ellipses

An **ellipsis** (...) is used to show that there is more to the quoted text than is necessary for the current discussion. Writers use them in place of words, lines, phrases, list content, or paragraphs that might just as easily have been omitted from a passage of writing. This can be done to save space or to focus only on the specifically relevant material.

> Exercise is good for some unexpected reasons. Watkins writes, "Exercise has many benefits such as ... reducing cancer risk."

In the example above, the ellipsis takes the place of the other benefits of exercise that are more expected.

The ellipsis may also be used to show a pause in sentence flow.

> "I'm wondering...how this could happen," Dylan said in a soft voice.

Commas

A **comma** (,) is the punctuation mark that signifies a pause—breath—between parts of a sentence. It denotes a break of flow. As with so many aspects of writing structure, authors will benefit by memorizing all of the different ways in which commas can be used so as not to abuse them.

In a complex sentence—one that contains a **subordinate** (**dependent**) clause or clauses—the use of a comma is dictated by where the subordinate clause is located. If the subordinate clause is located before the main clause, a comma is needed between the two clauses.

> *Because I don't have that much money*, I will not pay for the steak.

Generally, if the subordinate clause is placed after the main clause, no punctuation is needed.

> I did well on my exam *because I studied two hours the night before*.

Notice how the last clause is dependent because it requires the earlier independent clauses to make sense.

Use a comma on both sides of an interrupting phrase.

> I will pay for the ice cream, *chocolate and vanilla*, and then will eat it all myself.

The words forming the phrase in italics are nonessential (extra) information. To determine if a phrase is nonessential, try reading the sentence without the phrase and see if it's still coherent.

A comma is not necessary in this next sentence because no interruption—nonessential or extra information—has occurred. Read sentences aloud when uncertain.

I will pay for his chocolate and vanilla ice cream and then will eat it all myself.

If the nonessential phrase comes at the beginning of a sentence, a comma should only go at the end of the phrase. If the phrase comes at the end of a sentence, a comma should only go at the beginning of the phrase.

Other types of interruptions include the following:

- Interjections: Oh no, I am not going.
- Abbreviations: Barry Potter, M.D., specializes in heart disorders.
- Direct addresses: Yes, Claudia, I am tired and going to bed.
- Parenthetical phrases: His wife, lovely as she was, was not helpful.
- Transitional phrases: Also, it is not possible.

The second comma in the following sentence is called an Oxford comma.

I will pay for ice cream, syrup, and pop.

It is a comma used after the second-to-last item in a series of three or more items. It comes before the word *or* or *and*. Not everyone uses the Oxford comma; it is optional, but many believe it is needed. The comma functions as a tool to reduce confusion in writing. So, if omitting the Oxford comma would cause confusion, then it's best to include it.

Commas are used in math to mark the place of thousands in numerals, breaking them up so they are easier to read. Other uses for commas are in dates (*March 19, 2016*), letter greetings (*Dear Sally,*), and in between cities and states (*Louisville, KY*).

Semicolons

The **semicolon** (;) might be described as a heavy-handed comma. Take a look at these two examples:

I will pay for the ice cream, but I will not pay for the steak.

I will pay for the ice cream; I will not pay for the steak.

What's the difference? The first example has a comma and a conjunction separating the two independent clauses. The second example does not have a conjunction, but there are two independent clauses in the sentence, so something more than a comma is required. In this case, a semicolon is used.

Two independent clauses can only be joined in a sentence by either a comma and conjunction or a semicolon. If one of those tools is not used, the sentence will be a run-on. Remember that while the clauses are independent, they need to be closely related in order to be contained in one sentence.

Another use for the semicolon is to separate items in a list when the items themselves require commas.

The family lived in Phoenix, Arizona; Oklahoma City, Oklahoma; and Raleigh, North Carolina.

Colons

Colons (:) have many miscellaneous functions. Colons can be used to precede further information or a list. In these cases, a colon should only follow an independent clause.

> Humans take in sensory information through five basic senses: sight, hearing, smell, touch, and taste.

The meal includes the following components:

- Caesar salad
- Spaghetti
- Garlic bread
- Cake

Colons can also be used to introduce an appositive.

> The family got what they needed: a reliable vehicle.

While a comma is more common, a colon can also precede a formal quotation.

> He said to the crowd: "Let's begin!"

The colon is used after the greeting in a formal letter.

> Dear Sir:
> To Whom It May Concern:

In the writing of time, the colon separates the minutes from the hour (*4:45 p.m.*). The colon can also be used to indicate a ratio between two numbers (*50:1*).

Hyphens

The hyphen (-) is a small dash mark that can be used to join words to show that they are linked.

Hyphens can connect two words that work together as a single adjective (a compound adjective).

> honey-covered biscuits

Some words always require hyphens even if not serving as an adjective.

> merry-go-round

Hyphens always go after certain prefixes like *anti-* & *all-*.

Hyphens should also be used when the absence of the hyphen would cause a strange vowel combination (*semi-engineer*) or confusion. For example, *re-collect* should be used to describe something being gathered twice rather than being written as *recollect*, which means to remember.

Parentheses and Dashes

Parentheses are half-round brackets that look like this: *( )*. They set off a word, phrase, or sentence that is an afterthought, explanation, or side note relevant to the surrounding text but not essential. A pair of commas is often used to set off this sort of information, but parentheses are generally used for

information that would not fit well within a sentence or that the writer deems not important enough to be structurally part of the sentence.

> The picture of the heart (see above) shows the major parts you should memorize.
>
> Mount Everest is one of three mountains in the world that are over 28,000 feet high (K2 and Kanchenjunga are the other two).

See how the sentences above are complete without the parenthetical statements? In the first example, *see above* would not have fit well within the flow of the sentence. The second parenthetical statement could have been a separate sentence, but the writer deemed the information not pertinent to the topic.

The **em-dash** (—) is a mark longer than a hyphen used as a punctuation mark in sentences and to set apart a relevant thought. Even after plucking out the line separated by the dash marks, the sentence will be intact and make sense.

> Looking out the airplane window at the landmarks—Lake Clarke, Thompson Community College, and the bridge—she couldn't help but feel excited to be home.

The dashes use is similar to that of parentheses or a pair of commas. So, what's the difference? Many believe that using dashes makes the clause within them stand out while using parentheses is subtler. It's advised to not use dashes when commas could be used instead.

Quotation Marks

Quotation marks ("") are used in a number of ways. Here are some instances where quotation marks should be used:

- Dialogue for characters in narratives. When characters speak, the first word should always be capitalized, and the punctuation goes inside the quotes. For example:

  > Janie said, "The tree fell on my car during the hurricane."

- Around titles of songs, short stories, essays, and chapters in books
- To emphasize a certain word
- To refer to a word as the word itself

Apostrophes

This punctuation mark, the apostrophe ('), is a versatile little mark. It has a few different functions:

- Quotes: Apostrophes are used when a second quote is needed within a quote.
  - In my letter to my friend, I wrote, "The girl had to get a new purse, and guess what Mary did? She said, 'I'd like to go with you to the store.' I knew Mary would buy it for her."
- Contractions: Another use for an apostrophe in the quote above is a contraction. *I'd* is used for *I would.*

- Possession: An apostrophe followed by the letter *s* shows possession (*Mary's* purse). If the possessive word is plural, the apostrophe generally just follows the word.
    - The trees' leaves are all over the ground.

Practice Quiz

The next five questions are based upon the following passage:

The Myth of Head Heat Loss

It has recently been brought to my attention that most people believe that 75% of your body heat is lost through your head. I had certainly heard this before, and I'm not going to attempt to say I didn't believe it when I first heard it. It is natural to be gullible to anything said with enough authority. But the "fact" that the majority of your body heat is lost through your head is a lie.

Let me explain. Heat loss is proportional to surface area exposed. An elephant loses a great deal more heat than an anteater because it has a much greater surface area than an anteater. Each cell has mitochondria that produce energy in the form of heat, and it takes a lot more energy to run an elephant than an anteater.

So, each part of your body loses its proportional amount of heat in accordance with its surface area. The human torso probably loses the most heat, though the legs lose a significant amount as well. Some people have asked, "Why does it feel so much warmer when you cover your head than when you don't?" Well, that's because your head, because it is not clothed, is losing a lot of heat while the clothing on the rest of your body provides insulation. If you went outside with a hat and pants but no shirt, not only would you look stupid but your heat loss would be significantly greater because so much more of you would be exposed. So, if given the choice to cover your chest or your head in the cold, choose the chest. It could save your life.

1. What is the primary purpose of this passage?
    a. To provide evidence that disproves a myth
    b. To compare elephants and anteaters
    c. To explain why it is appropriate to wear clothes in winter
    d. To show how people are gullible

2. Which of the following best describes the main idea of the passage?
    a. It is better to wear a shirt than a hat.
    b. Heat loss is proportional to surface area exposed.
    c. It is natural to be gullible.
    d. The human chest loses the most heat.

3. Why does the author compare elephants and anteaters?
    a. To express an opinion
    b. To give an example that helps clarify the main point
    c. To show the differences between them
    d. To persuade why one is better than the other

4. Which of the following best describes the tone of the passage?
    a. Harsh
    b. Angry
    c. Casual
    d. Indifferent

5. Which of the following sentences provides the best evidence to support the main idea?
    a. "It is natural to be gullible to anything said with enough authority."
    b. "Each part of your body loses its proportional amount of heat in accordance with its surface area."
    c. "If given the choice to cover your chest or your head in the cold, choose the chest."
    d. "But the 'fact' that the majority of your body heat is lost through your head is a lie."

See answers on next page

Answer Explanations

1. A: Not only does the article provide examples to disprove a myth, the title also suggests that the article is trying to disprove a myth. Further, the sentence, "But the 'fact' that the majority of your body heat is lost through your head is a lie," and then the subsequent "let me explain," demonstrates the author's intention in disproving a myth. Choice *B* is incorrect because although the selection does compare elephants and anteaters, it does so in order to prove a point, and is not the primary reason that the selection was written. Choice *C* is incorrect because even though the article mentions somebody wearing clothes in the winter, and that doing so could save your life, wearing clothes in the winter is not the primary reason this article was written. Choice *D* is incorrect because the article only mentions that people are gullible once, and makes no further comment on the matter, so this cannot be the primary purpose.

2. B: If the myth is that most of one's body heat is lost through their head, then the fact that heat loss is proportional to surface area exposed is the best evidence that disproves it, since one's head has a great deal less surface area than the rest of the body, making Choice *B* the correct choice. "It is better to wear a shirt than a hat" does not provide evidence that disproves the fact that the head loses more heat than the rest of the body. Thus, Choice *A* is incorrect. Choice *C* is incorrect because gullibility is mentioned only once in this passage and the rest of the article ignores this statement, so clearly it is not the main idea. Finally, Choice *D* is incorrect because though the article mentions that the human chest probably loses the most heat, it is to provide an example of the evidence that heat loss is proportional to surface area exposed, so this is not the main idea of the passage.

3. B: Choice *B* is correct because the author is trying to demonstrate the main idea, which is that heat loss is proportional to surface area, and so they compare two animals with different surface areas to clarify the main point. Choice *A* is incorrect because the author uses elephants and anteaters to prove a point that heat loss is proportional to surface area, not to express an opinion. Choice *C* is incorrect because though the author does use them to show differences, they do so in order to give examples that prove the above points. Choice *D* is incorrect because there is no language to indicate favoritism between the two animals.

4. C: Because of the way the author addresses the reader and the colloquial language the author uses (e.g., "let me explain," "so," "well," "didn't," "you would look stupid"), Choice *C* is the best answer because it has a much more casual tone than the usual informative article. Choice *A* may be a tempting choice because the author says the "fact" that most of one's heat is lost through their head is a "lie" and that someone who does not wear a shirt in the cold looks stupid. However, this only happens twice within the passage, and the passage does not give an overall tone of harshness. Choice *B* is incorrect because again, while not necessarily nice, the language does not carry an angry charge. The author is clearly not indifferent to the subject because of the passionate language that they use, so Choice *D* is incorrect.

5. B: The primary purpose of the article is to provide evidence to disprove the myth that most of a person's heat is lost through their head. The fact that each part of the body loses heat in proportion to its surface area is the best evidence to disprove this myth. Choice *A* is incorrect because again, gullibility is not a main contributor to this article, but it may be common to see questions on the test that give the same wrong answer in order to try and trick the test taker. Choice *C* only suggests what you should do with this information; it is not the primary evidence itself. Choice *D,* while tempting, is actually not evidence. It does not give any reason for why it is a lie; it simply states that it is. Evidence is factual information that supports a claim.

Science

Reading for Meaning in Science

Claims and Evidence in Science

Finding Evidence that Supports a Finding

Science is one of the most objective, straightforward fields of study. Thus, it is no surprise that scientists and science articles are focused on **evidence**. When reading science passages, test takers are sometimes asked to find supporting evidence that reinforces a particular finding. A **finding** in science is a result of the investigation; it is what scientists find out. The majority of science passages tend to avoid opinions; instead, they focus on facts. Although no results are infallible just because the texts are scientific, most results are quantified. Quantified results mean they are expressed in numbers or measurements. Thus, when in doubt, go straight to the data, or numbers, that are offered. Sometimes data is embedded in the text; other times it appears in charts, tables, or graphs. These tools use numbers to demonstrate the patterns discussed in scientific texts, and they help readers to visualize concrete patterns. In order to find evidence to support a finding in scientific passage, all test takers should try collecting and analyzing the relevant data offered. Regardless of whether the data is coming from the text or a graph, it is helpful when making conclusions.

The following steps are helpful for identifying evidence that supports a finding in a science passage:

- Apply critical analysis and critical thinking by asking the right questions.
- Determine the weight of the information by figuring out its relevance.
- Identify trends in the numbers.
- Make inferences.
- Determine the most appropriate methods for either quantifying or communicating inferences.

Making Sense of Information that Differs Between Various Science Sources

Science is often a process of checks and balances, and GED students are expected to carry out this process of checks and balances as they analyze and compare information that differs between various science sources. Science demands a high degree of communication, which, in turn, demands a high degree of scientific literacy and numeracy. GED students must be prepared to analyze the different data and written conclusions of various texts. Contrary to popular belief, science is not an authoritarian field—scientific worldviews and inquiries can be wrong. It is more fruitful to think of science as a living library that is shaped by the complex activities carried out by different groups in different places. This living library is filled with ideas that are shaped by various sources and methods of research. The explanations, inferences, and discussions carried out by scientists are filled with facts that may be flawed or biased. Science, like any other field, cannot completely escape bias. Even though science is meant to be objective, its findings can still lend themselves to biases.

Thus, it is important for GED students to get in the practice of not only making sense of information that differs between various science sources, but also to begin synthesizing this information into a unique worldview. The peer review process is also necessary to ensure checks and balances within the scientific field. The key to making this happen while taking the GED is to maintain an acute awareness of when and where information or data differs. Pay close attention to the ways in which each scientist uses specific words or data to back their overall conclusions.

Below are some key reasons why data and interpretations can differ:

- Historical bias
- Cultural bias
- Interpretation or personal bias
- Lack of implementation and data collection fidelity
- Different data collection approaches
- Different data collection and data analysis tools
- Weak hypotheses
- Compounding variables
- Failure to recognize certain variables
- User error
- Changes in the environment between two studies
- Computation or statistical errors
- Interpretive blind spots
- Lack of understanding of context or environment

Science Vocabulary, Terms, and Phrases

Every field of study has its own specialized vocabulary, terms, and phrases. However, the field of science has one of the most unique living libraries when it comes to its specialized vocabulary, terms, and phrases. Many people mistakenly believe science is just about mathematical formulas. But scientific literacy is essential to becoming a marketable employee and an active global citizen. Thus, GED assessments try to test a student's scientific literacy by assessing their understanding of specialized vocabulary, terms, and phrases in passages, charts, graphs, and tables. Understanding the numbers is not enough to pass this portion of the exam. All students of science must have a basic understanding of science vocabulary, terms, and phrases in order to shape their scientific worldview, drive their scientific inquiry, and enhance their scientific enterprise.

Every person has the ability to formulate their own scientific worldview. Science is not only highly complex, but it is also tentative in nature—humans make educated guesses about the information and data they collect. This information and data change over time, and, as a result, new vocabulary, terms, and phrases are constantly shadowing new discoveries, data analysis, and findings. Scientific inquiry may begin with simple questions, or hypotheses, but it may end with new concepts and terminology. The more questions scientists ask, the more necessary it is to apply words to both the preconceived questions and logical answers. Scientific inquiry, in many ways, is a combination of logic and imagination, and scientific imagination is usually the force driving the creation of new specialized vocabulary, terms, and phrases. Scientific enterprise is a larger process of checks and balances, which allows scientific findings to be debated through intellectual dialogue. Words are an important component of the peer review process of scientific enterprise. Theories and findings always come into question, and GED students are expected to not only comprehend the words of passages, but also question their findings through intertextual analysis and data analysis.

Below are a few tables of commonly used scientific terms and their definitions:

Earth Science Terms
• **Carbon cycle**: The series of biochemical processes that transfer carbon, the main component of many biological compounds and minerals, into different reservoirs of the Earth's environment; these reservoirs include the Earth's interior, its geological sediments, its oceans and waterways, its terrestrial biosphere, and its atmosphere. • **Climate**: The weather in a particular location averaged over a period of time. • **Equator**: The line separating the Northern and Southern Hemispheres. • **Hemisphere**: Literally "half a sphere"; the earth is divided into two pairs of hemispheres (Northern and Southern, Eastern and Western). • **Orbit**: The path of a celestial body in its revolution about another. • **Prime meridian**: A human-made geographic line that runs South-to-North and separates the globe into two: the Eastern and Western Hemispheres. • **Revolve**: Turn on or around an axis. • **Seismic**: Caused by an earthquake or geological vibration. • **Solar system**: The Sun and the celestial bodies (for example, Earth and the other planets) that orbit it. • **Tectonic**: Pertaining to the structure or movement of the Earth's crust. • **Volcano**: A geological feature composed of a mountain or crevice that spews hot gases and magma into the atmosphere when agitated. • **Water**: The liquid that sustains life; a colorless, odorless liquid that helps shape geography (for example, rivers, lakes, streams, oceans, glaciers) and biological functions (for example, hydration, blood flow). • **Weather**: Atmospheric conditions such as temperature and precipitation. • **Wind**: Air moving from high pressure to low pressure.

Chemistry Terms

- **Acid**: a corrosive chemical substance that has the ability to neutralize alkali; opposite of a base on the pH scale.
- **Atom**: The microscopic building blocks of matter and the foundations of chemistry; every solid, liquid, and gas is composed of atoms.
- **Atomic mass**: Typically expressed in atomic mass units, atomic mass is the mass of an atom, which can be figured out by adding protons and neutrons to find the mass number.
- **Base**: Bases are substances that are the opposite of acids on the pH scale; when mixed with acids they create a chemical reaction that produces salts.
- **Boiling point**: A point at which a liquid reaches a temperature that allows it to transform into a vapor; the normal boiling point of water is 100 degrees Celsius.
- **Oxidation**: The process or result of oxidizing or being oxidized.
- **Chemical formula**: An arrangement of elemental symbols and subscripts that convey the structure of a compound.
- **Chemical reaction**: A process that transforms the molecular or ionic composition of a substance.
- **Condensation**: The conversion of a vapor or gas to a liquid.
- **Conductor**: Any material that can transmit sound, heat, or electricity; normally used to describe metals and other materials that serve as conduits for electricity.
- **Covalent bond**: The sharing of electrons between two atoms; sometimes called a molecular bond.
- **Decompose**: (With reference to a chemical compound) break down or cause to break down into component elements or simpler constituents.
- **Electron**: Subatomic particles that carry a negative charge; carries a charge that is opposite of a proton.
- **Ion**: Atoms or molecules that are not neutral in their charge; they are positively or negatively charged.
- **Ionic bond**: A type of ionic cohesion that occurs when two oppositely charged atoms or molecules attract one another.
- **Liquid**: A substance that is neither a solid nor a gas, but flows freely in a fluid-like state that is akin to oil or water.
- **Radioactivity**: A process by which atoms become unstable and emit radiation; an unstable, disintegrating atom losing energy.

- **Gas**: An air-like state of matter that has traits that are distinguishable from solids and liquids; gases are known for their ability to expand rapidly throughout free space because of their air-like qualities; in fact, air itself is a combination of gases.
- **Salt**: A substance created from a mixture of a base and an acid.
- **Solution**: A liquid combination of a solute (a chemical that dissolves in a solution) and a solvent (a chemical that other substances dissolve into)

Physics Terms

- **Acceleration**: Acceleration in physics can be found by dividing the change in velocity by the change in time; it is the rate of the overall change in velocity as analyzed in relationship to the overall change in time.
- **Activation energy**: The amount of energy that is required for a chemical reaction to be initiated; normally quantified by a measurement known as Joules (J).
- **Amplitude**: The peak strength of a vibration or wave, which is measured by its repetition over a single period.
- **Density**: The degree of compactness of a substance.
- **Electromagnetic spectrum**: The spectrum that includes all different types of electromagnetic radiation, including radio waves, infrared waves, visible light waves, ultraviolet waves, X-rays, and Gamma rays
- **Energy**: The scientific name describing the phenomenon that produces heat, light, or motion in an object; in biology, it is produced by cells and the body in order to fuel human functions.
- **Frequency**: The number of occurrences within a given period of time.
- **Friction**: The resistance when a body is moved in contact with another.
- **Gravity**: Discovered by Sir Isaac Newton, it is an invisible force that draws two objects or celestial bodies close together; this force is displayed in space when celestial objects orbit around one another.
- **Momentum**: Used by scientists to quantify the motion object.
- **Resistance:** The obstructing, slowing, or stopping effect from one object onto another.
- **Voltage**: The electrical potential between two items, expressed in a measurement known as volts.
- **Volume**: The amount of space that a three-dimensional geometrical object (whether solid, liquid, or gas) occupies.

General Science Terms

- **Atmosphere**: In science, it is the combinations of gases that contribute to the mass and shape of a celestial body, particularly the planet Earth.
- **Cause**: The beginning of a chain reaction or the root an event; a phenomenological starting point that produces an effect.
- **Conclusion**: A definitive decision, assumption, or statement that is rooted in logic.
- **Context**: In science, it is the places, perspectives, and circumstances that helped influence a particular experiment or hypothesis.
- **Effect**: An event, process, or phenomenon that results from another event, process, or phenomenon (which is known as a cause).
- **Experiment**: A scientific procedure that helps test hypotheses by carrying out the scientific method.
- **Evaluate**: To assess the nature, content, necessity, or effectiveness of a particular fact, theory, or philosophy.
- **Evidence**: The details or facts needed to prove a hypothesis, theory, case, or argument.
- **Fact**: Information that can be substantiated as true, using science or accepted theory; information that can be cross-referenced with others' understanding of reality.
- **Hypothesis**: A postulation or prediction that is assessed via the scientific method.
- **Inference**: An implicit conclusion that can be reached by combining the details of a document or experience with logically sound background knowledge.
- **Implication**: Something that is inferred.
- **Generalization**: The process of abstracting common properties of instances.
- **Research**: The process of consolidating information, ideas, and theories in a systematized fashion (typically via writing books, articles, or reports).
- **Scientific method**: The consolidation of ideas, observations, experiments, and theories, using tested hypotheses as a guide for understanding the world.
- **Scientist**: A researcher or practitioner devoted to the study of science, which includes: physics, Earth sciences, chemistry, and biology.
- **Theory**: A worldview, or a system of philosophies, ideas, perceptions, and conjectures, that tries to make sense of reality.

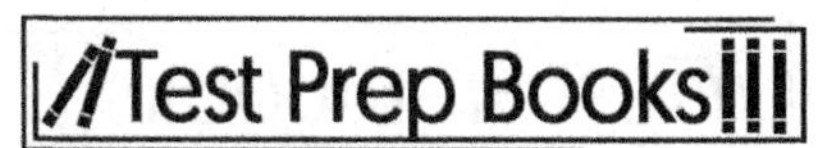

Understanding and Explaining Information from the Passages

Comprehension is a key component to passing the science portion of the GED. As previously mentioned, test takers must be able to make sense of the information presented in various scientific sources. This demands a well-rounded scientific literacy, which is the ability to understand complex scientific vocabulary, terms, and phrases. Making sense of science passages also requires scientific numeracy, which is the ability to understand scientific formulas, scientific equations, and scientific data. Literacy and numeracy are the skills that help test takers understand and explain the information in scientific passages.

Additionally, basic reasoning and language arts skills are helpful, such as understanding the purpose, details, and main idea of the passage. It is also important for test takers to recognize the method of arriving at the findings. Method is what sets apart a scientific text from a literary one. Each experiment or data collection technique has its own unique method. When reading scientific passages, test takers should be aware of the different ways that scientists carry out their experiments or data collection.

Understanding Symbols, Terms, and Phrases in Science

Much like in mathematics, scientific texts rely on symbols to convey certain messages. These symbols may be in a text, or they may be in graphs, charts, tables, or pictures. These symbols are key components of evaluating data and communicating results.

In physics-based passages, students may encounter symbols and variables that are particular to that field of science. For instance, in studies focusing on electricity and magnetism, students are likely to encounter a symbol that looks like this: λ. This symbol is the Greek letter "lambda." Scientists uses the λ symbol in order to communicate or compute a wavelength, measured in meters, of the electromagnetic spectrum. Scientists might also use a symbol like this: ƒ. This is a symbol that represents the frequency, measured in hertz, of the electromagnetic spectrum.

In chemistry, symbols are also used on a regular basis. For instance, when discussing temperature, whether in Celsius or Fahrenheit, scientists often use the following symbol: °. Instead of saying 35 degrees, a scientist might just present the finding as 35°. Chemistry also uses symbols for the periodic table. For example, mercury is represented on the periodic table by using the following symbol: Hg. All elements have their own unique symbols.

In most cases, test takers have access to a table that offers definitions for each symbol. At times, the symbols have units or need units attached to them in order to explain the measure of a particular property. The International System of Units (SI) is usually used for science. Some of the most frequently used standard measures include: the meter (m) for length, the kilogram (kg) for mass, the ampere (A) for electric current, the kelvin (K) for temperature, and the mole (mol) for the amount of a substance. It never hurts to familiarize oneself with these commonly repeated symbols in scientific texts.

Using Scientific Words to Express Science Information

Numbers and symbols alone, however, do not fully convey scientific knowledge. Scientists rely heavily on specialized words to express scientific information. Presenting graphs, tables, and charts without any words would create a lot of confusion. Scientists use words to enhance the numbers and symbols they record and evaluate. Scientific literacy, therefore, requires a specialized synthesis of numbers, symbols, and scientific words. Many of these words are not used much outside the field of science.

Take the Linnaean system of classification as an example. It was created by Carl Linnaeus, a Swedish scientist working in the 18th century. This classification system helps scientists organize all living organisms into different phyla, classes, orders, families, genera, and species. The Linnaean scheme for organizing living organisms is still in use today. However, the entire scheme is founded upon a highly specialized naming system that draws on an archaic Latin language. The American coyote for example carries a common name—most people refer to it simply as the "coyote," whether they are using French, Spanish, or English. However, its taxonomic name in the Linnaean system is *Canis latrans*. A difficult name like *Canis latrans* illustrates just how specialized scientific words can be. For someone taking the GED, it is not necessary to memorize the specialized names of all species and all chemical compounds. However, it is certainly important to understand that this highly specialized language may emerge within a passage to express scientific information. Together, along with symbols and numbers, these specialized words help create an entire scientific language. Scientific literacy at the GED level entails comprehending that such complex terms exist, and using context clues, dictionary definition keys, and other literacy-based tools to understand their meaning within the broader scope of the passage and its related assessment items.

Designing and Interpreting Science Experiments

Science Investigations

Designing a Science Investigation

Human beings are, by nature, very curious. Since long before the scientific method was established, people have been making and predicting outcomes, manipulating the physical world to create extraordinary things—from the first man-made fire in 6000 B.C.E. to the satellite that orbited Pluto in 2016. Although the history of the scientific method is sporadic and attributed to many different people, it remains the most reliable way to obtain and utilize knowledge about the observable universe. Designing a science investigation is based on the scientific method, which consists of the following steps:

- Make an observation
- Create a question
- Form a hypothesis
- Conduct an experiment
- Collect and analyze data
- Form a conclusion

The first step is to identify a problem based on an observation—the who, what, when, where, why, and how. An **observation** is the analysis of information using basic human senses: sight, sound, touch, taste, and smell. Observations can be two different types—qualitative or quantitative. A **qualitative observation** describes what is being observed, such as the color of a house or the smell of a flower. **Quantitative observations** measure what is being observed, such as the number of windows on a house or the intensity of a flower's smell on a scale of 1–5.

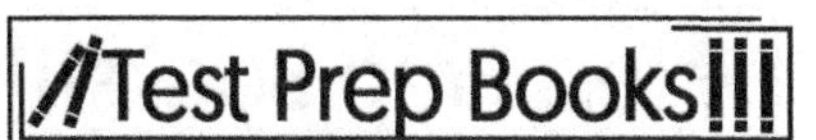

Observations lead to the identification of a problem, also called an **inference**. For example, if a fire truck is barreling down a busy street, the inferences could be:

- There's a fire.
- Someone is hurt.
- Some kid pulled the fire alarm at a local school.

Inferences are logical predictions based on experience or education that lead to the formation of a hypothesis.

Forming and Testing a Hypothesis

A hypothesis is a testable explanation of an observed scenario and is presented in the form of a statement. It's an attempt to answer a question based on an observation, and it allows a scientist to predict an outcome. A hypothesis makes assumptions on the relationship between two different variables, and answers the question: "If I do this, what happens to that?"

In order to form a hypothesis, there must be an independent variable and a dependent variable that can be measured. The **independent variable** is the variable that is manipulated, and the **dependent variable** is the result of the change.

For example, suppose a student wants to know how light affects plant growth. Based upon what he or she already knows, the student proposes (hypothesizes) that the more light to which a plant is exposed, the faster it will grow.

- Observation: Plants exposed to lots of light seem to grow taller.
- Question: Will plants grow faster if there's more light available?
- Hypothesis: The more light the plant has, the faster it will grow.
- Independent variable: The amount of time exposed to light (able to be manipulated)
- Dependent variable: Plant growth (the result of the manipulation)

Once a hypothesis has been formed, it must be tested to determine whether it's true or false. (How to test a hypothesis is described in a subsequent section.) After it has been tested and validated as true over and over, then a hypothesis can develop into a theory, model, or law.

Experimental Design

To test a hypothesis, one must conduct a carefully designed experiment. There are four basic requirements that must be present for an experiment to be valid:

- A control
- Variables
- A constant
- Repeated and collected data

The control is a standard to which the resultant findings are compared. It's the baseline measurement that allows for scientists to determine whether the results are positive or negative. For the example of light affecting plant growth, the control may be a plant that receives no light at all.

The independent variable is manipulated (a good way to remember this is I manipulate the Independent variable), and the dependent variable is the result of changes to the independent variable. In the plant example, the independent variable is the amount of time exposed to light, and the dependent variable is the resulting growth (or lack thereof) of the plant. For this experiment, there may be three plants—one that receives a minimal amount of light, the control, and one that receives a lot of light.

Finally, there must be constants in an experiment. A constant is an element of the experiment that remains unchanged. Constants are extremely important in minimizing inconsistencies within the experiment that may lead to results outside the parameters of the hypothesis. For example, some constants in the above case are that all plants receive the same amount of water, all plants are potted in the same kind of soil, the species of the plant used in each condition is the same, and the plants are stored at the same temperature. If, for instance, the plants received different amounts of water as well as light, it would be impossible to tell whether the plants responded to changes in water or light.

Once the experiment begins, a disciplined scientist must always record the observations in meticulous detail, usually in a journal. A good journal includes dates, times, and exact values of both variables and constants. Upon reading this journal, a different scientist should be able to clearly understand the experiment and recreate it exactly. The journal includes all collected data, or any observed changes. In this case, the data is rates of plant growth, as well as any other phenomena that occurred as a result of the experiment. A well-designed experiment also includes repetition in order to get the most accurate possible readings and to account for any errors, so several trials may be conducted.

Even in the presence of diligent constants, there are an infinite number of reasons that an experiment can (and will) go wrong, known as sources of error. All experimental results are inherently accepted as imperfect, if ever so slightly, because experiments are conducted by human beings, and no instrument can measure anything perfectly. The goal of scientists is to minimize those errors to the best of their ability.

Identifying and Explaining Independent and Dependent Variables

In an experiment, variables are the key to analyzing data, especially when data is in a graph or table. Variables can represent anything, including objects, conditions, events, and amounts of time.

Covariance is a general term referring to how two variables move in relation to each other. Take for example an employee that gets paid by the hour. For them, hours worked and total pay have a positive covariance. As hours worked increases, so does pay.

Constant variables remain unchanged by the scientist across all trials. Because they are held constant for all groups in an experiment, they aren't being measured in the experiment, and they are usually ignored. Constants can either be controlled by the scientist directly like the nutrition, water, and sunlight given to plants, or they can be selected by the scientist specifically for an experiment like using a certain animal species or choosing to investigate only people of a certain age group.

Independent variables are also controlled by the scientist, but they are the same only for each group or trial in the experiment. Each group might be composed of students that all have the same color of car or each trial may be run on different soda brands. The independent variable of an experiment is what is being indirectly tested because it causes change in the dependent variables.

Dependent variables experience change caused by the independent variable and are what is being measured or observed. For example, college acceptance rates could be a dependent variable of an experiment that sorted a large sample of high school students by an independent variable such as test

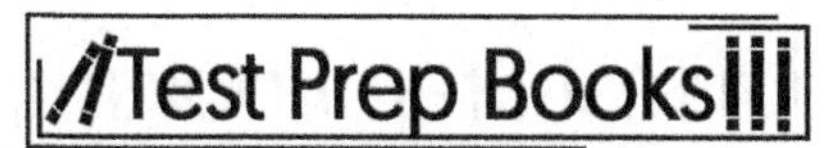

scores. In this experiment, the scientist groups the high school students by the independent variable (test scores) to see how it affects the dependent variable (their college acceptance rates).

Note that most variables can be held constant in one experiment, but also serve as the independent variable or a dependent variable in another. For example, when testing how well a fertilizer aids plant growth, its amount of sunlight should be held constant for each group of plants, but if the experiment is being done to determine the proper amount of sunlight a plant should have, the amount of sunlight is an independent variable because it is necessarily changed for each group of plants.

Identifying and Improving Hypotheses for Science Investigations

When presented with fundamental, scientific concepts, it is important to read for understanding. The most basic skill in achieving this literacy is to understand the concept of hypothesis and, moreover, to be able to identify it in a particular passage. A **hypothesis** is a proposed idea that needs further investigation in order to be proven true or false. While it can be considered an educated guess, a hypothesis goes more in depth in its attempt to explain something that is not currently accepted within scientific theory. It requires further experimentation and data gathering to test its validity and is subject to change, based on scientifically conducted test results. Being able to read a science passage and understand its main purpose, including any hypotheses, helps the test taker understand data-driven evidence. It helps the test taker to be able to correctly answer questions about the science excerpt they are asked to read.

When reading to identify a hypothesis, a test taker should ask, "What is the passage trying to establish? What is the passage's main idea? What evidence does the passage contain that either supports or refutes this idea?" Asking oneself these questions will help identify a hypothesis. Additionally, hypotheses are logical statements that are testable and use very precise language.

Review the following hypothesis example:

> Consuming excess sugar in the form of beverages has a greater impact on childhood obesity and subsequent weight gain than excessive sugar from food.

While this is likely a true statement, it is still only a conceptual idea in a text passage regarding how sugar consumption affects childhood obesity, unless the passage also contains tested data that either proves or disproves the statement. A test taker could expect the rest of the passage to cite data proving that children who drink empty calories and don't exercise will, in fact, be obese.

A hypothesis goes further in that, given its ability to be proven or disproven, it may result in further hypotheses that require extended research. For example, the hypothesis regarding sugar consumption in drinks, after undergoing rigorous testing, may lead scientists to state another hypothesis such as the following:

> Consuming excess sugar in the form of beverages as opposed to food items is a habit found in mostly sedentary children.

This new, working hypothesis further focuses not just on the source of an excess of calories, but tries an "educated guess" that empty caloric intake has a direct, subsequent impact on physical behavior.

The data-driven chart below is similar to an illustration a test taker might see in relation to the hypothesis on sugar consumption in children:

Behaviors of Healthy and Unhealthy Kids

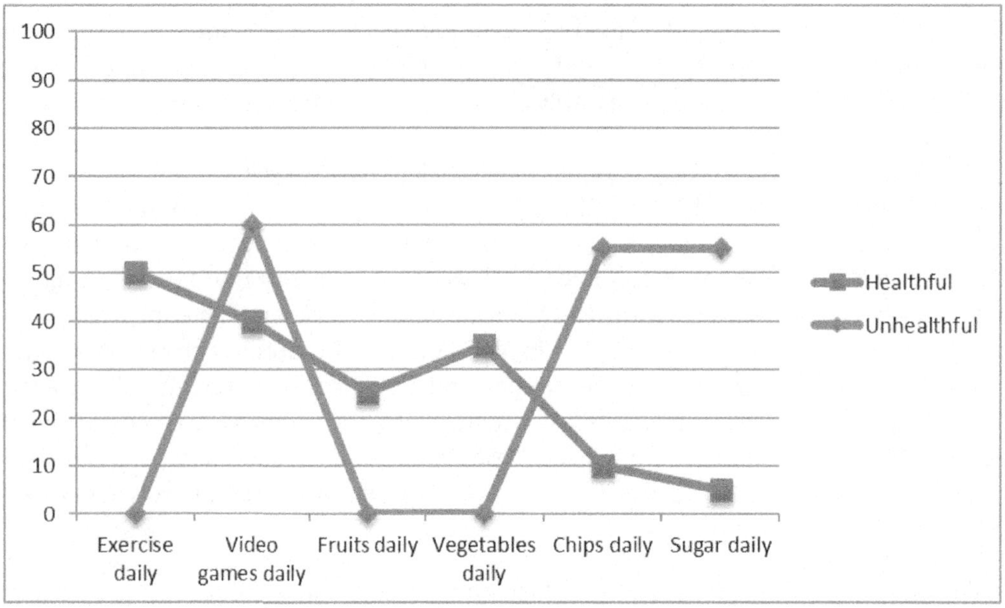

100
90
80
70
60
50
40
30
20
10
0
Exercise daily
Video games daily
Fruits daily
Vegetables daily
Chips daily
Sugar daily
Healthful
Unhealthful

While this guide will address other data-driven passages a test taker could expect to see within a given science excerpt, note that the hypothesis regarding childhood sugar intake and rate of exercise has undergone scientific examination and yielded results that support its truth.

When reading a science passage to determine its hypothesis, a test taker should look for a concept that attempts to explain a phenomenon, is testable, is logical, is precisely worded, and yields data-driven results. The test taker should scan the presented passage for any word or data-driven clues that will help identify the hypothesis, and then be able to correctly answer test questions regarding the hypothesis by using their critical thinking skills.

Identifying Possible Errors in a Science Investigation and Changing the Design to Correct Them

For a hypothesis to be proven true or false, all experiments are subject to multiple trials in order to verify accuracy and precision. A measurement is **accurate** if the observed value is close to the "true value." For example, if someone measured the pH of water at 6.9, this measurement would be considered accurate (the pH of water is 7). On the other hand, a measurement is **precise** if the measurements are consistent—that is, if they are reproducible. If someone had a series of values for a pH of water that were 6.9, 7.0, 7.2, and 7.3, their measurements would not be precise. However, if all measured values were 6.9, or the average of these values was 6.9 with a small range, then their measurements would be precise. Measurements can fall into the following categories:

- Both accurate and precise
- Accurate but not precise
- Precise but not accurate
- Neither accurate nor precise

The accuracy and precision of observed values most frequently correspond to the amount of error present in the experiment. Aside from general carelessness, there are two primary types of error: random and systematic. **Random errors** are unpredictable variations in the experiment that occur by chance. They can be difficult to detect, but they can often be nullified using a statistical analysis and minimized by taking repeated measurements and taking an average. **Systematic errors** occur when there are imperfections in the design of the experiment itself—usually errors that affect the accuracy of the measurements. These errors can be minimized by using the most accurate equipment available and by taking proper care of instruments and measuring techniques. Common examples of errors are listed below.

Random	Systematic
Environmental factors (random changes in vibration, temperature, humidity, etc.)	Poorly maintained instruments
	Old or out-of-date instruments
Differences in instrument use among scientists	Faulty calibration of instruments
Errors in judgment—can be affected by state of mind	Reading the instruments at an angle (parallax error) or other faulty reading errors
Incorrectly recorded observations	Not accounting for lag time

The most basic method to account for the possibility of errors is to take an average (also called a **mean**) of all observed values. To do so, one must divide the number of measurements taken from the sum of all measurements.

$$\frac{Sum\ of Measurements}{Total\ \#\ of\ Measurements}$$

For the above example of the pH values, the average is calculated by finding the sum of the pH values ascertained and dividing by the number of values recorded.

$$\frac{6.9 + 7.0 + 7.2 + 7.3}{4} = 7.1$$

The more observations recorded, the greater the precision. It's important to first assess the accuracy of measurements before proceeding to collect multiple trials of data. If a particular trial results in measurements that are vastly different from the average, it may indicate that a random or systematic error occurred during the trial. When this happens, a scientist might decide to "throw out" the trial and run the experiment again.

Identifying the Strengths and Weaknesses of Different Types of Science Investigations

In order to address the strengths and weaknesses of different types of scientific investigations, GED test takers must first strengthen their capacity for scientific literacy and numeracy. It is important to familiarize oneself with methods for decoding highly specialized scientific terms, formulas, and symbols. Additionally, test takers can take the following suggestions to help identify unique weaknesses and strengths in different types of scientific investigations:

- Using critical analysis, test takers begin asking questions about the accuracy of the methods used to collect, analyze, and display data. They should carefully look at text and graphics that show scientific findings.

- Test takers should determine whether or not the words, data, and symbols provided by the author actually offer information that is relevant for testing a hypothesis or making an inference.
- When two or more passages on the same topic are offered, test takers should cross-analyze the findings to determine what data is accurate or relevant and which findings are most objective.
- Although scientific research strives for objectivity, test takers should highlight any subjective biases that may be embedded in a text. In particular, they should be aware of certain historical or ethical biases that might appear.
- Test takers should double check for any computational inaccuracies.
- Test takers should make suggestions for better ways to present the findings in both texts and visual images.

Using Evidence to Draw Conclusions or Make Predictions

Deciding Whether Conclusions are Supported by Data

Drawing conclusions is the process of analyzing patterns in data and determining whether the relationship is **causal**, meaning that one variable is the cause of the change in the other. There are many correlations that aren't casual, such as a city where alcohol sales increase as crime increases. Although there's a positive correlation between the two, crime may not be the factor that causes an increase in alcohol sales. There could be other factors, such as an increase in unemployment, which increases both alcohol sales and crime rates. Although crime and alcohol sales are positively correlated, they aren't causally correlated.

For this reason, it's important for scientists to carefully design their experiments with all the appropriate constants to ensure that the relationships are causal. If a relationship is determined to be causal by isolating the variables from all other factors, only then can conclusions be drawn based on data. In the plant growth experiment, the conclusion is that light affects plant growth because the data shows they are causally correlated since the two variables were entirely isolated.

Making Conclusions Based on Data

The Science section of the GED will contain one data-driven science passage that require the test taker to examine evidence within a particular type of graphic. The test taker will then be required to interpret the data and answer questions demonstrating their ability to draw logical conclusions.

In general, there are two types of data: qualitative and quantitative. Science passages may contain both, but simply put, **quantitative** data is reflected numerically and qualitative is not. **Qualitative** data is based on its qualities. In other words, qualitative data tends to present information more in subjective generalities (for example, relating to size or appearance). Quantitative data is based on numerical findings such as percentages. Quantitative data will be described in numerical terms. While both types of data are valid, the test taker will more likely be faced with having to interpret quantitative data through one or more graphic(s), and then be required to answer questions regarding the numerical data. A test taker should take the time to learn the skills it takes to interpret quantitative data so that they can make sound conclusions.

An example of a line graph is as follows:

Cell Phone Use in Kiteville, 2000-2006

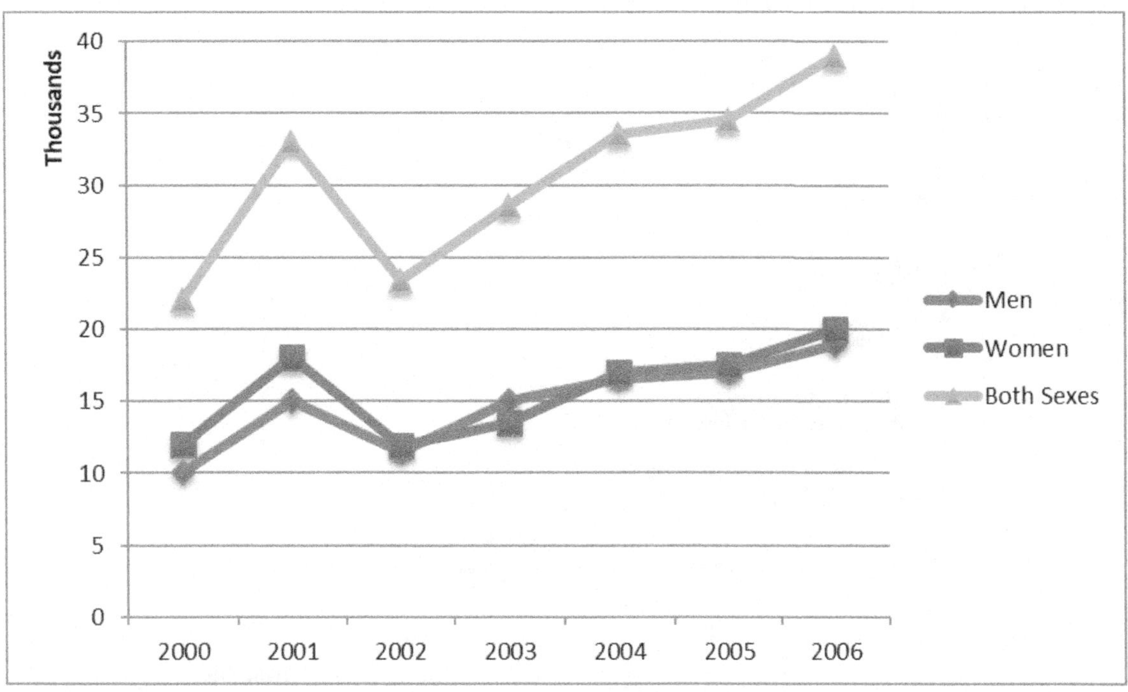

A **line graph** presents quantitative data on both horizontal (side to side) and vertical (up and down) axes. It requires the test taker to examine information across varying data points. When reading a line graph, a test taker should pay attention to any headings, as these indicate a title for the data it contains. In the above example, the test taker can anticipate the line graph contains numerical data regarding the use of cellphones during a certain time period. From there, a test taker should carefully read any outlying words or phrases that will help determine the meaning of data within the horizontal and vertical axes. In this example, the vertical axis displays the total number of people in increments of 5,000. Horizontally, the graph displays yearly markers, and the reader can assume the data presented accounts for a full calendar year. In addition, the line graph also uses different shapes to mark its data points. Some data points represent the number of men. Some data points represent the number of women, and a third type of data point represents the number of both sexes combined.

A test taker may be asked to read and interpret the graph's data, then answer questions about it. For example, the test may ask, *In which year did men seem to decrease cellphone use?* then require the test taker to select the correct answer. Similarly, the test taker may encounter a question such as *Which year yielded the highest number of cellphone users overall?* The test taker should be able to identify the correct answer as 2006.

A **bar graph** presents quantitative data through the use of lines or rectangles. The height and length of these lines or rectangles corresponds to the magnitude of the numerical data for that particular category or attribute. The data presented may represent information over time, showing shaded data over time or over other defined parameters. A bar graph will also utilize horizontal and vertical axes. An example of a bar graph is as follows:

Population Growth in Major U.S. Cities

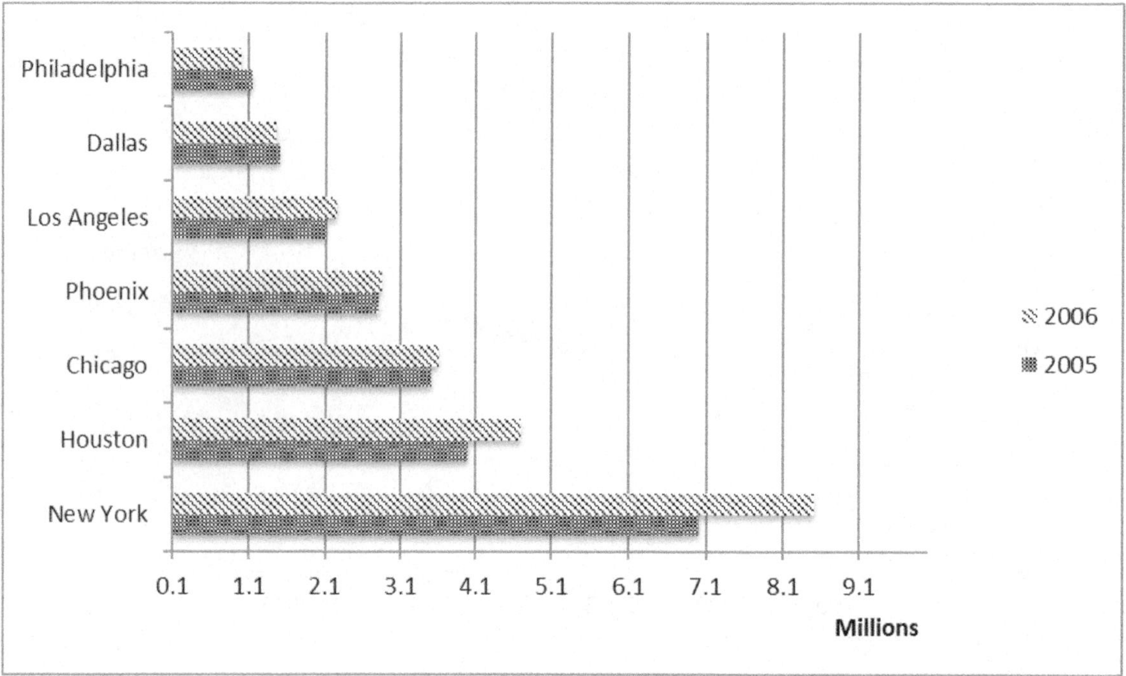

Reading the data in a bar graph is similar to the skills needed to read a line graph. The test taker should read and comprehend all heading information, as well as information provided along the horizontal and vertical axes. Note that the graph pertains to the population of some major U.S. cities. The "values" of these cities can be found along the left side of the graph, along the vertical axis. The population values can be found along the horizontal axes. Notice how the graph uses shaded bars to depict the change in population over time, as the heading indicates. Therefore, when the test taker is asked a question such as, *Which major U.S. city experienced the greatest amount of population growth during the depicted two year cycle,* the reader should be able to determine a correct answer of New York. It is important to pay particular attention to color, length, data points, and both axes, as well as any outlying header information in order to be able to answer graph-like test questions.

A **circle graph** (also sometimes referred to as a **pie chart**) presents quantitative data in the form of a circle. The same principles apply: the test taker should look for numerical data within the confines of the circle itself but also note any outlying information that may be included in a header, footer, or to the side of the circle. A circle graph will not depict horizontal or vertical axis information but will instead rely

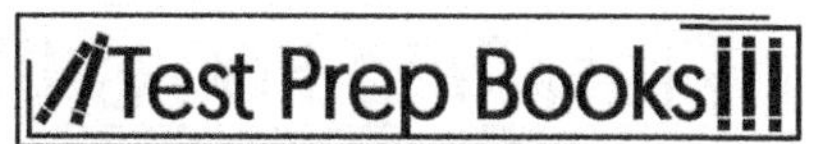

on the reader's ability to visually take note of segmented circle pieces and apply information accordingly. An example of a circle graph is as follows:

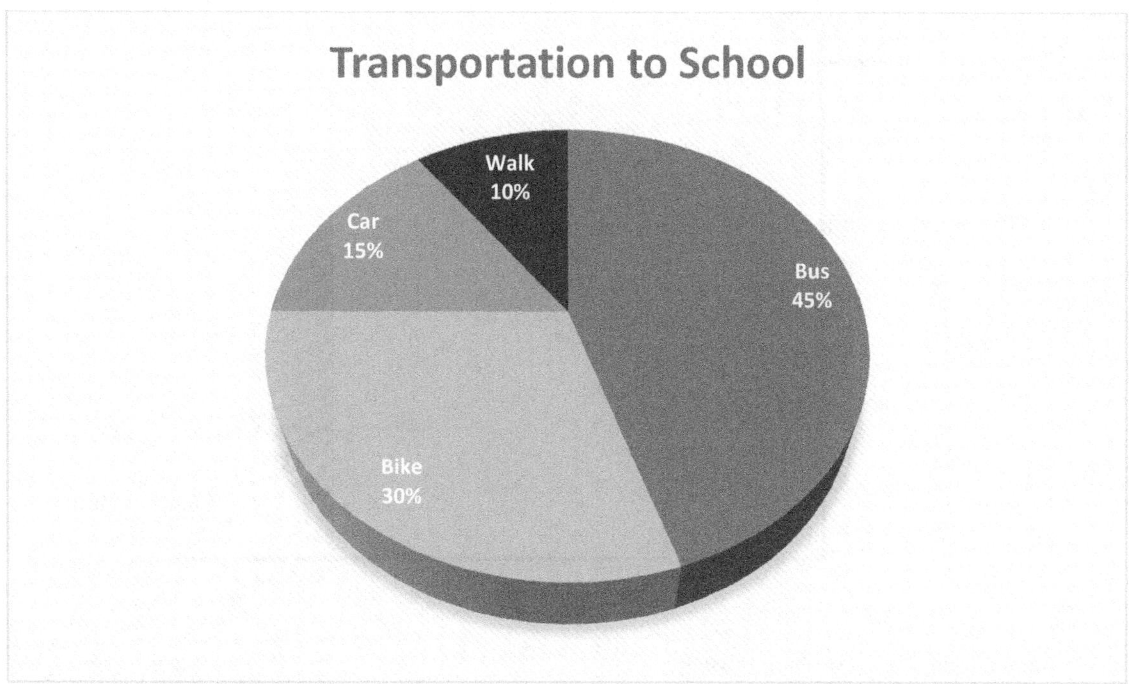

Notice the heading "Transportation to School." This should indicate to the test taker that the topic of the circle graph is how people traditionally get to school. To the right of the graph, the reader should comprehend that the data percentages contained within it directly correspond to the method of transportation. In this graph, the data is represented through the use shades and pattern. Each transportation method has its own shade. For example, if the test taker was then asked, *Which method of school transportation is most widely utilized,* the reader should be able to identify school bus as the correct answer.

Be wary of test questions that ask test takers to draw conclusions based on information that is not present. For example, it is not possible to determine, given the parameters of this circle graph, whether the population presented is of a particular gender or ethnic group. This graph does not represent data from a particular city or school district. It does not distinguish between student grade levels and, although the reader could infer that the typical student must be of driving age if cars are included, this is not necessarily the case. Elementary school students may rely on parents or others to drive them by personal methods. Therefore, do not read too much into data that is not presented. Only rely on the quantitative data that is presented in order to answer questions.

A **scatter plot** or **scatter diagram** is a graph that depicts quantitative data across plotted points. It will involve at least two sets of data. It will also involve horizontal and vertical axes.

An example of a scatter plot is as follows:

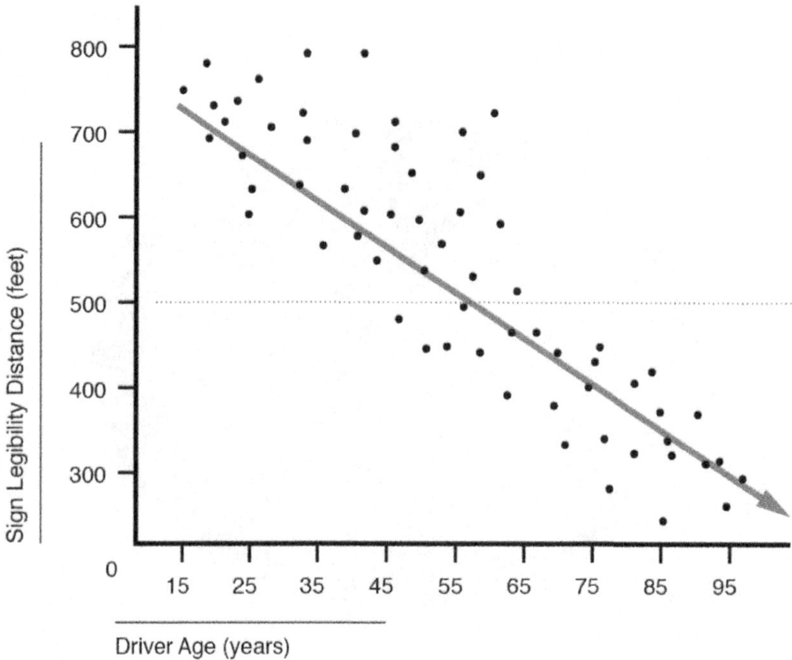

The skills needed to address a scatter plot are essentially the same as in other graph examples. Note any topic headings, as well as horizontal or vertical axis information. In the sample above, the reader can determine the data addresses a driver's ability to correctly and legibly read road signs as related to their age. Again, note the information that is absent. The test taker is not given the data to assess a time period, location, or driver gender. It simply requires the reader to note an approximate age to the ability to correctly identify road signs from a distance measured in feet. Notice that the overall graph also displays a trend. In this case, the data indicates a negative one and possibly supports the hypothesis that as a driver ages, their ability to correctly read a road sign at over 500 feet tends to decline over time. If the test taker were to be asked, *At what approximation in feet does a sixteen-year-old driver correctly see and read a street sign,* the answer would be the option closest to 500 feet.

Reading and examining scientific data in excerpts involves all of a reader's contextual reading, data interpretation, drawing logical conclusions based only on the information presented, and their application of critical thinking skills across a set of interpretive questions. Thorough comprehension and attention to detail is necessary to achieve test success.

Making Predictions Based on Data

Science is amazing in that it actually allows people to predict the future and see into the past with a certain degree of accuracy. Using numerical correlations created from quantitative data, one can see in a general way what will happen to *y* when something happens to *x*.

The best way to get a useful overview of quantitative data to facilitate predictions is to use a scatter plot, which plots each data point individually. As shown above, there may be slight fluctuations from the correlation line, so one may not be able to predict what happens with *every* change, but he or she will be able to have a general idea of what is going to happen to y with a change in x. To demonstrate, the graph with a line of best fit created from the plant growth experiment is below.

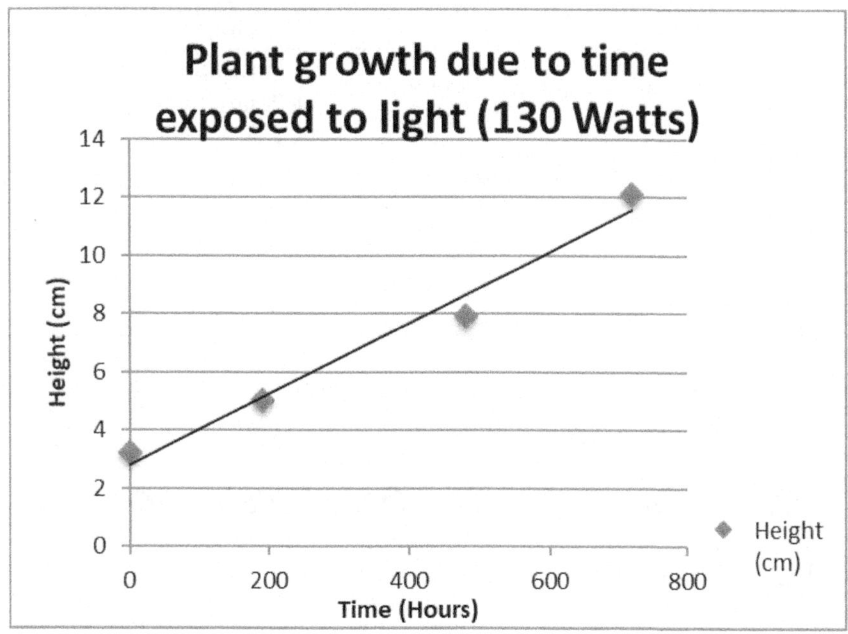

Using the trend line within the data, one can estimate what will happen to plant growth at a given length of time exposed to light. For example, it can be estimated that with 700 hours of time, the plant is expected to grow to a height of about 11 cm. The plant may not grow to exactly 11 cm, but it will likely grow to about that height based on previous data. This process allows scientists to draw conclusions based on data.

Science Theories and Processes

Theories, models, and laws have one thing in common: *they develop on the basis of scientific evidence that has been tested and verified by multiple researchers on many different occasions*. Listed below are their exact definitions:

- **Theory:** An explanation of natural patterns or occurrences—i.e., the theory of relativity, the kinetic theory of gases, etc.
- **Model:** A representation of a natural pattern or occurrence that's difficult or impossible to experience directly, usually in the form of a picture or 3-D representation—i.e., Bohr's atomic model, the double-helix model of DNA, etc.
- **Law:** A mathematical or concise description of a pattern or occurrence in the observable universe—i.e., Newton's law of gravity, the laws of thermodynamics, etc.

The terms *theory, model,* and *law* are often used interchangeably in the sciences, although there's an essential difference: theories and models are used to explain *how* and *why* something happens, while laws describe exactly *what* happens. A common misconception is that theories develop into laws. But theories and models never become laws because they inherently describe different things.

Type	Function	Examples
Theory	To explain how and why something happens	Einstein's Theory of Special Relativity The Big Bang Theory
Model	To represent how and why something happens	A graphical model or drawing of an atom
Laws	To describe exactly what happens	$E = mc^2$ $F = ma$ $PV = nRT$

In order to ensure that scientific theories are consistent, scientists continually gather information and evidence on existing theories to improve their accuracy.

Using Numbers and Graphics in Science

Science Formulas and Statistics

Applying Science Formulas

Scientific inquiry includes the fields of chemistry and physics. It incorporates mathematical problems, which are described with science formulas. Science formulas cannot be used haphazardly. In fact, these science formulas have very specific standards for use. These formulas stand at the intersection of mathematics and science. And, like math, science extracts all of its meaning through its specificity. On any standardized science test, the biggest challenge is knowing when to employ a particular science formula. All formulas are provided on the examination. Thus, the test taker does not need to memorize these formulas; they just need to use the formulas correctly.

Take the dynamics of motion as an example. In science, dynamics is the study of the relationship between motion and the forces affecting motion. In science, there is a formula that is universally used for force: F = m/a. This equation is shorthand for force (F) equals mass (m) divided by (/) acceleration (a). This equation is used to describe the relationship with three components of science: force, mass, and acceleration. For instance, an object remains at rest unless the force (F) is strong enough to move the mass (m) and cause the object to accelerate (a).

However, the equation F = m/a would NOT be helpful for figuring out the weight of an object. The weight of an object demands another formula: $W = m \times g$. This formula is shorthand for weight (W) equals mass (m) times (×) gravity (g). Force and weight have their own scientific formulas. The formulas do not need to be memorized, but every test taker needs to know *when* and *how* to use a particular formula. Otherwise, their results will be incorrect.

Using Statistics to Describe Science Data

The most common relationship examined in an experiment is between two variables (independent and dependent), most often referred to as *x* and *y*. The independent variable (*x*) is displayed on the horizontal axis of a coordinate plane, and the dependent variable (*y*) is displayed on the vertical axis.

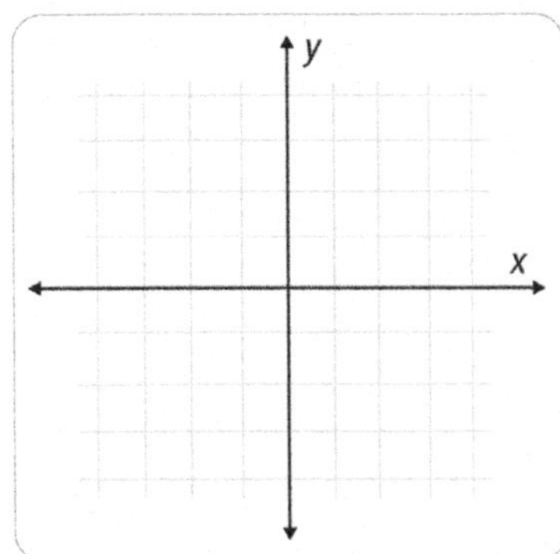

The placement of the variables in this way provides a visual representation of what happens to *y* when *x* is manipulated. In analyzing trends, *x* is used to predict *y*, and since *y* is the result of *x*, then *x* comes before *y* in time. For example, in the experiment on plant growth, the hours the plant was exposed to light had to happen before growth could occur.

When analyzing the relationship between the variables, scientists will consider the following questions:

- Does *y* increase or decrease with *x*, or does it do both?
- If it increases or decreases, how fast does it change?
- Does *y* stay steady through certain values of *x*, or does it jump dramatically from one value to the other?
- Is there a strong relationship? If given a value of *x*, can one predict what will happen to *y*?

If, in general, *y* increases as *x* increases, or *y* decreases and *x* decreases, it is known as a **positive correlation**. The data from the plant experiment show a positive correlation—as time exposed to light (*x*) increases, plant growth (*y*) increases. If the variables trend in the opposite direction of each other—that is, if *y* increases as *x* decreases, or vice versa—it is called a **negative correlation**. If there doesn't seem to be any visible pattern to the relationship, it is referred to as **no** or **zero correlation**.

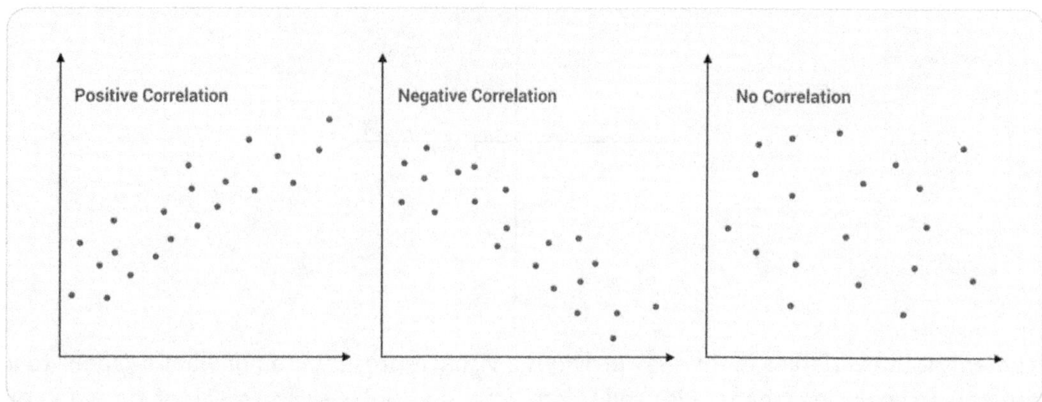

Experiments that show positive or negative correlation within their data indicate that the variables are related. This allows scientists to make predictions based on the data.

Probability and Sampling in Science

Determining the Probability or Likelihood of Something Happening

A **simple event** consists of only one outcome. The most popular simple event is flipping a coin, which results in either heads or tails. A **compound event** results in more than one outcome and consists of more than one simple event. An example of a compound event is flipping a coin while tossing a die. The result is either heads or tails on the coin and a number from one to six on the die. The probability of a simple event is calculated by dividing the number of possible outcomes by the total number of outcomes. Therefore, the probability of obtaining heads on a coin is $\frac{1}{2}$, and the probability of rolling a 6 on a die is $\frac{1}{6}$. The probability of compound events is calculated using the basic idea of the probability of simple events. If the two events are independent, the probability of one outcome is equal to the product of the probabilities of each simple event. For example, the probability of obtaining heads on a coin and rolling a 6 is equal to:

$$\frac{1}{2} \times \frac{1}{6} = \frac{1}{12}$$

The probability of either A or B occurring is equal to the sum of the probabilities minus the probability that both A and B will occur. Therefore, the probability of obtaining either heads on a coin or rolling a 6 on a die is:

$$\frac{1}{2} + \frac{1}{6} - \frac{1}{12} = \frac{7}{12}$$

The two events aren't mutually exclusive because they can happen at the same time. If two events are mutually exclusive, and the probability of both events occurring at the same time is zero, the probability

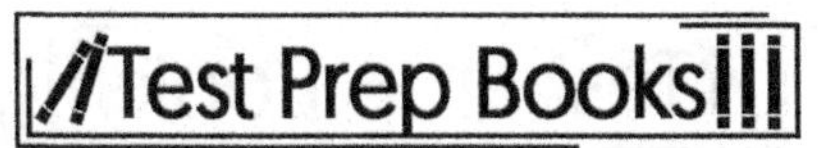

of event A or B occurring equals the sum of both probabilities. An example of calculating the probability of two mutually exclusive events is determining the probability of pulling a king or a queen from a deck of cards. The two events cannot occur at the same time.

Using a Sample to Answer Science Questions

When conducting a scientific experiment, once a hypothesis is conceived, it is important for scientists and students to adequately test their hypothesis. In order to test a hypothesis, scientists and students must analyze a particular **sample** of the larger population. Every sample must be composed of two comparable groups: a treatment (or experimental) group and a control group. Control groups can be used to acquire baseline measurements for analysis. When conducting the experiment, the treatment groups are the ones affected by experimental manipulation. From this sample, scientists and students can compare relevant data from each group to test their hypothesis.

If the experimental manipulation is effective, then scientists and students notice evident differences in the data collected from each sub-sample. In some cases, when scientists are merely carrying out observations, they may not split the sample into any subgroups but instead try to create new sub-samples through observation and data collection. Regardless of the approach, these kinds of samples, whether physical or observatory, are necessary for conducting scientific research. For the GED, test takers should be aware of how scientists use these samples, how they display their results, and how they compare samples through qualitative and quantitative data. Additionally, they should be prepared to extrapolate findings from the sample, comparing it to the larger population or other subpopulations. This extrapolation helps test takers better understand whether the sample is a good representation of the larger population or comparative to other subpopulations.

Using Counting to Solve Science Problems

In some instances, test takers have to use counting in order to solve science problems. Because the subject is science, a lot of quantitative data is offered in the form of charts, graphs, and tables. Additionally, numbers are referred to in science passages. At times, problems can be solved by counting the quantitative data offered in the text, charts, graphs, or tables. For example, if the scientific experiment compares two sub-samples of a larger sample of animals exposed to nuclear radiation, then the test taker may have to compute or count the number of animals from each sub-sample that are impacted by the radiation. Alternatively, test takers may have to compute or count the total number of animals from the larger population impacted by radiation. The author may choose to illustrate their findings with just text, just graphics, or a combination of text and graphics. Basic mathematics come in handy whenever quantitative data is offered. Basic mathematics consists of addition, subtraction, multiplication, and division. Complex formulas are not needed in these cases, but often test takers have to convey their ability to do basic arithmetic computations.

Presenting Science Information Using Numbers, Symbols, and Graphics

Using Graphics to Display Science Information

Observations made during a scientific experiment are organized and presented as data. Data can be collected in a variety of ways, depending on the purpose of the experiment. In testing how light exposure affects plant growth, for example, the data collected would be changes in the height of the plant relative to the amount of light it received. The easiest way to organize collected data is to use a **data table**.

A data table always contains a title that relates the two variables in the experiment. Each column or row must contain the units of measurement in the heading only. See the below example (note: this is not actual data).

Plant Growth During Time Exposed to Light (130 Watts)	
Time (Hours)	Height (cm)
0	3.2
192	5.0
480	7.9
720	12.1

Data must be presented in a concise, coherent way. Most data are presented in graph form. The fundamental rule for creating a graph based on data is that the independent variable (i.e., amount of time exposed to light) is on the x-axis, and the dependent variable (i.e., height of plant) is on the y-axis.

There are many types of graphs that a person may choose to use depending on which best represents the data.

The **illustrative diagram** provides a graphic representation or picture of some process. Questions may address specific details of the process depicted in the graphic. For example, "At which stage of the sliding filament theory of muscle contraction does the physical length of the fibers shorten (and contract)?"

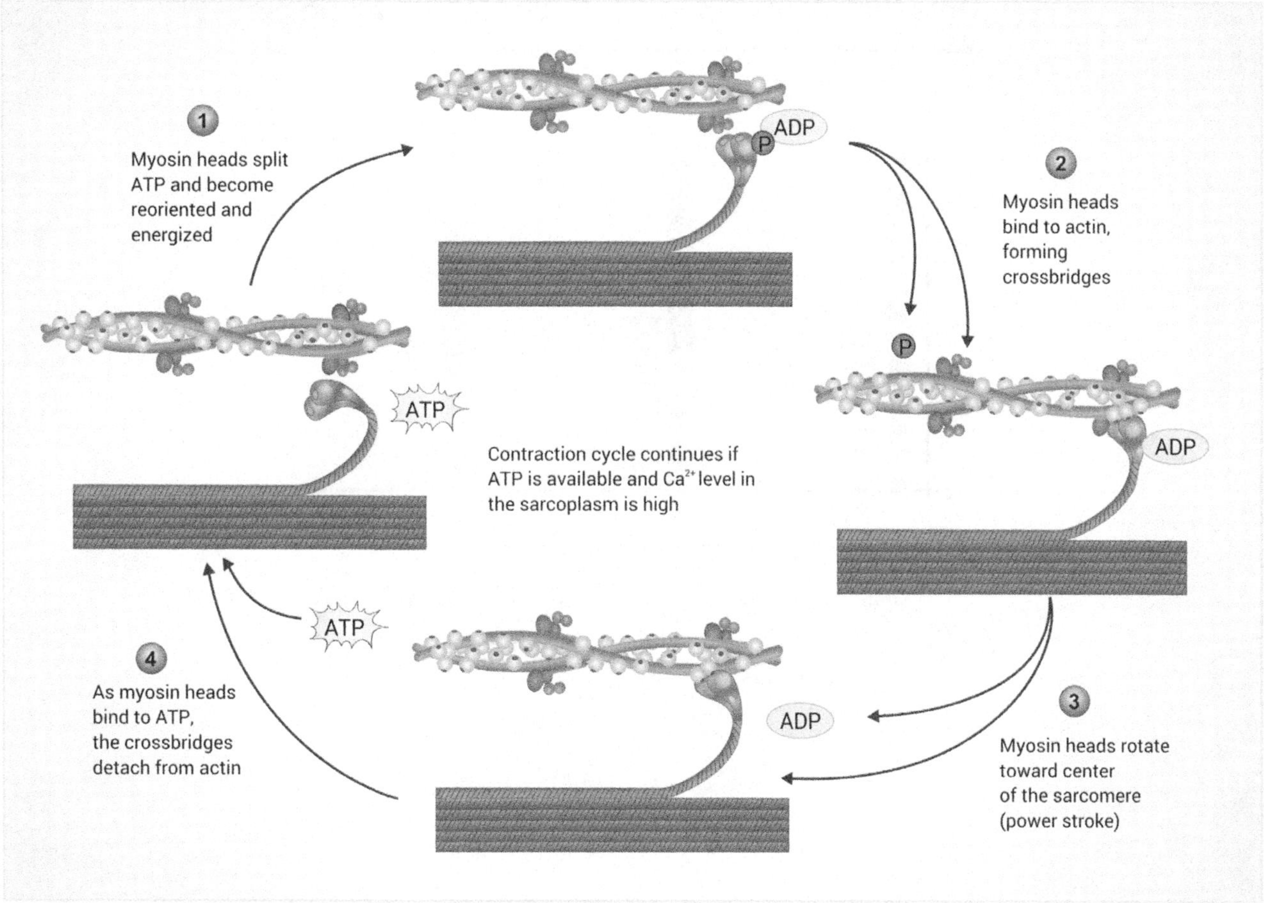

1 Myosin heads split ATP and become reoriented and energized

ADP P

2 Myosin heads bind to actin, forming crossbridges

P

ADP

ATP

Contraction cycle continues if ATP is available and Ca^{2+} level in the sarcoplasm is high

3 Myosin heads rotate toward center of the sarcomere (power stroke)

ADP

ATP

4 As myosin heads bind to ATP, the crossbridges detach from actin

Bar graphs depict the passage data as parallel lines of varying heights. GED bar graphs will be printed in black and white. Data may be oriented vertically or horizontally. Questions may ask, "During the fall season, in what habitat do bears spend the most time?"

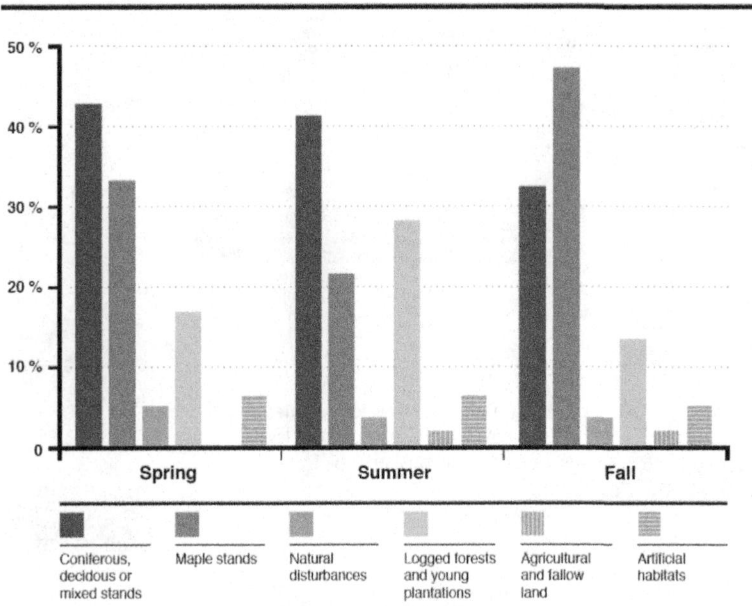

Bar graphs can also be horizontal, like the graph below.

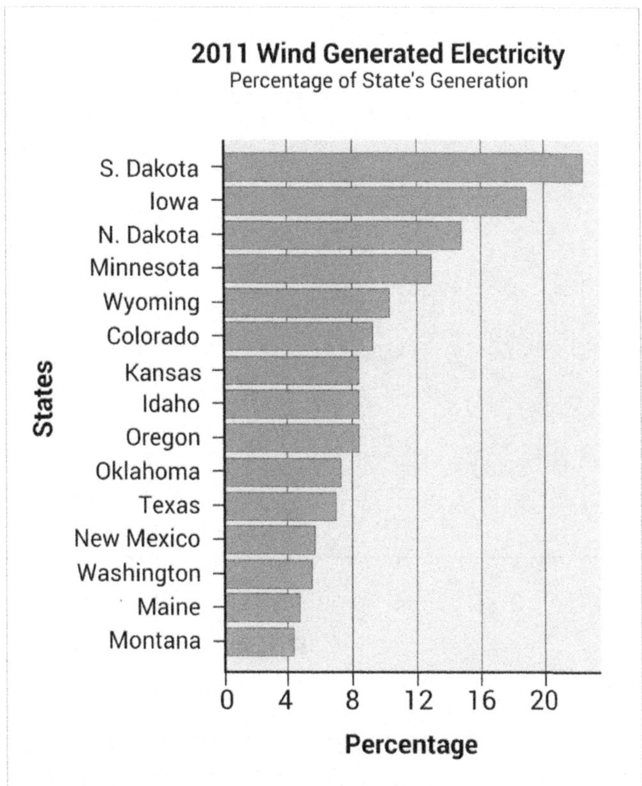

Recall that scatter plots provide a visual representation of the passage data along the x- and y-axes. This representation indicates the nature of the relationship between the two variables. It is important to note that correlation doesn't equal causation. The relationship may be linear, curvilinear, positive, negative, inverse, or there may be no relationship. Questions may ask "What is the relationship between x and y?"

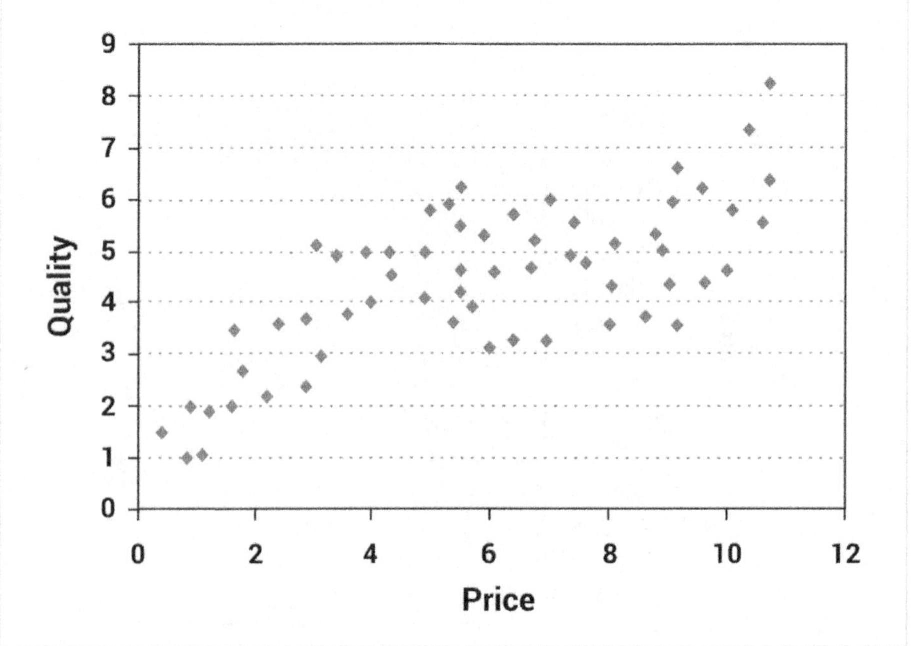

Line graphs are scatter plots that compare and contrast the relationships between two or more data sets. The horizontal axis represents the passage data sets that are compared over time. The vertical axis is the scale for measurement of that data. The scale points are equidistant from one another. There will always be a title for the line graph. Questions related to line graphs might ask," Which of the following conclusions is supported by the provided graph of tropical storms?"

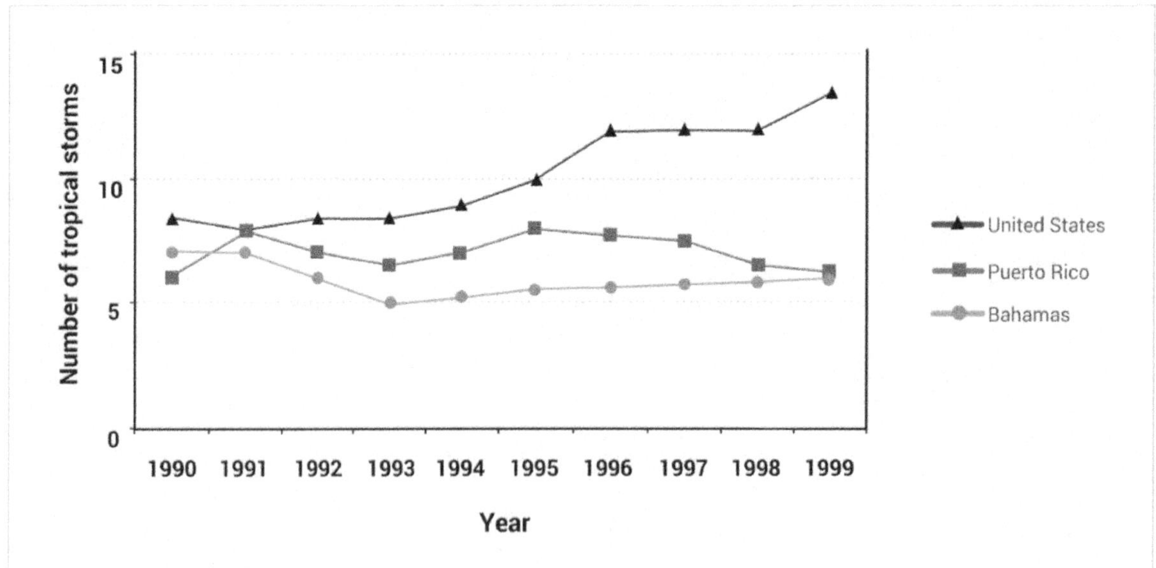

A **region graph** is a visual representation of the passage data set used to display the properties of a given substance under different conditions or at different points in time. Questions relating to this graph may ask, "According to the figure, what is the temperature range associated with liquid nitrogen?"

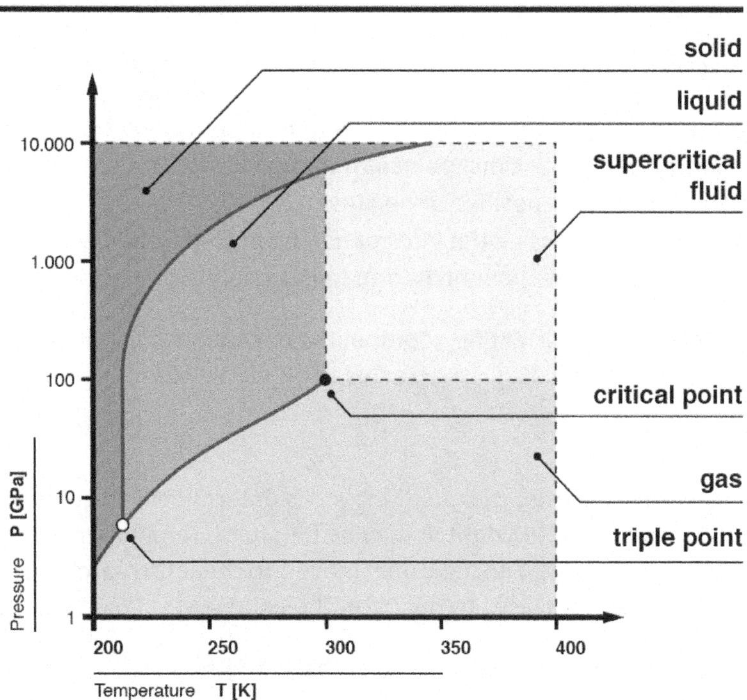

A pie or circle graph is used when the data sum to 100%, such as the percentage of students in each high school class interested in a trip to a local museum.

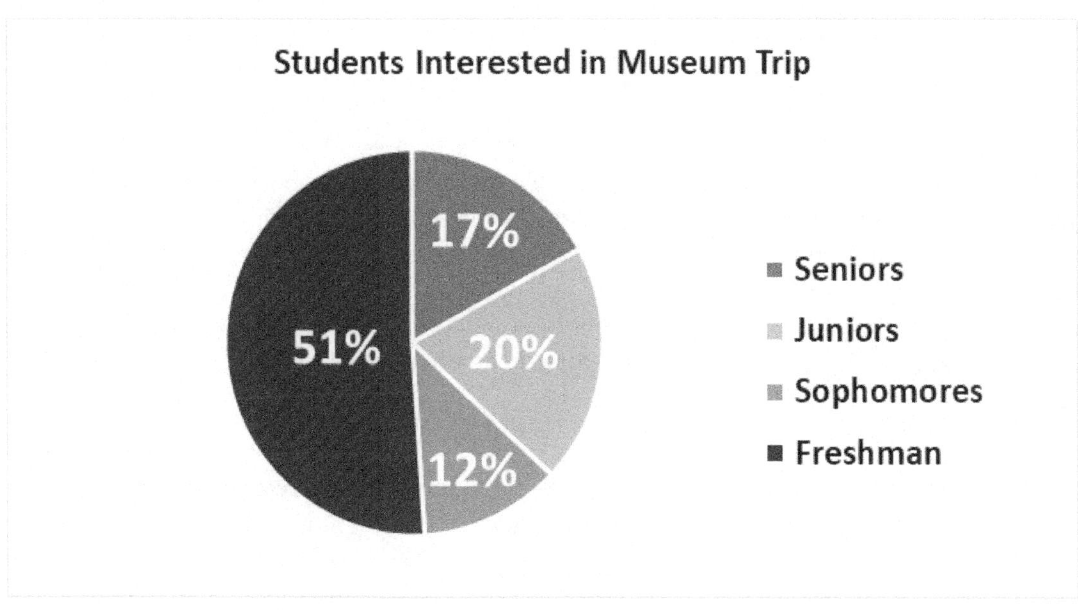

Using Numbers or Symbols to Display Science Information

Scientific Notation

Scientific notation is the conversion of extremely small or large numbers into a format that is easier to comprehend and manipulate. It changes the number into a product of two separate numbers: a digit term and an exponential term.

$$Scientific\ notation = digit\ term \times exponential\ term$$

To put a number into scientific notation, one should use the following steps:

- Move the decimal point to after the first non-zero number to find the digit number.
- Count how many places the decimal point was moved in step 1.
- Determine if the exponent is positive or negative.
- Create an exponential term using the information from steps 2 and 3.
- Combine the digit term and exponential term to get scientific notation.

For example, to put 0.0000098 into scientific notation, the decimal should be moved so that it lies between the last two numbers: 00000<u>9.8</u>. This creates the digit number:

$$9.8$$

Next, the number of places that the decimal point moved is determined; to get between the 9 and the 8, the decimal was moved six places to the right. It may be helpful to remember that a decimal moved to the right creates a negative exponent, and a decimal moved to the left creates a positive exponent. Because the decimal was moved six places to the right, the exponent is negative.

Now, the exponential term can be created by using the base 10 (this is *always* the base in scientific notation) and the number of places moved as the exponent, in this case:

$$10^{-6}$$

Finally, the digit term and the exponential term can be combined as a product. Therefore, the scientific notation for the number 0.0000098 is:

$$9.8 \times 10^{-6}$$

Significant Figures

Significant figures are numbers that contribute meaning to a measurement. Reporting values in significant figures reduces unnecessary numbers while increasing accuracy and minimizing confusion. For example, if a scale measures a sample to four significant figures, say, 12.56 grams, it would be inaccurate to write the number as 12.5600, because it very well may be more or less than 12.5600, but the scale cannot provide the measurement to that degree of precision. Therefore, all data must be presented with the number of figures that accurately reflect the precision of the measuring instrument.

There are rules for identifying the number of significant figures in a number:

- All non-zero digits are significant. For example, the number 23 has two significant figures, and the number 165.74 has five significant figures.

- Any zeros between two non-zero numbers are significant.
- For example, the number 203 has three significant figures: 2, 0, and 3.
- Leading zeros are never significant.
- For example, the value 0.000034 has two significant figures: 3 and 4.
- Trailing zeros (those following a non-zero number) are only significant after a decimal point.
- For example, the value 0.034500 has five significant figures: 3, 4, 5, 0, and 0.
- In numbers without decimals, trailing zeros may or may not be significant.
- For example, a number like 1,600 may have two or four significant figures, depending on if the number is precise to the nearest unit (four) or if it's just an estimate (two).

Scientific notation is often used to reduce numbers to significant figures. In scientific notation, the exponent doesn't count as a significant figure. For example, to reduce the number 0.0000098 (which has two significant figures) into a number that only has significant figures, it can be written in scientific notation;

$$9.8 \times 10^{-6}$$

where the 9 and the 8 are the only significant numbers. It's important to notice here that the number of significant figures remains the same, but one has an unnecessary number of zeros, and the other has none.

Different Ways in Which Scientific Information is Presented

The purpose of scientific experimentation is to gain knowledge and share it with others, particularly in the scientific field. In scientific practice, there are structures in place that allow scientists to share new ideas and groundbreaking discoveries with other scientists and potentially the public.

The following lists some outlets that scientists use to present information:

- **Scientific journals**: Scientific journals are magazines that publish scholarly articles relating to important discoveries or new research conducted by scientists. The articles in scientific journals are peer-reviewed, which means that other experts in the scientific community review the information for fallacies or bias before the information is published. Therefore, scholarly journals publish credible information written and reviewed by experts in the field.
- **Academic conferences**: In order to formally present new developments and meet up with others in the field, scientists frequently hold and attend scientific conferences. Presenting information is usually given by a panel or keynote speakers. Networking is an especially important part of academic conferences, as up-and-coming scientists have the opportunity to meet noteworthy experts in their field.
- **Popular media**: Communicating new research to the public is also an important way for scientists to gain acknowledgement and funding for their work. Scientists are able to reach a

large audience by using newspapers, magazines, or TV stations. A few examples of popular media outlets are *National Geographic*, *The New York Times*, and *CNN*, among others.

GED Science Questions

More so than simply presenting fact-based science questions that assess the test taker's knowledge of scientific concepts, the Science section of the GED primarily includes passage- and graphic-based questions. These questions test one's ability to interpret scientific data and concepts represented in a graphical format instead of written text. The following provides descriptions about what to expect:

Data Representation

Scientific data will be presented in tables, graphs, diagrams, or models designed to test one's ability to interpret scientific data represented in a graphical format instead of written text. These questions do *not* necessarily examine scientific content knowledge (e.g., the equation for photosynthesis); rather, they test students' ability to interpret raw data represented in a table or graph. Therefore, it's possible to do well on this portion of the exam without a detailed understanding of the scientific topic at hand. Questions may ask for factual information, identification of data trends, or graph calculations. For example:

- Based on the attached graph, how did Study 1 differ from Study 2?
- What is the nature of the relationship between Experiment 1 and Experiment 2?
- What is *x* at the given *y*-value?

Research Summaries

Passages present the design, implementation, and conclusion of various scientific experiments. These passages typically contain 5 or 6 questions designed to test one's ability to identify the following:

- What question is the experiment trying to answer?
- What is the researcher's predicted answer to the question?
- How did the researchers test the hypotheses?
- Based on data obtained from the experiments, was the prediction correct?
- What would happen if ...?
- 2 × 2 Matrix questions: "Yes, because ..." or "No, because ..."

Conflicting Viewpoints

This section will present a disagreement between two scientists about a specific scientific hypothesis or concept. The opinions of each researcher are presented in two separate passages. There are two formats for these questions. The test taker must demonstrate an understanding of the content or compare and contrast the main differences between the two opinions. For example:

- Based on the data presented by Scientist 1, which of the following is correct?
- What is the main difference between the conclusions of Expert A and Expert B?

Elements of Science Passages

Short Answer Questions

Short answer questions are usually one to five words long and require the reader to recall basic facts presented in the passage.

An example answer choice: "Research group #1 finished last."

Long Answer Questions

Long answer questions are composed of one to three sentences that require the reader to make comparisons, summaries, generalizations, or conclusions about the passage.

An example answer choice: "Scientist 2 disagreed with Scientist 1 on the effects of Bisphenol A pollution and its presumed correlation to birth defects in mice and humans. Scientist 2 proposes that current environmental Bisphenol A levels are not sufficient to cause adverse effects on human health."

Fact Questions

Fact questions are the most basic type of question on the test. They ask the reader to recall a specific term, definition, number, or meaning.

An example question/answer: "Which of the following organisms was present in fresh water samples from Pond #1?"

a. Water flea
b. Dragonfly nymph
c. Snail
d. Tadpole

Graphs

As mentioned, there are different graph types used in the GED Science Test to represent the passage data. Tables will also present passage data sets in tabular form. The **independent variable** is positioned on the left side, while the **dependent variable** is on the right side of the table. The content of the tables is always discussed in the corresponding passage. Knowledge of all table content isn't required.

Sample Table for Analysis

Data type	Seismic sources							
	Individual faults						Area/volume sources	
	Location	Activity	Length	Dip	Depth	Style	Area	Depth
Geological/Remote Sensing								
Detailed mapping	X	X	X	X		X		
Geomorphic data	X	X	X			X	X	
Quatenary surface rupture	X	X	X			X		
Fault trenching data	X	X		X		X		
Paleoliquefaction data	X	X					X	
Borehole data	X	X		X		X		
Aerial photography	X	X	X					
Low sun-angle photography	X	X	X					
Satellite imagery	X		X				X	
Regional structure	X			X		X	X	
Balanced Cross Section	X			X	X		X	
Geophysical/Geodetic								
Regional potential field data	X		X				X	X
Local potential field data	X		X	X	X	X		
High resolution reflection data	X	X		X		X		
Standard reflexing data	X			X		X		
Deep crustal reflection data	X			X	X		X	X
Tectonic geodetic/strain data	X	X		X	X	X	X	X
Regional stress data						X	X	
Seismological								
Reflected crustal phase data							X	X
Pre-instrumental earthquake data	X	X			X	X	X	
Teleseismic earthquake data							X	
Regional network seismicity data	X	X	X	X	X		X	X
Local network seismicity data	X	X	X	X	X			X
Focal mechanism data				X		X		

Practice Quiz

Questions 1–5 pertain to the following information:

Worldwide, fungal infections of the lung account for significant mortality in individuals with compromised immune function. Three of the most common infecting agents are *Aspergillus, Histoplasma*, and *Candida*. Successful treatment of infections caused by these agents depends on an early and accurate diagnosis. Three tests used to identify specific markers for these mold species include ELISA (enzyme-linked immunosorbent assay), GM Assay (Galactomannan Assay), and PCR (polymerase chain reaction).

Two important characteristics of these tests include sensitivity and specificity. Sensitivity relates to the probability that the test will identify the presence of the infecting agent, resulting in a true positive result. Higher sensitivity equals fewer false-positive results. Specificity relates to the probability that if the test doesn't detect the infecting agent, the test is truly negative for that agent. Higher specificity equals fewer false-negatives.

Figure 1 shows the timeline for the process of infection from exposure to the pathogen to recovery or death.

Figure 1:
Natural History of the Process of Infection

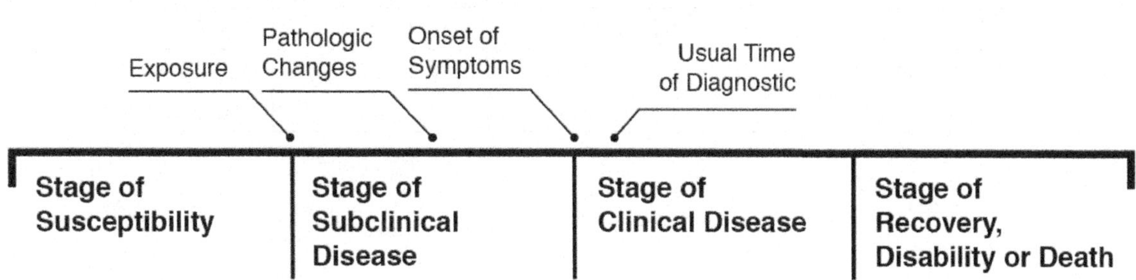

Figure 2 (below) shows the sensitivity and specificity for ELISA, GM assay and PCR related to the diagnosis of infection by *Aspergillus*, *Histoplasma* and *Candida*.

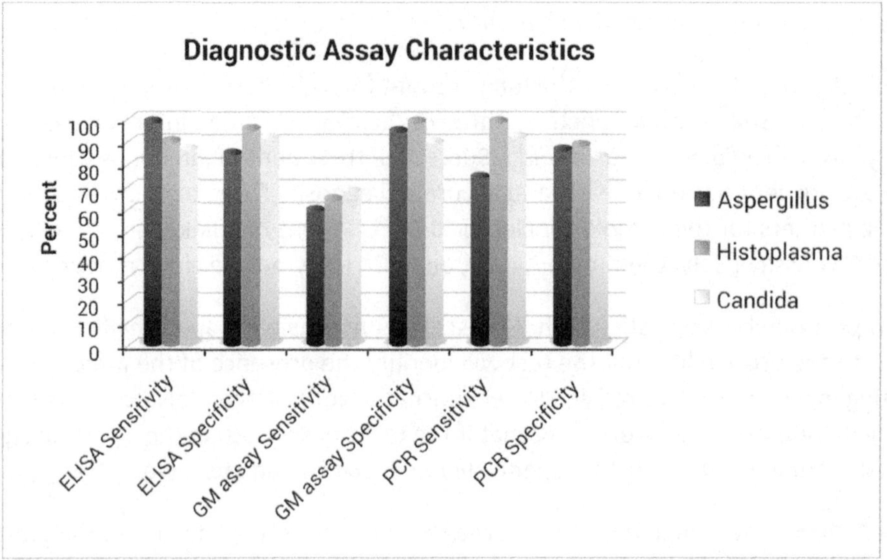

The table below identifies the process of infection (in days) from exposure for each of the species.

Process of Infection – Days Since Pathogen Exposure			
	Aspergillus	Histoplasma	Candida
Sub-clinical Disease	Day 90	Day 28	Day 7
Detection Possible	Day 118	Day 90	Day 45
Symptoms Appear	Day 145	Day 100	Day 120

Figure 3 (below) identifies the point at which each test can detect the organism. Time is measured in days from the time an individual is exposed to the pathogen.

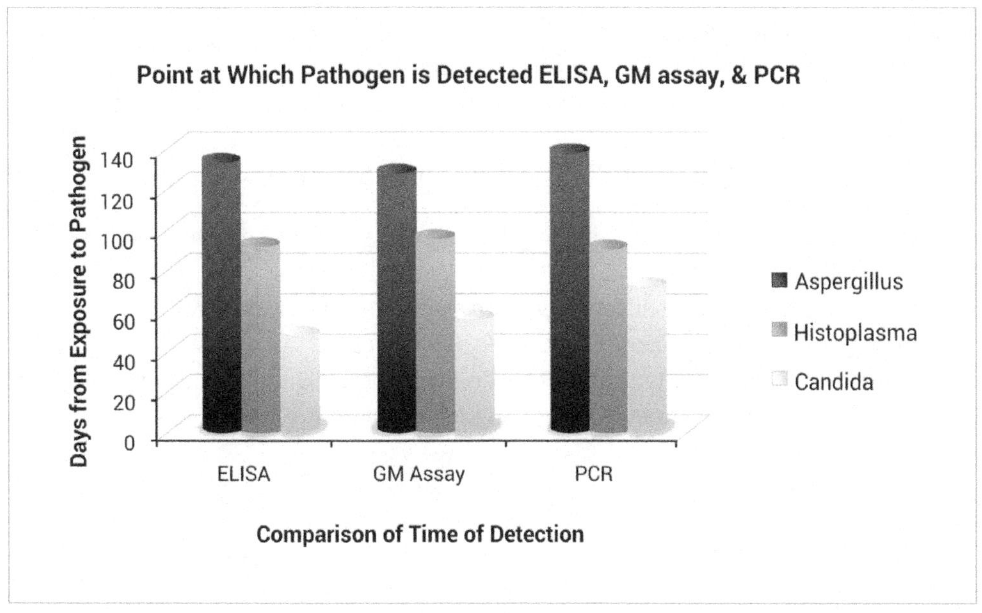

1. Which of the following statements is supported by Figure 2?
   a. For *Candida*, the GM assay will provide the most reliable results.
   b. ELISA testing for *Aspergillus* is the most specific of the three tests.
   c. PCR is the most sensitive method for testing *Histoplasma*.
   d. True positive rates were greater than 75% for all three testing methods.

2. In reference to the table and Figure 3, which pathogen from the options below can be detected earliest in the process of infection, and by which method?
   a. *Candida* by PCR testing
   b. *Aspergillus* by ELISA testing
   c. *Candida* by GM assay
   d. *Histoplasma* by PCR testing

3. In reference to Figure 2, which statement is correct?
   a. There is a 20% probability that ELISA testing will NOT correctly identify the presence of *Histoplasma.*
   b. When GM assay testing for *Candida* is conducted, there is a 31% probability that it will NOT be identified if the organism is present.
   c. The probability that GM assay testing for *Aspergillus* will correctly identify the presence of the organism is 99%.
   d. The false-negative probabilities for each of the three testing methods identified in Figure 2 indicate that the organism will be detected when present less than 70% of the time.

4. Physicians caring for individuals with suspected *Histoplasma* infections order diagnostic testing prior to instituting treatment. PCR testing results will not be available for 10 days. GM assay results can be obtained more quickly. The physicians opt to wait for the PCR testing. Choose the best possible rationale for that decision.
   a. The treatment will be the same regardless of the test results.
   b. The individual was not exhibiting any disease symptoms.
   c. The probability of PCR testing identifying the presence of the organism is greater than the GM assay.
   d. The subclinical disease phase for *Histoplasma* is more than 100 days.

5. Referencing the data in Figures 2 and 3, if ELISA testing costs twice as much as PCR testing, why might it still be the best choice to test for *Candida*?
   a. ELISA testing detects the presence of *Candida* sooner than PCR testing.
   b. ELISA testing has fewer false-positives than PCR testing.
   c. There is only a 69% probability that PCR testing will correctly identify the presence of *Candida.*
   d. PCR testing is less sensitive than ELISA testing for *Candida.*

See answers on next page

Answer Explanations

1. C: There is a 99% probability of PCR testing identifying *Histoplasma*. GM assay was more specific for identifying *Aspergillus,* 95% to 85%. True positive is defined by sensitivity. The sensitivity of GM assay testing is less than 70%.

2. D: *Histoplasma* is detectable 90 days from exposure; PCR testing, Choice *D*, is able to detect *Histoplasma* 91 days from exposure—one day after sufficient organisms exist for detection. *Candida* is detectable 45 days from exposure; PCR testing, Choice *A*, is able to detect *Candida* 72 days from exposure—27 days after a sufficient number of organisms exist for detection. GM assay testing, Choice *C*, is able to detect *Candida* 56 days from exposure—11 days after a sufficient number of organisms exist for detection. *Aspergillus* is detectable 118 days from exposure; ELISA testing, Choice *B*, is able to detect *Aspergillus* 134 days from exposure—16 days after a sufficient number of organisms exist for detection.

3. B: The probability that the GM assay will identify *Candida* is 69%. Therefore, there's a 31% probability that it won't be identified. ELISA sensitivity and specificity for *Histoplasma* are both greater than 80%. False-negative probabilities are represented by the specificity of a given testing method. The sensitivity and specificity for GM assay testing for *Aspergillus* is 59% and 94% respectively. All testing methods had greater than 80% specificity for the organisms.

4. C: The sensitivity of PCR testing for *Histoplasma* is 99%, and the test can identify the organism one day after it reaches a detectable colony size. The sensitivity for GM assay testing for *Histoplasma* is 65%. If physicians rely on GM assay testing, they may determine that the individual doesn't have the *Histoplasma* infection. Treatment will depend on the presence or absence of the infection as indicated by testing. Waiting for PCR testing is based on the sensitivity of the test, not the individual's current symptoms. The subclinical phase of *Histoplasma* is 28 days.

5. A: ELISA testing detects *Candida* three days after the organism is present in sufficient numbers to be recognized. PCR detects the organism more than three weeks after it is first detectable. ELISA testing sensitivity for *Candida* is 87% and PCR testing is 92%. However, the ability to identify the presence of the organism earlier in the process of infection (allowing early intervention) outweighs the differences in the probability of identifying the presence of the organism. There's a 92% probability that PCR testing will identify the presence of *Candida*. PCR testing is more sensitive than ELISA: 92% versus 87%.

Social Studies

Reading for Meaning in Social Studies

Main Ideas and Details in Social Studies Readings

Determining the Main Ideas

As mentioned, the **main idea** is more detailed than the topic of a piece of writing and it provides the author's central point of the text. It can be expressed through a complete sentence and is often found in the beginning, middle, or end of a paragraph. In most nonfiction books, the first sentence of the passage usually (but not always) states the main idea.

Using Details to Make Inferences or Claims

Once a reader has determined an author's thesis or main idea, he or she will need to understand how textual evidence supports interpretation of that thesis or main idea. Test takers will be asked direct questions regarding an author's main idea and may be asked to identify evidence that would support those ideas. This will require test takers to comprehend literal and figurative meanings within the text passage, be able to draw inferences from provided information, and be able to separate important evidence from minor supporting detail. It's often helpful to skim test questions and answer options prior to critically reading informational text; however, test takers should avoid the temptation to solely look for the correct answers. Just trying to find the "right answer" may cause test takers to miss important supporting textual evidence. Making mental note of test questions is only helpful as a guide when reading.

After identifying an author's thesis or main idea, a test taker should look at the supporting details that the author provides to back up their assertions, identifying those additional pieces of information that help expand the thesis. From there, test takers should examine the additional information and related details for credibility, the author's use of outside sources, and be able to point to direct evidence that supports the author's claims. It's also imperative that test takers be able to identify what is strong support and what is merely additional information that is nice to know but not necessary. Being able to make this differentiation will help test takers effectively answer questions regarding an author's use of supporting evidence within informational text.

Social Studies Vocabulary

Although general literacy is usually enough to understand social studies texts, some authors use specialized vocabulary for the field of social studies. Traditionally, these specialized vocabulary terms can be separated into eight major categories: people, places, events, groups, movements, eras, documents, and analytical trends. The field of social studies centers on those who have shaped history on both the microcosmic and macrocosmic levels. Much of the social studies vocabulary terms test takers encounter is focused on famous leaders or historical agents. An **agent** is someone who does something; historical agents do something historically significant.

Social studies concepts also include geography and are linked with geography in general, so it is important that test takers have a good understanding of place and its influences on history. Additionally, it is important for test takers to understand historical events: wars, assassinations, political victories,

resignations, marches, parades, and celebrations. Groups are also important to understanding social studies. In particular, some groups form social movements, factions of people devoted to some larger changes. At times, these movements succeed in changing history; at other times, they fail. Historians tend to also categorize history in segments of time known as eras. Eras can be as strict as decades (for example, the Roaring Twenties) or as fluid as ideas (for example, the Progressive Era).

Sometimes social studies texts also refer to the titles of primary and secondary texts, which have their own unique vocabulary terms. An example of an important primary text is the Declaration of Independence, while a secondary text might be a textbook discussing the Declaration of Independence. All these concepts—from people to documents—influence historical analyses, which are usually secondary texts. Historians and scholars may create their own analytical paradigms, which carry their own specialized vocabulary. For instance, some historians refer to themselves as quantitative historians because their analytical lenses are influenced heavily by quantitative data. Quantitative historians have their own specialized vocabulary for analytical trends.

Below are examples of the eight major categories of social studies vocabulary: people, places, events, groups, movements, eras, documents, and analytical trends.

People

King James I of England: The King of England who granted the charter that would help found the Jamestown Colony; the Jamestown colony is named after him.

John Smith: A famous English explorer who played an important role in the survival of the Jamestown colony.

Powhatan: A well-known Native American leader who led a tribe known as the Powhatans; he was the father of a famous Native American woman known as Pocahontas.

Pocahontas: A well-known Native American woman who served as a mediator between the Powhatans and the Jamestown colony; she was the daughter of a respected Native American chief known as Powhatan.

William Bradford: A famous Puritan settler who signed the Mayflower Compact, served as governor for nearly 30 years, and wrote *Of Plymouth Plantation*.

Bartolome de las Casas: Known as the "Protector of the Indians," he was a priest who wrote a treatise that shed light on the mistreatment of Native Americans in the New World.

Charles Townshend: British chancellor of the exchequer and responsible for the passage of the highly controversial Townshend Acts in 1767.

Crispus Attucks: Murdered by British soldiers in reaction to colonial protests, Crispus Attucks, a black colonist, became the first casualty of the so-called Boston Massacre. Some people even memorialize him as a martyr of the American Revolution, claiming that his bloodshed marked the beginning of the struggle for independence.

Thomas Paine: Thomas Paine was an English-born American political activist, philosopher, political theorist and revolutionary. He was the author of *Common Sense*, a foundational document that helped stir the American Revolution.

James Madison: Known as both a Founding Father and the Father of the Constitution, he served as the fourth president of the United States, preceded by Thomas Jefferson and succeeded by James Monroe.

Thomas Jefferson: A Founding Father who became the third president of the United States, Jefferson was famous for his involvement in the Declaration of Independence, the Louisiana Purchase, and the creation of the Jeffersonian Republican platform.

General Andrew Jackson: A famous general during the War of 1812, who led the United States to an impressive victory at the Battle of New Orleans. He later became a controversial US president known for expanding democracy while simultaneously perpetuating white supremacy.

James K. Polk: Known for his expansionist policies in an era that witnessed rapid westward annexation, occupation, and settlement, he is forever known as the president who led the United States in a (successful) border war with Mexico, the Mexican-American War.

Dred Scott: An escaped slave who catapulted the United States in a US Supreme Court case known as *Dred Scott v. Sanford* (1857). The Dred Scott decision, which reinforced the rights of slave owners and slave states, helped pave the way to the ideological battles over slavery that culminated in the Civil War.

Abraham Lincoln: Known for entering office when the nation was divided over slavery between the North and South, he is one of the most recognized presidents because of his involvement in the Civil War, his approval of the Emancipation Proclamation, and his untimely assassination by John Wilkes Booth.

Ulysses S. Grant: A famous Civil War general whose presidency was marred by corruptions such as the Whiskey Ring during the Gilded Age.

General Robert E. Lee: The most skilled Confederate military leader during the Civil War, Lee ended up surrendering at the Appomattox Courthouse in Virginia, which marked the end of the conflict between North and South.

Places

Mesoamerica: A historical region that includes modern-day Mexico and Central America.

Mississippi River: The longest river on the North American continent, the Mississippi is known for its vast estuaries and its cultural contributions to American history.

Great Lakes Region: A geographic region in North America that surrounds the large lakes that separate the modern-day United States and Canada

Reservations: Federal land, often of poor quality, set aside for Native Americans to live on in the United States.

Jamestown: Located on the coast of modern-day Virginia and founded in 1607, it became the first successful English colony in North America. Previous colonization attempts by the English (for example, Roanoke Island) were failures.

Plymouth: A religiously based English colony founded by Puritan Separatists in 1620.

Roanoke Island: A colony off the coast of Virginia that the English tried to settle in the 16th century.

James River: A river near coastal Virginia that served as a source of water for the Jamestown colony.

Chesapeake Bay: A large coastal estuary that served as a harbor for the early Jamestown colony.

Plymouth Harbor: The anchorage site of the ***Mayflower***; it is located in modern-day Massachusetts.

Massachusetts Bay Colony: An English colony composed of modern-day Maine, New Hampshire, Vermont, Massachusetts, and Connecticut; it was created through a joint-stock charter and eventually subsumed the old Plymouth Colony.

New England Colonies: The English colonies of the Northeast; this region included the Massachusetts Bay Colony (which acquired the Plymouth Colony), Rhode Island, Connecticut, and New Hampshire.

Middle Colonies: The English colonies located between the New England colonies and the Southern Colonies; this region included New York, New Jersey, Pennsylvania, and Delaware.

Southern Colonies: The English colonies located between Florida and the Middle Colonies; this region included Maryland, Virginia, North Carolina, South Carolina, and Georgia.

Mystic River Valley: A region in southeastern Connecticut that witnessed the massacre of the Pequot Native Americans by the English colonists.

Atlantic World: A word historians use to describe interactions that took place on either side of and on the Atlantic Ocean, particularly during the Age of Exploration and Colonization.

Appalachian Mountains: A well-known North American mountain range that extends from Georgia to Maine.

Louisiana Territory: A large tract of land west of the Mississippi River in North America. This land exchanged hands from one empire to the next throughout the 16th, 17th, and 18th centuries; the United States eventually purchased the land from the French in 1803.

Rio Grande River: The body of water that serves as a natural boundary between the United States and Mexico, flowing around the border of Texas and into the Gulf of Mexico.

Republic of Texas: Prior to American annexation, the name given to the independent state that emerged out of the Texas Revolution against Mexico; this republic lasted roughly ten years before statehood.

Trans-Appalachia: The region west of the Appalachian Mountains.

Confederate States of America: The name given to states that seceded from the United States Union during the Civil War. The Confederate States, also known as the Confederacy, formed a short-lived independent nation that lost to the Union during the Civil War.

Events

French and Indian War: English colonists in the New World fought against the French and their Native American allies. This conflict was an extension of a larger conflict between England and France called the Seven Years' War. The French and Indian War caused the Thirteen Colonies to accumulate a lot of debt, paving the way to the American Revolution.

American Revolution:https://en.wikipedia.org/wiki/American_Revolution A colonial revolt and war for independence that pitted American colonists against the British Crown.

Starving Time: Refers to a harsh period of struggle and starvation in the Jamestown colony in the winter of 1609–1610.

Pequot War: An armed conflict that pitted the English colonists and their Native American allies against the Pequot Indians of New England; this conflict lasted from 1636 to 1638.

King Philip's War: A bloody war pitting the English colonists and their allies against the Wampanoag indigenous tribe of New England and their chief, Metacom. The war resulted in over 5,000 deaths.

Boston Massacre: A conflict that stemmed from American protests over British quartering and taxation policies in the Thirteen Colonies. It led to the death of several American colonists and was sensationalized by Patriots as a strategic massacre.

Boston Tea Party: A famous protest that witnessed English colonists dumping dozens of tea crates into Boston harbor. It is known as one of the events that helped ignite the American Revolution.

Lexington and Concord: Often categorized as the locations of the first shots fired in the American War for Independence. These battles were fought in 1775, before the Declaration of Independence was even signed or even created.

Stamp Act Controversy: The controversy and protests in the American colonies surrounding the passage of the Stamp Act of 1765.

Constitutional Convention: A historical event, hosted in Philadelphia, Pennsylvania, that witnessed the end of the Articles of Confederation (and its coinciding Critical Period) and the adoption of a new national Constitution with a Bill of Rights.

Shays' Rebellion: Typically seen as a symbol of the weakness of the United States under the Articles of Confederation, it was a lengthy uprising by disaffected farmers in western Massachusetts under the leadership of Daniel Shays.

Great Compromise: A famous agreement during the Constitutional Convention that helped establish Congress into a two-part (or "bicameral") legislature with a House and Senate.

Three-Fifths Compromise: A controversial constitutional compromise that designated a slave as three fifths of a person when it came to census data, for electoral and legislative reasons.

Louisiana Purchase: This transaction, carried out by Thomas Jefferson, saw the United States expand by one-third and the French lose most of its territory in the New World.

War of 1812: A three-year war between the United States and Great Britain that witnessed the burning of the original White House and an eventual American victory in 1815.

Battle at Baltimore: The famous battle in the War of 1812 that inspired Francis Scott Key to write the "Star-Spangled Banner," a poem that later became the United States' national anthem.

Battle of New Orleans: A battle made famous by the leadership and victory of Andrew Jackson; it is considered part of the War of 1812, but it actually occurred after the war ended via official treaty between the United States and Great Britain.

Mexican-American War: An armed conflict that lasted between 1846 to 1848 that began as a skirmish over borders and territories, but ended with the official cession of one-third of the Mexican nation to the United States.

American Civil War: A deadly civil conflict between the North and South—the Union and Confederacy—that helped end slavery and eventually reunified a nation that had long been divided over the institution of slavery.

Battle of Gettysburg: A Civil War victory by the Union at Gettysburg, Pennsylvania in 1863 that helped turn the tide against the Confederates.

Groups

Olmec: The earliest Native American civilization in Mexico.

Maya: An early Mesoamerican civilization that began building its great pyramids around 250 CE and then disappeared around 900 CE.

Aztec: A Mesoamerican civilization that flourished in Mexico from about 1300 CE to 1521 CE but was eventually conquered by Spanish conquistadors under leadership of Hernán Cortés.

Inca: The largest civilization in the pre-Columbian Americas, it emerged in the highlands of Peru in the 13th century and was eventually conquered by Spanish conquistadors in 1572.

Iroquois: A political confederation of five northeastern Native American tribes that rose to prominence during colonial times.

Five Civilized Tribes: A group of prominent tribes in the Southeast region of North American continent that collaborated and traded with the colonists; the tribes included the Cherokee, Chickasaw, Choctaw, Creek, and Seminole tribes.

Separatists: Radical English Protestants who wanted to separate from the Church of England, this group founded Plymouth Colony.

Church of England: The official Protestant church of England; it separated from the Catholic Church in the 16th century under the leadership of King Henry VIII.

Pequot Indians: A group of Native Americans who originally resided in a territory that is now the modern-day state of Connecticut; this group fought against the English settlers in the Pequot War (1636–1638).

Mohegan: A Native American tribe that unified with the Pequot in present-day Connecticut during the era of European colonization.

Narragansett: An Algonquin Native American tribe that allied with the New England colonists during the Pequot War (1636–1638).

Parliament: The name given to the British legislature, which created taxes and acts that displeased the colonists in the years leading up to the American Revolution.

Patriots: The name given to the network of leaders, organizers, and militiamen who led a revolution against the British government in the Thirteen Colonies.

First Continental Congress: One of the first examples of colonial unity, it witnessed several colonies, represented by delegates, coming together to petition the alleged wrongdoings and overstepped boundaries of King George III and the British Crown in America.

Second Continental Congress: The second famous convening of the colonists during the revolutionary era in American history, which helped birth the Declaration of Independence on July 4, 1776.

Minutemen: A fast-acting group of civilian militiamen who were ready to form a standing army within a minute's time during the years of the American Revolution.

Tories: A group of American colonists who chose not to side with the revolutionists during the American War for Independence; they chose instead to stay loyal to the British.

Liberty Boys: A secret network of discontented colonists who strategically participated in both acts of protest and espionage against the British Crown in the Revolutionary Era.

Federalists: A group that emerged in the years leading up to the Constitutional Convention; they preferred federal rights over states' rights.

Anti-Federalists: A group that emerged in the years leading up to the Constitutional Convention; they preferred states' rights over federal rights.

Democratic-Republican Party: Also known as the Democratic Republicans and formed by Thomas Jefferson and James Madison around 1792, this American political party opposed the new Federalist Party's centralizing policies.

Jeffersonian Republicans: Named after Thomas Jefferson, the third president of the United States, this group trusted agrarian (farming) values.

Republican Party: Still in existence today as one of the main two political parties in the U.S., it was organized in the years prior to the Civil War. The first Republican President was Abraham Lincoln.

Democratic Party: Still in existence today as one of the main two political parties in the U.S., this political party emerged during the 1820s and 1830s with the democratic fervor surrounding the rise of President Andrew Jackson.

Movements

Women's Suffrage: The name given to the movement that secured women's right to vote in the United States in the early 20th century; women were the last group to gain this right in America.

Jacksonian Democracy: A phrase used to describe the rapid expansion of suffrage to include working class white men during Andrew Jackson's ascendancy to the presidency.

Eras

Industrial Revolution: The term used to refer to an era in global history that witnessed a paradigm shift in culture and economics; an 18th, 19th, and early 20th century global transformation that emphasized mechanized manufacturing processes over agrarian production.

Market Revolution: America's transition from an agrarian economy to a full-blown market economy, which eventually paved the way to the Industrial Revolution.

Critical Period: A phrase sometimes used to refer to the instability of the nation under the Articles of Confederation.

Age of Expansion: Refers to an era in US history following the Louisiana Purchase and extending all the way to the early 20th century, characterized by expansion of territories and borders.

Sectional Crisis: An era of political crisis in the United States in the antebellum period that created a division between North and South, free states and slave states.

Antebellum: Literally means "before the war"; it refers to the time period leading up to the American Civil War.

Populism: Support for the concerns of ordinary people.

Reconstruction: Deemed a failure by some historians because it perpetuated the oppression of African-Americans and resolved little tension between North and South, the era of Reconstruction directly followed the Civil War and tried to rebuild a devastated nation.

Documents

Mayflower Compact: The first governing document of the Plymouth Colony, which was signed by William Bradford and his fellow Puritan Separatists.

Declaration of Independence: A document adopted by the American colonies in 1776 to declare the colonies free from British rule.

Treaty of Paris: A treaty between the Spanish, British, and French Empires following the Seven Years' War; as a result of the treaty, the French relinquished a significant amount of land in North America.

Townshend Acts: These acts, created and implemented by Charles Townshend, a British Parliamentary leader, offended the American colonists because they enforced more taxes (on things such as tea) and greater British control over the colonies.

Tea Act of 1773: This law led to the Boston Tea Party because American colonists were enraged that the British would tax one of their favorite commodities, tea.

Proclamation of 1763: This royal directive angered American colonists because it stated that they were not allowed to transverse or settle territory west of the Appalachian Mountains.

Stamp Act of 1765: This act allowed the British to tax all stamps, which were needed on official documents in the colonies such as marriage licenses.

The Quartering Act: The colonists were angered by this act because it mandated that all colonists must house, or quarter, British soldiers without any royal compensation.

Treaty of Paris (1783): The documents, signed by the United States and Great Britain, that officially ended the American War for Independence in 1783.

Common Sense: A pamphlet written by Thomas Paine in 1775–76 advocating independence from Great Britain to people in the Thirteen Colonies.

Coercive Acts: Also known as the Intolerable Acts, a series of aggressive British statutes that were passed in 1774. They were designed to punish the Massachusetts colonists for their participation in the protests of Boston Tea Party; the colonists claimed the acts were "coercive" or "intolerable" in their revolutionary propaganda.

Quebec Act: A controversial act that instigated the Protestant sensitivities of the American colonists by making it legal for Roman Catholics to practice in Quebec.

Articles of Confederation: Created in 1777, this document established the first central government for the United States; it was replaced by the US Constitution in 1789.

US Constitution: The governing document of the United States that replaced the Articles of Confederation in 1789 and strengthened the federal government.

Bill of Rights: The first ten proposed and ratified amendments to the US Constitution, which spelled out specific personal rights such as the right to free speech.

Star-Spangled Banner: Written by Francis Scott Key at the Battle of Baltimore during the War of 1812, this poem became the national anthem of the United States 100 years after its creation.

Treaty of Ghent: The official end of the War of 1812 came about as a result of the signing of this treaty. However, some skirmishes between the United States and Great Britain continued for months after its signing, due to delays in communication.

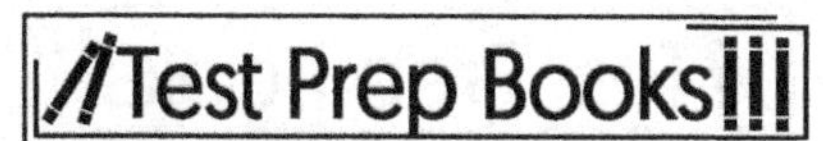

Indian Removal Act: A controversial act signed by President Andrew Jackson in 1830 that removed Native Americans to federal territory in the West, which resulted in the Trail of Tears.

Treaty of Guadalupe Hidalgo: Bringing about the end of the Mexican-American War, this 1848 treaty transitioned about one-third of Mexican territory into the hands of the United States.

Gadsden Purchase: Following the Mexican Cession after the Mexican-American War, this 1853 purchase from Mexico transferred a small sliver of northern Mexico (modern-day Arizona and New Mexico) into the possession of the United States.

Fugitive Slave Act: A divisive law created during the antebellum period in American history that made it illegal to house or assist runaway slaves in any capacity.

Emancipation Proclamation: The document that freed slaves in the United States; it was created by President Lincoln during the Civil War in 1863.

Gettysburg Address: A famous Abraham Lincoln speech, delivered in 1863 on the site of the Battle of Gettysburg, that is iconic for its passion and brevity

Jim Crow laws: Laws that reinforced the institutionalized segregation of the South from Reconstruction until the Civil Rights Movement of the 1960s.

Analytical Trends

Consensus History: A style of American historiography that downplays conflict and complexity, focusing on unity and nationalism.

Modernism: A philosophy that took hold in the late 19th and early 20th century that gave rise to histories and literature that emphasized the beauties and the pangs of modernity.

New Left: A 1960s political movement that championed such causes as anti-war activism, women's rights, and other issues.

Postmodernism: A departure from modernism, this literary, artistic, and architectural movement also affected history and philosophy. It focuses on the tenuousness of authority and truth and interpretation of texts.

Progressivism: A view of history and philosophy categorized by a larger search for order and a belief in human progress.

General Social Studies Terms

American Exceptionalism: A worldview that claims the United States is historically unique and more powerful than other nations.

Reductive: Oversimplifying a subject, debate, or narrative.

Nuanced: A subtly different view or varying argument that promotes a unique perspective.

Historically Accurate: Authentic or true, in terms of historical validity or honesty.

Indigenous People: A way of referring to any group who originated in a particular place, in contrast to people who arrived later, as conquerors, immigrants, or slaves.

Historical Narrative: A spoken or written account of history, as told from a specific viewpoint or perspective.

Eurocentrism: A worldview that favors a European narrative of progress.

Colonial Economy: A phrase used to describe the system of production, consumption, and trade that emerged during the period of European colonization.

Joint-Stock Company: A business entity in which shareholders own a share of the company's profit; many joint-stock companies are responsible for founding colonies in the New World.

Mayflower: The English ship that famously transported the Separatist Puritans to their new settlement at Plymouth.

Archive: To place or organize documents or materials in storage for future use.

Savage: A pejorative term the English used to describe the Native Americans as barbarous or uncivilized.

Bolster: A verb that means to support or reinforce.

Proselytizing: Trying to convert someone to a particular faith or religion.

Exploitation: Taking advantage of someone or something for selfish reasons, such as profit.

Genocidal: An adjective used to describe the systematic attempt to kill off an entire group of people, whether defined by religion, ethnicity, or race.

Paradigm Shifting: A phrase coined by Thomas Kuhn to describe large waves of historical and scientific change that fundamentally change the ways people understand the world around them.

Capitalism: The dominant political and economic philosophy of the United States, which focuses on creating a free market in which there is competition between businesses.

Slavery: An institution built upon the bondage and forced labor of human beings. Slavery preceded the foundation of the United States and continued until the Civil War era and the Emancipation Proclamation.

Protesting: When a person or group makes a public statement of disagreement; it can take the form of marches, gatherings, silences, and even boycotts.

Boycotting: A specific type of protest that focuses on finances and economics; it is the refusal to purchase or use a particular service or product, in an effort to force political or social change.

Electoral College: In the United States, it is a voting system that allows selected representatives to vote on behalf of the people. It is an example of limited democracy.

Industrialization: The widespread development of manufacturing industries in a region, country, or culture.

Agrarian: A term used to describe a society or culture that relies heavily on farming for trade and subsistence.

Republic: A classical form of government adopted by the United States (and the Republic of Texas) because it placed the power of the people in the hands of elected officials who are supposed to stand for public opinion.

Self-Sufficiency: Needing no outside help to sustain one's own life, especially when it comes to food production.

Virtue: Behavior showing high moral standards.

Yeoman: A term for a farmer who works a small, individually owned plot of land. Thomas Jefferson believed democracy could be sustained through the independence of yeoman farmers.

Discontent: A feeling of dissatisfaction, typically with the prevailing social or political situation.

Revisionism: The re-interpretation of the historical record, usually in a way that distorts or alters the prevailing understanding.

Sanitize: Literally, to clean; in social sciences it means to alter something regarded as less acceptable so as to make it more palatable.

Subjugation: The action of bringing someone or something under domination or control.

Terminological: Connected with the meanings of words, especially the technical words and expressions used in a particular subject.

Egalitarian: A term that is synonymous with ultimate equality or when people or society share material or immaterial power equally.

Anti-Egalitarian: Contrary to principles of social equality and fairness.

Cultural Milieu: The cultural and social environment that surrounds a person. It comes from a French term meaning "middle place."

Working Class: A term used as label for a laboring class that gained momentum during the Industrial Revolution.

White Supremacy: A system of beliefs that upholds white people as the supreme race while discriminating against other races.

Duel: An archaic way of resolving disputes that involved a highly structured form of violence; it was often performed with guns and involved a series of sport-like rules and procedures.

Immigration: The action of coming to live permanently in a foreign country.

Urbanization: The process of making an area more urban or populated.

Industrialization: The widespread development of manufacturing industries in a region, country, or culture.

Artisan: A worker who is highly skilled in a trade, especially one involving handicrafts.

Cash-Crop Agriculture: The growing of agricultural crops for money, in contrast to crops grown for subsistence. Before to the Civil War, cotton was an American cash crop.

Manufacturing: Using mechanized instruments or technology to make a particular good or product (for example, automobile manufacturing).

Suffrage: A term used to describe the right to vote; historically, it originally belonged to men or land-owners. It was extended gradually to other groups, with women being the last to earn the right.

Aristocratic: Having to do with a form of government that places strength in the hands of a small, privileged ruling class.

Insurgency: An act of rebellion or revolt against a government or ruler.

Elitism: A tendency to promote the wealthier portions of the population.

Hierarchical: Organized in order of rank.

Deference: Humble submission and respect.

Angst: Intense feelings of distress or anxiety that can be felt either personally or collectively.

Tyranny: Cruel and oppressive government or rule.

Spurious: Not what it purports to be; false or fake.

Rhetoric: The name given to any form of communication, written or oral, that carries power as an art and discourse; a personalized and recognizable style of personal or collective communication.

Plebeian: A commoner; a common person.

Racist: An individual who takes seriously the strict parameters of racial constructs and discriminates against other races as a result.

Racial Exclusivity: Excluding a person or group of persons because of their race.

Cotton Gin: A cotton-separating invention created by Eli Whitney in 1793 that was supposed to ease the burden of slavery through mechanized means but actually increased the demand for slave labor on cotton plantations.

Plantations: A large estate farmed by slaves or tenant farmers who live there but do not own the land. During the antebellum period in American history, plantations served as the epicenter of slave

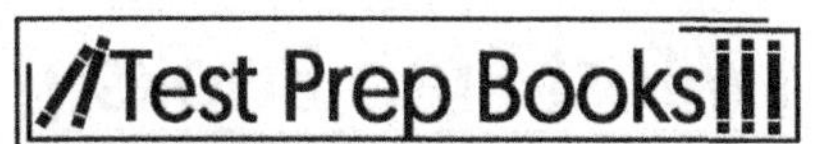

labor; these plantations capitalized on the institution of slavery to produce large cash crops such as tobacco and cotton.

How Authors Use Language in Social Studies

Often history is interpreted or taught as merely a timeline or a series of bland facts about the past, but history should also be understood as a "lived experience." All humans are *a part of* history—they are the historical actors and personas who make positive (or negative) changes in the world. Human beings are constantly interacting with the super-structural forces of history. History occurs in interlocking webs of mutual reciprocity.

History happens in a context of local and global events. The people recording that history (in whatever format) are part of that context and therefore shaped by it. No one merely records statistics, facts, and figures. Each thing recorded is done so because it is important for some reason to the one recording it. Those who study history must do their best to understand the people and places they study as well as understand themselves in their own historical context.

Good historians ask questions prior to reading or studying what has been left for them by prior generations. What was important to the person who left this record? Were they rich or poor? Were they weak or powerful? What was their particular view of the world? What was their view of themselves and the group(s) they belonged to and their perceived place in history? These and other questions are critical to better understanding what was recorded and why it was considered important. It also helps provide a context for understanding the record left for posterity.

The historian must also understand their own biases, worldview, preconceptions, and context so that they can be aware of who they are and what they believe, because it influences the way they read, interpret, and understand the historical record.

Social studies deal with many different documents and recordings, all using written or spoken language. Language can be found in diaries, journals, political cartoons, old maps, treatises, constitutions, treaties, laws, advertisements, deeds, archives, inventory reports, and financial receipts. These are all examples of **primary sources**. Social studies also uses language in textbooks, monographs, academic journals, encyclopedias, online blogs, contemporary maps, charts, tables, and graphs. These are all examples of **secondary sources**. Language can even be found on old artifacts, archeological discoveries, monuments, and museum exhibits. These are all examples of historical objects that can fall into the categories of either primary or secondary sources. Language is the primary method of capturing history and documenting its meaning. Although social studies can examine artifacts without language (for example, the artifacts used in anthropology and archeology), most social studies documents use language. The languages may change from culture to culture, but language use is itself a unifying component of all major cultural histories.

Thus, it is important for test takers to become detectives of social studies language. Every student must be prepared to understand the purpose and biases embedded in language. For instance, if a document repeatedly uses words such as *liberty*, *freedom*, and *inalienable rights*, it is likely that the authors of these documents believe in these concepts so much that they wanted to disseminate these words to a broader audience. Additionally, if advertisements consistently use the word "cool," then the creators of these advertisements are likely using this word for a specific purpose, such as to appeal to teenagers concerned with their image. Every language-based source carries its own perspective and biases. Thus, students must be prepared to link language to not only the historical context (for example, the era of the Early Republic), but also to the beliefs of the author(s).

Fact Versus Opinion

A fact is information that is true. If information can be disproven, it is not a fact. For example, water freezes at or below thirty-two degrees Fahrenheit. An argument stating that water freezes at seventy degrees Fahrenheit cannot be supported by data and is therefore not a fact. Facts tend to be associated with science, mathematics, and statistics.

Opinions are information open for debate. Opinions are often tied to subjective concepts like feelings, desires, or manners. They can also be controversial. An affirmative argument for a position—such as gun control—can be just as effective as an opposing argument against it.

Biases and stereotypes are viewpoints based in opinion and held despite evidence that they are incorrect. A bias is an individual prejudice. Biased people ignore evidence that contradicts their position while offering as proof any evidence that supports it. A stereotype is a widely held belief projected onto a group. Those who stereotype tend to make assumptions based on what others have told them and usually have little firsthand experience with the group or item in question.

Readers must read critically to discern between fact and opinion and to notice bias and stereotypes.

Claims and Evidence in Social Studies

Determining Whether a Claim Is or Is Not Supported by Evidence

Valid claims must have sufficient evidence that fully support the claims and conclusions. Critical readers examine the facts and evidence used to support an author's claim. They check the facts against other sources to be sure those facts are correct. They also check the validity of the sources used to be sure those sources are credible, academic, and/or peer-reviewed. Consider that when an author uses another person's opinion to support their argument, even if it is an expert's opinion, it is still only an opinion and should not be taken as fact. A strong argument uses valid, measurable facts to support ideas. Even then, the reader may disagree with the argument as it may be rooted in their personal beliefs.

An authoritative argument may use the facts to sway the reader. For example, in a paper on global warming, many experts differ in their opinions of what alternative fuels can be used to aid in offsetting it. Because of this, a writer may choose to only use the information and expert opinion that supports their viewpoint.

Students must be able to distinguish between reliable and unreliable sources in order to develop a well-written research report. When choosing print sources, typically published works that have been edited and clearly identify the author or authors are considered credible sources. Peer-reviewed journals and research conducted by scholars are likewise considered to be credible sources of information.

When deciding on what Internet sources to use, it is also a sound practice for researchers to look closely at each website's universal resource locator, the *URL*. Generally speaking, websites with .edu, .gov, or .org as the Top Level Domain are considered reliable, but the researcher must still question any possible

political or social bias. Personal blogs, tweets, personal websites, online forums, and any site that clearly demonstrates bias, strong opinions, or persuasive language are considered unreliable sources.

Comparing Information that Differs Between Sources

If one were to analyze current events, they will get a clearer view of how this works. The same event can be recorded by two different people and sound like two different events because of the way the information is reported. For example, two people might report on an event during a time of war. The first might be a pacifist and therefore would be opposed to the war and that bias would be seen in how they reported on the conflict. Someone else might speak of the same events and make them seem heroic because they are very much in favor of their country's involvement in the conflict. The same historical event is being recorded but with two very different intents, understandings, and interpretations.

The historian who comes to this information (or the modern reader in the current events case) needs to also be aware of their personal views and how that affects their understanding of what they are reading. They may read sympathetically if they share the bias of the original author. They may also react in great opposition to what was recorded if their own view varies sharply from that of the original recorder.

Awareness of the times, backgrounds, purposes, and influences on both the original recorder and the one examining the record must be taken into account when analyzing historical sources.

Analyzing Historical Events and Arguments

Making Inferences

Inference refers to the reader's ability to understand the unwritten text, i.e., "read between the lines" in terms of an author's intent or message. The strategy asks that a reader not take everything he or she reads at face value but instead, add their own interpretation of what the author seems to be trying to convey. A reader's ability to make inferences relies on their ability to think clearly and logically about the text. It does not ask that the reader make wild speculation or guess about the material but demands that he or she be able to come to a sound conclusion about the material.

An author's use of less literal words and phrases requires readers to make more inference when they read. Since inference involves **deduction**—deriving conclusions from ideas assumed to be true—there's more room for interpretation. Still, critical readers who employ inference, if careful in their thinking, can still arrive at the logical, sound conclusions the author intends.

Connections Between Different Social Studies Elements (People, Events, Places, Processes)

Analyzing Cause-and-Effect Relationships

Every time someone studies history, it is very much a collision of past, present, and future. Historians are concerned for the past, rooted in the present, and thinking about the future. Historical analysis is, therefore, a process infusing the present in the past in hopes of predicting (or deterring) certain social interactions in the future.

When examining the historical narratives of events, it is important to understand the relationship between causes and effects. A cause can be defined as something, whether an event, social change, or other factor, that contributes to the occurrence of certain events; the results of causes are called effects. Those terms may seem simple enough, but they have drastic implications on how one explores history. Events such as the American Revolution or the Civil Rights Movement may appear to occur spontaneously, but a closer examination will reveal that these events depended on earlier phenomena and patterns that influenced the course of history.

There can be multiple causes and effects for any situation. The existence of multiple causes can be seen through the settling of the American West. Many historians have emphasized the role of manifest destiny—the national vision of expanding across the continent—as a driving force behind the growth of the United States. Yet there were many different influences behind the expansion westward. Northern abolitionists and southern planters saw the frontier as a way to either extend or limit slavery. Economic opportunities in the West also encouraged travel westward, as did the gradual pacification, relocation, or eradication of Native American tribes. In fact, manifest destiny as well as economic and political reasons played significant roles in justifying the pacification, relocation, or eradication of the Native American tribal nations.

Even an individual cause can be subdivided into smaller factors or stretched out in a gradual process. Although there were numerous issues that led to the Civil War, slavery was the primary cause. However, that topic stretched back to the very founding of the nation, and the existence of slavery was a controversial topic during the creation of the Declaration of Independence and the Constitution. The abolition movement as a whole did not start until the 1830s, but nevertheless, slavery is a cause that gradually grew more important over the following decades. In addition, opponents of slavery were divided by different motivations—some believed that it stifled the economy, while others focused on moral issues.

On the other end of the spectrum, a single event can have numerous results. The rise of the telegraph, for example, had several effects on American history. The telegraph allowed news to travel much quicker and turned events into immediate national news, such as the sinking of the USS Maine, which sparked the Spanish-American War. In addition, the telegraph helped make railroads run more efficiently by improving the links between stations. The faster speed of both travel and communications led to a shift in time itself, and localized times were replaced by standardized time zones across the nation.

By looking at different examples of cause and effect closely, it becomes clear that no event occurs without one—if not multiple—causes behind it, and that each historical event can have a variety of direct and indirect consequences.

One of the most critical elements of cause-and-effect relationships is how they are relevant not only in studying history but also in contemporary events. People must realize that events and developments today will likely have a number of consequences later on. Therefore, the study of cause and effect remains vital in understanding the past, the present, and the future.

Describing the Connections Between People, Places, Environments, Processes, and Events

The primary role of social studies is to illuminate connections between people, places, environments, processes, and events. Therefore, test takers must be prepared to examine correlations and causations in social studies. Correlations are connections that do not necessarily show any signs of causation. Two things are correlated when they happen to the same people, or in the same circumstances, or at the

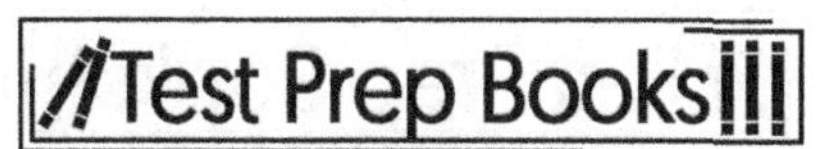

same time. For example, the increased popularity of apocalyptic literature in 2008 and 2009 can be **correlated** with the Great Recession that occurred around that time. However, these two events might not be **causally related**. A relationship is causal when one thing causes another to happen. In other words, the rise in apocalyptic literature may be caused by other cultural changes, such as an increasing disenchantment with humanity, a disenchantment caused by an increase in global wars and genocide.

Other connections can be discovered by analyzing causation. For instance, the mass immigration of Irish workers to the United States in the 19th century can likely be understood as a cause and effect scenario spawned by the great potato famine of that era—immigrants had to flee Ireland because their families were going to starve to death. In this instance, one thing caused another. Students of social studies must constantly be on the search for these connections. They must study the ways in which geography (for example, the Rio Grande River) affects immigration patterns (for example, undocumented immigration from Mexico to America in the 20th and 21st centuries). They must even be aware of the ways in which people (for example, Adolf Hitler) influence events (the rise of Nazi Germany in the 1930s and 1940s).

Connections are discussed in passages, political cartoons, and test questions. Test takers must be able to contextualize, historicize, and analyze connections. Too often the field of social studies is taught as a linear timeline. But, in reality, the field of social studies is more like a complex web of ideas, characters, events, eras, movements, counter-movements, and belief systems. Additionally, views of historical events change throughout history. Today we may analyze slavery differently than the era in which slavery was legal in the United States. Therefore, students of social studies must also be aware of their own connections to history and all the variables that form its foundations. Below is one example of a cognitive map showing the connections between people, places, environments, processes, and events in social studies.

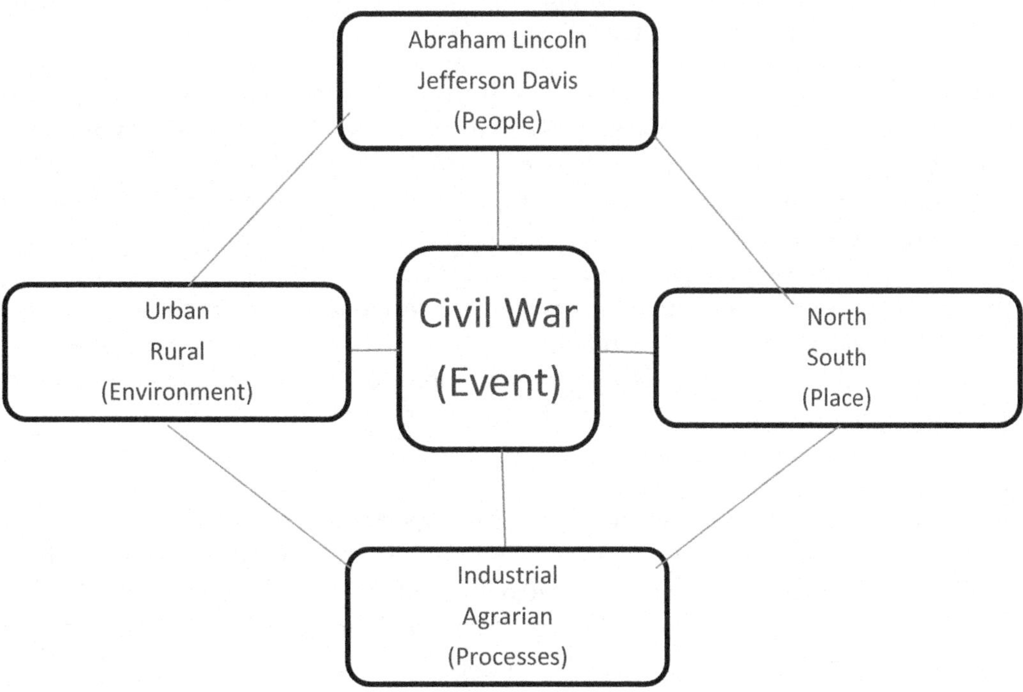

Putting Events in Order and Understanding the Steps in a Process

Social studies students must understand how to determine the timeline/chronology of events through a process called sequencing. Sequencing allows students to gain a better understanding of change over time in history. Social studies classrooms often employ test questions that force students to recall the correct chronology, or time order, of important historical events.

Along with sequencing, social studies students should be able to carry out a process known as categorizing. Categorizing is the process by which historical themes, events, agents, persons, movements, or ideas are placed in designated categories that help students understand their historical significance. Categorization is usually most effective when certain words or phrases are organized by themes or concepts. For instance, the categorical concept of "economic depression" could help students better understand such historical events as the Panic of 1819, the Great Depression, and the Great Recession. Categorization allows students to link unrelated events in history.

Identifying associations and cause-and-effect relationships strengthens a student's ability to sequence events in history. All U.S. history is a series of associated events leading to still other events. A cause is what made something happen. An effect is what happens because of something. Understanding cause-and-effect helps students to understand the proverbial *why* of history; it helps them breathe more meaning into history.

Comparing and contrasting is another strategy that will make students more historically informed. In history, we often compare two or more things to understand their similarities and differences better. Part of the historical process is understanding what historical characteristics are unique or utterly common. Students might, for instance, compare and contrast the American Revolution to the Texas Revolution to gain a better understanding of the ways in which such variables as time, geographic location, and contributing persons affect history.

Summarizing is a strategy that is also used often throughout the historical process in a social studies classroom. Students will not only have to summarize the meaning of historical events or eras, but they will also need to know how to summarize the important points of primary and secondary sources. Summaries allow students to convey their knowledge in a short, concise, digestible fashion. Part of summarizing requires that students find the main idea of a particular article, source, or paragraph. Main ideas help students make their summaries even more concise and effective. Summarizing sometimes requires students to make generalizations or draw inferences/conclusions. Often there are "gaps of information" in the sources provided to students. Students will have to use background knowledge and critical-thinking skills to fill in these gaps with generalizations (broad, sweeping statements) or inferences/conclusions (educated guesses, predictions, or assumptions).

Analyzing the Relationship of Events, Processes, and/or Ideas

Events, processes, and ideas can be related in different ways. Earlier events don't necessarily *cause* later ones; in many cases, they simply occurred prior to the later event. For example, although the battles at Concord and Lexington may seem to be instantaneous eruptions of violence during the American Revolution, they stemmed from a variety of factors. The most obvious influences behind those two battles were the assortment of taxes and policies imposed on the Thirteen Colonies following the French and Indian War from 1754 to 1763. Taxation without direct representation, combined with the deployment of British soldiers to enforce these policies, greatly increased American resistance. Earlier events, such as the Boston Massacre and the Boston Tea Party, similarly stemmed from conflicts

between British soldiers and local colonists over perceived tyranny and rebelliousness. Therefore, the start of the American Revolution progressed from earlier developments.

The Effect of Different Social Studies Concepts on an Argument or Point Of View

Analyzing How Events and Situations Shape the Author's Point of View

Many people want to rise above their historical contexts, but it is an impossibility. Whether one likes it or not, the ideas of humanity are always influenced by the forces of history. The individual and collective consciousness of humanity is often dictated by historical events and situations. A Jew writing in Germany during World War II would inevitably be affected in some capacity by the anti-Semitic tendencies of Nazism. A Texas-based Mexican national writing during the Mexican-American War of the 1840s would inevitably be influenced by American expansionism. A college student writing and liking posts on Facebook during the Great Recession of 2008 would inevitably be exposed to the effects of the stock market's decline. Even if the author does not comment on these events, they still shape the author's point of view. When analyzing a history text or a historical cartoon, test takers should first ask key questions: "When, where, and why was this documented created?" Often the answers to these questions provide test takers with the evidence they need to properly analyze the documents and answer multiple choice questions.

In some cases, the author of a document explicitly comments on history. The author may refer to historical persons, events, or dates. Test takers should take note of these persons, events, and dates because they offer evidence for answering questions or prompts. For instance, a primary source such as Anne Frank's diary directly refers to the events of World War II and the aggressions of Germans. In other cases, it is up to the test taker to decode the implicit messages embedded in a text in order to gain a better understanding of historical influences. A good place to start with this decoding process is the date the document was created. If test takers know the date of a document, they can begin to illuminate historical correlations. For instance, a historian writing in the 1960s might not explicitly discuss the historical opinions of the New Left (a political movement of the 1960s), but a test taker may be able to decode the implicit messages embedded in the text and infer that the historian may have been influenced by that era of political thought.

Evaluating Whether the Author's Evidence is Factual, Relevant, and Sufficient

It's important to read any piece of writing critically. The goal is to discover the point and purpose of what the author is writing about through analysis. It's also crucial to establish the point or stance the author has taken on the topic of the piece. After determining the author's perspective, readers can then more effectively develop their own viewpoints on the subject.

If the argument is that wind energy is the best solution, the author will use facts that support this idea. That same author may leave out relevant facts on solar energy. The way the author uses facts can influence the reader, so it's important to consider the facts being used, how those facts are being presented, and what information might be left out.

Making Judgments About How Different Ideas Impact the Author's Argument

To reach supportable judgments and conclusions in social studies, teachers and students must be prepared to categorize and synthesize a variety of primary and secondary sources, paying close attention to which sources are legitimate sources of fact or opinion. Students must also be able to justifiably quote information from these sources to establish historical generalizations, or "general statements that identify themes that unite or separate source materials." Often, a generalization identifies key features, relationships, or differences found throughout multiple sources.

Identifying Bias

Bias exists in all forms of written and visual documentation. In social studies, it is especially important to look out for bias, in both primary and secondary sources. Bias can stem from various sources, including: historical context, cultural background, personal beliefs, political affiliation, and religious values. All these things shape the way an individual sees and writes about history and society. For example, a conservative author writing in the late 1980s may have been likely to support the political initiative known as the War on Drugs.

This likelihood is due to political affiliation and historical context. The 1980s was a conservative era in American politics, thanks to the rise of President Ronald Reagan. It was also a historical era that responded accordingly to the crack epidemic and gained conservative support for expanded police enforcement. Additionally, a communist political cartoonist in the Soviet Union during the Cold War may be likely to paint a picture of the United States as an aggressor. That era of history pitted the Soviet Union against the United States on a global level. Biases even emerge in secondary sources; people analyzing history are influenced by their own cultural-historical contexts.

Propaganda in Social Studies Readings

There are times in which biases are so extreme that they take the form of propaganda. Propaganda means written, spoken, or visual texts that try to influence or control the opinions of audiences. Two examples of propaganda are the texts and political cartoons published by Nazi Germany during Adolf Hitler's era of leadership. These materials tried to influence or control the beliefs of Germany by exposing them to extreme biases. GED test takers often have to decode texts and political cartoons by exposing biases or propagandistic tendencies.

Using Numbers and Graphics in Social Studies

Using Data Presented in Visual Form, Including Maps, Charts, Graphs, and Tables

Making Sense of Information that is Presented in Different Ways

Primary sources contain firsthand documentation of a historical event or era. Primary sources are provided by people who have experienced an historical era or event. Primary sources capture a specific moment, context, or era in history. They are valued as eyewitness accounts and personal perspectives. Examples include diaries, memoirs, journals, letters, interviews, photographs, context-specific artwork, government documents, constitutions, newspapers, personal items, libraries, and archives. Another example of a primary source is the Declaration of Independence. This historical document captures the revolutionary sentiment of an era in American history.

Authors of secondary sources write about events, contexts, and eras in history with a relative amount of experiential, geographic, or temporal distance. Normally, secondary source authors aren't firsthand witnesses. In some cases, they may have experienced an event, but they are offering secondhand, retrospective accounts of their experience. All scholars and historians produce secondary sources—they gather primary source information and synthesize it for a new generation of students. Monographs, biographies, magazine articles, scholarly journals, theses, dissertations, textbooks, and encyclopedias

are all secondary sources. In some rare instances, secondary sources become so enmeshed in their era of inquiry that they later become primary sources for future scholars and analysts.

Both primary and secondary sources of information are useful. They both offer invaluable insight that helps the writer learn more about the subject matter. However, researchers are cautioned to examine the information closely and to consider the time period as well as the cultural, political, and social climate in which accounts were given. Learning to distinguish between reliable sources of information and questionable accounts is paramount to a quality research report.

Analyzing Information from Maps, Tables, Charts, Photographs, and Political Cartoons

Geographers utilize a variety of maps in their study of the spatial world. Projections are maps that represent the spherical globe on a flat surface. Conformal projections attempt to preserve shape but distort size and area. For example, the most well-known projection, the Mercator projection, drastically distorts the size of land areas at the poles. In this particular map, Antarctica, one of the smallest continents, appears massive, while the areas closer to the equator are depicted more accurately.

Other projections attempt to lessen the amount of distortion; the equal-area projection, for example, attempts to accurately represent the size of landforms. However, equal-area projections alter the shapes and angles of landforms regardless of their positioning on the map. Other projections are hybrids of the two primary models. For example, the Robinson projection tries to balance form and area in order to create a more visually accurate representation of the spatial world. Despite the efforts to maintain consistency with shapes, projections cannot provide accurate representations of the Earth's surface due to their flat, two-dimensional nature. In this sense, projections are useful symbols of space, but they do not always provide the most accurate portrayal of reality.

Unlike projections, topographic maps display contour lines, which represent the relative elevation of a particular place and are very useful for surveyors, engineers, and/or travelers. For example, hikers may refer to topographic maps to calculate their daily climbs.

Similar to topographic maps, **isoline maps** are also useful for calculating data and differentiating between the characteristics of two places. These maps use symbols to represent values and lines to connect points with the same value. For example, an isoline map could display average temperatures of a given area. The sections which share the same average temperature would be grouped together by lines. Additionally, isoline maps can help geographers study the world by generating questions. For example, is elevation the only reason for differences in temperature? If not, what other factors could cause the disparity between the values?

Thematic maps are also quite useful because they display the geographical distribution of complex political, physical, social, cultural, economic, or historical themes. For example, a thematic map could indicate an area's election results using a different color for each candidate. There are several different kinds of thematic maps, including dot-density maps and flow-line maps. A *dot-density map* uses dots to illustrate volume and density; these dots could represent a certain population, or the number of specific events that have taken place in an area. Flow-line maps utilize lines of varying thicknesses to illustrate the movement of goods, people, or even animals between two places. Thicker lines represent a greater number of moving elements, and thinner lines represent a smaller number.

Representing Textual Data into Visual Form

Students should not only be able to analyze maps and other infographics, but they should also be able to create graphs, charts, tables, documents, maps, timelines, and other visual materials to represent geographic, political, historical, economic, and cultural features. Students should be made aware of the different options they have to present data. They should understand that maps visually display geographic features, and they can be used to illustrate key relationships in human geography and natural geography. Maps can indicate themes in history, politics, economics, culture, social relationships, and demographic distributions.

Students can also choose to display data or information in a variety of graphs: Bar graphs compare two or more things with parallel bars; line graphs show change over time with strategic points placed carefully between vertical and horizontal axes; and pie graphs divide wholes into percentages or parts. Likewise, students can choose to use timelines or tables to present data/information. Timelines arrange events or ideas into chronological order, and tables arrange words or numbers into columns or rows. These are just some of the visual tools teachers and students can use to help visually convey their historical questions or ideas.

Using Graphs with Appropriate Labeling, and Using the Data to Predict Trends

Being "literate" in social studies means that teachers and students must be ready to interpret a variety of forms of data. In social studies, data is usually numerical or statistical information offered in the form of a graph, chart, table, document, map, or timeline.

Sometimes valuable data can also be embedded in documents, maps, or timelines. Thus, it is important that every student is also exposed to these data-based tools in a social studies classroom. Much like all sources, students should be challenged to determine the validity of the data presented in graphs, charts, tables, documents, maps, and timelines.

Dependent and Independent Variables

As mentioned, the independent variable in an experiment or process is the one that is manipulated, while the dependent one experiences change because of the manipulations to the independent variable.

Correlation Versus Causation

In social studies, much like in basic statistics, correlation does not always imply causation. Correlation means events occur together, in a relation of more than just random chance. Causation means one thing causes other another. In social studies, one event can be shown to lead to another. For example, the bombing of Pearl Harbor by the Japanese led to the entrance of the United States in the Second World War. The bombing of Pearl Harbor encouraged President Franklin Delano Roosevelt and the United States Congress to declare war on Japan. This example shows a clear line of cause and effect, one that is indisputable in terms of historical evidence.

However, when discussing the Great Depression in America, historians are far less likely to come to a consensus about the cause. Since there are a multitude of variables contributing to the Great Depression, delineating a clear line of causation is more difficult. Instead, historians can discuss the correlation of factors that led to the Depression, which include: increased inflation, increased debt, various taxes and policies, fear, isolationism, corruption, and the excesses of the Roaring Twenties. It is

hard to come up with a clear formula of "this equaled that" when it comes to the Great Depression. Thus, it is more applicable to discuss the historical correlations between people, trends, and events.

Using Statistics in Social Studies

Mean, Median, Mode, and Range of a Data Set

Recall that the center of a set of data (statistical values) can be represented by its mean, median, or mode. These are sometimes referred to as measures of central tendency. Measures of central tendency can also be used to analyze and understand data related to history and social studies.

The mean is the average of the data set. The mean can be calculated by adding the data values and dividing by the sample size (the number of data points). Suppose a student has test scores of 93, 84, 88, 72, 91, and 77. To find the mean, or average, the scores are added and the sum is divided by 6 because there are 6 test scores:

$$\frac{93+84+88+72+91+77}{6}=\frac{505}{6}=84.17$$

Given the mean of a data set and the sum of the data points, the sample size can be determined by dividing the sum by the mean. Suppose you are told that Kate averaged 12 points per game and scored a total of 156 points for the season. The number of games that she played (the sample size or the number of data points) can be determined by dividing the total points (sum of data points) by her average (mean of data points): $\frac{156}{12}=13$. Therefore, Kate played in 13 games this season.

If given the mean of a data set and the sample size, the sum of the data points can be determined by multiplying the mean and sample size. Suppose you are told that Tom worked 6 days last week for an average of 5.5 hours per day. The total number of hours worked for the week (sum of data points) can be determined by multiplying his daily average (mean of data points) by the number of days worked (sample size):

$$5.5\times 6=33$$

Therefore, Tom worked a total of 33 hours last week.

The median of a data set is the value of the data point in the middle when the sample is arranged in numerical order. To find the median of a data set, the values are written in order from least to greatest. The lowest and highest values are simultaneously eliminated, repeating until the value in the middle remains. Suppose the salaries of math teachers are: $35,000; $38,500; $41,000; $42,000; $42,000; $44,500; $49,000. The values are listed from least to greatest to find the median. The lowest and highest values are eliminated until only the middle value remains. Repeating this step three times reveals a median salary of $42,000. If the sample set has an even number of data points, two values will remain after all others are eliminated. In this case, the mean of the two middle values is the median. Consider the following data set: 7, 9, 10, 13, 14, 14. Eliminating the lowest and highest values twice leaves two values, 10 and 13, in the middle. The mean of these values $\left(\frac{10+13}{2}\right)$ is the median. Therefore, the set has a median of 11.5.

The mode of a data set is the value that appears most often. A data set may have a single mode, multiple modes, or no mode. If different values repeat equally as often, multiple modes exist. If no value repeats, no mode exists. Consider the following data sets:

- A: 7, 9, 10, 13, 14, 14
- B: 37, 44, 33, 37, 49, 44, 51, 34, 37, 33, 44
- C: 173, 154, 151, 168, 155

Set A has a mode of 14. Set B has modes of 37 and 44. Set C has no mode.

The range of a data set is the difference between the highest and the lowest values in the set. The range can be considered the span of the data set. To determine the range, the smallest value in the set is subtracted from the largest value. The ranges for the data sets A, B, and C above are calculated as follows:

A: $14 - 7 = 7$

B: $51 - 33 = 18$

C: $173 - 151 = 22$

Practice Quiz

The next three questions refer to the passage below:

> It hath been shewn to have been the constant Opinion of there being a North-west Passage, from the Time soon after which the South Sea was discovered near the Western Part of America, and that this Opinion was adopted by the greatest Men not only in the Time they lived, but whose Eminence and great Abilities are revered by the present Age. That there is a Sea to Westward of Hudson's Bay, there hath been given the concurrent Testimony of Indians; and of Navigators and Indians that there is a Streight which unites such Sea with the Western Ocean. The Voyage which lead us into these Considerations, hath so many Circumstances relating to it, which, now they have been considered, shew the greatest Probability of its being authentick; which carry with them as much the Evidence of a Fact, afford as great a Degree of Credibility as we have for any Transaction done a long Time since, which hath not been of a publick Nature and transacted in the Face of the World, so as to fall under the Notice of every one, though under the Disadvantage that the Intent on one Part must have been to have it concealed and buried in Oblivion.

Excerpt from *The Great Probability of a Northwest Passage* by Thomas Jefferys, 1768

1. Which of the following events most directly triggered increased interest in the maritime route described in the passage?
   a. Vasco da Gama sailing around the Cape of Good Hope in 1488.
   b. Christopher Columbus reaching the Caribbean in 1492.
   c. Ferdinand Magellan's expedition circumnavigating the world in 1522.
   d. Henry Hudson exploring the Hudson Bay in 1611.

2. Which of the following was a long-term consequence of explorers looking for a "North-west passage"?
   a. European powers gained a faster route to the Pacific Ocean.
   b. European powers abandoned international trade networks.
   c. European powers forged alliances with Amerindian empires.
   d. European powers colonized the Americas.

3. Which of the following people most likely funded the expeditions alluded to in the passage?
   a. Monarch
   b. Feudal lord
   c. Leader of a merchant trade guild
   d. Military general

Questions 4–5 refer to the passage below:

> What is dangerous for Japan is, not the imitation of the outer features of the West, but the acceptance of the motive force of the Western nationalism as her own. Her social ideals are already showing signs of defeat at the hands of politics. I can see her motto, taken from science, "Survival of the Fittest," writ large at the entrance of her present-day history—the motto whose meaning is, "Help yourself, and never heed what it costs to others"; the motto of the blind man who only believes in what he can touch, because he cannot see. But those who can see know that men are so closely knit that when you strike others the blow comes back to yourself. The moral law, which is the greatest discovery of man, is the discovery of this wonderful truth, that man becomes all the truer the more he realizes himself in others. This truth has not only a subjective value but is manifested in every department of our life. And nations who sedulously cultivate moral blindness as the cult of patriotism will end their existence in a sudden and violent death.

Excerpt from the essay "Nationalism in Japan" by Rabindranath Tagore, 1917

4. Which of the following BEST summarizes the "outer features of the West" that Japan adopted in the nineteenth century?
    a. Japan enacted a written constitution and modernized its military in the nineteenth century.
    b. Japan outlawed Shintoism and orchestrated mass conversions to Christianity.
    c. Japan encouraged nationalism to strengthen the Shogun.
    d. Japan adopted European moral laws and other positive social ideals.

5. Nationalism had the LEAST influence on which one of the following world events?
    a. German unification
    b. Latin American wars of independence
    c. Russo-Turkish War
    d. War of the Spanish Succession

See answers on next page

Answer Explanations

1. B: Jefferys is referencing the Northwest Passage. There were rumors about a Northwest Passage to Asia prior to Columbus reaching the Caribbean, and his voyage ignited a firestorm of interest. From 1492 to 1800, European powers sponsored many hundreds of expeditions to locate the route. Thus, Choice *B* is the correct answer. Vasco da Gama sailing around the Cape of Good Hope led to increased European trade with East Africa, India, and China, but his journey around Africa was unrelated to the Northwest Passage. So, Choice *A* is incorrect. Ferdinand Magellan's circumnavigation of the world didn't increase interest in a Northwest Passage because his expedition traveled to Asia across the southern portion of the Atlantic Ocean. So, Choice *C* is incorrect. Choice *D* is the second best answer. European explorers believed the Northwest Passage was located to the west of Hudson Bay, and the passage mentions Hudson Bay. However, the voyage of Christopher Columbus was the inciting incident for the entire Age of Discovery, so Choice *D* is incorrect.

2. D: European explorers never found the Northwest Passage, but the search uncovered the Americas' economic potential. European colonization started almost immediately after Columbus reached the Caribbean, and it spread across both continents as explorers continued to search for the elusive route to Asia. Thus, Choice *D* is the correct answer. Although Ferdinand Magellan found a passage to Asia through the southern Atlantic, it was much slower than sailing around the Cape of Good Hope. So, Choice *A* is incorrect. The search for a Northwest Passage exponentially increased international trade, so Choice *B* is incorrect. European powers occasionally made strategic short-term alliances with individual Amerindian tribes, but alliances weren't a long-term consequence of European exploration in the Americas. As such, Choice *C* is incorrect.

3. A: European monarchies were the primary sponsors of maritime expeditions that searched for an alternative route to Asia via a Northwest Passage in the Atlantic Ocean. Thus, Choice *A* is the correct answer. Feudal political systems collapsed in the fifteenth century, and the passage was published in 1768. So, Choice *B* is incorrect. Choice C is the second-best answer. Some wealthy merchants invested in joint-stock companies that sponsored expeditions, but maritime expeditions typically required a royal charter. As such, the monarchy was still always involved in maritime expeditions during the eighteenth century. In addition, joint-stock companies were independent legal entities, so they were rarely connected to trade guilds. Therefore, Choice *C* is incorrect. Although maritime expeditions usually included a militarized component, military generals were not a primary source of funding. So, Choice *D* is incorrect.

4. A: The passage mentions that Japan has already imitated the "outer features of the West" before issuing a warning against nationalism. During the late nineteenth century, Japan followed the example of great European powers by modernizing its navy and adopting the Meiji Constitution in writing. Both of these reforms fall under the category of "outer features of the West" as the phrase is used in the passage. Nationalism is defined in spiritual terms throughout the passage, so it would be an "inner feature of the West." Thus, Choice *A* is the correct answer. Shintoism is a traditional Japanese religion, and it's not mentioned in the passage. Japan also didn't orchestrate mass conversions to Christianity, so Choice *B* is incorrect. The Shogun was a Japanese military dictatorship that held power between 1185 and 1868. Japanese modernization efforts dissolved the Shogun, and nationalism was adopted under the new imperial Japanese regime. So, Choice *C* is incorrect. Choice *D* is incorrect because Japan didn't adopt European moral laws or social ideals; rather, Japan embraced nationalism in the late-eighteenth and early-nineteenth centuries.

5. D: The Prussian political leader Otto von Bismarck leveraged nationalism to rally support for German unification, which occurred in 1871. So, Choice *A* is incorrect. Mexican nationalists defeated Spanish colonizers in the Mexican Revolution, and Simon Bolivar led nationalist revolts across South America during the early nineteenth century. So, Choice *B* is incorrect. The Russo-Turkish War was largely caused by nationalist revolts in Bulgaria, Montenegro, and Romania against the Ottoman Empire, so Choice *C* is incorrect. The War of the Spanish Succession was fought in the early eighteenth century, which predates the rise of nationalism in continental Europe. Thus, Choice *D* is the correct answer.

GED Practice Test #1

Reading Comprehension

Questions 1–5 are based upon the following passage:

A Scandal in Bohemia

To Sherlock Holmes she is always *the* woman. I have seldom heard him mention her under any other name. In his eyes she eclipses and predominates the whole of her sex. It was not that he felt any emotion akin to love for Irene Adler. All emotions, and that one particularly, were abhorrent to his cold, precise but admirably balanced mind. He was, I take it, the most perfect reasoning and observing machine that the world has seen, but as a lover he would have placed himself in a false position. He never spoke of the softer passions, save with a gibe and a sneer. They were admirable things for the observer—excellent for drawing the veil from men' s motives and actions. But for the trained reasoner to admit such intrusions into his own delicate and finely adjusted temperament was to introduce a distracting factor which might throw a doubt upon all his mental results. Grit in a sensitive instrument, or a crack in one of his own high-power lenses, would not be more disturbing than a strong emotion in a nature such as his. And yet there was but one woman to him, and that woman was the late Irene Adler, of dubious and questionable memory.

I had seen little of Holmes lately. My marriage had drifted us away from each other. My own complete happiness, and the home-centred interests which rise up around the man who first finds himself master of his own establishment, were sufficient to absorb all my attention, while Holmes, who loathed every form of society with his whole Bohemian soul, remained in our lodgings in Baker Street, buried among his old books, and alternating from week to week between cocaine and ambition, the drowsiness of the drug, and the fierce energy of his own keen nature. He was still, as ever, deeply attracted by the study of crime, and occupied his immense faculties and extraordinary powers of observation in following out those clues, and clearing up those mysteries which had been abandoned as hopeless by the official police. From time to time I heard some vague account of his doings: of his summons to Odessa in the case of the Trepoff murder, of his clearing up of the singular tragedy of the Atkinson brothers at Trincomalee, and finally of the mission which he had accomplished so delicately and successfully for the reigning family of Holland. Beyond these signs of his activity, however, which I merely shared with all the readers of the daily press, I knew little of my former friend and companion.

One night—it was on the twentieth of March, 1888—I was returning from a journey to a patient (for I had now returned to civil practice), when my way led me through Baker Street. As I passed the well-remembered door, which must always be associated in my mind with my wooing, and with the dark incidents of the Study in Scarlet, I was seized with a keen desire to see Holmes again, and to know how he was employing his extraordinary powers. His rooms were brilliantly lit, and, even as I looked up, I saw his tall, spare figure pass twice in a dark silhouette against the blind. He was pacing the room swiftly, eagerly, with his head sunk upon his chest and his hands clasped behind him. To me, who knew his every mood and habit, his attitude and manner told their own story. He was at work again. He had risen out of his drug-created dreams and was hot upon the scent of some new problem. I rang the bell and was shown up to the chamber which had formerly been in part my own.

His manner was not effusive. It seldom was; but he was glad, I think, to see me. With hardly a word spoken, but with a kindly eye, he waved me to an armchair, threw across his case of cigars, and indicated a spirit case and a gasogene in the corner. Then he stood before the fire and looked me over in his singular introspective fashion.

Excerpt from The Adventures of Sherlock Holmes by A. Conan Doyle

1. Who is the narrator of this passage?
   a. An omniscient narrator
   b. A physician
   c. A police officer
   d. A resident of Baker Street

2. How did the narrator learn of Sherlock Holmes' latest cases?
   a. Reading the newspaper
   b. Reviewing police reports
   c. Talking with Holmes
   d. Watching the cases unfold

3. Which of the following is true about Sherlock Holmes?
   a. He admired the effects of love on people.
   b. He appreciated the way love made him feel.
   c. He loved Irene Adler openly and freely.
   d. He valued the use of love to help him solve cases.

4. What is the meaning of the word *singular* in the following sentence?

   Then he stood before the fire and looked me over in his singular introspective fashion.

   a. Exceptional
   b. Friendly
   c. Only
   d. Typical

5. What is the main purpose of the passage?
   a. To argue that Holmes never solves crimes alone
   b. To describe the history between Holmes the narrator
   c. To provide details on Holmes' current case
   d. To summarize Holmes' feelings on emotions

Questions 6–11 are based upon the following passage:

Who Will Save the Birds?

Three years ago, I think there were not many bird-lovers in the United States who believed it possible to prevent the total extinction of both egrets from our fauna. All the known rookeries accessible to plume-hunters had been totally destroyed. Two years ago, the secret discovery of several small, hidden colonies prompted William Dutcher, President of the National Association of Audubon Societies, and Mr. T. Gilbert Pearson, Secretary, to attempt the protection of those colonies. With a fund contributed for the

purpose, wardens were hired and duly commissioned. As previously stated, one of those wardens was shot dead in cold blood by a plume hunter. The task of guarding swamp rookeries from the attacks of money-hungry desperadoes to whom the accursed plumes were worth their weight in gold, is a very chancy proceeding. There is now one warden in Florida who says that "before they get my rookery they will first have to get me."

Thus far the protective work of the Audubon Association has been successful. Now there are twenty colonies, which contain all told, about 5,000 egrets and about 120,000 herons and ibises which are guarded by the Audubon wardens. One of the most important is on Bird Island, a mile out in Orange Lake, central Florida, and it is ably defended by Oscar E. Baynard. To-day, the plume hunters who do not dare to raid the guarded rookeries are trying to study out the lines of flight of the birds, to and from their feeding-grounds, and shoot them in transit. Their motto is—"Anything to beat the law, and get the plumes." It is there that the state of Florida should take part in the war.

The success of this campaign is attested by the fact that last year a number of egrets were seen in eastern Massachusetts—for the first time in many years. And so to-day the question is, can the wardens continue to hold the plume-hunters at bay?

Excerpt from *Our Vanishing Wildlife,* by William T. Hornaday

6. The author's use of first-person pronouns in the following text does NOT have which of the following effects?

> Three years ago, I think there were not many bird-lovers in the United States who believed it possible to prevent the total extinction of both egrets from our fauna.

a. The phrase "I think" acts as a sort of hedging, where the author's tone is less direct and absolute.
b. It allows the reader to more easily connect with the author.
c. It encourages the reader to empathize with the egrets.
d. It distances the reader from the text by overemphasizing the story.

7. What purpose does the quote serve at the end of the first paragraph?

a. The quote shows proof of a hunter threatening one of the wardens.
b. The quote lightens the mood by illustrating the colloquial language of the region.
c. The quote provides an example of a warden protecting one of the colonies.
d. The quote provides much needed comic relief in the form of a joke.

8. What is the meaning of the word *rookeries* in the following text?

> To-day, the plume hunters who do not dare to raid the guarded rookeries are trying to study out the lines of flight of the birds, to and from their feeding-grounds, and shoot them in transit.

a. Houses in a slum area
b. A place where hunters gather to trade tools
c. A place where wardens go to trade stories
d. A colony of breeding birds

9. What is on Bird Island?
   a. Hunters selling plumes
   b. An important bird colony
   c. Bird Island Battle between the hunters and the wardens
   d. An important egret with unique plumes

10. What is the main purpose of the passage?
   a. To persuade the audience to act in preservation of the bird colonies
   b. To show the effect hunting egrets has had on the environment
   c. To argue that the preservation of bird colonies has had a negative impact on the environment
   d. To demonstrate the success of the protective work of the Audubon Association

11. Why are hunters trying to study the lines of flight of the birds?
   a. To further their studies of ornithology
   b. To help wardens preserve the lives of the birds
   c. To have a better opportunity to hunt the birds
   d. To build their homes under the lines of flight because they believe it brings good luck

Questions 12–18 are based on the following passage:

What is the "Business of the Holes"?

In the quest to understand existence, modern philosophers must question if humans can fully comprehend the world. Classical western approaches to philosophy tend to hold that one can understand something, be it an event or object, by standing outside of the phenomena and observing it. It is then by unbiased observation that one can grasp the details of the world. This seems to hold true for many things. Scientists conduct experiments and record their findings, and thus many natural phenomena become comprehensible. However, several of these observations were possible because humans used tools in order to make these discoveries.

This may seem like an extraneous matter. After all, people invented things like microscopes and telescopes in order to enhance their capacity to view cells or the movement of stars. While humans are still capable of seeing things, the question remains if human beings have the capacity to fully observe and see the world in order to understand it. It would not be an impossible stretch to argue that what humans see through a microscope is not the exact thing itself, but a human interpretation of it.

This would seem to be the case in the "Business of the Holes" experiment conducted by Richard Feynman. To study the way electrons behave, Feynman set up a barrier with two holes and a plate. The plate was there to indicate how many times the electrons would pass through the hole(s). Rather than casually observe the electrons acting under normal circumstances, Feynman discovered that electrons behave in two totally different ways depending on whether or not they are observed. The electrons that were observed had passed through either one of the holes or were caught on the plate as particles. However, electrons that weren't observed acted as waves instead of particles and passed through both holes. This indicated that electrons have a dual nature.

Electrons seen by the human eye act like particles, while unseen electrons act like waves of energy.

This dual nature of the electrons presents a conundrum. While humans now have a better understanding of electrons, the fact remains that people cannot entirely perceive how electrons behave without the use of instruments. We can only observe one of the mentioned behaviors, which only provides a partial understanding of the entire function of electrons. Therefore, we're forced to ask ourselves whether the world we observe is objective or if it is subjectively perceived by humans. Or, an alternative question: can man understand the world only through machines that will allow them to observe natural phenomena?

Both questions humble man's capacity to grasp the world. However, those ideas don't take into account that many phenomena have been proven by human beings without the use of machines, such as the discovery of gravity. Like all philosophical questions, whether man's reason and observation alone can understand the universe can be approached from many angles.

12. What is the author's motivation for writing the passage?
    a. Bring to light an alternative view on human perception by examining the role of technology in human understanding.
    b. Educate the reader on the latest astroparticle physics discovery and offer terms that may be unfamiliar to the reader.
    c. Argue that humans are totally blind to the realities of the world by presenting an experiment that proves that electrons are not what they seem on the surface.
    d. Reflect on opposing views of human understanding.

13. Which of the following most closely resembles the way in which paragraph four is structured?
    a. It offers one solution, questions the solution, and then ends with an alternative solution.
    b. It presents an inquiry, explains the detail of that inquiry, and then offers a solution.
    c. It presents a problem, explains the details of that problem, and then ends with more inquiry.
    d. It gives a definition, offers an explanation, and then ends with an inquiry.

14. For the classical approach to understanding to hold true, which of the following must be required?
    a. The person observing must use a telescope.
    b. The person observing must prove their theory beyond a doubt.
    c. Multiple witnesses must be present.
    d. The person observing must be unbiased.

15. Which best describes how the electrons in the experiment behaved like waves?
    a. The electrons moved up and down like actual waves.
    b. The electrons passed through both holes and then onto the plate.
    c. The electrons converted to photons upon touching the plate.
    d. Electrons were seen passing through one hole or the other.

16. The author mentions gravity in the last paragraph in order to do what?
    a. In order to show that different natural phenomena test man's ability to grasp the world.
    b. To prove that since man has not measured it with the use of tools or machines, humans cannot know the true nature of gravity.
    c. To demonstrate an example of natural phenomena humans discovered and understood without the use of tools or machines.
    d. To show an alternative solution to the nature of electrons that humans have not thought of yet.

17. Which situation best parallels the revelation of the dual nature of electrons discovered in Feynman's experiment?
    a. A man is born color-blind and grows up observing everything in lighter or darker shades. With the invention of special goggles he puts on, he discovers that there are other colors in addition to different shades.
    b. The coelacanth was thought to be extinct, but a live specimen was just recently discovered. There are now two living species of coelacanth known to man, and both are believed to be endangered.
    c. In the Middle Ages, blacksmiths added carbon to iron, thus inventing steel. The consequences of this important discovery would have its biggest effects during the industrial revolution.
    d. In order to better examine and treat broken bones, the x-ray machine was invented and put to use in hospitals and medical centers.

18. Which statement about technology would the author likely disagree with?
    a. Technology can help expand the field of human vision.
    b. Technology renders human observation irrelevant.
    c. Developing tools used in observation and research indicates growing understanding of our world in itself.
    d. Studying certain phenomena necessitates the use of tools and machines.

Questions 19–24 are based upon the following passage:

The Life of Frederick Douglass

Frederick Douglass's experiences as a slave established his authority on the subject matter. "What to the American Slave is the Fourth of July?" was a self-referential speech that based much of its criticisms on Douglass's personal encounters.

Frederick Douglass was born Frederick Augustus Washington Bailey in Talbot County, Maryland, in 1818. His mother, Harriet Bailey, was a slave, and his father was an unknown[20] white man, rumored to be his slave owner at the time. To these rumors, Douglass would later write in his autobiography, "that my master was my father, may or may not be true...is of but little consequence...The slaveholder, in cases not a few, sustains to his slaves the double relation of master and father" (Chesebrough 246).

Early on, Frederick recognized the injustices of slavery. Many of his experiences as a young man were later reflected in his rhetoric. Not long after Douglass's birth, he was separated from his mother and sent to live twelve miles away with his grandparents, Isaac and Betsey. From then on, Douglass recalled seeing his mother only a few times before her death when he was only seven years old. He later reflected, "For what this

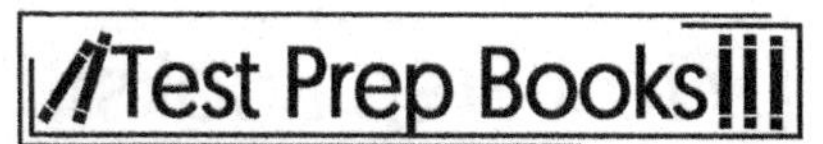

separation is done, I do not know, unless it be to hinder the development of the child's affection toward its mother, and to blunt and destroy the natural affection of the mother for the child. This is the inevitable result" (Pitts 288). During the nineteenth century, slaveholders often removed children from the care of their parents to destabilize their family structures. This was done in order to keep slaves feeling isolated and to ensure that slave parents remained focused on their work. Later on in his life, Douglass acknowledged the cruel separation of mother and child as a way for slaveholders to foster familial detachment and racial injustice.

Frederick spent the next twenty-one years of his life as a slave. His experiences during these years shaped much of the oratory and rhetorical style he employed later on in his career. His speeches were all the more powerful because he had first-hand anecdotes reflecting the brutal nature of slavery. Douglass developed his ethos as a speaker by simply living the life of a slave. Throughout his life, Frederick moved to numerous plantations and was forced to work under the lash of many masters. Each plantation was characterized by new and repulsive horrors.[21] Douglass witnessed "the screams for mercy, the shrieks of agony, the sound of the lash upon bare flesh, and the gory sight of flowing blood" (Chesebrough 7). Scenes of slave mothers ripped from their children and Black folk being beaten until they could not stand fueled the bitterness Douglass felt and later referenced in his speeches. Not until Douglass moved to Baltimore to live with Hugh and Sophia Auld did he feel any ounce of gratitude toward his masters. In Baltimore, Sophia treated Douglass with compassion, and taught him to read and write.

Much to the dismay of her husband, Sophia introduced Douglass to the Bible, the dictionary, and the American novel. Teaching a slave to read or write was against the law in the nineteenth century. After his initial taste of literacy, Douglass became conscious that his race was not what declared him inferior to whites, but the suppressive institution of slavery that produced his illiteracy and ignorance. With this knowledge, Douglass knew that achieving literacy was what could set him apart from the stereotypical slave. He took advantage of every opportunity to read books, magazines, advertisements, newspapers, and the Bible. He was obsessed with Webster's Spelling Book and was inspired by famous speeches from Caleb Bingham's volume, The Columbian Orator (Burke 11). Douglass was especially drawn to slave narratives and speeches given by early abolitionists. Douglass's introduction to the Bible also sparked an interest in religion. He recognized the irony of the white man's devotion to religion, yet his contradictory adherence to slavery. "He observed the use of religion to justify slavery, to support the doctrine of racial superiority and inferiority, and condone the use of the whip[22] and other forms of brutality to keep the people of color in their 'God-ordained places" (Chesebrough 8).

Annoyed with Frederick's dedication to literacy and his peculiar tendency to defy authority, Thomas Auld (Hugh's brother) sent him to live with Edward Covey. Covey succeeded in breaking Frederick by crushing his spirits and diminishing any desire he had to read. The tables were turned one morning when Frederick refused to be whipped. This incident led to a two-hour fight between Frederick and Covey, which ultimately brought Covey's beatings to an end. Douglass claimed that this moment was "the turning point in my career as a slave. My long-crushed spirit rose, cowardice departed, bold defiance took its place; and I now resolved that, however long I might remain a slave in form, the day had passed forever when I could be a slave in fact" (Chesebrough 10). Following this fight and Douglass's enlightenment, he was sent to live with a surprisingly tolerable master, William Friedland. Douglass made plans to escape, failed, and was once again sent to Baltimore under the control of Hugh Auld. On Monday, September 3, 1838, Frederick finally carried out a successful escape. He met a woman named Anna Murray, married her, and moved to Bedford, Massachusetts to begin their new life.

Once in Bedford, he was quickly introduced to William Lloyd Garrison's abolitionist paper entitled Liberator, which centered on bold criticisms of slavery. Douglass closely identified with the words of Garrison and not long after began attending abolitionist meetings. Frederick became a prominent member at anti-slavery meetings[23], speaking on the injustices of slavery and quickly making a name for himself. He was asked to speak by The Massachusetts Anti-Slavery Society and by his idol, William Lloyd Garrison (Chesebrough 18). Douglass spoke about equality, the abolition of slavery, the disjointed union, and religious irony. He rapidly earned recognition among abolitionists and harsh criticisms from pro-slavery supporters.

On July 5, 1852, Frederick Douglass delivered his most compelling anti-slavery speech to an audience of six hundred, mostly white abolitionist Americans. Douglass's speech, entitled "What to the American slave is the Fourth of July?" was an eloquent performance meant to both praise America's Founders and condemn his audience for not continuing their vision of a free and equal nation. I argue that Douglass's Fourth of July address was the most successful abolition speech of the nineteenth century, and it serves as a model for all anti-slavery orators.

Excerpt from *The Genre of Abolition Rhetoric and Frederick Douglass's 'What to the American Slave is the Fourth of July?* by Kelsey Lauren Fisher; 2011

19. What is the meaning of the following sentence?

The slaveholder, in cases not a few, sustains to his slaves the double relation of master and father.

a. Many slaveholders also fathered children with their slaves.
b. Many slaveholders insisted on being treated as fathers by their slaves.
c. Many slaveholders treated young slaves like their own children.
d. Many slaveholders were the closest thing slave children had to a father.

20. How did Douglas's separation from his mother at a young age affect their relationship?
a. It made him more eager to visit with her when he could.
b. It made him resent his mother for not keeping him.
c. It strengthened his bond with his grandparents.
d. It weakened his bond with his mother.

21. What is the mostly likely reason it was illegal to teach a slave to read or write in the nineteenth century?
    a. Reading was the only thing that made slave owners feel superior to slaves.
    b. Reading was unnecessary for the duties slaves performed.
    c. Reading would empower slaves to question their circumstances.
    d. Reading would strengthen the bond among slave families.

22. What observation did Douglas make about slave owners that highlighted their hypocrisy?
    a. They claimed to be religious but treated slaves poorly.
    b. They taught slaves to read even though it was illegal.
    c. They treated slaves like their own children but also whipped them.
    d. They valued family but separated slave families.

23. How did Douglas's "What to the American slave is the Fourth of July?" speech relate to slavery in the nineteenth century?
    a. The 4th of July was meant to end slavery in America, but it had not.
    b. The 4th of July symbolized a free and equal nation for all Americans.
    c. The 4th of July symbolized freedom for America but not for slaves.
    d. The 4th of July marked the end of slavery in America.

24. What is the purpose of this passage?
    a. To argue that Douglass's experiences as a slave made him a compelling speaker.
    b. To inform the reader about the horrendous conditions of slavery.
    c. To persuade the reader that slaves should have been taught to read.
    d. To question whether Douglas's life would have been different if he had been born free.

25. The following exchange occurred after the Baseball Coach's team suffered a heartbreaking loss in the final inning.

> Reporter: The team clearly did not rise to the challenge. I'm sure that getting zero hits in twenty at-bats with runners in scoring position hurt the team's chances at winning the game. What are your thoughts on this devastating loss?
>
> Baseball Coach: Hitting with runners in scoring position was not the reason we lost this game. We made numerous errors in the field, and our pitchers gave out too many free passes. Also, we did not even need a hit with runners in scoring position. Many of those at-bats could have driven in the run by simply making contact. Our team did not deserve to win the game.

Which of the following best describes the main point of dispute between the reporter and baseball coach?
    a. The loss was heartbreaking.
    b. Getting zero hits in twenty at-bats with runners in scoring position caused the loss.
    c. Numerous errors in the field and pitchers giving too many free passes caused the loss.
    d. The team deserved to win the game.

26. Read the following opinions of two opposing politicians:

> Conservative Politician: Social welfare programs are destroying our country. These programs are not only adding to the annual deficit, which increases the national debt, but they also discourage hard work. Our country must continue producing leaders who bootstrap their way to the top. None of our country's citizens truly *need* assistance from the government; rather, the assistance just makes things easier.
>
> Liberal Politician: Our great country is founded on the principle of hope. The country is built on the backs of immigrants who came here with nothing, except for the hope of a better life. Our country is too wealthy not to provide basic necessities for the less fortunate. Recent immigrants, single mothers, historically disenfranchised, disabled persons, and the elderly all require an ample safety net.

What is the main point of dispute between the politicians?

a. Spending on social welfare programs increases the national debt.
b. Certain classes of people rely on social welfare programs to meet their basic needs.
c. Certain classes of people would be irreparably harmed if the country failed to provide a social welfare program.
d. All of the country's leaders have bootstrapped their way to the top.

27. Which of the following passages best displays clarity, fluency, and parallelism?

a. Ernest Hemingway is probably the most noteworthy of expatriate authors. Hemingway's concise writing style, void of emotion and stream of consciousness, had a lasting impact, one which resonates to this very day. In Hemingway's novels, much like in American cinema, the hero acts without thinking, is living in the moment, and is repressing physical and emotional pain.
b. Ernest Hemingway is probably the most noteworthy of expatriate authors since his concise writing style is void of emotion and stream of consciousness and has had a lasting impact on Americans which has resonated to this very day, and Hemingway's novels are much like in American cinema. The hero acts. He doesn't think. He lives in the moment. He represses physical and emotional pain.
c. Ernest Hemingway is probably the most noteworthy of authors. His concise writing style, void of emotion and consciousness, had a lasting impact, one which resonates to this very day. In Hemingway's novels, much like in American cinema, the hero acts without thinking, lives in the moment, and represses physical and emotional pain.
d. Ernest Hemingway is probably the most noteworthy of expatriate authors. His concise writing style, void of emotion and stream of consciousness, had a lasting impact, one which resonates to this very day. In Hemingway's novels, much like in American cinema, the hero acts without thinking, lives in the moment, and represses physical and emotional pain.

28. Which of the following sentences shows correct word usage?

a. It's often been said that work is better then rest.
b. Its often been said that work is better then rest.
c. It's often been said that work is better than rest.
d. Its often been said that work is better than rest.

29. Which word or words would best link these sentences?

> Polls show that more and more people in the US distrust the government and view it as dysfunctional and corrupt. Every election, the same people are voted back into office.

a. Not surprisingly,
b. Understandably,
c. And yet,
d. Therefore,

30. Which of the following pronoun pairs should be used in the blanks below?

> The realtor showed __________ and __________ a house on Wednesday afternoon.

a. She, I
b. She, me
c. Me, her
d. Her, me

31. Read the sentence below and then follow the directions that come afterward:

> Student loan debt is at an all-time high, which is why many politicians are using this issue to gain the attention and votes of students, or anyone with student loan debt.

Rewrite, beginning with Student loan debt is at an all-time high. the next words will be which of the following:

a. because politicians want students' votes.
b. , so politicians are using the issue to gain votes.
c. , so voters are choosing politicians who care about this issue.
d. , and politicians want to do something about it.

32. Read the sentence below and then follow the directions that come afterward:

> Seasoned runners often advise new runners to get fitted for better quality running shoes because new runners often complain about minor injuries like sore knees or shin splints.

Rewrite, beginning with Seasoned runners often advise new runners to get fitted for better quality running shoes. The next words will be which of the following:

a. to help them avoid minor injuries.
b. because they know better.
c. , so they can run further.
d. to complain about running injuries.

33. A student writes the following in an essay:

> Protestors filled the streets of the city. Because they were dissatisfied with the government's leadership.

Which of the following is an appropriately-punctuated correction for this sentence?

a. Protestors filled the streets of the city, because they were dissatisfied with the government's leadership.
b. Protesters, filled the streets of the city, because they were dissatisfied with the government's leadership.
c. Because they were dissatisfied with the government's leadership protestors filled the streets of the city.
d. Protestors filled the streets of the city because they were dissatisfied with the government's leadership.

Read the selection about traveling in an RV and answer Questions 34-40:

> I have to admit that when my father bought a recreational vehicle (RV), I thought he was making a huge mistake. I didn't really know anything about RVs, but I knew that my dad was as big a "city slicker" as there was. (34) In fact, I even thought he might have gone a little bit crazy. On trips to the beach, he preferred to swim at the pool, and whenever he went hiking, he avoided touching any plants for fear that they might be poison ivy. Why would this man, with an almost irrational fear of the outdoors, want a 40-foot camping behemoth?
>
> (35) The RV was a great purchase for our family and brought us all closer together. Every morning (36) we would wake up, eat breakfast, and broke camp. We laughed at our own comical attempts to back The Beast into spaces that seemed impossibly small. (37) We rejoiced as "hackers." When things inevitably went wrong and we couldn't solve the problems on our own, we discovered the incredible helpfulness and friendliness of the RV community. (38) We even made some new friends in the process.
>
> (39) Above all, it allowed us to share adventures. While traveling across America, which we could not have experienced in cars and hotels. Enjoying a campfire on a chilly summer evening with the mountains of Glacier National Park in the background, or waking up early in the morning to see the sun rising over the distant spires of Arches National Park are memories that will always stay with me and our entire family. (40)

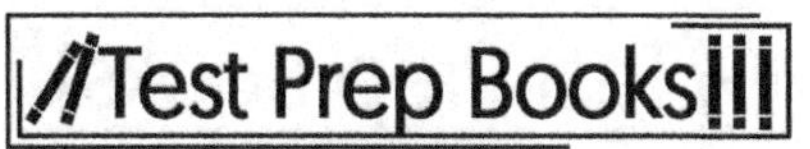

Those are also memories that my siblings and me have now shared with our own children.

34. Which of the following would be the best choice for this sentence?
    a. Leave it where it is now.
    b. Move the sentence so that it comes before the preceding sentence.
    c. Move the sentence to the end of the first paragraph.
    d. Omit the sentence.

35. Which of the following would be the best choice for this sentence?
    a. NO CHANGE
    b. Not surprisingly, the RV
    c. Furthermore, the RV
    d. As it turns out, the RV

36. Which of the following would be the best choice for this sentence?
    a. NO CHANGE
    b. we would wake up, eat breakfast, and break camp.
    c. would we wake up, eat breakfast, and break camp?
    d. we are waking up, eating breakfast, and breaking camp.

37. Which of the following would be the best choice for this sentence?
    a. NO CHANGE
    b. To a nagging problem of technology, we rejoiced as "hackers."
    c. We rejoiced when we figured out how to "hack" a solution to a nagging technological problem.
    d. To "hack" our way to a solution, we had to rejoice.

38. Which of the following would be the best choice for this sentence?
    a. NO CHANGE
    b. In the process was the friends we were making.
    c. We are even making some new friends in the process.
    d. We will make new friends in the process.

39. Which of the following would be the best choice for this sentence?
    a. NO CHANGE
    b. Above all, it allowed us to share adventures while traveling across America
    c. Above all, it allowed us to share adventures; while traveling across America
    d. Above all, it allowed us to share adventures—while traveling across America

40. Which of the following would be the best choice for this sentence?
    a. NO CHANGE
    b. Those are also memories that me and my siblings
    c. Those are also memories that my siblings and I
    d. Those are also memories that I and my siblings

41. Which of the following examples uses correct punctuation?
    a. Recommended supplies for the hunting trip include the following: rain gear, large backpack, hiking boots, flashlight, and non-perishable foods.
    b. I left the store, because I forgot my wallet.
    c. As soon as the team checked into the hotel; they met in the lobby for a group photo.
    d. None of the furniture came in on time: so they weren't able to move in to the new apartment.

42. Which word choices will correctly complete the sentence?

    Increasing the price of bus fares has had a greater [affect / effect] on ridership [then / than] expected.

    a. affect; then
    b. affect; than
    c. effect; then
    d. effect; than

43. Which pronoun makes the following sentence grammatically correct?

    ___________ ordered the flowers?

    a. Whose
    b. Whom
    c. Who
    d. Who've

44. Which pronoun makes the following sentence grammatically correct?

    The giraffe nudged ___________ baby.

    a. it's
    b. hers
    c. them
    d. its

45. Which sentence shows incorrect subject/verb agreement?
    a. All of the kittens in the litter show their courage.
    b. The black kitten pounce on the ball of yarn.
    c. The calico kitten eats voraciously.
    d. My favorite kitten snuggles with its mother.

Extended Response

Read both of the passages carefully all the way through. Then, choose which passage you think is better supported by evidence. In your response, be sure to use your own evidence from the passages. You will have forty-five minutes to plan, write, and edit your response. Your essay should be around 500 words.

Passage I

Lethal force, or deadly force, is defined as the physical means to cause death or serious harm to another individual. The law holds that lethal force is only accepted when you or another person are in immediate and unavoidable danger of death or severe bodily harm. For example, a person could be beating someone in such a way that the victim is suffering severe trauma that could result in death or serious harm. This would be an instance where lethal force would be acceptable and possibly the only way to save the victim from irrevocable damage.

Another example of when to use lethal force would be when someone enters your home with a deadly weapon. The intruder's presence and possession of the weapon indicate mal-intent and the ability to inflict death or severe injury to you and your loved ones. Again, lethal force can be used in this situation. Lethal force can also be applied to prevent the harm of another individual. If a woman is being brutally assaulted and is unable to fend off an attacker, lethal force can be used to defend her as a last-ditch effort. If she is in immediate jeopardy of rape, harm, and/or death, lethal force could be the only response that could effectively deter the assailant.

The key to understanding the concept of lethal force is the term *last resort*. Deadly force cannot be taken back; it should be used only to prevent severe harm or death. The law does distinguish whether the means of one's self-defense is fully warranted, or if the individual goes out of control in the process. If you continually attack the assailant after they are rendered incapacitated, this would be causing unnecessary harm, and the law can bring charges against you. Likewise, if you kill an attacker unnecessarily after defending yourself, you can be charged with murder. This would move lethal force beyond necessary defense, making it no longer a last resort but rather a use of excessive force.

Passage II

Assault is the unlawful attempt of one person to apply apprehension on another individual by an imminent threat or by initiating offensive contact. Assaults can vary, encompassing physical strikes, threatening body language, and even provocative language. In the case of the latter, even if a hand has not been laid, it is still considered an assault because of its threatening nature.

Let's look at an example: A homeowner is angered because his neighbor blows fallen leaves into his freshly mowed lawn. Irate, the homeowner gestures a fist to his neighbor and threatens to bash his head in for littering on his lawn. The homeowner's physical motions and verbal threats herald a physical threat against the other neighbor. These factors classify the homeowner's reaction as an assault. If the angry neighbor hits the threatening homeowner in retaliation, that would constitute an assault as well because he physically hit the homeowner.

Assault also centers on the involvement of weapons in a conflict. If someone fires a gun at another person, it could be interpreted as an assault unless the shooter acted in self-defense. If an individual drew a gun or a knife on someone with the intent to harm them, it would be considered assault. However, it's also considered an assault if someone simply aimed a weapon, loaded or not, at another person in a threatening manner.

Mathematical Reasoning

No Calculator Questions

1. What is the product of two irrational numbers?
   a. Irrational
   b. Rational
   c. Contradictory
   d. Irrational or rational

2. The number –4 can be classified as which of the following?
   a. Real, rational, integer, whole, natural
   b. Real, rational, integer, natural
   c. Real, rational, integer
   d. Real, irrational

3. What is the y-intercept for $y = x^2 + 3x - 4$?
   a. $y = 1$
   b. $y = -4$
   c. $y = 3$
   d. $y = 4$

4. In an office, there are 50 workers. A total of 60% of the workers are women, and the chances of a woman wearing a skirt is 50%. If no men wear skirts, how many workers are wearing skirts?
   a. 12
   b. 15
   c. 16
   d. 20

5. What is the type of function that is modeled by the values in the following table?

x	$f(x)$
1	2
2	4
3	8
4	16
5	32

a. Linear
b. Exponential
c. Quadratic
d. Cubic

Calculator Questions

6. Which of the following is the result of simplifying the expression:

$$\frac{4a^{-1}b^3}{a^4b^{-2}} \times \frac{3a}{b}$$

a. $12a^3b^5$
b. $12\frac{b^4}{a^4}$
c. $\frac{12}{a^4}$
d. $7\frac{b^4}{a}$

7. The graph shows the position of a car over a 10-second time interval. Which of the following is the correct interpretation of the graph for the interval 1 to 3 seconds?

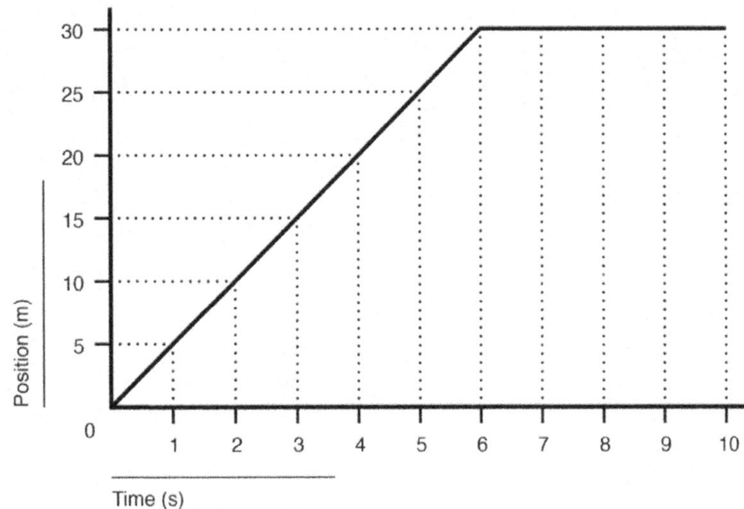

a. The car remains in the same position.
b. The car is traveling at a speed of 5 m/s.
c. The car is traveling up a hill.
d. The car is traveling at 5 mph.

8. What is 60 percent of 75?
a. 29
b. 30
c. 59
d. 45

9. What are the zeros of the function: $f(x) = x^3 + 4x^2 + 4x$?
a. -2
b. 0, -2
c. 2
d. 0, 2

10. A closet is filled with red, blue, and green shirts. If $\frac{1}{3}$ of the shirts are green and $\frac{2}{5}$ are red, what fraction of the shirts are blue?
a. $\frac{4}{15}$
b. $\frac{1}{5}$
c. $\frac{7}{15}$
d. $\frac{1}{2}$

11. $(2x - 4y)^2 =$
a. $4x^2 - 16xy + 16y^2$
b. $4x^2 - 8xy + 16y^2$
c. $4x^2 - 16xy - 16y^2$
d. $2x^2 - 8xy + 8y^2$

12. Mo needs to buy enough material to cover the walls around the stage for a theater performance. If he needs 79 feet of wall covering, what is the minimum number of yards of material he should purchase if the material is sold only by whole yards?
a. 23 yards
b. 25 yards
c. 26 yards
d. 27 yards

13. If $\sqrt{1 + x} = 4$, what is x?
a. 10
b. 15
c. 20
d. 25

14. Ten students take a test. Five students get a 50. Four students get a 70. If the average score is 55, what was the last student's score?
    a. 20
    b. 40
    c. 50
    d. 60

15. What is the volume of a cube with the side equal to 5 centimeters?
    a. $10\ cm^3$
    b. $15\ cm^3$
    c. $50\ cm^3$
    d. $125\ cm^3$

16. What is the solution for the following equation?

$$\frac{x^2 + x - 30}{x - 5} = 11$$

    a. x=–6
    b. There is no solution.
    c. $x = 16$
    d. $x = 5$

17. Mom's car drove 72 miles in 90 minutes. How fast did she drive in feet per second?
    a. 0.8 feet per second
    b. 48.9 feet per second
    c. 0.009 feet per second
    d. 70.4 feet per second

18. How do you solve $V = lwh$ for h?
    a. $lwV = h$
    b. $h = \frac{V}{lw}$
    c. $h = \frac{Vl}{w}$
    d. $h = \frac{Vw}{l}$

19. What is the domain for the function $y = \sqrt{x}$?
    a. All real numbers
    b. $x \geq 0$
    c. $x > 0$
    d. $y \geq 0$

20. If Sarah reads at an average rate of 21 pages in four nights, how long will it take her to read 140 pages?
    a. 6 nights
    b. 26 nights
    c. 8 nights
    d. 27 nights

21. The phone bill is calculated each month using the equation $c = 50g + 75$. The cost of the phone bill per month is represented by c, and g represents the gigabytes of data used that month. What is the value and interpretation of the slope of this equation?

   a. 75 dollars per day
   b. 75 gigabytes per day
   c. 50 dollars per day
   d. 50 dollars per gigabyte

22. Round to the nearest tenth: 8.067

   a. 8.70
   b. 8.1
   c. 8.0
   d. 8.07

23. Karen gets paid a weekly salary and a commission for every sale that she makes. The table below shows the number of sales and her pay for different weeks.

Sales	2	7	4	8
Pay	\$380	\$580	\$460	\$620

Which of the following equations represents Karen's weekly pay?

   a. $y = 90x + 200$
   b. $y = 90x - 200$
   c. $y = 40x + 300$
   d. $y = 40x - 300$

24. Christie is building a shed with a base of 7 feet by 3.5 feet. If she plans to make the walls seven feet tall, how many 7-foot-long, 3.5-inch-wide boards will it take to completely surround the base, if there is no overlap?

   a. 36
   b. 48
   c. 72
   d. 108

25. What are the zeros of $f(x) = x^2 + 4$?

   a. $x = -4$
   b. $x = \pm 2i$
   c. $x = \pm 2$
   d. $x = \pm 4i$

26. Twenty is 40 percent of what number?

   a. 500
   b. 8
   c. 200
   d. 50

27. Simplify $1.2 \times 10^{12} \div 3.0 \times 10^{8}$ and write the result in scientific notation.
   a. 0.4×10^{4}
   b. 4.0×10^{4}
   c. 4.0×10^{3}
   d. 3.6×10^{20}

28. You measure the width of your door to be 36 inches. The true width of the door is 35.75 inches. What is the relative error in your measurement?
   a. 0.7%
   b. 0.007%
   c. 0.99%
   d. 0.1%

29. What is the value of x in the following equation?

$$13 - \frac{3x}{4} = -11$$

   a. -32
   b. 19
   c 16
   d. 32

30. How could the following function be rewritten to identify the zeros?

$$y = 3x^3 + 3x^2 - 18x$$

   a. $y = 3x(x + 3)(x - 2)$
   b. $y = x(x - 2)(x + 3)$
   c. $y = 3x(x - 3)(x + 2)$
   d. $y = (x + 3)(x - 2)$

31. A line goes through the point $(-4, 0)$ and the point $(0,2)$. What is the slope of the line?
   a. 2
   b. 4
   c. $\frac{3}{2}$
   d. $\frac{1}{2}$

32. Given the following triangle, what is the length of the missing side? Round the answer to the nearest tenth.

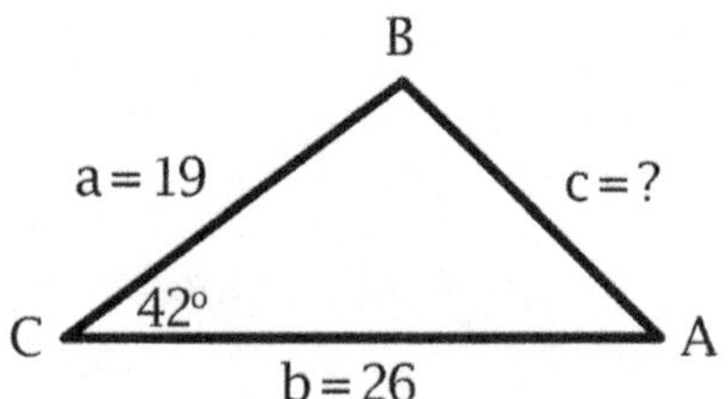

a. 17.0
b. 17.4
c. 18.0
d. 18.4

33. How many possible two-number pairs are there for the numbers 1, 2, 3, 4, and 5 if each number can only be used once and order DOES matter?

a. 120
b. 60
c. 20
d. 10

34. A piggy bank contains 12 dollars' worth of nickels. A nickel weighs 5 grams, and the empty piggy bank weighs 1,050 grams. What is the total weight of the full piggy bank?

a. 1,110 grams
b. 1,200 grams
c. 2,150 grams
d. 2,250 grams

35. A particle moves along the x-axis, so that at any time $t \geq 0$, its velocity is given by $v(t) = \frac{6}{t+3}$. What is the acceleration of the particle at time $t = 5$?

a. $-\frac{2}{3}$
b. $-\frac{3}{32}$
c. $\frac{3}{4}$
d. $\frac{2}{3}$

36. If the volume of a sphere is 288π cubic meters, what are the radius and surface area of the same sphere?

a. Radius: 6 meters, Surface Area: 144π *square meters*
b. Radius: 36 meters, Surface Area: 144π *square meters*
c. Radius: 6 meters, Surface Area: 12π *square meters*
d. Radius: 36 meters, Surface Area: 12π *square meters*

37. The triangle shown below is a right triangle. What is the value of x?

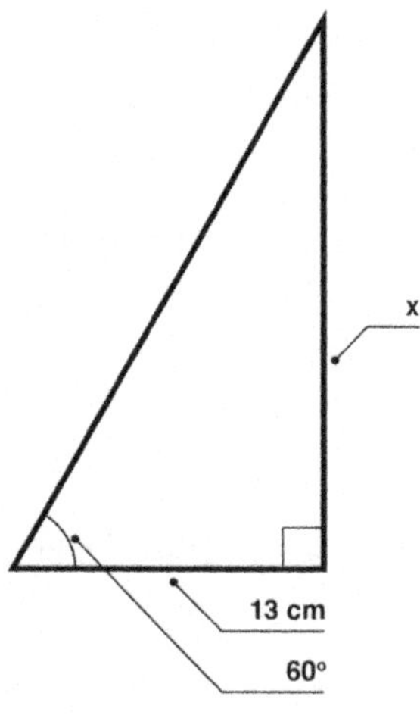

a. $x = 1.73$
b. $x = 0.57$
c. $x = 13$
d. $x = 22.52$

38. What is the midpoint of a line segment with endpoints $(-1, 2)$ and $(3, -6)$?
a. $(1, 2)$
b. $(1, 0)$
c. $(-1, 2)$
d. $(1, -2)$

39. Add and express in reduced form $\frac{5}{12} + \frac{4}{9}$
a. $\frac{9}{17}$
b. $\frac{1}{3}$
c. $\frac{31}{36}$
d. $\frac{3}{5}$

40. The height, in feet, of a baseball falling t seconds after it has reached its peak after being hit by a bat can be found by $-16t^2 + 170$. What is the baseball's altitude 1.5 seconds after it has reached its peak?
a. 134 ft
b. 154 ft
c. 206 ft
d. 184 ft

41. What is the answer to $(3 + 3i)(3 - 3i)$?
    a. 18
    b. $18i$
    c. 9
    d. $9i$

42. A right triangle has a hypotenuse of 10 inches, and one leg is 8 inches. How long is the other leg?
    a. 6 in
    b. 18 in
    c. 80 in
    d. 13 in

43. Which of the following statements is true about the two lines below?

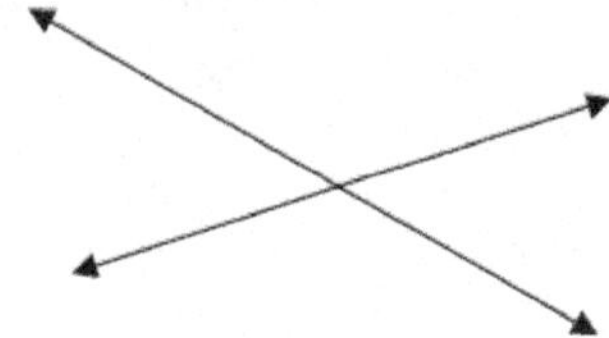

    a. The two lines are parallel but not perpendicular.
    b. The two lines are perpendicular but not parallel.
    c. The two lines are both parallel and perpendicular.
    d. The two lines are neither parallel nor perpendicular.

44. What is the probability of rolling a 6 exactly once in two rolls of a die?
    a. $\frac{1}{3}$
    b. $\frac{1}{36}$
    c. $\frac{1}{6}$
    d. $\frac{11}{36}$

45. What is the area of a circle, in terms of π, with a radius of 10 centimeters?
    a. $10\,\pi$ cm ^{2}
    b. $20\,\pi$ cm ^{2}
    c. $100\,\pi$ cm ^{2}
    d. $200\,\pi$ cm ^{2}

46. Solve the following radical equation: $\sqrt{16 - x} - x = 4$.
    a. {0}
    b. {4}
    c. {0, -9}
    d. Ø

Science

Questions 1–3 pertain to the following information:

Molecules are composed of a group of atoms connected by chemical bonds, which are the result of attractive forces between the electrons and protons in those atoms. Molecules contain unique atoms or elements that have a level of attraction for electrons. The level of attraction or tendency of an atom to attract electrons is called electronegativity. Table 1 below shows a list of electronegativity values for specific elements.

Table 1: Electronegativity values

H 2.1	C 2.5	N 3.0	O 3.5	F 4.0
Li 1.0	Si 1.8	P 2.1	S 2.5	Cl 3.0
Na 0.9	Ge 1.8	As 2.0	Se 2.4	Br 2.8

The polarity of a chemical bond describes the difference in electronegativity of a bond (ΔEN). For example, the difference in electronegativity of the C-H bond can be determined by subtracting the electronegativity values of carbon and hydrogen.

$$\Delta EN(C - H) = |EN_C - EN_H| = |2.5 - 2.1| = 0.4$$

A C-H bond is classified as nonpolar covalent, as indicated in Table 2 below. To distinguish which atoms carry more electrons, a partial negative sign ($\delta -$) is placed over the atom. For atoms in a chemical bond that have fewer electrons, a partial positive sign is placed over the atom ($\delta +$). The placement of the signs for the C-H bond, is shown below.

$$C^{\delta-} - H^{\delta+}$$

Since the carbon atom has a greater electronegativity value than hydrogen, it is slightly electron-rich, whereas the hydrogen atom is electron deficient.

Table 2. Bond polarity scale

Bond type	ΔEN value
Nonpolar covalent or slightly polar	Less than or equal to 0.4
Polar covalent	0.4 < ΔEN < 1.7
Ionic	Greater than or equal to 1.7

1. In general, the trend in electronegativity values shown in Table 1 indicates that the values will do which of the following?

    a. Decrease left to right and increase top to bottom.

b. Increase left to right and increase top to bottom.
c. Increase left to right and decrease top to bottom.
d. Decrease left to right and decrease top to bottom.

2. Which of the following choices provides the correct ΔEN and bond type for C-Cl?
   a. 0.5 and polar covalent
   b. 5.5 and ionic
   c. -0.5 and nonpolar covalent
   d. 5.5 and polar covalent

3. Which of the following bonds shows the correct partial charges on each respective atom?
   a. $H^{\delta-} - Se^{\delta+}$
   b. $H^{\delta-} - Si^{\delta+}$
   c. $P^{\delta-} - Cl^{\delta+}$
   d. $Se^{\delta-} - Br^{\delta+}$

Questions 4–6 pertain to the following information:

> A geologist can use two types of evidence to determine the interior of the Earth's crust. The first method requires gathering direct evidence from samples of rock. Typically, holes are drilled into the Earth's crust and rock samples are brought up for analysis. The second method is indirect and involves the use of seismic waves. Earthquakes can produce seismic waves, and researchers measure the speed at which these waves travel

through the planet's crust. Figure 1 shows the velocity of seismic waves with respect to the depth of the Earth's crust.

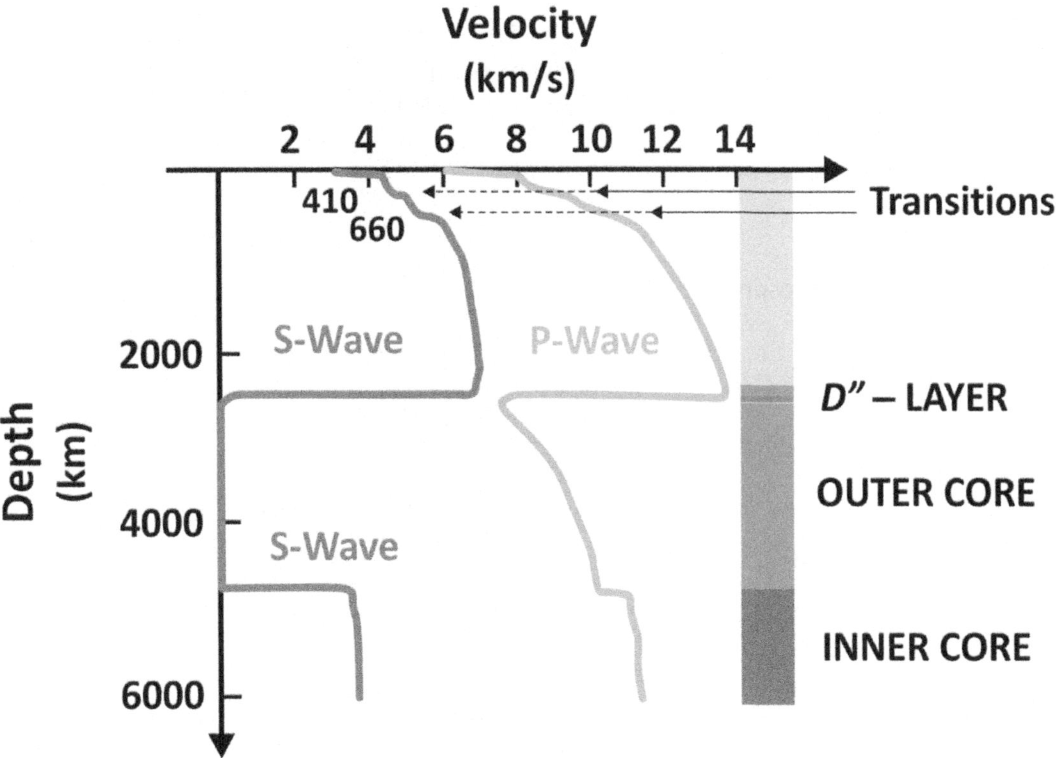

Figure 1. Velocity of the wave vs. the depth

The S and P waves are called body waves and travel through Earth's Interior. The velocity for each wave varies with respect to the depth. For example, the S wave has a velocity of over 3 km/s up to about 2,000 km/s, which corresponds to the mantle region. Seismic waves generally travel faster through denser materials, and the density gradually increases toward the Earth's center.

The Earth's structural layer is divided into three layers called the crust, upper mantle, and lower mantle (Figure 2). The solid layer of rock that makes up the outer shell or skin of the Earth is the crust; this layer comprises the ocean floor and dry land. There are different types of crust. The crust that forms the continents contains granite, and the crust from the ocean consists of rock called basalt. The mantle is a layer of hot solid rock that spans nearly 4,000 kilometers beneath the Earth's crust. There are several layers within the mantle, which can be divided into an upper and lower layer. The upper layer is called the lithosphere and is about 100 kilometers deep. The asthenosphere is the lower layer, which is hotter and softer. The remaining lower portion of the mantle is solid and connects to the Earth's core. The core consists mostly of metals such as nickel and iron. The outer portion of the core is molten metal, whereas the inner core is dense and solid metal.

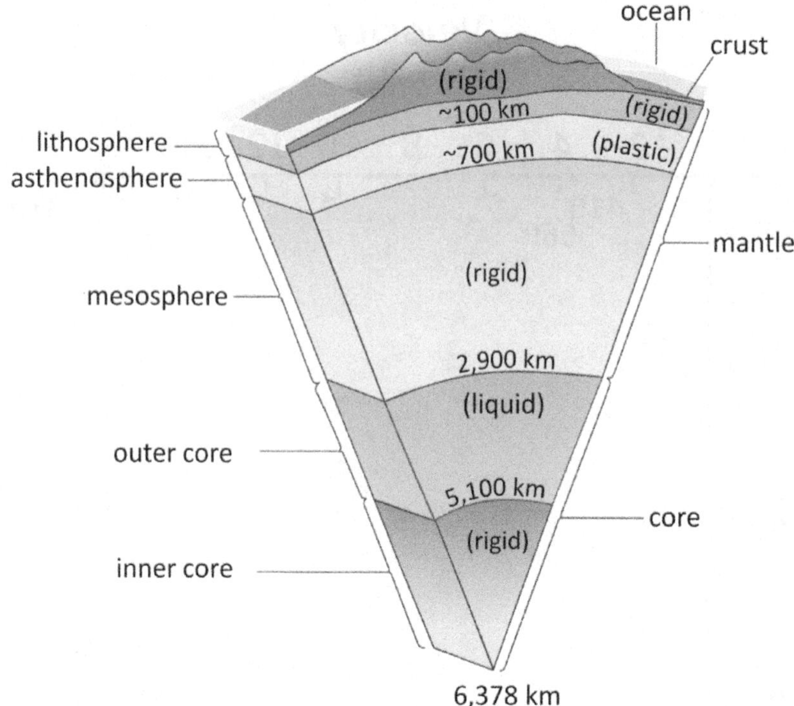

Figure 2.

4. Based on the passage's discussion of seismic waves, the maximum velocity of a body wave was recorded at about 14 km/s. Which choice represents the correct body wave and depth associated with a velocity of 14 km/s?
   a. P wave and 2,500 km depth
   b. S wave and 2,500 km depth
   c. P wave and 6,000 km depth
   d. S wave and 6,000 km depth

5. Which of the following choices represents the thickest layer of the Earth?
   a. Mesosphere
   b. Core
   c. Inner core
   d. Crust

6. Which of the following statements is accurate?
   a. Seismic waves gradually travel more slowly from the Earth's mantle to molten metal.
   b. Seismic waves gradually travel more slowly from the Earth's mantle to solid metal.
   c. Seismic waves travel faster in solid metal compared to molten metal
   d. Seismic waves travel faster in molten metal compared to solid metal.

Questions 7–11 pertain to the following information:

Worldwide, fungal infections of the lung account for significant mortality in individuals with compromised immune function. Three of the most common infecting agents are *Aspergillus, Histoplasma*, and *Candida*. Successful treatment of infections caused by these agents depends on an early and accurate diagnosis. Three tests used to identify specific markers for these mold species include ELISA (enzyme-linked immunosorbent assay), GM Assay (Galactomannan Assay), and PCR (polymerase chain reaction).

Two important characteristics of these tests include sensitivity and specificity. Sensitivity relates to the probability that the test will identify the presence of the infecting agent, resulting in a true positive result. Higher sensitivity equals fewer false-positive results. Specificity relates to the probability that if the test doesn't detect the infecting agent, the test is truly negative for that agent. Higher specificity equals fewer false-negatives.

Figure 1 shows the timeline for the process of infection from exposure to the pathogen to recovery or death.

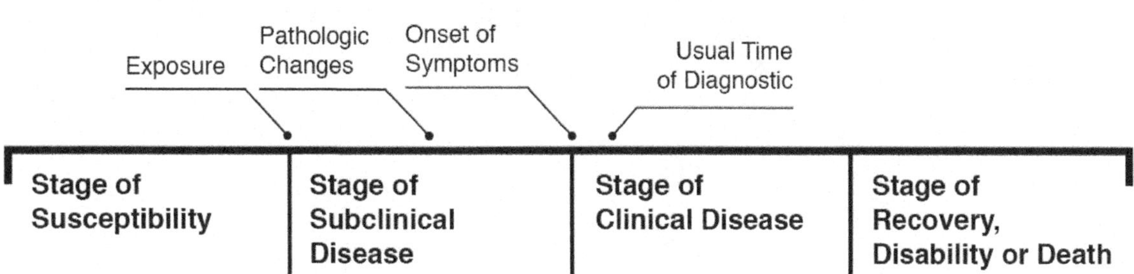

Figure 1.

Figure 2 shows the sensitivity and specificity for ELISA, GM assay and PCR related to the diagnosis of infection by *Aspergillus*, *Histoplasma* and *Candida*.

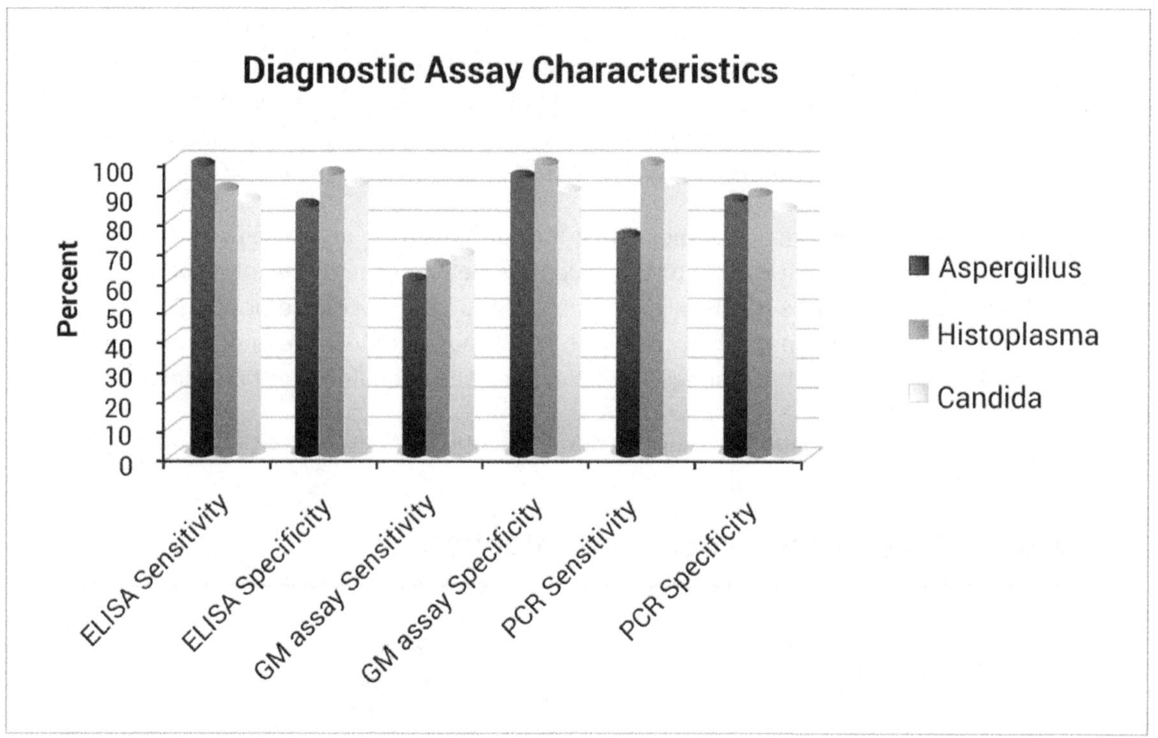

Figure 2.

The table below identifies the process of infection (in days) from exposure for each of the species.

Process of Infection – Days Since Pathogen Exposure			
	Aspergillus	Histoplasma	Candida
Sub-clinical Disease	Day 90	Day 28	Day 7
Detection Possible	Day 118	Day 90	Day 45
Symptoms Appear	Day 145	Day 100	Day 120

Figure 3 identifies the point at which each test can detect the organism. Time is measured in days from the time an individual is exposed to the pathogen.

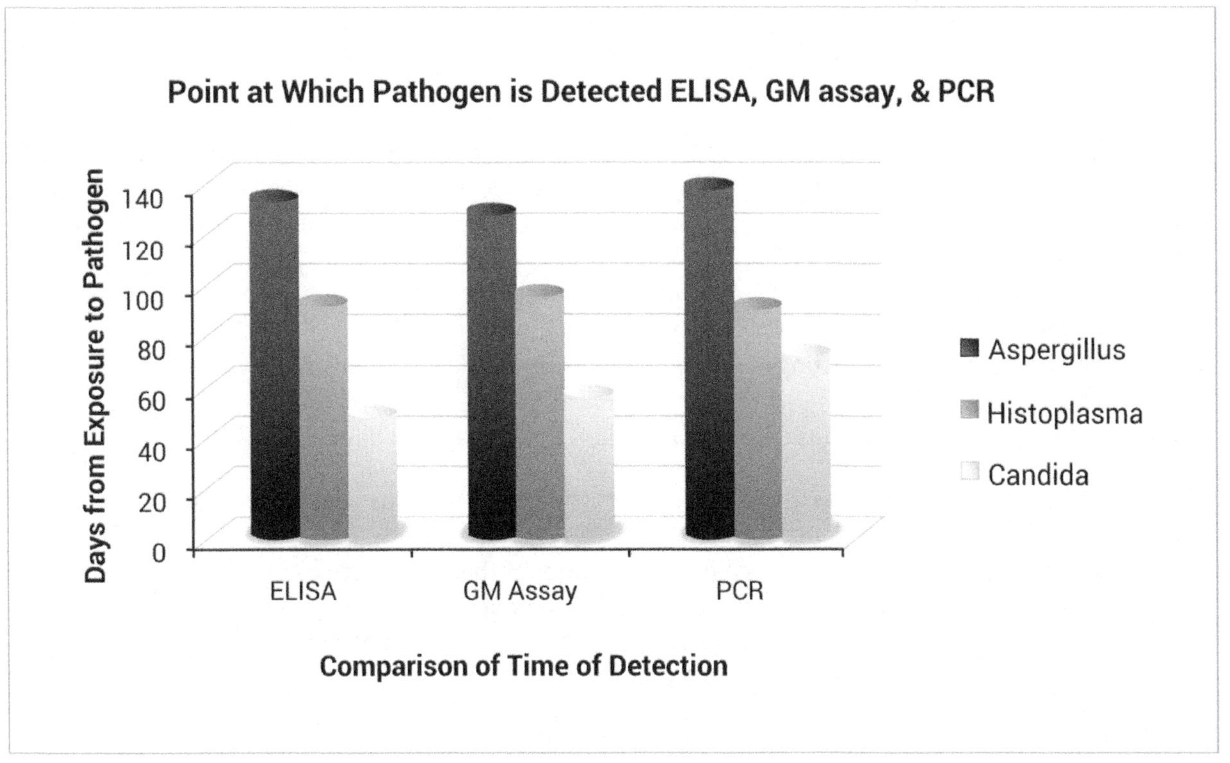

Figure 3.

7. Which of the following statements is supported by Figure 2?
   a. For *Candida*, the GM assay will provide the most reliable results.
   b. ELISA testing for *Aspergillus* is the most specific of the three tests.
   c. PCR is the most sensitive method for testing *Histoplasma*.
   d. True positive rates were greater than 75% for all three testing methods.

8. In reference to the table and Figure 3, which pathogen from the options below can be detected earliest in the process of infection, and by which method?
   a. *Candida* by PCR testing
   b. *Aspergillus* by ELISA testing
   c. *Candida* by GM assay
   d. *Histoplasma* by PCR testing

9. In reference to Figure 2, which statement is correct?
   a. There is a 20% probability that ELISA testing will NOT correctly identify the presence of *Histoplasma.*
   b. When GM assay testing for *Candida* is conducted, there is a 31% probability that it will NOT be identified if the organism is present.
   c. The probability that GM assay testing for *Aspergillus* will correctly identify the presence of the organism is 99%.
   d. The false-negative probabilities for each of the three testing methods identified in Figure 2 indicate that the organism will be detected when present less than 70% of the time.

10. Physicians caring for individuals with suspected *Histoplasma* infections order diagnostic testing prior to instituting treatment. PCR testing results will not be available for 10 days. GM assay results can be obtained more quickly. The physicians opt to wait for the PCR testing. Choose the best possible rationale for that decision.
   a. The treatment will be the same regardless of the test results.
   b. The individual was not exhibiting any disease symptoms.
   c. The probability of PCR testing identifying the presence of the organism is greater than the GM assay.
   d. The subclinical disease phase for *Histoplasma* is more than 100 days.

11. Referencing the data in Figures 2 and 3, if ELISA testing costs twice as much as PCR testing, why might it still be the best choice to test for *Candida*?
   a. ELISA testing detects the presence of *Candida* sooner than PCR testing.
   b. ELISA testing has fewer false-positives than PCR testing.
   c. There is only a 69% probability that PCR testing will correctly identify the presence of *Candida.*
   d. PCR testing is less sensitive than ELISA testing for *Candida.*

Questions 12–16 pertain to the following information:

> A national wholesale nursery commissioned research to conduct a cost/benefit analysis of replacing existing fluorescent grow lighting systems with newer LED lighting systems. LEDs (light-emitting diodes) are composed of various semi-conductor materials that allow the flow of current in one direction. This means that LEDs emit light in a predictable range, unlike conventional lighting systems that give off heat and light in all directions. The wavelength of light of a single LED is determined by the properties of the specific semi-conductor. For instance, the indium gallium nitride system is used for blue, green, and cyan LEDs. As a result, growing systems can be individualized for the specific wavelength requirements for different plant species. In addition, LEDs don't emit significant amounts of heat compared to broadband systems, so plant hydration can be controlled more efficiently.

Figure 1 identifies the visible spectrum with the wavelength expressed in nanometers.

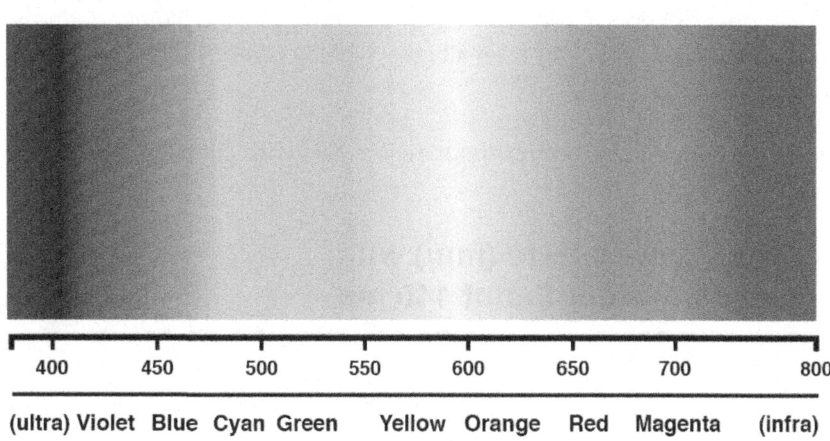

Figure 1.

Figure 2 identifies the absorption rates of different wavelengths of light.

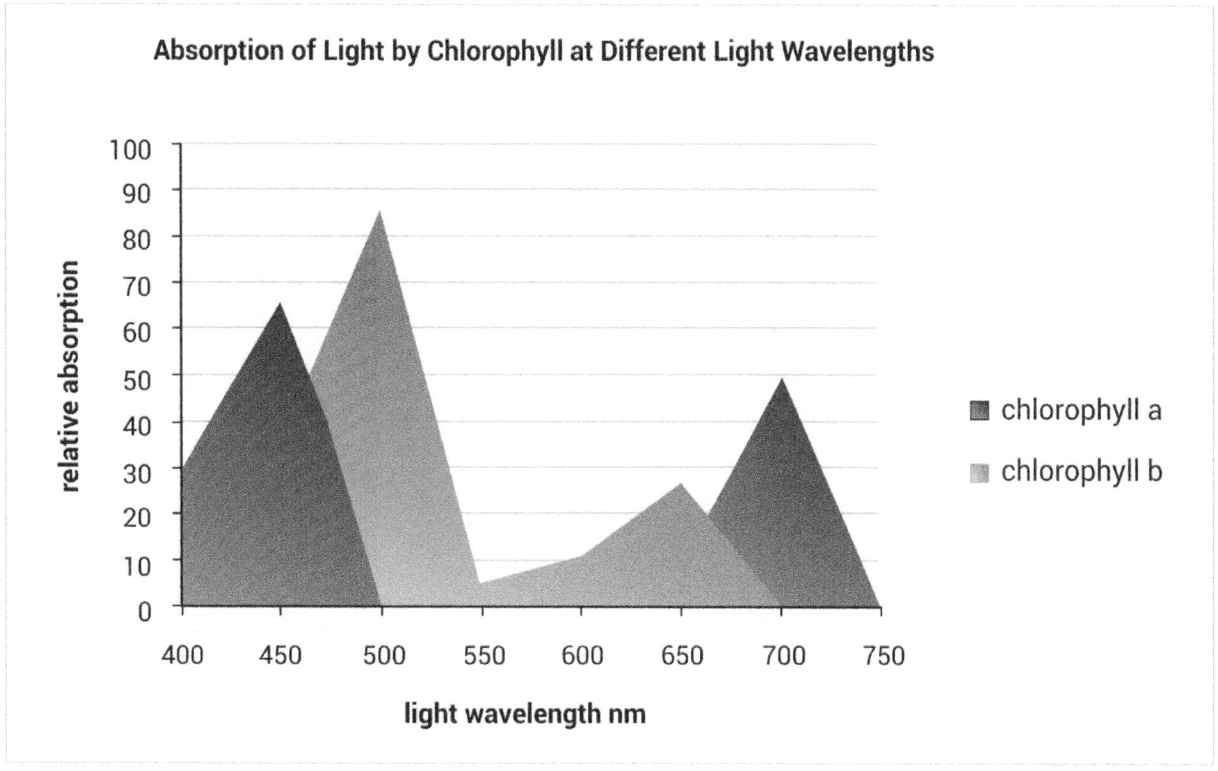

Figure 2.

Researchers conducted three trials and hypothesized that LEDs would result in greater growth rates than conventional lighting or white light. They also hypothesized that using a combination of red, blue, green, and yellow wavelengths in the LED lighting system would result in a greater growth rate than using red or blue wavelengths alone. Although green and yellow wavelengths are largely reflected by the plant (Figure 2), the absorption rate is sufficient to make a modest contribution to plant growth. Fifteen Impatiens walleriana seed samples were planted in the same growing medium. Temperature, hydration, and light intensity were held constant. Plant height in millimeters was recorded as follows.

Figure 3 identifies the plant growth rate in millimeters with light wavelengths of 440 nanometers.

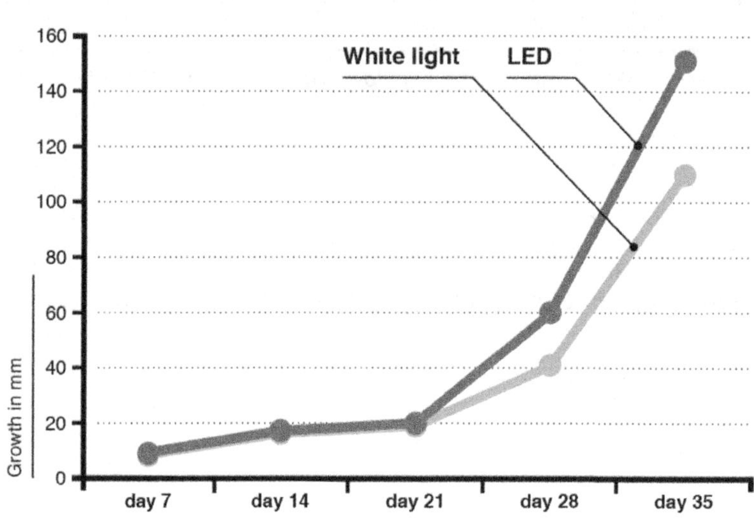

Figure 3.

Figure 4 identifies the plant growth rate in millimeters with light wavelengths of 650 nanometers.

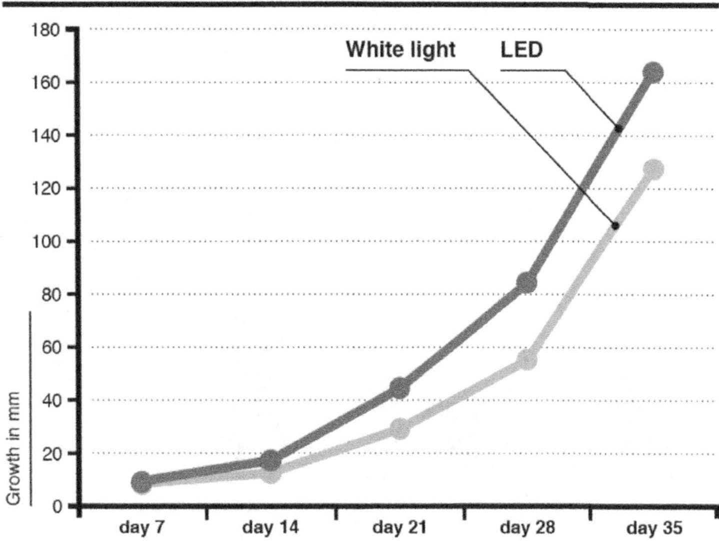

Figure 4.

Figure 5 identifies the plant growth rate in millimeters with combined light wavelengths of 440, 550, and 650 nanometers.

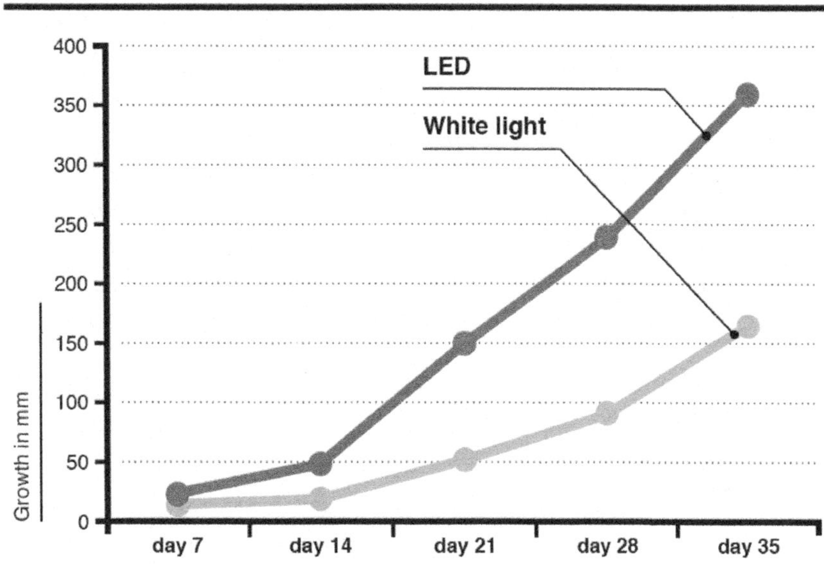

Figure 5.

Figure 6 identifies average daily plant growth rate in millimeters.

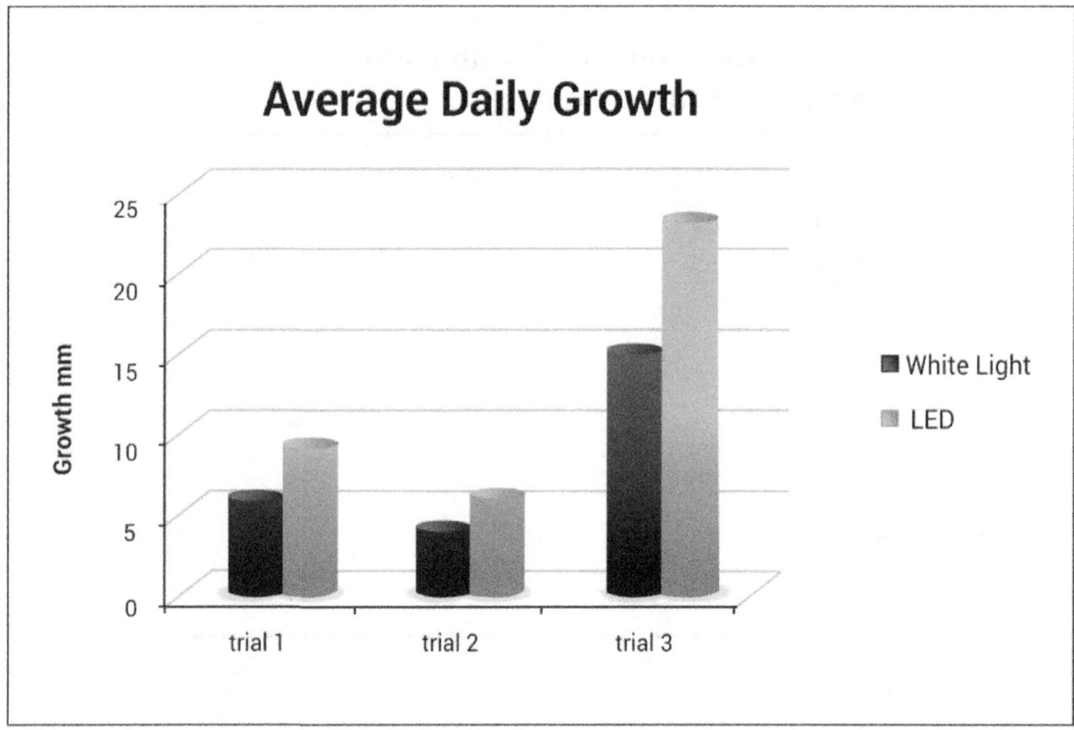

Figure 6.

12. If the minimum plant height required for packaging a plant for sale is 150 millimeters, based on plant growth, how much sooner will the LED plants be packaged compared to the white light plants?

   a. 14 days
   b. 21 days
   c. 35 days
   d. 42 days

13. Plants reflect green and yellow light wavelengths. Do the results of the three trials support the view that plants also absorb and use green and yellow light wavelengths for growth?

   a. Yes, green and yellow light wavelengths were responsible for plant growth in trial 3.
   b. No, white light alone was responsible for measurable plant growth.
   c. Yes, the growth rates in trial 3 were greater than the rates in trials 1 and 2.
   d. No, only the red and blue wavelengths were effective in stimulating plant growth.

14. When did the greatest rate of growth occur for both groups in trial 1 and trial 2?

   a. From 7 days to 14 days
   b. From 28 days to 35 days
   c. From 21 days to 28 days
   d. From 14 days to 21 days

15. If an LED lighting system costs twice as much as a white light system, based only on the average daily growth rate as noted above, would it be a wise investment?
    a. No, because multiple different semi-conductors would be necessary.
    b. Yes, growth rates are better with LEDs.
    c. No, the LED average daily growth rate was not two times greater than the white light rate.
    d. Yes, LEDs use less electricity and water.

16. If the researchers conducted an additional trial, trial 4, to measure the effect of green and yellow wavelengths on plant growth, what would be the probable result?
    a. The growth rate would equal trial 1.
    b. The growth rate would equal trial 2.
    c. The growth rate would equal trial 3.
    d. The growth rate would be less than trial 1 or trial 2.

Questions 17–21 pertain to the following passage:

A biome is a major terrestrial or aquatic environment that supports diverse life forms. Freshwater biomes—including lakes, streams and rivers, and wetlands—account for 0.01% of the Earth's fresh water. Collectively, they are home to 6% of all recognized species. Standing water bodies may vary in size from small ponds to the Great Lakes. Plant life in lakes is specific to the zone of the lake that provides the optimal habitat for a specific species, based on the depth of the water as it relates to light. The photic layer is the shallower layer where light is available for photosynthesis. The aphotic layer is deeper, and the levels of sunlight are too low for photosynthesis. The benthic layer is the bottom-most layer, and its inhabitants are nourished by materials from the photic layer. Light-sensitive cyanobacteria and microscopic algae are two forms of phytoplankton that exist in lakes. As a result of nitrogen and phosphorus from agriculture and sewage run-off, algae residing near the surface can multiply abnormally so that available light is diminished to other species. Oxygen supplies may also be reduced when large numbers of algae die.

Recently, concerns have been raised about the effects of agriculture and commercial development on the quality of national freshwater bodies. In order to estimate the effect of human impact on freshwater, researchers examined plant life from the aphotic layer of three freshwater lakes of approximately the same size located in three different environments. Lake A was located in a remote forested area of western Montana. Lake B was located in central Kansas. Lake C was located in a medium-size city on the west coast of Florida. The researchers hypothesized that the microscopic algae and cyanobacteria populations from Lake A would approach appropriate levels for the size of the lake. They also hypothesized that the remaining two samples would reveal abnormal levels of the phytoplankton. In addition, the researchers measured the concentration of algae at different depths at four different times in another lake identified as having abnormal algae growth. These measurements attempted to identify the point at which light absorption in the photic layer was no longer sufficient for the growth of organisms in the aphotic layer. Resulting data is identified below.

Figure 1 illustrates the zones of the freshwater lake.

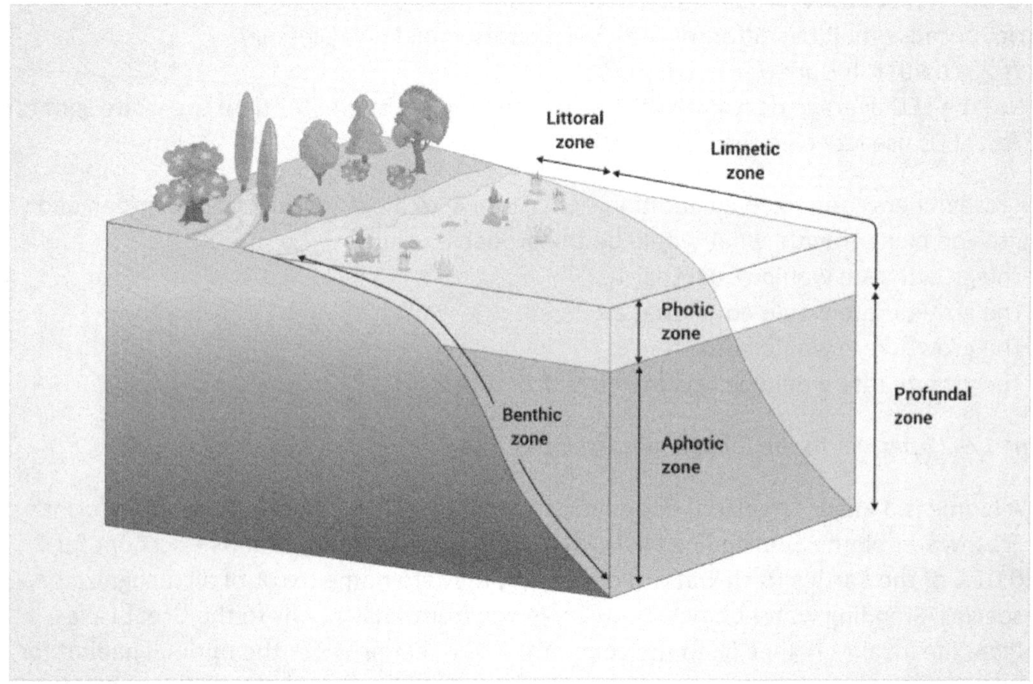

Figure 1.

Figure 2 identifies algae and cyanobacteria levels in parts per million for Lake A over six measurements.

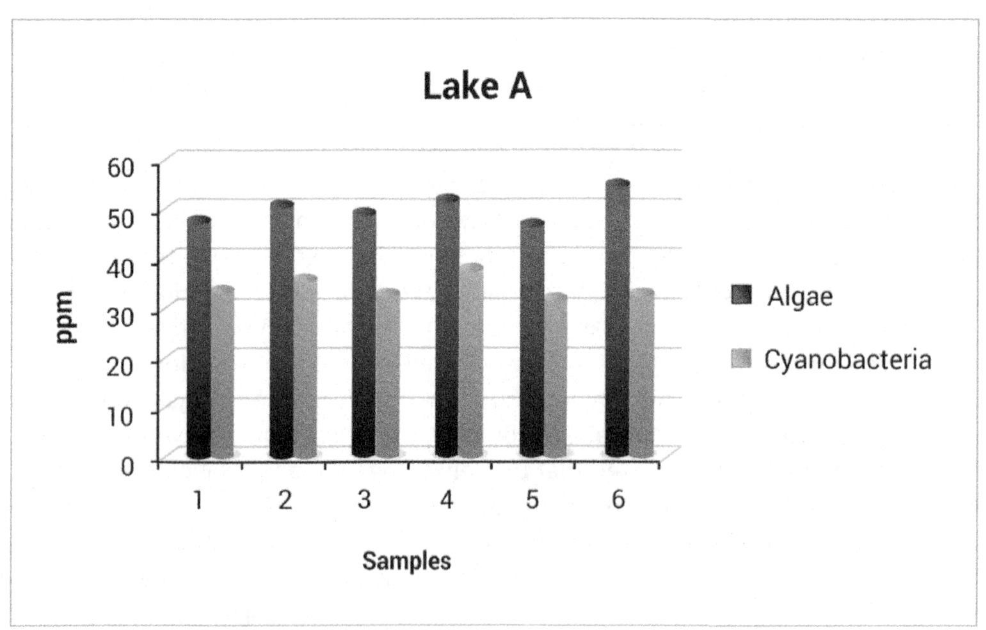

Normal: Algae 50 ppm, Cyanobacteria 35 ppm

Figure 2.

Figure 3 identifies algae and cyanobacteria levels in parts per million for Lake B over six measurements.

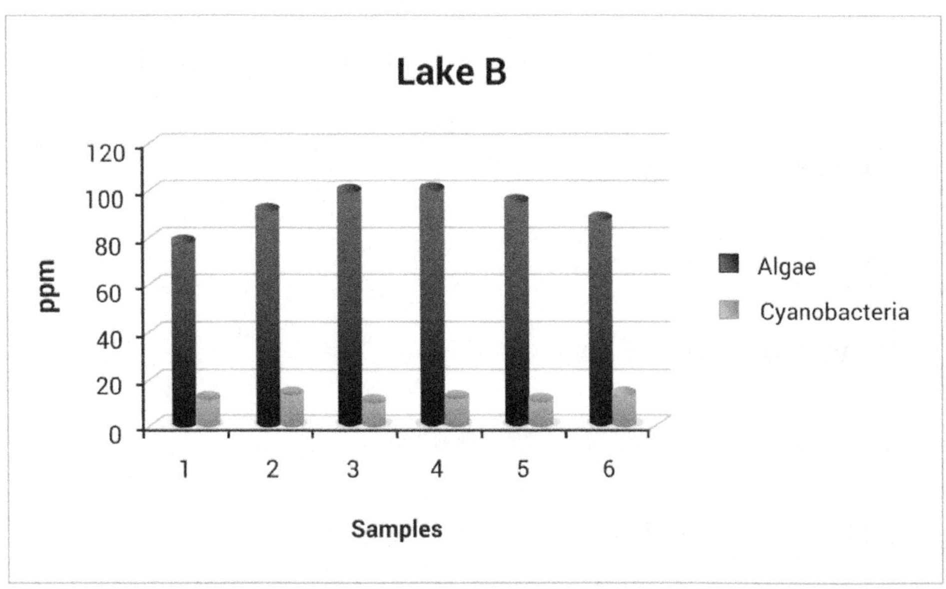

Normal: Algae 50 ppm, Cyanobacteria 35 ppm

Figure 3.

Figure 4 identifies algae and cyanobacteria levels in parts per million for Lake C over six measurements.

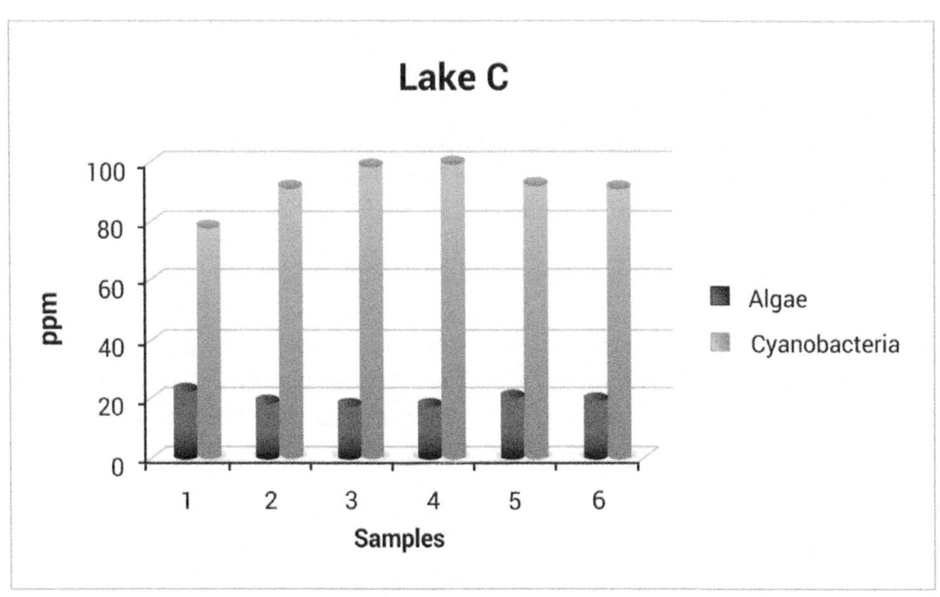

Normal: Algae 50 ppm, Cyanobacteria 35 ppm

Figure 4.

Figure 5 identifies cyanobacteria levels at different depths over time.

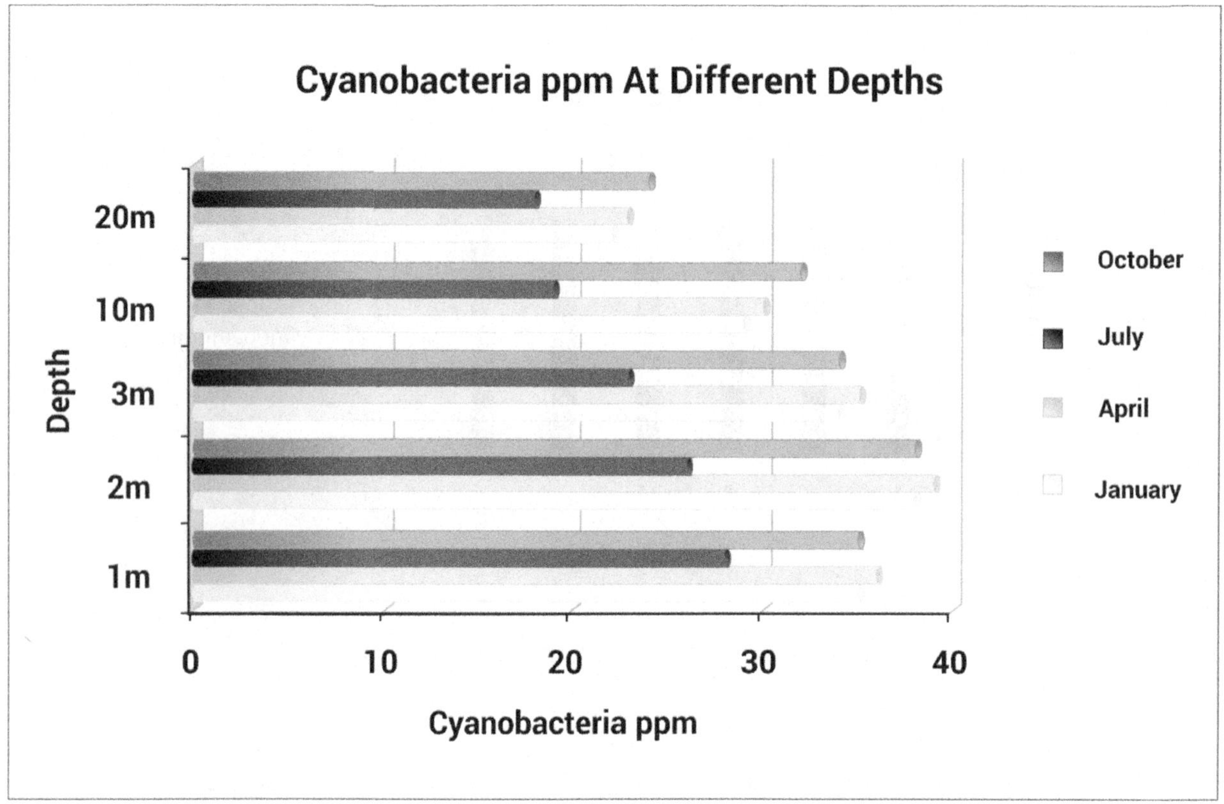

Figure 5.

17. Based on Figure 2, was the researchers' hypothesis confirmed?
    a. No, the phytoplankton levels were not elevated in the first trial.
    b. Yes, the phytoplankton levels were raised above normal in each sample.
    c. No, the Lake A numbers clearly disproved the hypothesis.
    d. Yes, algae levels were above normal in Lake C.

18. In Lake B, cyanobacteria were decreased and algae were increased. Which of the following is a possible explanation for this finding?
    a. The overgrowth of algae decreased the light energy available for cyanobacteria growth.
    b. Lake B experienced severe flooding, causing the water levels in the lake to rise above normal.
    c. Agricultural chemical residue depleted the food source for cyanobacteria.
    d. Cyanobacteria cannot survive in the cold winter weather in Lake B.

19. As algae levels increase above normal, what happens to organisms in the aphotic level?
    a. Growth is limited but sustained.
    b. Species may eventually die due to decreased oxygenation.
    c. Cyanobacteria increase to unsafe levels.
    d. Aerobic bacteria multiply.

20. Referencing Figures 3 and 4, which environment would favor organisms in the benthic layer of the corresponding lake?
    a. Figure 4, because the cyanobacteria are protective.
    b. Figure 3, because increased numbers of algae provide more light.
    c. Figure 4, because cyanobacteria are able to survive.
    d. Figure 3, because the levels of both species are normal.

21. Which of the following statements is supported by the data in Figure 5?
    a. Algae growth is greater in July than April.
    b. Cyanobacteria can't exist at 20 meters in this lake.
    c. There's insufficient light in the aphotic layer at 3 meters to support algae growth.
    d. Cyanobacteria growth rates are independent of algae growth at 1 meter.

Questions 22–26 pertain to the following information:

A meteorologist uses many different tools to predict the weather. They study the atmosphere and changes that are occurring to predict what the weather will be like in the future. Listed below are some of the tools that a meteorologist uses:

- Thermometer: measures air temperature
- Barometer: measures air pressure
- Rain gauge: measures rainfall over a specific time
- Anemometer: measures air speed
- Wind vane: shows which direction the wind is blowing

Figure 1 shows data that is collected by a meteorologist.

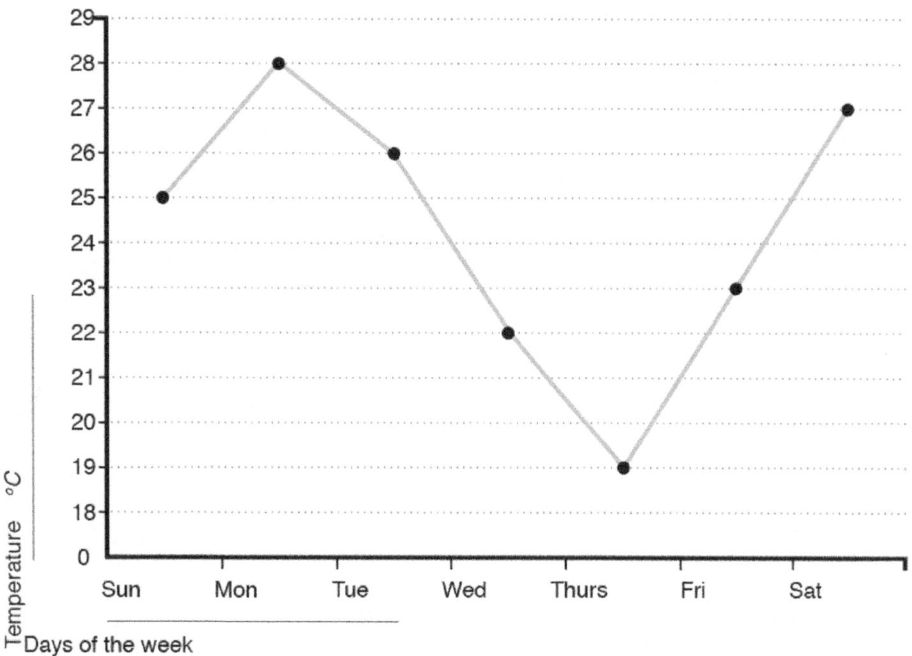

Figure 1.

Figure 2 shows data collected from a rain gauge.

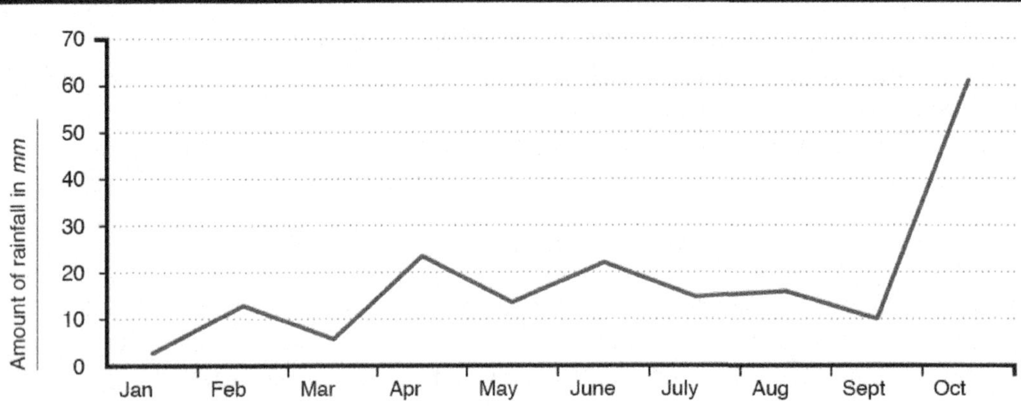

Figure 2.

22. What tool would a meteorologist use to find out how fast the wind is blowing?
    a. Anemometer
    b. Barometer
    c. Thermometer
    d. Wind vane

23. What tool was used to collect the data shown in Figure 1?
    a. Rain gauge
    b. Thermometer
    c. Barometer
    d. Anemometer

24. The wind vane is pointing north. What does this tell us?
    a. Wind is blowing in an eastern direction.
    b. A storm is coming.
    c. The wind is blowing in a northern direction.
    d. The wind is blowing in a southern direction.

25. Looking at Figure 2, which month had the lowest rainfall?
    a. January
    b. April
    c. September
    d. October

26. Looking at Figure 2, what was the approximate amount of rain that fell in June?
    a. 0 mm
    b. 10 mm
    c. 50 mm
    d. 20 mm

Questions 27–31 pertain to the following information:

The density of a substance is equal to the mass of the substance over the volume of the substance.

$$d = \frac{m}{V}$$

The units of mass are given in grams (g), and the volume is in cubic centimeters (cm^3). When measuring the volume of liquids, chemists use specific instruments that measure the volume in milliliters (mL). Some liquids include oil and water. One cubic centimeter (cm^3) is equal to one milliliter (mL); other instruments used when finding the density are shown below.

Top loading balance: measures the mass of a substance with an accuracy of 0.1 g

Analytical balance: measures the mass of a substance with an accuracy of 0.0001 g

Metric ruler: measures the length of an object in meters or centimeters

Graduated cylinder: measures the volume of a liquid in milliliters.

The density of a substance, such as freshwater, depends on the temperature, as indicated in Figure 1. For a given volume of water, the mass will remain constant as the temperature increases and the kinetic energy of the water increases. The water molecules will move rapidly and expand at increasing temperatures.

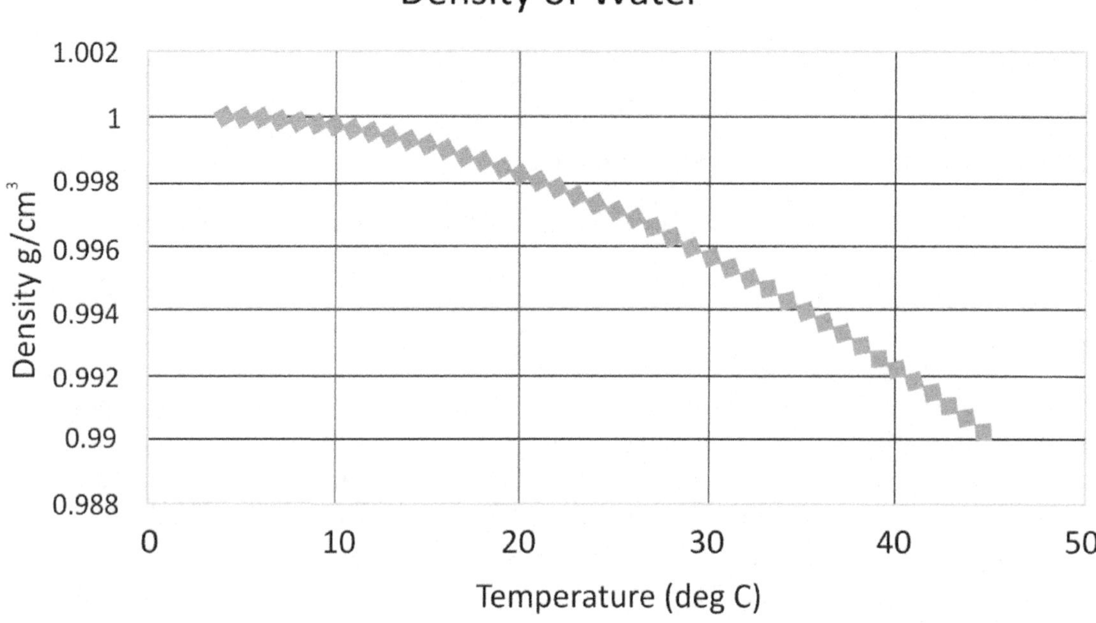

Figure 1. The density of fresh water

27. During an experiment in a lab room, a chemist measured 30.0 mL of water. The temperature of the room was approximately 25 °C, which was greater than the outside temperature of 20 °C. What is the approximate density of the substance?
   a. 0.998 g/cm^3
   b. 0.997 g/cm^3
   c. 0.996 g/cm^3
   d. 0.995 g/cm^3

28. Which of the following instruments would be useful to measure the volume of a liquid?
   a. A metric ruler
   b. An analytical balance
   c. A graduated cylinder
   d. A top-loading balance

29. During an experiment, a chemist measured 30.0 mL of water using a graduated cylinder. If the temperature of the room was approximately 20 °C, which expression below can be used to find the mass of water?
   a. $mass = \left(30.0\frac{g}{cm^3}\right)/(0.998cm^3)$
   b. $mass = \left(0.996\frac{g}{cm^3}\right)(30.0cm^3)$
   c. $mass = \left(0.998\frac{g}{cm^3}\right)(30.0cm^3)$
   d. $mass = \left(30.0\frac{g}{cm^3}\right)/(0.996cm^3)$

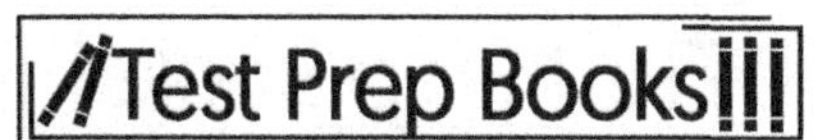

30. Which of the following is an accurate statement regarding the relationship between density and temperature?
    a. As the temperature increases, the density of freshwater increases.
    b. As the temperature decreases, the density of freshwater increases.
    c. As the density of freshwater decreases, the temperature decreases.
    d. As the density of freshwater increases, the temperature remains constant.

31. The passage indicates the kinetic energy of a water molecule increases with temperature. Based on the passage, the density of water changes with temperature because:
    a. The volume of liquid water expands with increasing temperature, which increases the density.
    b. The mass of water increases as temperature rises, which increases the density.
    c. The mass of water increases as temperature rises, which decreases the density.
    d. The volume of liquid water expands with increasing temperature, which decreases the density.

Use the following information to answer Questions 32–34:

> Chemical reactions are conveyed using chemical equations. **Chemical equations** must be balanced with equivalent numbers of atoms for each type of element on each side of the equation. Antoine Lavoisier, a French chemist, was the first to propose the **Law of Conservation of Mass** for the purpose of balancing a chemical equation. The law states, "Matter is neither created nor destroyed during a chemical reaction." The **reactants** are located on the left side of the arrow, while the **products** are located on the right side of the arrow. **Coefficients** are the numbers in front of the chemical formulas. **Subscripts** are the numbers to the lower right of chemical symbols in a formula. The coefficient times the subscript of each element should be the same on both sides of the equation.

32. Explain the Law of Conservation of Mass as it applies to this reaction: $2\ H_2 + O_2 \rightarrow 2\ H_2O$.
    a. Electrons are lost.
    b. The hydrogen loses mass.
    c. New oxygen atoms are formed.
    d. There is no decrease or increase of matter.

33. What coefficients are needed to balance the following combustion equation?

$$\_\ C_2H_{10} + \_\ O_2 \rightarrow \_\ H_2O + \_\ CO_2$$

    a. 1:5:5:2
    b. 1:9:5:2
    c. 2:9:10:4
    d. 2:5:10:4

34. Which coefficient would fill in the blank in the following equation to correctly balance the chemical reaction between iron oxide and carbon monoxide: $FeO_3 + 3CO \rightarrow Fe + \_\_CO_2$?

a. 1
b. 3
c. 2
d. 6

Questions 35–40 pertain to the following information:

Scientists disagree about the cause of Bovine Spongiform Encephalopathy (BSE), also known as "mad cow disease." Two scientists discuss different explanations about the cause of the disease.

Scientist 1

Mad cow disease is a condition that results in the deterioration of brain and spinal cord tissue. This deterioration manifests as sponge-like defects or holes that result in irreversible damage to the brain. The cause of this damage is widely accepted to be the result of an infectious type of protein, called a prion. Normal proteins are located in the cell wall of the central nervous system and function to preserve the myelin sheath around the nerves. Prions are capable of turning normal proteins into other prions by a process that is still unclear, thereby causing the proteins to be "refolded" in abnormal and harmful configurations. Unlike viruses and bacteria, the harmful prions possibly don't contain DNA or RNA, based on the observation of infected tissues in the laboratory that remain infected after immersion in formaldehyde or exposure to ultraviolet light. The transformation from normal to abnormal protein structure and function in a given individual is thought to occur as the result of proteins that are genetically weak or abnormally prone to mutation, or through transmission from another host through food, drugs, or organ transplants from infected animals. The abnormal prions also don't trigger an immune response. After prions accumulate in large enough numbers, they form damaging conglomerations that result in the sponge-like holes in tissues, which eventually cause the loss of proper brain function and death.

Figure 1 depicts formation of abnormal prions that results from the abnormal (right) folding of amino acids.

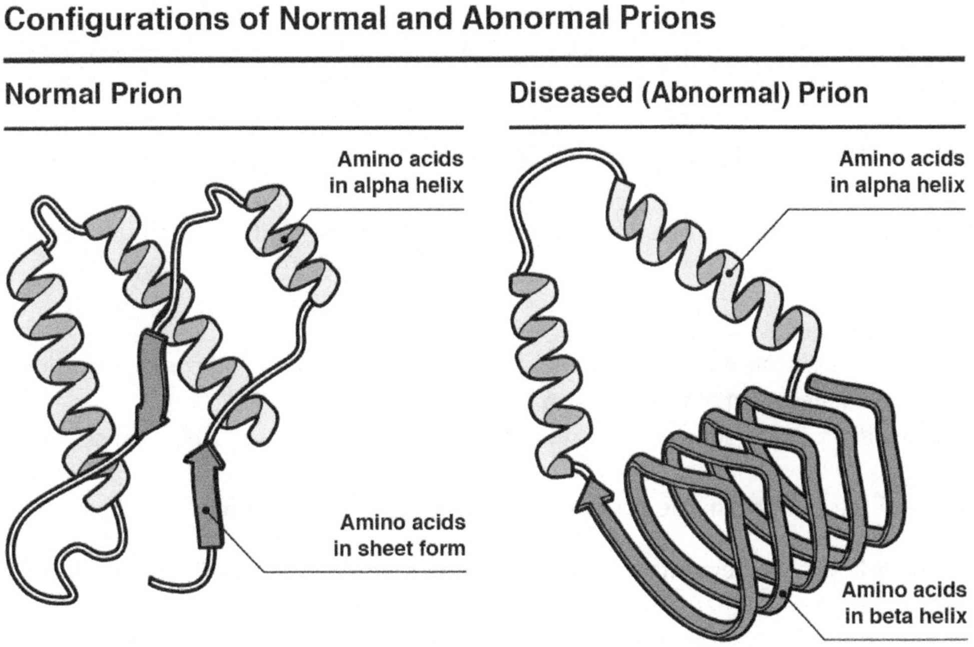

Configurations of Normal and Abnormal Prions

Normal Prion

Amino acids in alpha helix

Amino acids in sheet form

Diseased (Abnormal) Prion

Amino acids in alpha helix

Amino acids in beta helix

Figure 1.

Scientist 2

The degeneration of brain tissue in animals afflicted with mad cow disease is widely considered to be the result of prions. This theory fails to consider other possible causes, such as viruses. Recent studies have shown that infected tissues often contain small particles that match the size and density of viruses. In order to demonstrate that these viral particles are the cause of mad cow disease, researchers used chemicals to inactivate the viruses. When the damaged, inactivated viruses were introduced into healthy tissue, no mad cow disease symptoms were observed. This result indicates that viruses are likely the cause of mad cow disease. In addition, when the infected particles from an infected animal are used to infect a different species, the resulting particles are identical to the original particles. If the infecting agent was a protein, the particles would not be identical because proteins are species-specific. Instead, the infective agent is viewed as some form of a virus that has its own DNA or RNA configuration and can reproduce identical infective particles.

35. Which statement below best characterizes the main difference in the scientists' opinions?

   a. The existence of species-specific proteins
   b. Transmission rates of mad cow disease
   c. The conversion process of normal proteins into prions
   d. The underlying cause of mad cow disease

36. Which of the following statements is NOT correct?
    a. Scientist 2 proposes that viruses aren't the cause of mad cow disease because chemicals inactivated the viruses.
    b. Scientist 1 suggests that infectious proteins called prions are the cause of mad cow disease.
    c. Scientist 1 indicates that the damaging conglomerations formed by prions eventually result in death.
    d. Scientist 2 reports that infected tissues often contain particles that match the size profile of viruses.

37. Which of the following is true according to Scientist 1?
    a. Normal proteins accumulate in large numbers to produce damaging conglomerations.
    b. Prions can change normal proteins into prions.
    c. Species-specific DNA sequences of infected tissues indicate that proteins cause mad cow disease.
    d. Prions are present only in the peripheral nervous system of mammals.

38. Which of the following statements would be consistent with the views of both scientists?
    a. Resulting tissue damage is reversible.
    b. The infecting agent is composed of sheets of amino acids in an alpha helix configuration.
    c. Species-specific DNA can be isolated from infected tissue.
    d. Cross-species transmission of the illness is possible.

39. How does the conglomeration described in the passage affect function?
    a. Synapses are delayed.
    b. Sponge-like tissue formations occur.
    c. Space-occupying lesions compress the nerves.
    d. The blood supply to surrounding tissues is decreased.

40. Which of the following statements is supported by this passage?
    a. Scientist 1 favors the claim that viruses are the cause of mad cow disease.
    b. Prions are a type of infectious virus.
    c. The process that results in the formation of the abnormal prion is unclear.
    d. Mad cow disease is caused by normal proteins.

Social Studies

Questions 1–3 refer to the passage below:

> I believe that this was the first moving line ever installed. The idea came in a general way from the overhead trolley that the Chicago packers use in dressing beef. We had previously assembled the fly-wheel magneto in the usual method. With one workman doing a complete job he could turn out from thirty-five to forty pieces in a nine-hour day, or about twenty minutes to an assembly. What he did alone was then spread into twenty-nine operations; that cut down the assembly time to thirteen minutes, ten seconds. Then we raised the height of the line eight inches—this was in 1914—and cut the time to seven minutes. Further experimenting with the speed that the work should move at cut the time down to five minutes. In short, the result is this: by the aid of scientific study one man is now able to do somewhat more than four did only a

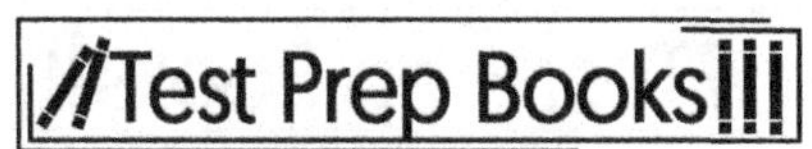

comparatively few years ago. That line established the efficiency of the method and we now use it everywhere. The assembling of the motor, formerly done by one man, is now divided into eighty-four operations—those men do the work that three times their number formerly did. In a short time we tried out the plan on the chassis.

Excerpt from *My Life and My Work* by Henry Ford, 1922

1. According to the passage, which one of the following best describes the primary economic benefit of this innovation?
   a. The innovation increased workers' ability to multi-task.
   b. The innovation decreased labor costs per worker.
   c. The innovation increased productivity in terms of both speed and quantity.
   d. The innovation decreased the size of the industrial workforce.

2. Which one of the following is the name for this type of production?
   a. Assembly line
   b. Assembly trolley
   c. Automated assembly
   d. Elevated assembly

3. According to the passage, how did this new method of production improve over time?
   a. The method improved by adopting the exact practices of other industries.
   b. The method improved after it was applied to the chassis.
   c. The method improved by continually increasing the number of operations per product.
   d. The method improved progressively through experimentation.

Question 4 is based on the following passage:

Hand in hand with this we must frankly recognize the overbalance of population in our industrial centers and, by engaging on a national scale in a redistribution, endeavor to provide a better use of the land for those best fitted for the land. The task can be helped by definite efforts to raise the values of agricultural products and with this the power to purchase the output of our cities. It can be helped by preventing realistically the tragedy of the growing loss through foreclosure of our small homes and our farms. It can be helped by insistence that the Federal, State, and local governments act forthwith on the demand that their cost be drastically reduced. It can be helped by the unifying of relief activities which today are often scattered, uneconomical, and unequal. It can be helped by national planning for and supervision of all forms of transportation and of communications and other utilities which have a definitely public character. There are many ways in which it can be helped, but it can never be helped merely by talking about it. We must act and act quickly.

Finally, in our progress toward a resumption of work we require two safeguards against a return of the evils of the old order; there must be a strict supervision of all banking and credits and investments; there must be an end to speculation with other people's money, and there must be provision for an adequate but sound currency.

Excerpt from President Franklin D. Roosevelt's Inaugural Address, March 4, 1933

4. Which of the following best describes President Roosevelt's underlying approach to government?
   a. Government must be focused on redistribution of land.
   b. Government must "act and act quickly" to intervene and regulate the economy.
   c. Government must exercise "strict supervision of all banking."
   d. Government must prevent the "growing loss through foreclosure."

Question 5 is based on the following diagram:

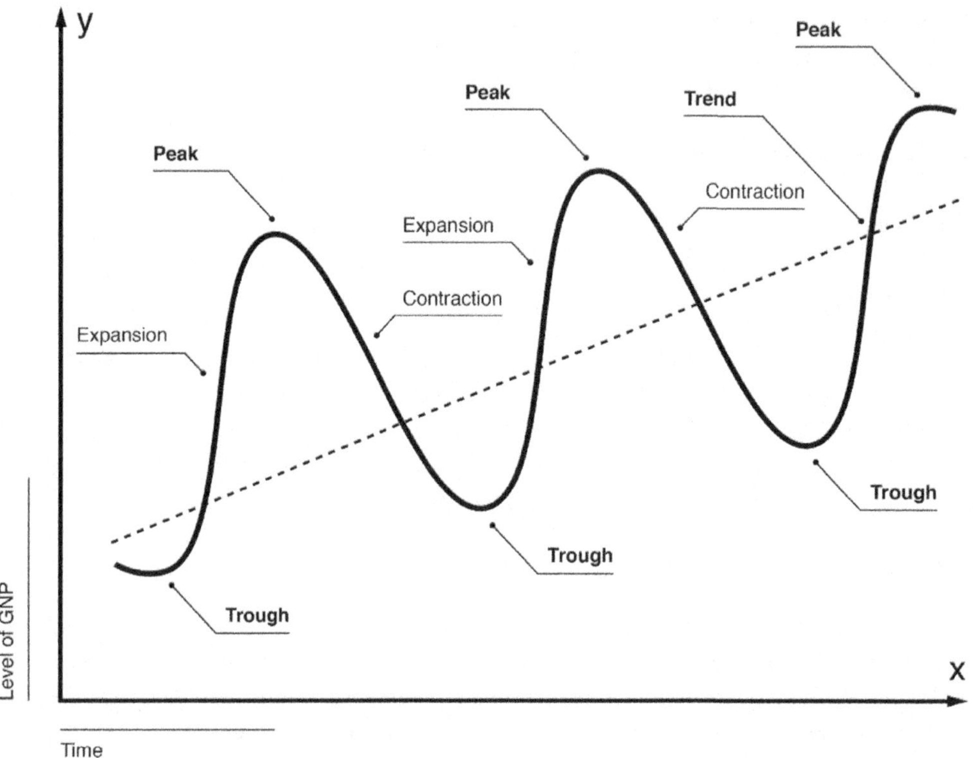

5. Which of the following phases of a business cycle occurs when there is continual growth?
   a. Expansion
   b. Peak
   c. Contraction
   d. Trough

Use the following passages to answer questions 6 and 7:

> Spain had three main motivators in colonizing the Americas: God, Gold, and Glory. The Spanish wanted to convert natives to Christianity (God). They had heard of the gold and silver deposits in South America and wanted to profit from these (Gold). They also wanted to claim and conquer land in the name of Spain (Glory).
>
> In colonizing the Americas, England was motivated in part by religion. Dissenting sects of religion could be persecuted by the king for their non-conformity. Therefore, many of

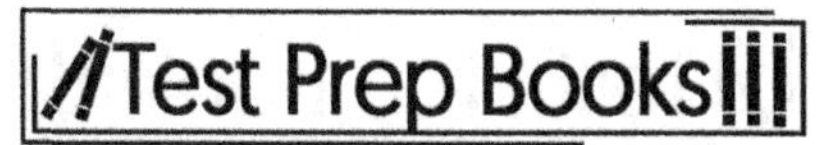

them desired religious freedom. Missionaries with the aim of converting Natives also became a part of English colonization. The English were motivated by economic reasons as well, in part from the raw materials of the Americas. They had also heard of the Northwest Passage—a potential new trade route to Asia. Additionally, they were motivated by the ability to cultivate land, giving them some grounding in the Americas as well as creating new settlements for England.

The French were primarily motivated to colonize the Americas in order to take part in the fur trade. The few settlements made by the French were primarily for trade. Eventually, French missionaries who aimed to convert Natives to Catholicism became a part of their colonization.

The Netherlands' initial motivation was to discover a new trade route to Asia (the Northwest Passage) in order to make financial gain through this new route. However, they ended up with similar motivations as the French after seeing the profits of the fur trade. The Dutch then began to participate in the fur trade and had a small number of settlements for the sake of the fur trade.

6. Of the above listed motivations, which of the given motivations most closely line up with Spain's motivation of Gold?

a. The English's motivation to benefit from the raw materials in the Americas
b. The French missionaries' motivation to convert Native peoples to Catholicism
c. The Netherlands' motivation to profit from the fur trade
d. None of these motivations are similar to Spain's motivation of Gold

7. Based upon the given information about the different European countries' motivations for the colonization of America, which two countries were overall the most similar in their motivations?

a. Spain and the Netherlands
b. England and France
c. England and Spain
d. France and the Netherlands

Questions 8 and 9 are based on the graphic that follows a brief introduction to the topic:

The United States Constitution directs Congress to conduct periodic censuses to determine the country's population. The United States Census Bureau carries out the surveys and collects both population numbers and demographic information. In 1790, then Secretary of State Thomas Jefferson conducted the first census, and the most recent U.S. census was in 2020. The last U.S. census was the first to be issued primarily through the internet.

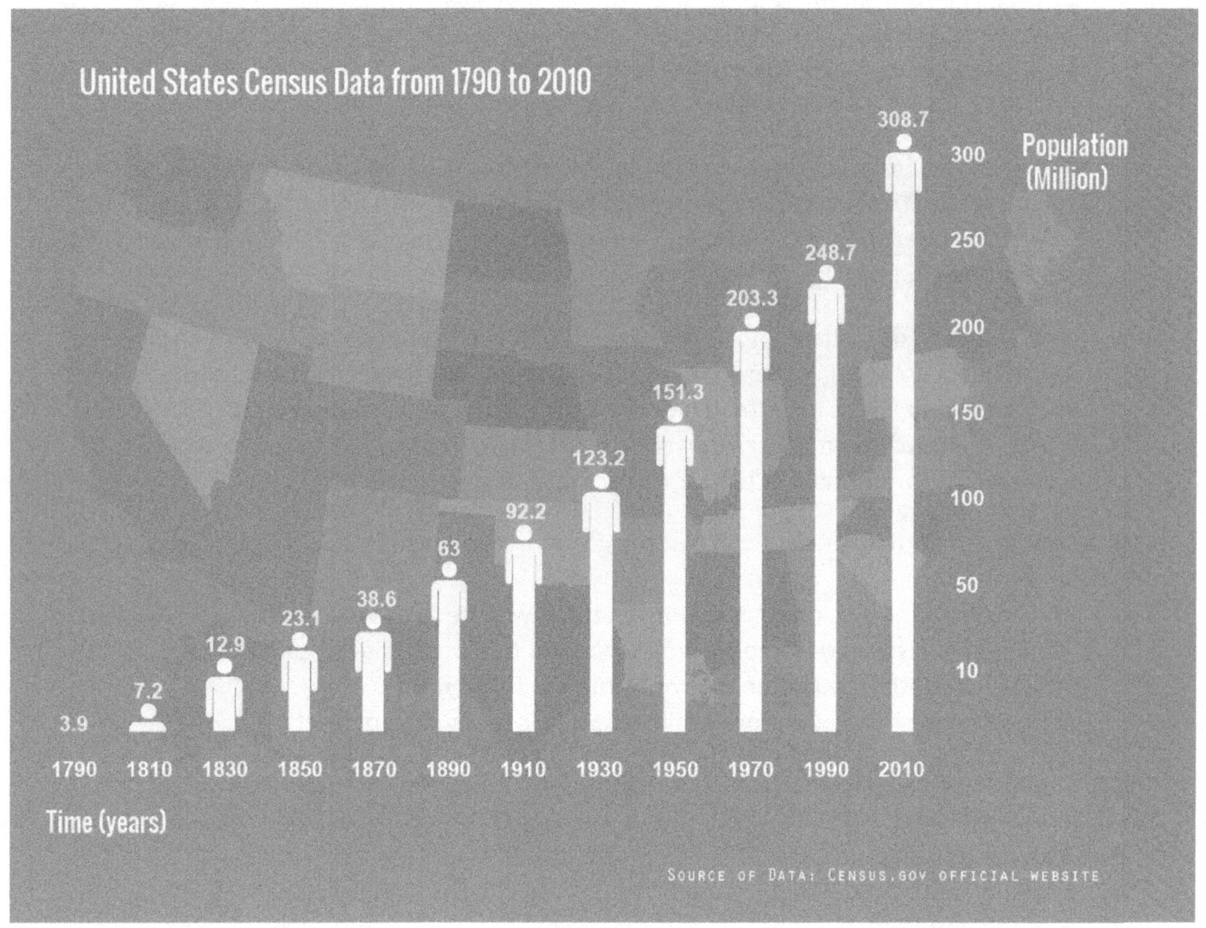

8. In which of the following years was the United States population less than it was in 1930?
   a. 1950
   b. 1970
   c. 1910
   d. 1990

9. In what twenty-year interval did the population increase the most?
   a. From 1930 to 1950
   b. From 1950 to 1970
   c. From 1970 to 1990
   d. From 1990 to 2010

Use the following map to help answer question 10:

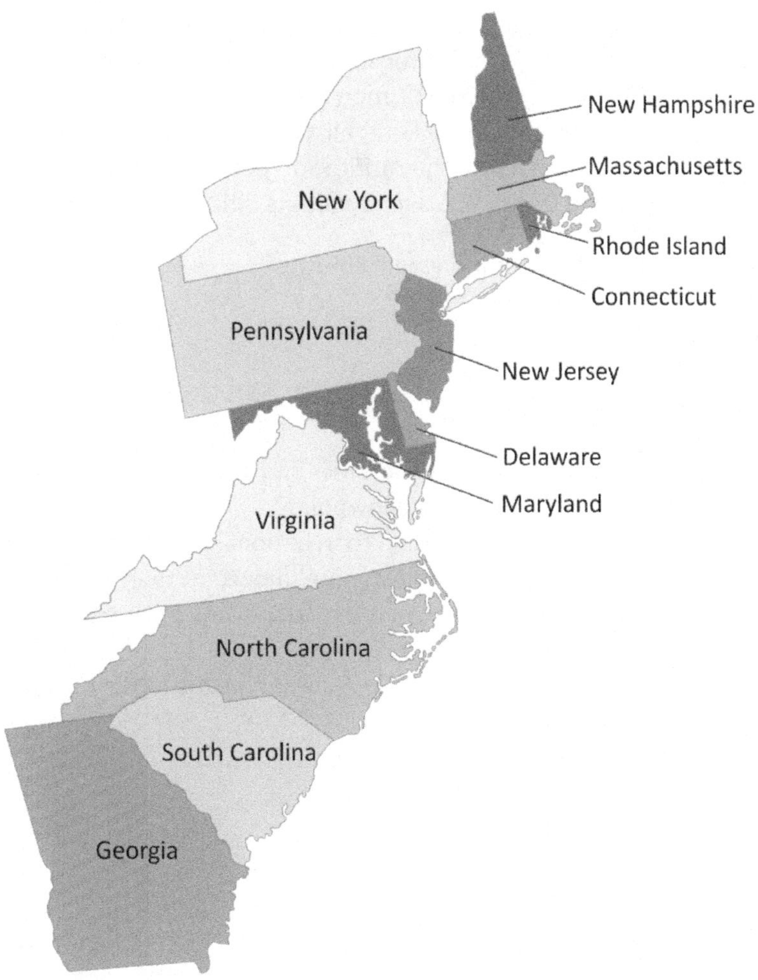

10. In 1850, the ten most populous cities in the United States, in order from most populous to least were: New York, NY; Baltimore, MD; Boston, MA; Philadelphia, PA; New Orleans, LA; Cincinnati, OH; Brooklyn, NY; St. Louis, MO, Spring Garden, PA; Albany, NY. How many of these cities are located in a state that was one of the original thirteen colonies?

   a. 6
   b. 7
   c. 8
   d. 9

Use the following passage to answer Questions 11 and 12:

> Federalists supported strong national government over strong state governments. Federalists also believed that having three branches of government protected people's rights. Each branch was equal to one another; therefore, they could not assume control over each other. Federalists were in support of a Constitution for the United States. In support of the Constitution, Alexander Hamilton, John Jay, and James Madison wrote a series of essays in 1788 titled the Federalist Papers. However, anti-Federalists were

concerned about the lack of individual liberties explicitly afforded in the new Constitution. Anti-Federalists were more concerned about national government gaining excessive amounts of power and favored strong state governments and a weaker national/centralized government. In response to the Constitution, many state conventions and opponents of the Constitution asked for amendments of explicit liberties of citizens as individuals. Many Federalists agreed to an addition in order to gain more anti-Federalist support for the ratification of the Constitution. Once ratified, the Bill of Rights was added in order to accommodate citizens' individual rights.

11. What was this addition that wrote out individual liberties?
    a. The Judiciary Act of 1789
    b. The Bill of Rights
    c. The Virginia Plan
    d. The Federalist Papers

12. Based upon the differing viewpoints of the Federalists and anti-Federalists in the passage above, which statement best lines up with the Federalist viewpoint?
    a. State government should be more powerful than national government.
    b. A strong, centralized national government is more important than state governments.
    c. Individual liberties should be focused on in order to prevent a too-powerful centralized government.
    d. The Constitution should not be ratified until it guarantees the rights of states and individuals.

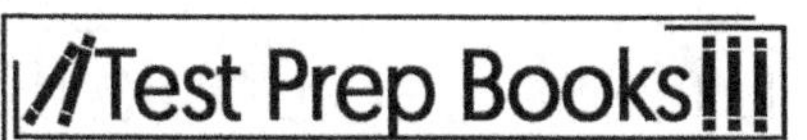

Use the following figure to answer Questions 13–15:

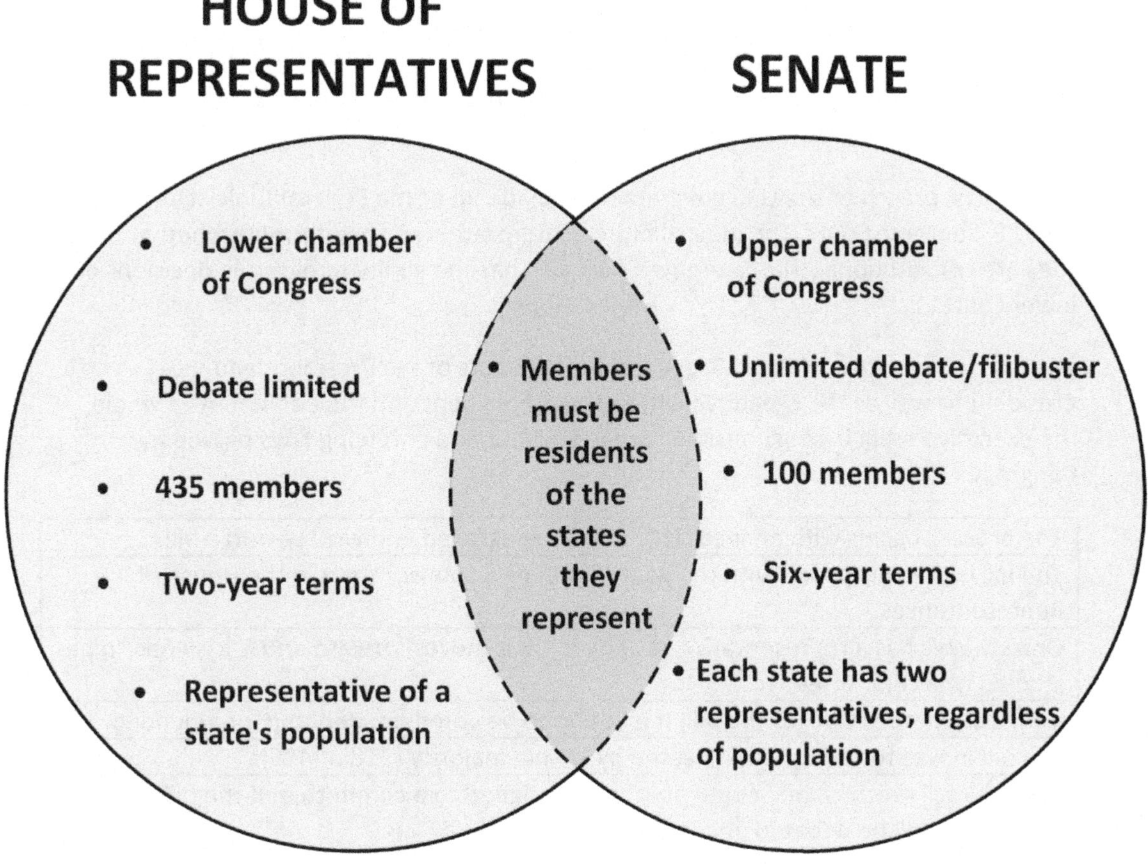

13. Referencing the figure above, which of the following could be placed as a similarity between the U.S. House of Representatives and the U.S. Senate?
    a. Both the House and the Senate have 100 members each.
    b. Congress officials serve four-year terms.
    c. Representatives must live within the state they represent.
    d. Both have a middle chamber of the congress.

14. Which of the following statements is true based on the information provided in *Figure 1*?
    a. The House is more politically powerful than the Senate.
    b. Limited debate is the expectation/requirement of both the House and the Senate.
    c. Each state has an equal number of representatives in both the House and the Senate.
    d. There are 535 members of the U.S. Congress.

15. Monroe, Omar, and Hansen are members of Congress and represent the same state. They are in the same part of Congress (House or Senate). Which part of Congress are they members of?
    a. The House of Representatives
    b. The Senate
    c. Neither of these is correct.

d. There is not enough information to determine which part of Congress they are members of.

Use the following passage and table to answer Questions 16–18:

The legislative branch of the U.S. government consists of the Congress, which is made up of the House of Representatives and the Senate. The legislative branch has many powers, including creating laws and regulating things such as interstate and foreign commerce.

The judicial branch of the U.S. government is made up of the Federal Judicial Center and the U.S. Supreme Court. The judicial branch interprets laws to determine whether or not they are constitutional. The Supreme Court also has the ability to overrule decisions of lower courts.

The executive branch of the U.S. government consists of the President and Vice President as well as the Executive Office of the President and the Cabinet. As a whole, the executive branch is responsible for carrying out and enforcing laws passed by Congress.

The process begins with an idea. This idea is researched and written into a bill.
The bill is then proposed with the goal of gaining a sponsor for it in the House of Representatives.
Once the bill has a representative to sponsor it, it moves forward and is assigned to be studied by a committee.
If the committee releases the bill, it is set up to be voted on, debated, or amended.
The bill moves to the Senate if passed by simple majority (218 of 435).
Once the bill reaches the Senate, it is again assigned to a committee. If the bill is released, it will be debated and voted on.
If there are any changes to the bill, it moves back to the House.
After this, the bill returns to both the House and the Senate for their final approval.
Finally, once the bill is approved by the House and the Senate, the President has 10 days to either veto it or sign it into law.

16. The table describes what process?
    a. The legislative process
    b. The judicial process
    c. The executive process
    d. None of these answers are correct.

17. Which statement does NOT accurately describe the process listed in the table?
    a. Both the House and the Senate must first approve of a bill before it moves forward.
    b. A bill does not need a sponsor to move forward in the process.
    c. The President makes the last decision in the process, either vetoing a bill or signing it into law.
    d. The approval of only two of the three different governmental branches is needed to pass a law.

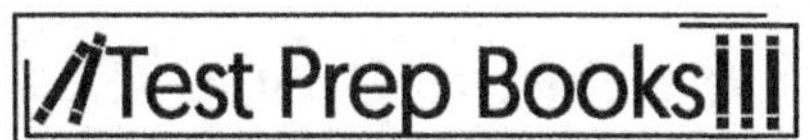

18. The constitutionality of a law has been brought into question. Which branch of the U.S. government has the power to determine whether a law is constitutional?
   a. Legislative
   b. Executive
   c. Judicial
   d. None of these

Use the following passage and Venn diagram to answer Question 19:

> To strengthen the central government, while still appeasing the individual states who preferred to remain sovereign over their territories, the framers of the Constitution based the new government upon the principle of Federalism—a compound government system that divides powers between a central government and various regional governments. The Constitution clearly defined the roles of both the state governments and the new federal government, specifying the limited power of the federal government and reserving all other powers not specifically granted by the Constitution to the federal government to the states in the Tenth Amendment to the Constitution, commonly referred to as the Reservation Clause.
>
> The Constitution establishes the specific powers granted to the federal and state governments:
>
> - **Delegated powers**: the specific powers granted to the federal government by the Constitution
> - **Implied powers**: the unstated powers of the federal government that can be reasonably inferred from the Constitution
> - **Inherent powers**: the reasonable powers required by the federal government to manage the nation's affairs and maintain sovereignty
> - **Reserved powers**: the unspecified powers belonging to the states that are not expressly granted to the federal government or denied to the state governments by the Constitution
> - **Concurrent powers**: the powers shared between the federal and state governments

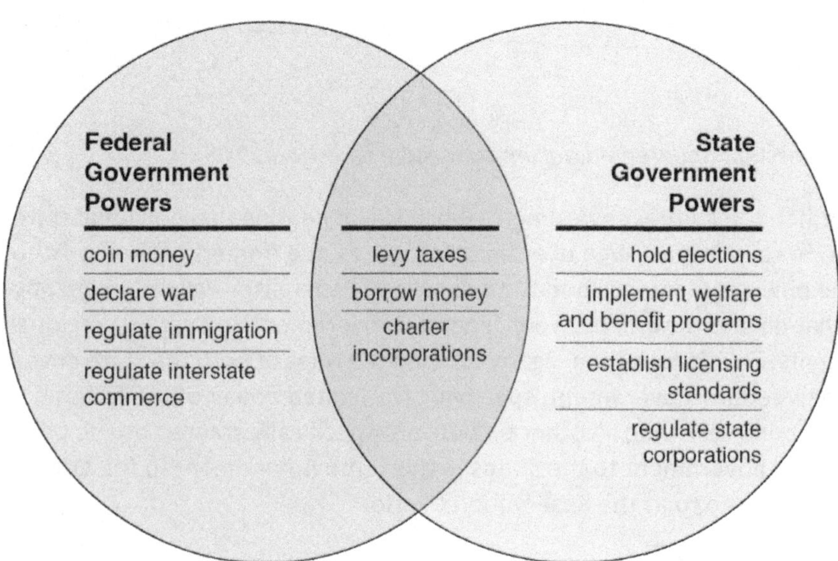

19. Which of the following terms best describes the missing title?
    a. Reserved powers
    b. Implied powers
    c. Delegated powers
    d. Concurrent powers

Questions 20 and 21 pertain to the following passage:

When the people cast their votes for president in the general election, they are casting their votes for the *electors* from the *Electoral College* who will elect the president. In order to win the presidential election, a nominee must win a majority of the electoral votes. The number of electors is equal to the total number of senators and representatives from each state plus three electoral votes for Washington D.C. which does not have any voting members in the legislative branch.

The electors typically vote based on the popular vote from their states. Although the Constitution does not require electors to vote for the popular vote winner of their state, no elector voting against the popular vote of their state has ever changed the outcome of an election. Due to the Electoral College, a nominee may win the popular vote and still lose the election.

If no one wins the majority of electoral votes in the presidential election, the House of Representatives decides the presidency, as required by the Twelfth Amendment. They may only vote for the top three candidates, and each state delegation votes as a single bloc. A simple majority is required to elect the president. The House has only elected the president twice, in 1801 and 1825.

20. Which party's candidate won the 2000 presidential election?

Electoral College Results (2000)		
Party	**Popular Votes**	**Electoral Votes**
Constitution	98,020	0
Democratic	50,999,897	266
Green	2,882,955	0
Libertarian	384,431	0
Natural Law	83,714	0
Reform	448,895	0
Republican	50,456,002	271
Other	51,186	0
Abstention	n/a	1

a. Democratic
b. Green
c. Libertarian
d. Republican

21. Who won the presidential election of 1824?

Presidential Election of 1824			
Candidate	Electoral Votes	Popular Votes	State Votes in the House of Representatives
Andrew Jackson	99	153,544	7
John Quincy Adams	84	108,740	13
William H. Crawford	41	46,618	4
Henry Clay	37	47,136	0

a. Andrew Jackson
b. John Quincy Adams
c. William H. Crawford
d. Henry Clay

Question 22 refers to the following diagram:

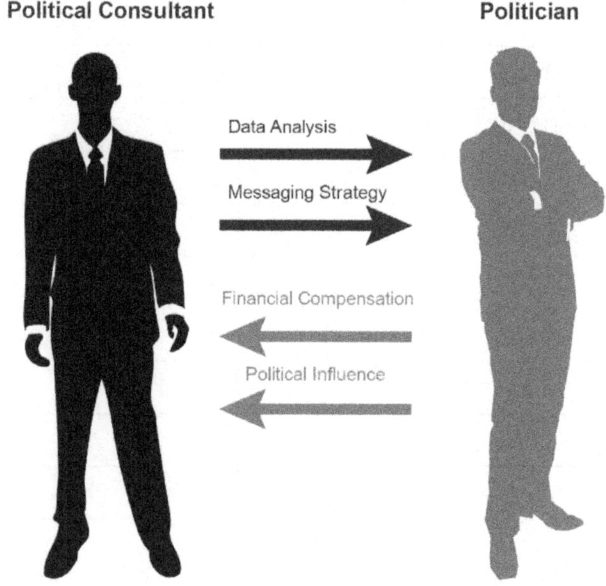

22. Which of the following statements BEST describes how the politician benefits from the relationship depicted above?
   a. The politician will likely be able to spend less money during their election cycle.
   b. The politician will likely enhance the effectiveness of their campaign communication through tailored advertisements.
   c. The politician will likely increase their popularity by appearing more genuine and relatable to voters.
   d. The politician will be able to better analyze economic data to develop policies that benefit an increased number of constituents.

23. Following the Civil War, Congress passed the **Fifteenth Amendment** (1870) to prohibit denying the vote based on "race, color, or previous condition of servitude." During the early twentieth century, the **Seventeenth Amendment** (1913) expanded political participation by establishing the popular election of U.S. Senators. Prior to the Seventeenth Amendment, state legislatures selected the U.S. Senators. How does the Fifteenth Amendment compare to the Seventeenth Amendment in regard to the expansion of democracy in the United States?
   a. The Fifteenth Amendment increased the number of eligible voters, and the Seventeenth Amendment allowed more input from the public.
   b. The Fifteenth Amendment guaranteed the right to vote for people regardless of sex, and the Seventeenth Amendment established the popular election of U.S. Senators.
   c. The Fifteenth Amendment prohibited discrimination based on race, and the Seventeenth Amendment limited political corruption by prohibiting the sale of alcohol.
   d. The Fifteenth Amendment lowered the eligible voting age, and the Seventeenth Amendment created the Electoral College.

Please use the graphic below to answer Questions 24 and 25:

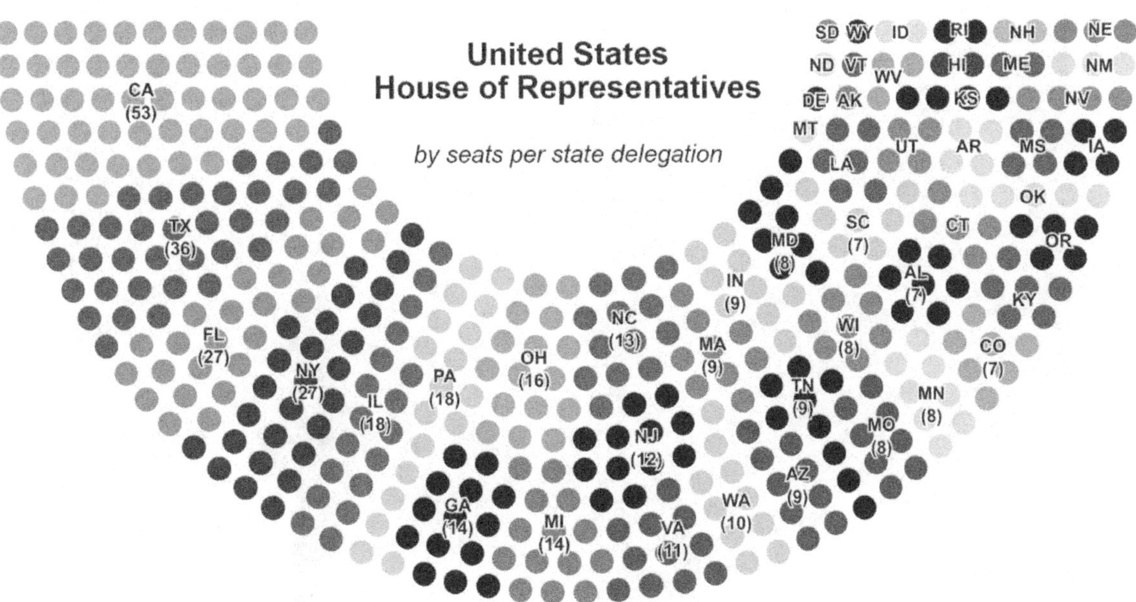

24. Which of the following statements is reflected in the graphic?
    a. The ten least-populated states possess a greater collective representation than the two most-populated states.
    b. The two most-populated states possess a greater collective representation than the ten least-populated states.
    c. The two most-populated states and ten least-populated states possess an equal number of representation.
    d. The ten most-populated states and two least-populated states possess an equal number of representatives.

25. Which of the following states would have the most votes within the Electoral College?
    a. Ohio
    b. Iowa
    c. Michigan
    d. South Dakota

Please use the map below to answer Questions 26 and 27:

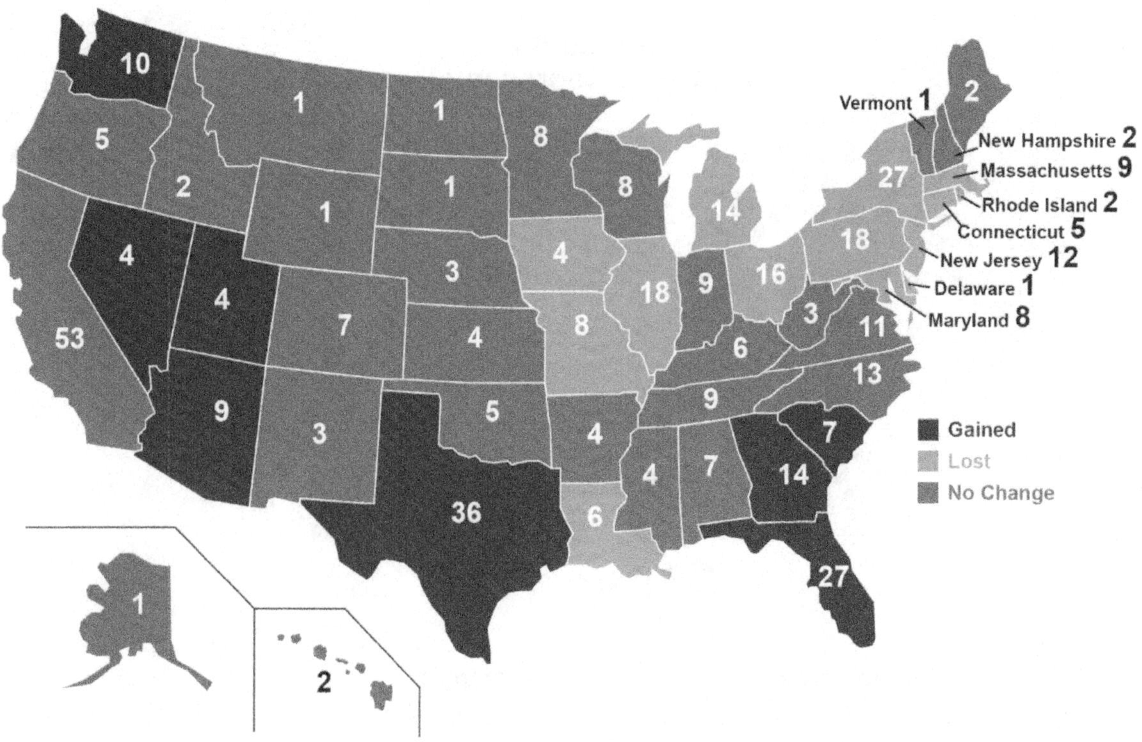

26. How many total electoral votes are accounted for by the states that gained representatives as a result of the 2010 U.S. census?
   a. 123
   b. 111
   c. 97
   d. 88

27. Which of the following statements is reflected in the map?
   a. More states gained or lost representatives than experienced no change at all.
   b. Most states that gained representatives were concentrated in the Pacific Northwest and Great Plains regions.
   c. Most states that lost representatives were concentrated in the Midwest and Northeast.
   d. More less-populous states lost representatives than more-populous states.

Please read the passage below and use it to answer Question 28:

> The idea of a council to the Executive, which has so generally obtained in the State constitutions, has been derived from that maxim of republican jealousy which considers power as safer in the hands of a number of men than of a single man. If the maxim should be admitted to be applicable to the case, I should contend that the advantage on that side would not counterbalance the numerous disadvantages on the opposite side. But I do not think the rule at all applicable to the executive power. I clearly concur in

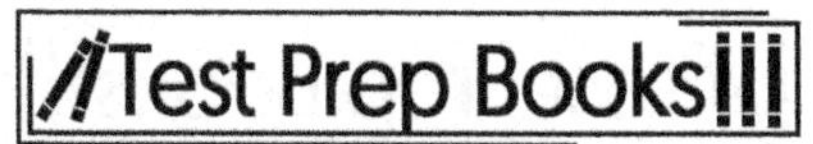

opinion, in this particular, with a writer whom the celebrated Junius pronounces to be "deep, solid, and ingenious," that "the executive power is more easily confined when it is ONE;" that it is far more safe there should be a single object for the jealousy and watchfulness of the people; and, in a word, that all multiplication of the Executive is rather dangerous than friendly to liberty.

Excerpt from Alexander Hamilton, Federalist No. 70

28. Which of the following statements is MOST consistent with the author's argument in the passage?
    a. Republican values dictate that it is in the best interest of the U.S. government to multiply executive power by electing multiple leaders to executive office.
    b. A single president would result in a single object of jealousy and watchfulness, which would ultimately threaten liberty through dictatorship.
    c. The multiplication of the executive office would be more of a threat to liberty than the election of single executive leader.
    d. The power of the executive office should be invested in state governments and constitutions, which would help balance executive power in the American Republic.

Question 29 is based on the following passage:

Now, therefore I, Abraham Lincoln, President of the United States, by virtue of the power in me vested as Commander-in-Chief, of the Army and Navy of the United States in time of actual armed rebellion against the authority and government of the United States, and as a fit and necessary war measure for suppressing said rebellion...

And by virtue of the power, and for the purpose aforesaid, I do order and declare that all persons held as slaves within said designated States, and parts of States, are, and henceforward shall be free; and that the Executive government of the United States, including the military and naval authorities thereof, will recognize and maintain the freedom of said persons.

Excerpt from President Abraham Lincoln's Emancipation Proclamation, January 1, 1863

29. How does President Lincoln justify freeing the slaves in designated areas of the South?
    a. Emancipation is necessary since slavery is evil.
    b. Emancipation is necessary to boost the morale of the North.
    c. Emancipation is necessary to punish the South for seceding from the Union.
    d. Emancipation is necessary to strengthen the war effort of the North.

Use the following passages to answer Questions 30–32:

During the Great Depression, there were many different perspectives about how to help lift the economy back up. The route the U.S. went was ultimately decided with the election of Franklin D. Roosevelt. When Roosevelt took office in 1933, he began a series of programs and projects that have impacts still to this day. These programs and projects were a part of the New Deal, which is considered to have occurred in its initial introduction from 1933–1936. One of the early parts of the New Deal is the Agricultural Adjustment Act (May 1933), though there were many laws passed during this time (the Glass-Steagall Act, the Tennessee Valley Authority Act, the Emergency Banking Act, and many more). Many of the acts passed in 1933 were passed within the first 100 days of Roosevelt taking office. The National Industrial Recovery Act (June 1933) is a particularly important law for workers because it guarantees workers the right to unionize as well as bargain for better conditions and wages. Later aspects of the New Deal, often considered the Second New Deal, include the Social Security Act, the Works Progress Administration, and many other programs and laws.

The Social Security Act (1935) guaranteed a pension to Americans through setting up a system of unemployment insurance. It included the federal government caring for the disabled and (dependent) children. The Social Security program that this act created still exists today. To help provide jobs for those that were unemployed, the Works Progress Administration was created (also 1935). This included many different types of jobs, including building things intended for public use such as post offices and highways, but it also included more creative jobs such as those of musicians and writers.

Many Americans approved of aspects of the New Deal yet also disapproved of others. There were many setbacks in trying to incorporate new laws, with the more conservative Supreme Court arguing that these laws often were unconstitutional because the federal government was reaching too far. Once Roosevelt planned on packing the Court with more liberal justices, the conservative Supreme Court then voted more in favor of the New Deal programs and acts in hopes of preventing this action. Eventually, the U.S. entered World War II, which stimulated the economy enough to effectively end the Great Depression.

30. Which of these aspects of the New Deal was first passed/created?
    a. The National Industrial Recovery Act
    b. The Agricultural Adjustment Act
    c. The Social Security Act
    d. The Works Progress Administration

31. Which of these statements is an accurate representation of the New Deal?
    a. While the New Deal was beneficial at the time, there were not any laws or programs that are still around and impactful to this day.
    b. The New Deal was widely and openly supported by other branches of the government and American citizens.
    c. The New Deal was designed to provide relief following the tough conditions of the Great Depression, and it still has an impact on U.S. citizens of today.
    d. None of these statements accurately represent the New Deal.

32. After Jack was laid off from his job, he was able to get assistance in finding a job working in the construction of the new local library. Which act or program is responsible for the assistance that Jack received?
    a. The Works Progress Administration
    b. The Tennessee Valley Authority Act
    c. The Emergency Banking Act
    d. The Glass-Steagall Act

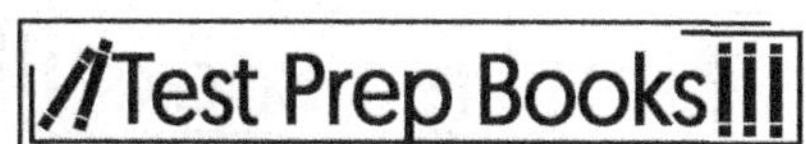

Question 33 is based on the following passage:

> Those who are opposed to this proposition tell us that the issue of paper money is a function of the bank and that the government ought to go out of the banking business. I stand with Jefferson rather than with them, and tell them, as he did, that the issue of money is a function of the government and that the banks should go out of the governing business.
>
> If they dare to come out in the open field and defend the gold standard as a good thing, we shall fight them to the uttermost, having behind us the producing masses of the nation and the world. Having behind us the commercial interests and the laboring interests and all the toiling masses, we shall answer their demands for a gold standard by saying to them, you shall not press down upon the brow of labor this crown of thorns. You shall not crucify mankind upon a cross of gold.

Excerpt from William Jennings Bryan, *Cross of Gold* speech, 1896

33. What is the main idea presented in the excerpt?
   a. Banks prefer the gold standard.
   b. Most Americans dislike the gold standard.
   c. Violence is justified when the government oppresses the masses.
   d. The government should set the monetary policy based on the will of the people.

Question 34 is based on the following graph:

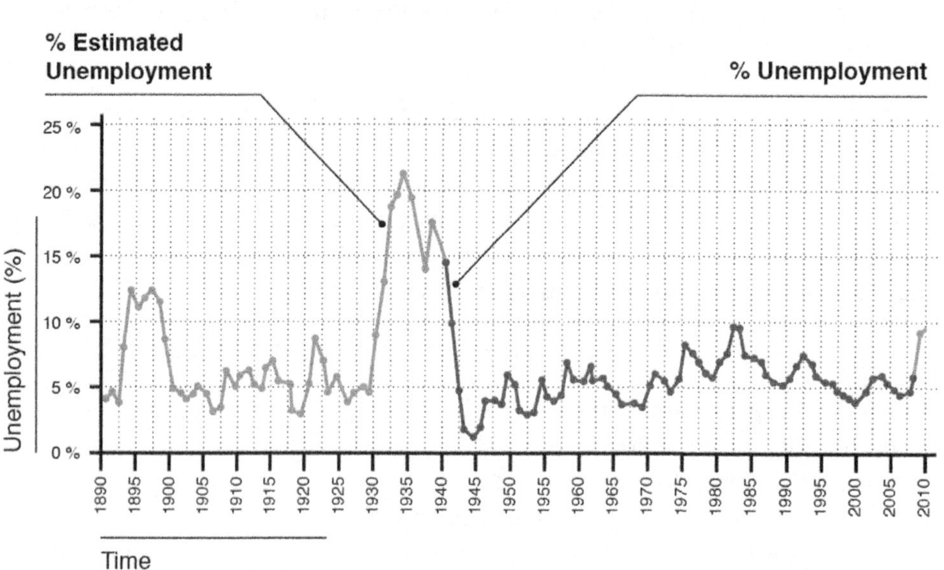

34. Which event caused the second-largest increase in unemployment in American history?
    a. Panic of 1893
    b. Depression of 1920
    c. Depression of 1929
    d. Great Recession of 2007

Question 35 is based on the following passage:

> George Washington's **Farewell Address** is one of the most famous speeches in American history. While Washington reluctantly served as president, he had near-unanimous popular support. Washington realized that future American presidents would not enjoy that luxury, and he hoped the country wouldn't fracture when divisive issues arose. The revolutionary hero turned first president felt it was his duty to impart some words of wisdom to the country as it embarked on its first regime change.
>
> Washington primarily warned of the dangers of **factionalism**. He argued that the United States would be safe and prosperous as long as it was a cohesive entity and then proceeded to give a number of warnings about factionalism. He believed political factionalism would grind the new constitutional system to a halt and possibly lead to state disintegration. To prevent partisan bickering, Washington cautioned against the establishment of political parties, believing that they would consolidate power and dissolve the core tenets of representative government. The Farewell Address is also famous for Washington cautioning America against getting entangled in European rivalries, foreign disputes, and permanent foreign alliances. Washington pointed to the

benefits of America's geographic location and urged the government to continue developing prosperous and peaceful relations with foreign powers whenever possible.

35. What was a concern that George Washington warned of in his Farewell Address?
    a. The danger of political parties
    b. To be prepared to intervene in Europe’s affairs
    c. The abolition of slavery
    d. To protect states’ rights through sectionalism

Answer Explanations for Practice Test #1

Reading Comprehension

1. B: The first line in the last paragraph, "...I was returning from a journey to a patient (for I had now returned to civil practice..." indicates that the narrator is a physician. Choice *A* is incorrect because the narrator admits to not knowing about Holmes' recent activities beyond what he's read in the press. Choice *C* is incorrect because there's no evidence for it. Choice *D* is incorrect because while the narrator mentions once living at Baker Street, he is only led past it on a walk in the last paragraph. This suggests that he doesn't presently live there.

2. A: The line "Beyond these signs of his activity, however, which I merely shared with all the readers of the daily press, I knew little of my former friend and companion," suggests that the narrator learned of the cases mentioned in the press, another name for the newspaper. Choice *B* is incorrect because there is no mention of police reports. Choices *C* and *D* are incorrect because the narrator admits that he has not recently had direct contact with Holmes or his cases for some time.

3. D: The first paragraph describes Holmes' reaction to emotions, including love, as abhorrent, or disgusting. However, he finds them "...excellent for drawing the veil from men's motives and actions," which would allow him to gather clues for solving cases, Choice *D*. Holmes' clearly negative feelings toward love and other emotions make the positive feelings described in Choices *A*, *B*, and *C* incorrect.

4. A: *Singular* could mean referring to one thing or remarkable. Holmes is described in the passage as complex and thoughtful, so it is unlikely that introspection is his only, Choice *C*, characteristic. Instead, the word is being used to describe his remarkable and exceptional skills of introspection, Choice *A*. Choices *B* and *D* are incorrect definitions for the word singular.

5. B: The passage gives the reader information about Holmes as a character as well as how Holmes and the narrator formerly lived and worked together but have not seen each other for some time. Choice *A* is incorrect because while the narrator worked on a case with Holmes, they did not collaborate on several other cases mentioned. Choice *C* is incorrect because no details on the current case are provided in this passage. Choice *D* is incorrect because while Holmes' feelings on emotions are discussed, that is only one portion of the passage that helps to set up the rest of the story; it is not the main purpose.

6. D: The use of *I* could serve to have a "hedging" effect, allow the reader to connect with the author in a more personal way, and cause the reader to empathize more with the egrets. However, it doesn't distance the reader from the text, making Choice *D* the answer to this question.

7. C: The quote provides an example of a warden protecting one of the colonies. Choice *A* is incorrect because the speaker of the quote is a warden, not a hunter. Choice *B* is incorrect because the quote does not lighten the mood but shows the danger of the situation between the wardens and the hunters. Choice *D* is incorrect because there is no humor found in the quote.

8. D: A *rookery* is a colony of breeding birds. Although *rookery* could mean Choice *A*, houses in a slum area, it does not make sense in this context. Choices *B* and *C* are both incorrect, as this is not a place for hunters to trade tools or for wardens to trade stories.

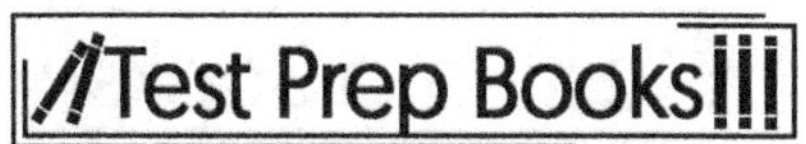

9. B: The previous sentence is describing "twenty colonies" of birds, so what follows should be a bird colony. Choice *A* may be true, but we have no evidence of this in the text. Choice *C* does touch on the tension between the hunters and wardens, but there is no official "Bird Island Battle" mentioned in the text. Choice *D* does not exist in the text.

10. D: The text mentions several different times how and why the association has been successful and gives examples to back this fact. Choice *A* is incorrect because although the article, in some instances, calls certain people to act, it is not the purpose of the entire passage. There is no way to tell if Choices *B* and *C* are correct, as they are not mentioned in the text.

11. C: Choice *A* might be true in a general sense, but it is not relevant to the text. Choice *B* is incorrect because the hunters are not studying lines of flight to help wardens, but to hunt birds. Choice *D* is incorrect because nothing in the text mentions that hunters are trying to build homes underneath lines of flight of birds for good luck.

12. A: This is a challenging question because the author's purpose is somewhat open-ended. The author concludes by stating that the questions regarding human perception and observation can be approached from many angles. Thus, they do not seem to be attempting to prove one thing or another. Choice *B* is incorrect because we cannot know for certain whether the electron experiment is the latest discovery in astroparticle physics because no date is given. Choice *C* is a broad generalization that does not reflect accurately on the writer's views. While the author does appear to reflect on opposing views of human understanding, Choice *D*, the best answer is Choice *A*.

13. C: The beginning of this paragraph literally "presents a conundrum," explains the problem of partial understanding, and then ends with more questions, or inquiry. There is no solution offered in this paragraph, making Choices *A* and *B* incorrect. Choice *D* is incorrect because the paragraph does not begin with a definition.

14. D: Looking back in the text, the author describes that classical philosophy holds that understanding can be reached by careful observation. This will not work if they are overly invested or biased in their pursuit. Choices *A* and *C* are in no way related and are completely unnecessary. A specific theory is not necessary to understanding, according to classical philosophy mentioned by the author. Again, the key to understanding is observing the phenomena outside of it, without bias or predisposition. Thus, Choice *B* is wrong.

15. B: Choices *A* and *C* are incorrect because such movement is not mentioned at all in the text. In the passage, the author says that electrons that were physically observed appeared to pass through one hole or another. Remember, the electrons that were observed doing this were described as acting like particles. Therefore, Choice *D* is incorrect. Recall that the plate actually recorded electrons passing through both holes simultaneously and hitting the plate. This behavior, the electron activity that wasn't seen by humans, was characteristic of waves. Thus, Choice *B* is the correct answer.

16. C: Choice *A* mirrors the language in the beginning of the paragraph but is incorrect in its intent. Choice *B* is incorrect; the paragraph mentions nothing of "not knowing the true nature of gravity." Choice *D* is incorrect as well. There is no mention of an "alternative solution" in this paragraph.

17. A: The important thing to keep in mind is that we must choose a scenario that best parallels, or is most similar to, the discovery of the experiment mentioned in the passage. The important aspects of the experiment can be summed up like so: humans directly observed one behavior of electrons and then through analyzing a tool (the plate that recorded electron hits), discovered that there was another electron behavior that could not be physically seen by human eyes. This best parallels the scenario in Choice *A*. Like Feynman, the colorblind person is able to observe one aspect of the world but through the special goggles (a tool) he is able to see a natural phenomenon that he could not physically see on his own. While Choice *D* is compelling, the x-ray helps humans see the broken bone, not necessarily revealing that the bone is broken in the first place. The other Choices do not parallel the scenario in question. Therefore, Choice *A* is the best choice.

18. B: The author would not agree that technology renders human observation irrelevant. Choice *A* is incorrect because much of the passage discusses how technology helps humans observe what cannot be seen with the naked eye, therefore the author would agree with this statement. This line of reasoning is also why the author would agree with Choice *D*, making it incorrect as well. As indicated in the second paragraph, the author seems to think that humans create inventions and tools with the goal of studying phenomena more precisely. This indicates increased understanding as people recognize limitations and develop items to help bypass the limitations and learn. Therefore, Choice *C* is incorrect as well. Again, the author doesn't attempt to disprove or dismiss classical philosophy.

19. D: The implication that Douglass was unsure who his father was combined with the discussion about slaveholders' desire to separate slave families, suggests that many slave children lacked a father or father figure other than the slaveholder himself. Choices *A* and *B* are incorrect because these points are not discussed or implied anywhere in the passage. Choice *C* is incorrect because the passage repeatedly discusses how cruelly slaves were treated by their masters.

20. D: Douglass states that his master sending him away from his mother was meant to destroy the relationship between mother and child and that "[t]his is the inevitable result," meaning it had done exactly that. Choice *A* is incorrect because Douglas does not mention positive feelings toward his mother after having been separated from her. Choice *B* is incorrect because it was not his mother's choice to send him to his grandparents. Choice *C* is incorrect because he does not describe or imply how this impacted his relationship with his grandparents.

21. C: Douglass suggests that learning to read allowed him to realize that he was not considered inferior because of his race but because one of the goals of slavery was to limit his opportunities and oppress him. Choice *A* is incorrect because slaveholders felt superior to slaves in many ways, as evidenced by the way they kept and treated their slaves. Choice *B* is incorrect because while they did not need to read to perform their work, Choice *C* is a more likely reason based on the information in the passage. Choice *D* is incorrect because there is no information or implication related to the effect of reading on slave families in the passage.

22. A: When Douglass learned to read and discovered religion, he found it ironic that slaveholders were religious but kept and whipped slaves, which seemed contrary to their religious beliefs. Choice *B* is incorrect because it was illegal to teach slaves to read, and most slaveholders avoided doing it. Choice *C* is incorrect because most slaveholders were cruel to their slaves and did not treat them like their own children. Choice *D* is not mentioned or implied in the passage, so we can't know if Douglass made this observation.

23. C: The 4th of July signifies the independence of America from Britain; however, Americans chose to continue to enslave people in their country even after they fought for their freedom from British rule.

Choices *A*, *B*, and *C* are incorrect because the 4th of July was not directly related to the end of slavery in America or freedom and equality for slaves.

24. A: Both the first sentence and the last paragraph highlight that all of the details described about Douglass's life during and after his experience as a slave made him a remarkable abolitionist speaker. Choice *B* is incorrect because while the awful conditions are discussed, they are mentioned as a means of showing how they shaped Douglass's skill as a speaker; the conditions are not the main purpose. Choice *C* is incorrect because Douglass learning to read is one discussion point in the passage but is not the purpose of the whole passage. Choice *D* is incorrect because there is no speculation in the passage about how Douglass's life would have differed had he been born free.

25. B: Choice *A* uses similar language, but it is not the main point of disagreement. The reporter calls the loss devastating, and there's no reason to believe that the coach would disagree with this assessment. Eliminate this choice.

Choice *B* is strong since both passages mention the at-bats with runners in scoring position. The reporter asserts that the team lost due to the team failing to get such a hit. In contrast, the coach identifies several other reasons for the loss, including fielding and pitching errors. Additionally, the coach disagrees that the team even needed a hit in those situations.

Choice *C* is mentioned by the coach, but not by the reporter. It is unclear whether the reporter would agree with this assessment. Eliminate this choice.

Choice *D* is mentioned by the coach but not by the reporter. It is not stated whether the reporter believes that the team deserved to win. Eliminate this choice.

Therefore, Choice *B* is the correct answer.

26. C: Choice *A* is incorrect. The Conservative Politician definitely believes that spending on social welfare programs increases the national debt. However, the Liberal Politician does not address the cost of those programs.

Choice *B* is a strong answer choice. The Liberal Politician explicitly agrees that certain classes of people rely on social welfare programs. The Conservative Politician actually agrees that people rely on the programs, but thinks this reliance is detrimental. This answer choice is slightly off base. Eliminate this choice.

Choice *C* improves on Choice *B*. The Liberal Politician definitely believes that certain classes of people would be irreparably harmed. In contrast, the Conservative Politician asserts that the programs are actually harmful since people become dependent on the programs. The Conservative Politician concludes that people don't need the assistance and would be better off if left to fend for themselves. This is definitely the main point of disagreement.

Choice *D* is not the main point of dispute. Neither of the politicians discusses whether *all* of the nation's leaders have bootstrapped their way to the top. Eliminate this choice.

Therefore, Choice *C* is the best answer.

27. D: This passage displays clarity (the author states precisely what he or she intended), fluency (the sentences run smoothly together), and parallelism (words are used in a similar fashion to help provide rhythm). Choice *A* lacks parallelism. When the author states, "the hero acts without thinking, is living in the moment, and is repressing physical and emotional pain," the words *acts, is living* and *is repressing* are in different tenses, and, consequently, jarring to one's ears. Choice *B* runs on endlessly in the first half ("Ernest Hemingway is probably the most noteworthy of expatriate authors since his concise writing style is void of emotion and stream of consciousness and has had a lasting impact on Americans which has resonated to this very day, and Hemingway's novels are much like in American cinema.") It demands some type of pause and strains the readers' eyes. The second half of the passage is choppy: "The hero acts. He doesn't think. He lives in the moment. He represses physical and emotional pain." For Choice *C*, leaving out *expatriate* is, first, vague, and second, alters the meaning. The correct version claims that Hemingway was the most notable of the expatriate authors while the second version claims he's the most notable of any author *ever*, a very bold claim indeed. Also, leaving out *stream of* in "stream of consciousness" no longer references the non-sequential manner in which most people think. Instead, this version sounds like all the characters in the novel are in a coma!

28. C: This question focuses on the correct usage of the commonly confused word pairs of *it's/its* and *then/than*. *It's* is a contraction for *it is* or *it has*. *Its* is a possessive pronoun. The word *than* shows comparison between two things. *Then* is an adverb that conveys time. Choice *C* correctly uses *it's* and *than*. *It's* is a contraction for *it has* in this sentence, and *than* shows comparison between *work* and *rest*. None of the other answer choices use both of the correct words.

29. C: The second sentence tells of an unexpected outcome of the first sentence. Choice *A*, Choice *B*, and Choice *D* indicate a logical progression, which does not match this surprise. Only Choice *C* indicates this unexpected twist.

30. D: The object pronouns *her* and *me* act as the indirect objects of the sentence. If *me* is in a series of object pronouns, it should always come last in the series. Choice *A* is incorrect because it uses subject pronouns *she* and *I*. Choice *B* is incorrect because it uses the subject pronoun *she*. Choice *C* uses the correct object pronouns, but they are in the wrong order.

31. B: The original sentence focuses on how politicians are using the student debt issue to their advantage, so Choice *B* is the best answer choice. Choice *A* says politicians want students' votes but suggests that it is the reason for student loan debt, which is incorrect. Choice *C* shifts the focus to voters, when the sentence is really about politicians. Choice *D* is vague and doesn't best restate the original meaning of the sentence.

32. A: This answer best matches the meaning of the original sentence, which states that seasoned runners offer advice to new runners because they have complaints of injuries. Choice *B* may be true, but it doesn't mention the complaints of injuries by new runners. Choice *C* may also be true, but it does not match the original meaning of the sentence. Choice *D* does not make sense in the context of the sentence.

33. D: The problem in the original passage is that the second sentence is a dependent clause that cannot stand alone as a sentence; it must be attached to the main clause found in the first sentence. Because the main clause comes first, it does not need to be separated by a comma. However, if the dependent clause came first, then a comma would be necessary, which is why Choice *C* is incorrect. *A* and *B* also insert unnecessary commas into the sentence.

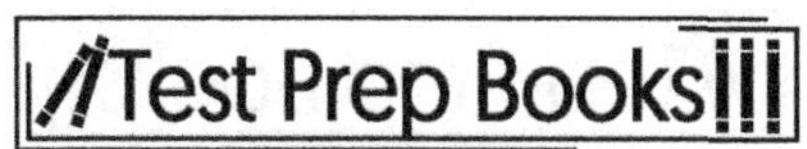

34. B: Move the sentence so that it comes before the preceding sentence. For this question, place the underlined sentence in each prospective choice's position. To keep it as-is is incorrect because the father "going crazy" doesn't logically follow the fact that he was a "city slicker." Choice *C* is incorrect because the sentence in question is not a concluding sentence and does not transition smoothly into the second paragraph. Choice *D* is incorrect because the sentence doesn't necessarily need to be omitted since it logically follows the very first sentence in the passage.

35. D: Choice *D* is correct because "As it turns out" indicates a contrast from the previous sentiment, that the RV was a great purchase. Choice *A* is incorrect because the sentence needs an effective transition from the paragraph before. Choice *B* is incorrect because the text indicates it *is* surprising that the RV was a great purchase because the author was skeptical beforehand. Choice *C* is incorrect because the transition "Furthermore" does not indicate a contrast.

36. B: This sentence calls for parallel structure. Choice *B* is correct because the verbs "wake," "eat," and "break" are consistent in tense and parts of speech. Choice *A* is incorrect because the words "wake" and "eat" are present tense while the word "broke" is in past tense. Choice *C* is incorrect because this turns the sentence into a question, which doesn't make sense within the context. Choice *D* is incorrect because it breaks tense with the rest of the passage. "Waking," "eating," and "breaking" are all present participles, and the context around the sentence is in past tense.

37. C: Choice *C* is correct because it is clear and fits within the context of the passage. Choice *A* is incorrect because "We rejoiced as 'hackers'" does not give a reason why hacking was rejoiced. Choice *B* is incorrect because it does not mention a solution being found and is therefore not specific enough. Choice *D* is incorrect because the meaning is eschewed by the helping verb "had to rejoice," and the sentence suggests that rejoicing was necessary to "hack" a solution.

38. A: The original sentence is correct because the verb tense as well as the meaning aligns with the rest of the passage. Choice *B* is incorrect because the order of the words makes the sentence more confusing than it otherwise would be. Choice *C* is incorrect because "We are even making" is in present tense. Choice *D* is incorrect because "We will make" is future tense. The surrounding text of the sentence is in past tense.

39. B: Choice *B* is correct because there is no punctuation needed if a dependent clause ("while traveling across America") is located behind the independent clause ("it allowed us to share adventures"). Choice *A* is incorrect because there are two dependent clauses connected and no independent clause, and a complete sentence requires at least one independent clause. Choice *C* is incorrect because of the same reason as Choice *A*. Semicolons have the same function as periods: there must be an independent clause on either side of the semicolon. Choice *D* is incorrect because the dash simply interrupts the complete sentence.

40. C: The rules for "me" and "I" is that one should use "I" when it is the subject pronoun of a sentence, and "me" when it is the object pronoun of the sentence. Break the sentence up to see if "I" or "me" should be used. To say "Those are memories that I have now shared" is correct, rather than "Those are memories that me have now shared." Choice *D* is incorrect because "my siblings" should come before "I."

41. A: In this example, a colon is correctly used to introduce a series of items. Choice *B* places an unnecessary comma before the word *because*. A comma is not needed before the word *because* when it introduces a dependent clause at the end of a sentence and provides necessary information to understand the sentence. Choice *C* is incorrect because it uses a semi-colon instead of a comma to join a dependent clause and an independent clause. Choice *D* is incorrect because it uses a colon in place of a comma and coordinating conjunction to join two independent clauses.

42. D: In this sentence, the first answer choice requires a noun meaning *impact* or *influence*, so *effect* is the correct answer. For the second answer choice, the sentence is drawing a comparison. *Than* shows a comparative relationship whereas *then* shows sequence or consequence. *A* and *C* can be eliminated because they contain the choice *then*. *B* is incorrect because *affect* is a verb while this sentence requires a noun.

43. C: The word *who* in the sentence is a subjective interrogative pronoun and the sentence needed a subject that begins a question. Choice *A* is incorrect. The word *whose* is a possessive pronoun and it is not being asked who owns the flowers. Choice *B* is incorrect. The word *whom* is always an objective pronoun—never a subjective one; a subjective pronoun is needed in this sentence. Choice *D* is incorrect. The word *who've* is a contraction of the words *who* and *have*. We would not say, *"Who have ordered the flowers?"*

44. D: The word *its* in the sentence is the singular possessive form of the pronoun that stands in place for the word *giraffe's*. There is one baby that belongs to one giraffe. Choice *A* is incorrect. It is a contraction of the words *it* and *is*. You would not say, *"The giraffe nudged it is baby."* Choice *B* is incorrect. We do not know the gender of the giraffe and if it was female the proper word would be *her* baby not *hers* baby. Choice *C* is incorrect. The word *them* is a plural objective pronoun and we need a singular possessive pronoun because *there* is only one giraffe doing the nudging.

45. B: The *kitten* is a singular subject and so the singular verb *pounces* should be used instead of *pounce*. Choice *A* is incorrect because the plural subject *kittens* agrees with the plural verb *show*. Choice *C* is incorrect because the singular subject *kitten* agrees with the singular verb *eats*. Choice *D* is incorrect because the singular subject *kitten* agrees with the singular verb *snuggles*.

Mathematical Reasoning

No Calculator Questions

1. D: The product of two irrational numbers can be rational or irrational. Sometimes the irrational parts of the two numbers cancel each other out, leaving a rational number. For example, $\sqrt{2} \times \sqrt{2} = 2$ because the roots cancel each other out. Technically, the product of two irrational numbers is a complex number, because real numbers are a type of complex number. However, Choice *D* is incorrect because the product of two irrational numbers is not an imaginary number.

2. C: The terms "whole numbers" and "natural numbers" include all the ordinary counting numbers $(1, 2, 3, 4, 5, \ldots)$, and sometimes zero depending on the definition used, but no negative numbers. The term "integers" includes all those numbers, their negatives, and zero. So –4 is not a whole number or a natural number, but it is an integer. It is also rational because it can be written as a ratio of two integers ($-\frac{4}{1}$); all integers are rational. It is a real number because it does not have an imaginary component (symbolized by the letter i); all integers are real numbers.

3. B: The y-intercept of an equation is found where the x-value is zero. Plugging zero into the equation for x, the first two terms cancel out, leaving -4.

4. B: If 60% of 50 workers are women, then there are 30 women working in the office. If half of them are wearing skirts, then that means 15 women wear skirts. Since none of the men wear skirts, this means there are 15 people wearing skirts.

5. B: The table shows values that are increasing exponentially. The differences between the inputs are the same, while the differences in the outputs are changing by a factor of 2. The values in the table can be modeled by the equation $f(x) = 2^x$.

Calculator Questions

6. B: To simplify the given expression, the first step is to make all exponents positive by moving them to the opposite place in the fraction. This expression becomes:

$$\frac{4b^3b^2}{a^1a^4} \times \frac{3a}{b}$$

Then the rules for exponents can be used to simplify. Multiplying the same bases means the exponents can be added. Dividing the same bases means the exponents are subtracted. Thus, after multiplying the exponents in the first fraction, the equation becomes:

$$\frac{4b^5}{a^5} \times \frac{3a}{b}$$

Therefore, we can first multiply to get:

$$\frac{12ab^5}{a^5b}$$

Then, simplifying yields:

$$12\frac{b^4}{a^4}$$

7. B: The car is traveling at a speed of 5 meters per second. On the interval from 1 to 3 seconds, the position changes by 10 meters. This is 10 meters in 2 seconds, or 5 meters in each second.

8. D: To find 60 percent of 75, multiple 75 by .60:

$$75 \times .60 = 45$$

9. B: There are two zeros for the function $x = 0, -2$. The zeros can be found several ways, but this particular equation can be factored into:

$$f(x) = x(x^2 + 4x + 4) = x(x + 2)(x + 2)$$

By setting each factor equal to zero and solving for x, there are two solutions. On a graph, these zeros can be seen where the line crosses the x-axis.

10. A: The total fraction taken up by green and red shirts will be:

$$\frac{1}{3}+\frac{2}{5}=\frac{5}{15}+\frac{6}{15}=\frac{11}{15}$$

The remaining fraction is:

$$1-\frac{11}{15}=\frac{15}{15}-\frac{11}{15}=\frac{4}{15}$$

11. A: To expand a squared binomial, it's necessary to use the First, Outer, Inner, Last (FOIL) Method.

$$(2x-4y)^2$$

$$(2x)(2x)+(2x)(-4y)+(-4y)(2x)+(-4y)(-4y)$$

$$4x^2-8xy-8xy+16y^2$$

$$4x^2-16xy+16y^2$$

12. D: In order to solve this problem, the number of feet in a yard must be established. There are 3 feet in every yard. The equation to calculate the minimum number of yards is:

$$79 \div 3 = 26\frac{1}{3}$$

If the material is sold only by whole yards, then Mo would need to round up to the next whole yard in order to cover the extra $\frac{1}{3}$ yard. Therefore, the answer is 27 yards. None of the other choices meets the minimum whole yard requirement.

13. B: Start by squaring both sides to get $1+x=16$. Then subtract 1 from both sides to get $x=15$.

14. A: Let the unknown score be x. The average will be:

$$\frac{5\times 50+4\times 70+x}{10}=\frac{530+x}{10}=55$$

Multiply both sides by 10 to get $530+x=550$, or $x=20$.

15. D: The volume of a cube is the length of the side cubed, and 5 centimeters cubed is 125 cm^3. Choice *A* is not the correct answer because that is 2×5 centimeters. Choice *B* is not the correct answer because that is 3×5 centimeters. Choice *C* is not the correct answer because that is 5×10 centimeters.

16. B: The equation can be solved by factoring the numerator into $(x+6)(x-5)$. Since that same factor exists on top and bottom, that factor $(x-5)$ cancels. This leaves the equation $x+6=11$. Solving the equation gives the answer $x=5$. When this value is plugged into the equation, it yields a zero in the denominator of the fraction. Since this is undefined, there is no solution.

17. D: This problem can be solved by using unit conversion. The initial units are miles per minute. The final units need to be feet per second. Converting miles to feet uses the equivalence statement $1\text{ mi}=$

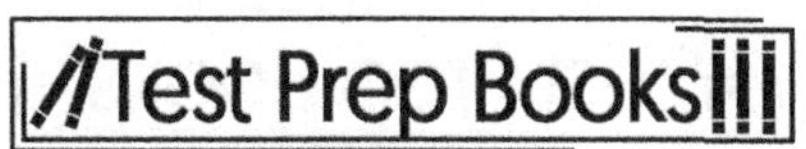

5,280 ft. Converting minutes to seconds uses the equivalence statement $1 \text{ min} = 60 \text{ s}$. Setting up the ratios to convert the units is shown in the following equation:

$$\frac{72 \text{ mi}}{90 \text{ min}} \times \frac{1 \text{ min}}{60 \text{ s}} \times \frac{5{,}280 \text{ ft}}{1 \text{ mi}} = 70.4 \frac{\text{ft}}{\text{s}}$$

The initial units cancel out, and the new units are left.

18. B: The formula can be manipulated by dividing both the length, l, and the width, w, on both sides. The length and width will cancel on the right, leaving height, h, by itself.

19. B: The domain is all possible input values, or x-values. For this equation, the domain is every number greater than or equal to zero. There are no negative numbers in the domain because taking the square root of a negative number results in an imaginary number.

20. D: This problem can be solved by setting up a proportion involving the given information and the unknown value. The proportion is:

$$\frac{21 \text{ pages}}{4 \text{ nights}} = \frac{140 \text{ pages}}{x \text{ nights}}$$

We can cross-multiply to get $21x = 4 \times 140$. Solving this, we find $x \approx 26.67$. Since this is not an integer, we round up to 27 nights. 26 nights would not give Sarah enough time.

21. D: The slope from this equation is 50, and it is interpreted as the cost per gigabyte used. Since the g-value represents number of gigabytes and the equation is set equal to the cost in dollars, the slope relates these two values. For every gigabyte used on the phone, the bill goes up 50 dollars.

22. B: 8.1

To round 8.067 to the nearest tenths place, use the digit in the hundredths place.

6 in the hundredths place is greater than 5, so round up in the tenths place.

8.0̲67

0 becomes a 1.

8.1

23. C: $y = 40x + 300$. In this scenario, the variables are the number of sales and Karen's weekly pay. The weekly pay depends on the number of sales. Therefore, weekly pay is the dependent variable (y), and the number of sales is the independent variable (*x*). Each pair of values from the table can be written as an ordered pair (*x*, *y*): (2, 380), (7, 580), (4, 460), (8, 620). The ordered pairs can be substituted into the equations to see which create true statements (both sides equal) for each pair. Even if one ordered pair produces equal values for a given equation, the other three ordered pairs must be checked.

The only equation which is true for all four ordered pairs is $y = 40x + 300$:

$$380 = 40(2) + 300 \rightarrow 380 = 380$$

$$580 = 40(7) + 300 \rightarrow 580 = 580$$

$$460 = 40(4) + 300 \rightarrow 460 = 460$$

$$620 = 40(8) + 300 \rightarrow 620 = 620$$

24. C: Christie would need 72 boards. The total can be found by converting the length and width of the base into inches and finding the number of boards for each side. Start by finding the dimensions in inches:

$$7 \text{ ft} \times \frac{12 \text{ in}}{1 \text{ ft}} = 84 \text{ in}$$

$$3.5 \text{ ft} \times \frac{12 \text{ in}}{1 \text{ ft}} = 48 \text{ in}$$

Next, divide the length of each side by 3.5 inches per board to find the number of boards needed to cover that side, and multiply by 2 to account for the opposite walls:

$$84 \text{ in} \times \frac{1 \text{ board}}{3.5 \text{ in}} \times 2 = 48 \text{ boards}$$

$$48 \text{ in} \times \frac{1 \text{ board}}{3.5 \text{ in}} \times 2 = 24 \text{ boards}$$

Finally, sum the numbers for both lengths and widths to arrive at the total number of boards needed:

$$48 \text{ boards} + 24 \text{ boards} = 72 \text{ boards}$$

25. B: The zeros of this function can be found by using the quadratic formula:

$$x = \frac{-b \pm \sqrt{b^2 - 4ac}}{2a}$$

Identifying a, b, and c can also be done from the equation because it is in standard form. The formula becomes:

$$x = \frac{0 \pm \sqrt{0^2 - 4(1)(4)}}{2(1)} = \frac{\sqrt{-16}}{2}$$

Since there is a negative underneath the radical, the answer is a complex number:

$$x = \pm 2i$$

26. D: Setting up a proportion is the easiest way to represent this situation. The proportion is $\frac{20}{\text{x}} = \frac{40}{100}$, and cross-multiplication can be used to solve for x. Here, $40\text{x} = 2{,}000$, so $\text{x} = 50$. The answer can also be found by observing the two fractions as equivalent, knowing that twenty is half of forty, and fifty is half of one-hundred.

27. C: It may help to look at this problem as a fraction: $\frac{(1.2\times10^{12})}{(3.0\times10^{8})}$. We can calculate $\frac{1.3}{3} = 0.4$, and using the rules of exponents, we can see that $\frac{10^{12}}{10^{8}} = 10^{(12-8)} = 10^{4}$. This gives us an answer of 0.4×10^{4}, which is Choice *A*, but our answer is not yet in scientific notation because the first term, 0.4, is not between 1 and 10. We can rewrite 0.4×10^{4}, multiplying the first term by 10 and subtracting 1 from the exponent, which gives 4.0×10^{3}, Choice *C*.

28. A: The relative error can be found by finding the absolute error and making it a percent of the true value. The absolute error is $36 - 35.75 = 0.25$. This error is then divided by 35.75—the true value—to find 0.7%.

29. D: To solve for x, isolate the variables from the constants. First, subtract 13 from both sides:

$$13 - 13 - \frac{3x}{4} = -11 - 13$$

$$-\frac{3x}{4} = -24$$

Next, multiply both sides by 4 to eliminate the fraction:

$$-\frac{3x}{4} \times 4 = -24 \times 4$$

$$-3x = -96$$

Finally, multiply by -3 to solve for x:

$$\frac{-3x}{-3} = \frac{-96}{-3}$$

$$x = 32$$

Therefore, the value of x is 32.

30. A: The function can be factored to identify the zeros. First, the term $3x$ is factored out to the front because each term contains $3x$. Then, the quadratic is factored into $(x + 3)(x - 2)$.

31. D: The slope is given by the change in y divided by the change in x. The change in y is $2 - 0 = 2$, and the change in x is:

$$0 - (-4) = 4$$

The slope is $\frac{2}{4} = \frac{1}{2}$.

32. B: Because this isn't a right triangle, the SOHCAHTOA mnemonic can't be used. However, the law of cosines can be used:

$$c^2 = a^2 + b^2 - 2ab\cos C$$

$$c^2 = 19^2 + 26^2 - 2 \times 19 \times 26 \times \cos 42° = 302.773$$

Taking the square root and rounding to the nearest tenth results in $c = 17.4$.

33. C: Because order *does* matter, the total number of permutations needs to be computed.

$$P(5,2) = \frac{5!}{(5-2)!} = \frac{120}{6} = 20$$

represents the number of ways that two objects can be arranged from a set of five.

34. D: A dollar contains 20 nickels. Therefore, if there are 12 dollars' worth of nickels, there are:

$$12 \times 20 = 240 \text{ nickels}$$

Each nickel weighs 5 grams. Therefore, the weight of the nickels is $240 \times 5 = 1{,}200$ grams.

Adding in the weight of the empty piggy bank, the filled bank weighs 2,250 grams.

35. B: The acceleration of the particle can be found by taking the derivative of the velocity equation. This equation is:

$$v'(t) = \frac{0 - 6(1)}{(t+3)^2} = \frac{-6}{(t+3)^2}$$

Finding the acceleration at time $t = 5$ can be found by plugging five in for the variable t in the derivative. The equation and answer are:

$$v'(5) = \frac{-6}{(5+3)^2} = \frac{-6}{64} = \frac{-3}{32}$$

36. A: Because the volume of the given sphere is 288π cubic meters, this gives:

$$\frac{4}{3}\pi r^3 = 288\pi$$

This equation is solved for r to obtain a radius of 6 meters. The formula for surface area is $4\pi r^2$, so:

$$SA = 4\pi 6^2 = 144\pi \text{ square meters}$$

37. D: We are given an angle (60°), the length of the opposite side (x), and the length of the adjacent side (13 cm). We can use the mnemonic "SOHCAHTOA," where the "TOA" reminds us that tangent equals the opposite side over the adjacent side. In other words, $\tan 60° = \frac{x}{13}$. Since $\tan 60° = \sqrt{3}$, we can calculate:

$$x = 13 \tan 60 = 13 \times \sqrt{3} = 22.52$$

38. D: The midpoint formula should be used.

$$M = \left(\frac{x_1 + x_2}{2}, \frac{y_1 + y_2}{2}\right) = \left(\frac{-1+3}{2}, \frac{2+(-6)}{2}\right) = (1, -2)$$

39. C: Set up the problem and find a common denominator for both fractions.

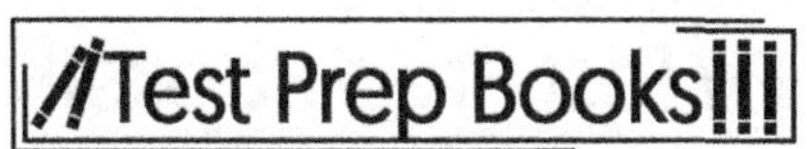

$$\frac{5}{12}+\frac{4}{9}$$

Multiply each fraction across by 1 to convert to a common denominator.

$$\frac{5}{12}\times\frac{3}{3}+\frac{4}{9}\times\frac{4}{4}$$

Once over the same denominator, add across the top. The total is over the common denominator.

$$\frac{15+16}{36}=\frac{31}{36}$$

40. A: This amount can be found by plugging $t = 1.5$ into the expression. Therefore, the baseball's altitude is equal to $-16(1.5^2) + 170 = -16(2.25) + 170 = -36 + 170 = 134$ ft.

41. A: This answer is correct because $(3 + 3i)(3 - 3i)$, using the FOIL method and rules for imaginary numbers, is:

$$9 - 9i + 9i - 9i^2 = 18$$

42. A: Using the Pythagorean theorem, we can determine the length of the hypotenuse by plugging in the lengths of the sides $a^2 + b^2 = c^2$, or $a^2 + 8^2 = 10^2$. The Pythagorean theorem tells us that $8^2 + x^2 = 10^2$, where x is the unknown side. This simplifies to $64 + x^2 = 100$, so $x^2 = 100 - 64 = 36$, and $x = \sqrt{36} = 6$ inches.

43. D: The two lines are neither parallel nor perpendicular. Parallel lines will never intersect or meet. Therefore, the lines are not parallel. Perpendicular lines intersect to form a right angle (90°). Although the lines intersect, they do not form a right angle, which is usually indicated with a box at the intersection point. Therefore, the lines are not perpendicular.

44. D: If we roll a die twice, there are 6 possibilities for the first roll and 6 for the second roll, which gives $6 \times 6 = 36$ total possibilities. Now, how many ways are there to roll exactly one 6? We could get a 6 & 1, or 6 & 2, or 6 & 3, or 6 & 4, or 6 & 5. Or the 6 could come on the second roll; we could get a 1 & 6, or 2 & 6, or 3 & 6, or 4 & 6, or 5 & 6. Counting these up, we find a total of 10 different ways to roll exactly one 6. That means our event happens in 10 out of 36 possible rolls, so the probability is $\frac{10}{36}$, which reduces to $\frac{5}{18}$.

45. C: The formula for the area of the circle is πr^2 and 10^2 is 100. Choice *A* is not the correct answer because 10 is not squared. Choice *B* is not the correct answer because that is 2×10. Choice *D* is not the correct answer because that is $r^2 \times 2$.

46. A: First, isolate the radical by adding x to both sides to obtain $\sqrt{16 - x} = x + 4$. Then, square both sides to obtain $16 - x = x^2 + 8x + 16$. This is a quadratic equation, so put it in standard form by adding x to both sides and subtracting 16 off both sides. The result is the equation $x^2 + 9x = 0$. This can be solved by factoring and setting each factor equal to zero. Therefore, $x(x + 9) = 0$ results in the two potential solutions $x = 0$ and $x = -9$. Because the original equation has a radical, these solutions must be checked to see if they are not extraneous. Plugging $x = 0$ results in $\sqrt{16 - 0} - 0 = 4$, which is true. However, plugging $x = -9$ results in $\sqrt{16 + 9} + 9 = 4$, which is not true. The only solution is 0.

Science

1. C: Choice *C* is correct. The electronegativity values increase from left to right along a row and decrease from top to bottom within a column. For example, C has a value of 2.5, and F on the right side has a value of 4.0. From F to Br, the electronegativity value decreases from 4.0 to 2.8.

2. A: Choice *A* is correct. The difference in electronegativity values between the carbon and chlorine atom is:

$$\Delta EN(C - Cl) = |EN_C - EN_{cl}| = |2.5 - 3.0| = 0.5$$

Since the value of $\Delta EN = 0.5$, the bond is polar covalent. Choice *C* is incorrect; the difference in electronegativity takes the absolute value of the difference, which should be a positive number. Choices *B* and *D* are both incorrect, since the calculated value gives the sum of the electronegativity values.

3. B: Choice *B* is correct. For a chemical bond, the atom that is more electronegative has a partial negative charge, and the atom that is the least electronegative bears a partial positive charge. The following table indicates the respective partial charges and electronegativity values. The H-Si has the correct partial charges, which are based on the electronegativity values. The electronegativity value for hydrogen is 2.0, and for silicon, it is 1.8. Hydrogen bears the partial negative charge, and silicon the partial positive charge.

Left Atom	Right Atom
H ($\delta +$) 2.1	Se ($\delta -$) 2.4
H ($\delta -$) 2.0	Si ($\delta +$) 1.8
P ($\delta +$) 2.1	Cl ($\delta -$) 3.0
Se ($\delta +$) 2.4	Br ($\delta -$) 2.8

4. A: Choice *A* is the correct answer. The S wave has a maximum velocity of 7 km/s and decreases as the depth increases, so Choices *B* and *C* can both be eliminated. Choice *C* can be eliminated as the velocity of the P wave, 12 km/s, is associated with a depth of 6,000 km. The P wave has two velocity peaks: 14 km/s, which corresponds to a depth of 2,500 km.

5. B: Choice *B* is correct. According to Figure 1, the core spans a depth ranging from 2,900 km to 63,78 km, which is 3,478 km thick. Choice *A* is incorrect since the mesosphere spans a depth from 800 km to 2,900 km, which is about 2,100 km thick. Choice *C* is incorrect since the inner core spans a depth from 5,100 km to 6,328 km, which is 1,228 km thick. The crust, Choice *D*, is incorrect because it is the thinnest layer.

6. C: Choice *C* is correct. In general seismic waves will move faster in denser regions. The passage indicates that seismic waves move faster through denser regions. Since the density increases gradually towards the Earth's center, the velocity of the seismic waves increases, which makes Choices *A* and B

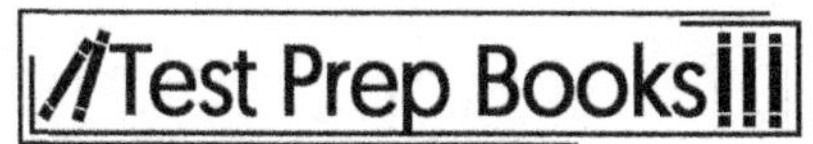

incorrect. Solid metal is denser than molten or liquid metal, which makes Choice *C* correct and Choice *D* incorrect.

7. C: There is a 99% probability of PCR testing identifying *Histoplasma*. GM assay was more specific for identifying *Aspergillus,* 95% to 85%. True positive is defined by sensitivity. The sensitivity of GM assay testing is less than 70%.

8. D: *Histoplasma* is detectable 90 days from exposure; PCR testing, Choice D, is able to detect *Histoplasma* 91 days from exposure—one day after sufficient organisms exist for detection. *Candida* is detectable 45 days from exposure; PCR testing, Choice A, is able to detect *Candida* 72 days from exposure—27 days after a sufficient number of organisms exist for detection. GM assay testing, Choice C, is able to detect *Candida* 56 days from exposure—11 days after a sufficient number of organisms exist for detection. *Aspergillus* is detectable 118 days from exposure; ELISA testing, Choice B, is able to detect *Aspergillus* 134 days from exposure—16 days after a sufficient number of organisms exist for detection. *Candida* is detectable 45 days from exposure. GM assay testing is able to detect *Candida* 56 days from exposure—11 days after a sufficient number of organisms exist for detection.

9. B: The probability that the GM assay will identify *Candida* is 69%. Therefore, there's a 31% probability that it won't be identified. ELISA sensitivity and specificity for *Histoplasma* are both greater than 80%. False-negative probabilities are represented by the specificity of a given testing method. The sensitivity and specificity for GM assay testing for Aspergillus is 59% and 94% respectively. All testing methods had greater than 80% specificity for the organisms.

10. C: The sensitivity of PCR testing for *Histoplasma* is 99%, and the test can identify the organism one day after it reaches a detectable colony size. The sensitivity for GM assay testing for *Histoplasma* is 65%. If physicians rely on GM assay testing, they may determine that the individual doesn't have the *Histoplasma* infection. Treatment will depend on the presence or absence of the infection as indicated by testing. Waiting for PCR testing is based on the sensitivity of the test, not the individual's current symptoms. The subclinical phase of *Histoplasma* is 28 days.

11. A: ELISA testing detects *Candida* three days after the organism is present in sufficient numbers to be recognized. PCR detects the organism more than three weeks after it is first detectable. ELISA testing sensitivity for *Candida* is 87% and PCR testing is 92%. However, the ability to identify the presence of the organism earlier in the process of infection (allowing early intervention) outweighs the differences in the probability of identifying the presence of the organism. There's a 92% probability that PCR testing will identify the presence of *Candida*. PCR testing is more sensitive than ELISA: 92% versus 87%.

12. A: In trial 3, the plants grown with the combined-wavelength LED's reached 150 millimeters by day 21. The plants grown with white light reached 160 millimeters by day 35. Therefore, the LED plants will be packaged 14 days sooner than the white light plants.

13. C: In trial 3, with LED lighting that included green and yellow wavelengths, plant growth was greater than trial 1 or trial 2 with either blue or red wavelengths. However, from the available information, it can only be said that green and yellow wavelengths *contributed to* plant growth in trial 3, but not that green and yellow wavelengths *alone* were responsible for plant growth in trial 3. There was plant growth in all lighting conditions.

14. B: In trial 1, from day 28 to day 35, white light growth increased by 71 millimeters, and blue light increased by 92 millimeters. In trial 2, from day 28 to day 35, white light growth increased by 71 millimeters, and red light increased by 80 millimeters. The other time periods show less growth than the span from day 28 to 35.

15. C: The average daily growth with LED lighting was not twice the white light average daily growth. LED systems did result in better growth rates and they do require less water and electricity. However, the question is based on recorded average daily growth, and that rate was not double the white light rate.

16. D: The passage says that green and yellow wavelengths are reflected by the plant. Therefore, it's expected that those wavelengths would result in slower growth than the blue or red wavelengths, which are absorbed.

17. A: Based only on Figure 2, the researchers' hypothesis was not confirmed. However, the data from Lake A did not disprove the researchers' theory, as the levels were normal. Subsequent trials were needed to confirm the hypothesis.

18. A: Increased algae levels can block sunlight, limiting growth of species inhabiting lower zones. The passage doesn't identify the effects of rainfall or cold temperatures on phytoplankton growth, so Choices *B* and *D* are incorrect. The passage identifies the effect of phosphorus and nitrogen residue on algae growth, but not as a food source for cyanobacteria.

19. B: As algae levels increase above normal, organisms in the aphotic level plants don't receive adequate light for normal growth and oxygen levels are decreased, resulting in the death of oxygen-dependent species.

20. C: Algae block the sunlight, which limits growth.

21. A: Algae growth was greater in July, which limited the amount of light reaching the lower zones of the lake, decreasing the levels of cyanobacteria. Cyanobacteria existed in less-than-normal concentrations at 20 meters, but there were measurable levels of the organisms. Algae growth at 3 meters wasn't measured. The passage states that cyanobacteria growth is associated with algae growth, not independent of algae growth.

22. A: An anemometer measures air speed. Wind is the movement of air, so an anemometer would be able to measure wind speed. A barometer, Choice *B*, measures air pressure. A thermometer, Choice *C*, measures temperature. A wind vane, Choice *D*, shows which direction the wind is blowing.

23. B: Figure 1 is a graph showing the temperature on different days. Temperature is measured using a thermometer. A rain gauge, Choice *A*, would allow a meteorologist to record amounts of rainfall. A barometer, Choice *C*, measures air pressure. An anemometer, Choice *D*, measures air speed.

24. C: A wind vane shows which direction the wind is blowing. If it is pointing north, the wind is blowing in a northern direction. It would not be blowing in an eastern direction, Choice *A*, or a southern direction, Choice *D*, since that is the opposite direction of north. A wind vane simply tells wind direction and does not determine whether a storm is coming, Choice *B*.

25. A: Looking at the line graph in Figure 2, the lowest point is marked for January, with approximately 2 mm of rainfall. April, Choice *B*, has approximately 23 mm rainfall; September, Choice *C*, has 10 mm of rainfall; and October, Choice *D*, has the highest rainfall at 60 mm.

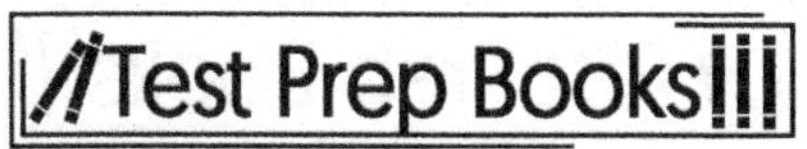

26. D: Reading the graph in Figure 2, at June, the rainfall is approximately 20 mm. The trend line marks all of the data collected for each month. For June, the trend line is just about at the 20 mm mark from the vertical axis on the left side of the graph.

27. B: Choice *B* is correct. The temperature of the lab room is 25 °C. Using Figure 1 above, if the temperature is x = 25 °C, then moving vertically along the y-axis until intersecting the graph, the density would be 0.997 g/cm^3. Choice *A* is incorrect and would refer to the density corresponding to the temperature outside, which was 25 °C. Choice *C* is incorrect since the density corresponds to a temperature of 30 °C. Choice *D* is incorrect and corresponds to a temperature near 32 °C.

28. C: Choice *C* is correct. A graduated cylinder is designed to measure the volume of any liquid in milliliters. Graduated cylinders may be indicated by the volume capacity; for example, a 10, 30, or 50 mL graduated cylinder. Choice *A* is incorrect and is used to measure the distance of solids, but can also be used to find the volume of a solid cube. Choices *C* and *D* are both incorrect and are used to find the mass of a substance.

29. C: Choice *C* is correct. The mass is the product of the density and volume.

$$d = \frac{m}{V} \rightarrow m = d \times V$$

Choices *A* and *D* can be eliminated since the formulas incorporate a division operation, which is incorrect. Choice *C* is correct, since the density of 0.998 g/cm^3 corresponds to a temperature of 20 °C.

30. B: Choice *B* is correct. As the temperature decreases from right to left (45 → 5°C), the density increases from 0.990 → 1 g/cm^3. Choice *A* is incorrect since it indicates that temperature and density are proportional; as temperature increases, the density should decrease. Choice *C* is incorrect since, like Choice *A,* it indicates a proportional relationship. Choice *D* is not accurate, since the temperature is an independent variable that changes. A more accurate statement would be: As the temperature increases, the density of water converges to a density of one or remains constant.

31. D: Choice *D* is correct. When the temperature increases, the kinetic energy (KE) of the molecules increases. The water molecules move rapidly and allow liquid water to expand. In the density formula, the volume is located in the denominator. When the volume expands, the denominator will become larger, thereby decreasing the density. As the passage indicated, the mass remains fixed based on the law of the conservation of mass. However, the volume will change due to the expansion of the water molecules with greater kinetic energy. Choice *A* can be eliminated since it's not consistent with the density/temperature relationship shown in Figure 1. Choices *B* and *C* can both be eliminated since they states that the mass of water changes, which is not consistent with the passage.

32. D: The law states that matter cannot be created or destroyed in a closed system. In this equation, there are the same number of molecules of each element on either side of the equation. Matter is not gained or lost, although a new compound is formed. As there are no ions on either side of the equation, no electrons are lost. The law prevents the hydrogen from losing or gaining mass and prevents oxygen atoms from being spontaneously spawned.

33. C: These are the coefficients that follow the law of conservation of matter. The coefficient times the subscript of each element should be the same on both sides of the equation.

34. B: For a chemical equation to be balanced, the same quantity of each element must be present on each side of the equation. On the left side of the equation, there is one Fe atom, and there are six oxygen atoms and three carbon atoms. On the right side of the equation, there is one iron atom and the rest of the oxygen and carbon atoms must be accounted for by the carbon dioxide molecules. Having three carbon dioxide molecules would give three carbon atoms and six oxygen atoms, which is equivalent to the reactants' side of the equation.

35. D: The main difference in the scientists' opinions is related to the cause of mad cow disease. The existence of species-specific proteins was used by Scientist 2 to support viral infection as the cause of the disease. Transmission rates of the disease and the conversion of normal proteins to prions were not debated in the passage.

36. A: Scientist 2 proposed that viruses were the cause of mad cow disease because chemicals inactivated the viruses. The remaining Choices are correct.

37. B: According to Scientist 1, abnormal prions are capable of "refolding" normal proteins into harmful prions. Abnormal proteins accumulate to produce the damaging conglomerations. Scientist 2 didn't find species-specific DNA and used this fact to support viruses as the cause of mad cow disease. According to Scientist 1, prions are located in the central nervous system, not the peripheral nervous system.

38. D: Mad cow disease can be spread between animal species and from animals to humans through consumption of diseased animal products. The resulting damage to the central nervous system is irreversible and will eventually cause the death of the animal. Scientist 2 would not agree that the infecting agent contained amino acids, as they form proteins, and Scientist 2 believes that a virus causes the disease. Scientist 2 demonstrated that the infected tissue of animals that were infected by a different species didn't contain species-specific DNA, which would have been the expected outcome if the infecting agent were a protein.

39. B: The accumulated masses of abnormal prions eventually form sponge-like holes in the brain and spinal cord that result in death. The passage doesn't mention the effects of the synapses, nerves, or blood supply.

40. C: The actual process of "refolding" the normal protein into the abnormal protein isn't clear from this passage. Scientist 1 claims that prions cause the disease. Prions are an abnormal protein, not a virus. Scientist 1 claims that mad cow disease is caused by abnormal proteins.

Social Studies

1. C: The innovation's primary economic benefit was to increase productivity in terms of both speed and quantity. The passage contains several examples of how the assembly increased the production of fly-wheel magnetos and motors. For example, at the end of the passage, Ford claims that the assembly line tripled the productivity for motors. Thus, Choice *C* is the correct answer. The innovation is that each worker is assigned one single operation to be completed on every product, which is the opposite of multi-tasking. So, Choice *A* is incorrect. Although the innovation might have decreased labor costs by standardizing tasks, the passage doesn't reference labor costs. Therefore, Choice *B* is incorrect. Choice *D* is the second-best answer choice. Ford mentions that men can perform three times the amount of work, but it's unclear whether this means the workforce decreased. In other words, the workforce could've remained the same or even increased to support mass production. As such, Choice *D* is incorrect.

2. A: The passage is describing an assembly line, which Henry Ford used to mass produce his famous Model T cars. An assembly line is a method of production where workers are each assigned a single task, and the products are progressively built as they slide down the assembling line. The passage mentions how the assembly was divided into operations, and the product was assembled along a line. Thus, Choice *A* is the correct answer. Although Ford mentions how his assembly line has aspects of an overhead trolley, this method of production was not called the assembly trolley. So, Choice *B* is incorrect. The assembly line did use more automation than previous methods of industrial production, but the method of assembly wasn't referred to as automated assembly. Therefore, Choice *C* is incorrect. Choice *D* is incorrect because this method also wasn't called elevated assembly, though Ford did raise the height of the assembly line to increase the speed of production.

3. D: The method improved progressively through experimentation. Ford describes how he first got the idea from the overhead trolley used by Chicago beef packers and then they later elevated the height of the assembly line. In addition, the passage explicitly references "experimenting with the speed" of line and making use of "scientific study." Thus, Choice *D* is the correct answer. Choice *A* is the second-best answer choice because the Chicago beef packing industry influenced Ford. However, Ford claims it was only loosely based on the beef industry's overhead trolley, and he repeatedly describes experimenting with the height and speed. So, Choice *A* is incorrect. The passage ends with Ford stating his intention to test the new method on a chassis, which is the automobile's frame. As such, the chassis didn't improve the method as described in the passage, so Choice *B* is incorrect. Choice *C* is incorrect because the increased number of operations was a consequence of Ford's experimentation; the method didn't improve simply because the number of operations increased. So, Choice *C* is incorrect.

4. B: President Franklin D. Roosevelt introduced the New Deal, a series of executive orders and laws passed by Congress in response to the Great Depression. The excerpt describes how President Roosevelt intended to fight poverty by using the government's power to intervene and regulate the economy. Although Choices *A*, *C*, and *D* correctly identify specific activities referenced in the excerpt, they are specific examples of the underlying philosophy in action. The underlying philosophy is an active role for government in the nation's economic affairs.

5. A: A business cycle is when the gross domestic product (GDP) moves downward and upward over a long-term growth trend, and the four phases are expansion, peak, contraction, and trough. An expansion is the only phase where employment rates and economic growth continually grow. Choice *C* is incorrect because contraction is the opposite of expansion. Choices *B* and *D* are incorrect because the peaks and troughs are the extreme points on the graph.

6. A: The correct answer is Choice *A*. Spain's Gold motivation was to profit from the raw materials (specifically the gold and silver deposits) of the Americas. England had similar motivations to profit from these raw materials, which is Choice *A* and lines up with the Spain motivation given. Choice *B* is incorrect because it deals with the religious motivations rather than the motivation of profit from raw materials. Choice *C* is incorrect because while it deals with the Netherlands' financial motivation, it is different from the goal of benefiting from raw materials. Choice *D* is incorrect because there is a given answer that is similar.

7. C: Choice *C* is the correct answer. Both England and Spain had religious motivation, including converting Natives to their religion. Both had the goal of profiting from raw materials of the Americas. Both had motivation to create settlements in the name of their countries. This gives England and Spain three common motivations. Choice *A* is incorrect because Spain and the Netherlands did not have much similarity in their motivations. The Dutch didn't colonize with religious intent, while Spain did. They both wanted to profit, but Spain wanted to profit from raw materials and the Dutch wanted to profit from a potential new trade route and the fur trade. They both had settlements; however, the Netherlands had them for fur trade, and Spain had them for domination. Choice *B* is incorrect, because England and France fewer shared motivations in common than England and Spain had. Both had religious and financial motivation. However, their financial motivations came from different areas—England from raw materials and other means, France from the fur trade. France had less interest than England in creating new settlements in the name of their country. France's interest was in the fur trade. Choice *D* is incorrect as well. The similarities between France and the Netherlands pertain to the fur trade.

8. C: The correct answer choice is *C*, 1910. There are two ways to arrive at the correct answer. You could find the four answer Choices on the graph, or you could have identified that the population never dips at any point. Thus, the correct answer needs to be the only answer choice that is earlier in time than the others, Choice *C*.

9. D: The population increased the most between 1990 and 2010. The question is asking you to identify the rate of change for each interval. Between 1990 and 2010, the population increased by approximately 60 million. Thus, Choice *D* is the correct answer. The slope of the graph is also the steepest in this interval, which represents its higher increase. Choice *A* is incorrect because between 1930 and 1950, the population increased by approximately 28 million. Choice *B* is incorrect because between 1950 and 1970, the population increased by approximately 52 million. Choice *C* is incorrect because between 1970 and 1990, the population increased by approximately 45 million.

10. B: The original thirteen colonies were Virginia, New York, Massachusetts, Maryland, Rhode Island, Connecticut, New Hampshire, Delaware, North Carolina, South Carolina, New Jersey, Pennsylvania, and Georgia. Thus, all but three cities on the list (New Orleans, Cincinnati, St. Louis) are in states that were one of the original thirteen colonies, so the correct answer is Choice *B, 7*.

11. B: Choice *B* is correct. The Bill of Rights was strongly supported by anti-Federalists as a way to protect citizens against any vagueness in the Constitution and aimed to offer specific protection against tyrannical national government since the Constitution did not have specific protection against this. The Bill of Rights was used to ensure ratification of the Constitution by gaining anti-Federalist support of the Constitution's ratification. Choice *A* is incorrect because the Judiciary Act of 1789 was created to establish a federal court system. Choice *C* is incorrect because the Virginia Plan outlined a national government with three different branches (executive, judicial, and legislative). Choice *D* is incorrect because the Federalist Papers were a series of essays to support the ratification of the new Constitution.

12. B: Choice *B* is correct. Federalists supported a strong national/centralized government over strong state governments. Choice *A* states that state governments, rather than national government, should be more powerful. This aligns more with the beliefs of the anti-Federalists, who favored strong state governments and a weaker centralized government. Choice *C* focuses on individual liberties over centralized government, which is also more in line with anti-Federalists' beliefs than Federalists'. Choice *D* is incorrect because Federalists supported the Constitution prior to the addition of the addition of explicit individual liberties.

13. C: Choice *C* is correct. Members of both the House of Representatives and the Senate must be residents of the states that they represent. Choice *A* is incorrect because the Senate has 100 members, whereas the House has 435. Choice *B* is incorrect because no member of Congress serves a four-year

term—the House members have two-year terms, and Senate members have six-year terms. Choice *D* is incorrect because the Senate is considered the upper chamber of congress and the House is considered the lower chamber of congress—no middle chamber exists.

14. D: Choice *D* is correct. There are 435 members of the House and 100 members of the Senate; therefore, there are 535 members of the U.S. Congress. Choice *A* is incorrect, as the Senate is considered to be the upper chamber of Congress. Choice *B* is also incorrect, as the Senate has unlimited debate/the filibuster. Choice *C* is incorrect because while each state has two members of the Senate, the number of House members they have is dependent on their population; therefore, many states have more House representatives than they do Senate representatives.

15. A: Choice *A* is the correct answer. While each state has only two Senators, each has a number of representatives in the House that is dependent on the population. Therefore, states can have more than two members of the House—and Choice *A* refers to three members of the same part of Congress all for the same state. Similarly, Choice *B* is incorrect because each state is limited to two representatives in the Senate, and three were given. Choice *C* is incorrect because a correct answer is given. Choice *D* is incorrect because enough information is given to determine that the example representatives would be a part of the House rather than the Senate.

16. A: Choice *A* is correct. The process listed is considered the legislative process, or the process in which a bill becomes a law. Much of the process specifically involves the legislative branch of the U.S. government (the House of Representatives and the Senate). Choice *B* is incorrect because the judicial process would refer to the judicial branch, involving the likes of the U.S. Supreme Court, which is not involved in the passing of laws. The judicial process would refer to legal proceedings. Choice *C* is incorrect, as the executive process is not an official process, but rather simply refers to the executive branch of the government. While there is some involvement of the President in the passing of laws, the process is not referred to as the executive process. Choice *D* is incorrect because there is a correct answer listed above.

17. B: Choice *B* is correct. It is the only inaccurate statement about the process listed in *Table 1.* A bill is supposed to have a sponsor in order to move forward in the process of becoming a law. Choice *A* is incorrect because it is true that the House and the Senate must approve of a bill before it moves forward to the President. Choice *C* is incorrect because the President does make the final decision in the process, by either vetoing the bill or signing it into law. Choice *D* is incorrect because only two of the three branches of the government are involved in passing a law, meaning that the approval of only two of the three branches is needed to pass a law.

18. C: Choice *C* is the correct answer. The Supreme Court has the power to determine whether laws are constitutional, and the Supreme Court is part of the judicial branch. Choice *A* is incorrect because the legislative branch has the power to create laws but does not determine their constitutionality. Choice *B* is incorrect because, again, the executive branch (specifically the President) is involved in creating laws but not in determining their constitutionality. Choice *D* is incorrect because the correct answer is listed in the prior choices.

19. D: The missing title is in the overlap between federal and state government powers. Concurrent powers are shared between federal and state governments. Choice *A* is incorrect because reserved powers are the unspecified powers of the states not expressly granted to the federal government or denied to the states by the Constitution, and left to the states by the Tenth Amendment. Choice *B* is incorrect because implied powers are the unstated powers that can be reasonably inferred from the specific powers outlined in the Constitution. Choice *C* is incorrect because delegated powers are the specific powers granted to the federal government by the Constitution.

20. D: The Electoral College is how presidential elections are decided in the United States. Presidential candidates must win a majority of electoral votes to win the election. The table shows that the Republican candidate won 271 electoral votes, which constitutes a majority of the total electoral votes. Thus, Choice *D* is correct. Although the Democratic candidate won the popular vote, the Electoral College only counts electoral votes; therefore, Choice *A* is incorrect. Choices *B* and *C* are both incorrect because neither party's candidate won a single electoral vote.

21. B: The Electoral College determines the winner of presidential races, but if a candidate doesn't win a majority of electoral votes, the Twelfth Amendment requires the House of Representatives to decide the presidency, with each state delegation voting as a single bloc. The candidate with the most votes in the House wins the election. The total number of Electoral Votes in the table provided is 261; because no candidate has a majority of the votes (131), the vote went to the House of Representatives. Choice *A* is incorrect because the table shows that Andrew Jackson won a plurality of electoral and popular votes, but he didn't receive a majority. Choices *C* and *D* are incorrect because John Quincy Adams received the most votes in the House of Representatives, so he won the presidency.

22. B: The diagram illustrates a politician's relationship with a political consultant. The politician is paying money and providing access to power in exchange for assistance with data analytics and messaging strategy. As such, the politician would likely be using the political consultant's expertise in those areas for the purpose of tailoring advertisements to voters' values and priorities. Thus, Choice *B* is correct. The politician is paying the political consultant, and there's no evidence that this relationship will save the politician money during the election cycle, so Choice *A* is incorrect. Data analysis and messaging strategy is more closely related to political advertising than increasing a candidate's personal popularity, so Choice *C* is incorrect. Choice *D* is incorrect because the diagram doesn't reference a populist economic program.

23. A: The Fifteenth Amendment expanded democracy by prohibiting the denial of voting rights based on "race, color, or previous condition of servitude," which increased the number of eligible voters. The Seventeenth Amendment expanded democracy by establishing the popular election of U.S. Senators, which gave the public more input. Thus, Choice *A* is correct. Choice *B* is incorrect because the Nineteenth Amendment guaranteed the right to vote for people regardless of sex. Choice *C* is incorrect because the Fourteenth Amendment prohibited discrimination based on race, and the Eighteenth Amendment prohibited the sale of alcohol. Choice *D* is incorrect because the Twenty-Sixth Amendment lowered the eligible voting age, and the Twelfth Amendment reformed the Electoral College.

24. B: The two most-populous states (California and Texas) possess a greater collective representation (eighty-nine representatives) than the ten least-populous states. All other answer Choices do not reflect accurate comparisons of representation.

25. A: Each state has a number of electoral college votes equal to its representatives plus its senators (which is always two). States with more representatives have more electoral college votes. Of this list, Ohio would have the most votes (16+2=18) compared to Iowa (4+2=6), Michigan (14+2=16), and South Dakota (1+2=3).

26. B: If you add up the representatives in states that gained representatives (South Carolina, Georgia, Florida, Texas, Arizona, Utah, Nevada, and Washington), the total is 111. Therefore, Choices *A*, *C*, and *D* are incorrect.

27. C: Most states that lost representatives are located in the Rust Belt—the Midwest and Northeast—as illustrated by the light grey states on the map. Choice *A* is incorrect because more states remained unchanged than lost or grained representation. Choice *B* is incorrect because most states that gained representation were scattered in the South and the West, not the Pacific Northwest and Great Plains. Choice *D* is incorrect because this map does not provide information on population levels in the various states.

28. C: Hamilton, the foremost federalist authority in the Early Republic, argued that a strong government is best reflected in strong federal leadership with one executive power instead of multiple state powers. He believed multiplying executive power is a threat to liberty. While a single executive is imperfect, and may be the target of resentment from citizens, it is the best option, according to the source. Choice *A* is incorrect because the document actually attacks classical republican values. Choice *B* is incorrect because Hamilton saw a single executive as a source of dissatisfaction, but not a major threat to liberty. Choice *D* is incorrect because its language, which is not reflected in the document, actually conveys Anti-Federalist sentiments.

29. D: President Lincoln issued the Emancipation Proclamation to free the slaves in the Confederacy, allowing the institution to continue in states and territories that didn't secede. The excerpt justifies the decision as a "fit and necessary war measure for suppressing said rebellion." Therefore, per the excerpt, emancipation was necessary to strengthen the war effort for the North. Choice *C* is the second-best answer, but the excerpt supports the contention that emancipation was part of an active war effort, rather than merely a punishment. Choices *A* and *B* are incorrect because nothing in the excerpt describes the evil of slavery or the effect of emancipation on morale in the North.

30. B: Choice *B* is the correct answer. The Agricultural Adjustment Act was signed in May of 1933, which is the earliest of all of the given options. Choice *A* is incorrect because the National Industrial Recovery Act was signed in June of 1933. Choice *C* is incorrect because the Social Security Act was signed in 1935. Choice *D* is incorrect because the Works Progress Administration was created in 1935.

31. C: Choice *C* is the correct answer. The New Deal was Franklin D. Roosevelt's response to the Great Depression, and some aspects of the New Deal still affect people today. Choice *A* is incorrect because there are parts of the New Deal that are still impactful today, namely the Social Security Act. Choice *B* is incorrect because, although it saw some support, the New Deal saw the disapproval of conservative Supreme Court justices. Additionally, many Americans had parts of the New Deal that they did not support. Choice *D* is incorrect because there is a correct statement that is given about the New Deal.

32. A: Choice *A* is the correct answer. The Works Progress Administration was created in 1935 to provide jobs to those that were unemployed. There were many types of jobs created by this program, including in the construction of new public buildings. Choice *B* is incorrect, as the Tennessee Valley Authority Act was an act that supported the building of dams within the Tennessee Valley region. Choice *C* is incorrect because the Emergency Banking Act was intended to stabilize the system of banking. Choice *D* is incorrect because the Glass-Steagall Act was a law that created the Federal Deposit Insurance Corporation and separated commercial and investment banking.

33. D: William Jennings Bryan's "Cross of Gold" is one of the most famous speeches in American history, launching his candidacy in the 1896 presidential election. The speech advocates for abolishing the gold standard and adopting a bimetallic system to provide more government control over monetary policy. The excerpt condemns the influence of banks in monetary policy, and states that the masses should act to remove the gold standard. Choices *A, B,* and *C* are incorrect. Although some of the other answer choices accurately state assertions from the excerpt, they aren't the main idea.

34. A: The Depression of 1929, commonly referred to as the Great Depression, is the largest increase to unemployment, but the question asks for the second-largest increase. According to the graph, the Panic of 1893 increased unemployment by approximately 10 percentage points; the Depression of 1920 increased unemployment by approximately 6 percentage points; the Depression of 1929 increased unemployment by approximately 15 percentage points; and the Great Recession of 2007 increased unemployment by approximately 4 percentage points. Thus, the Panic of 1893 marks the second-largest increase to unemployment.

35. A: George Washington was a slave owner himself in life, so he did not make abolition a theme in his Farewell Address. On the other hand, he was concerned that sectionalism could potentially destroy the United States, and he warned against it. Furthermore, he believed that Americans should avoid getting involved in European affairs. However, one issue that he felt was especially problematic was the formation of political parties, and he urged against it in his farewell.

GED Practice Tests #2 & #3

To keep the size of this book manageable, save paper, and provide a digital test-taking experience, the 2n and 3rd practice test can be found online. Scan the QR code or go to this link to access it:

testprepbooks.com/bonus/ged

The first time you access the test, you will need to register as a "new user" and verify your email address.

If you have any issues, please email support@testprepbooks.com

Index

Abraham Lincoln, 216, 220, 223
Absolute Value, 13, 17, 23, 24, 83
Academic Conferences, 205
Acceleration, 179, 194
Accurate, 184, 186, 187, 188
Acid, 178, 179
Activation Energy, 179
Addition, 23, 25, 52, 76, 80, 81, 83, 85, 90, 93, 103, 109, 155, 189, 197, 230
Addition Rule, 76
Adjective, 13
Adversative Conjunctions, 160
Age of Expansion, 221
Agent, 214
Agrarian, 220, 221, 225
Allusions, 135
Alternate Interior Angle Theorem, 119
Alternative Conjunctions, 160
American Civil War, 219
American Exceptionalism, 223
American Revolution, 215, 216, 218, 220, 221, 230, 232
Amplitude, 179
Angst, 226
Antebellum, 221, 223, 226
Antecedent, 160, 162
Anti-Egalitarian, 225
Anti-Federalists, 220
Apostrophe, 152, 165, 169, 170
Apothem, 56, 57
Appalachian Mountains, 217, 218, 222
Arc, 59, 60
Arc Length, 60
Archive, 224
Area, 48, 54, 55, 56, 57, 58, 59, 67, 68, 69, 70, 71, 90, 94, 226, 266, 323
Aristocratic, 226
Articles of Confederation, 218, 221, 222
Artisan, 226
Associative Property, 14
Associative Property of Addition, 25
Atlantic World, 217
Atmosphere, 177, 180
Atom, 178, 194
Atomic Mass, 178
Atoms, 287, 327
Author, 315
Axis of Symmetry, 102, 115, 116
Aztec, 219
Bar Graph, 64, 150, 189, 190, 200, 201, 236
Bar Graphs, 200, 201, 236
Bartolome De Las Casas, 215
Base, 26, 27, 51, 55, 56, 68, 70, 71, 113, 114, 178, 179, 204
Basic, 14, 27, 33
Battle at Baltimore, 219
Battle of Gettysburg, 219, 223
Battle of New Orleans, 216, 219
Bill of Rights, 218, 222
Boiling Point, 178
Bolster, 224
Boston Massacre, 215, 218, 232
Boston Tea Party, 218, 222, 232
Box Plot, 61
Box-and-Whisker Plot, 61
Boycotting, 224
Capitalism, 224
Carbon Cycle, 177
Cash-Crop Agriculture, 226
Causal, 188, 231
Causally Related, 231
Cause and Effect Structure, 138
Celsius, 42
Center, 56, 59, 61, 75, 237
Charles Townsend, 215, 222
Chemical, 287
Chemical Equations, 287
Chemical Formula, 178
Chemical Reaction, 178, 179
Chemical Reactions, 287
Chesapeake Bay, 217
Chronology, 126, 232
Church of England, 219, 220
Circle, 59, 60, 65, 70, 100, 101, 137, 191, 203, 266, 323
Circle Graph, 65, 191, 203
Circumference, 59
Classification/Division, 135

Climate, 177, 235
Climax, 137
Closed, 90
Coefficient, 42, 287, 327
Coefficients, 81, 84, 85, 98, 287
Coercive Acts, 222
Collective Noun, 156, 162
Collective Nouns, 162
Colon, 315
Colonial Economy, 224
Colons, 168
Comma, 28, 166, 167, 168, 314, 315
Common Denominator, 24, 33, 38, 39
Common Sense, 139, 216, 222
Commutative Property, 14, 21
Commutative Property of Addition, 25
Commutative Property of Multiplication, 25
Comparison/Contrast, 135
Comparison-Contrast Paragraph Structure, 138
Complex Fraction, 92
Composite Numbers, 14
Compound Event, 79, 196
Conclusion, 3, 131, 140, 141, 143, 144, 146, 147, 148, 149, 151, 180, 182, 188, 206, 229
Conclusions, 127, 139, 140, 143, 144, 145, 146, 175, 176, 188, 191, 192, 193, 202, 206, 207, 228, 229, 232, 233
Concurrent Powers, 299
Condensation, 178
Conditional Probability, 77, 78
Conductor, 178
Cone, 49, 70, 72, 84
Confederate States of America, 218
Conjunctions, 159, 160
Connotation, 133, 134
Consensus History, 223
Constant Variables, 184
Constitutional Convention, 218, 220
Context, 122, 139, 151, 152, 176, 180, 182, 227, 228, 234
Contrast, 315
Conversion Factor, 41, 47
Coordinates, 59, 97, 102, 107, 108, 110
Coordinating, 160
Correlated, 188, 230
Cotton Gin, 226
Counterargument, 131, 143, 144
Covalent Bond, 178
Covariance, 184
Crispus Attucks, 215
Critical Period, 218, 221
Cube, 53, 67, 68
Cube Root, 53
Cultural Milieu, 225
Cumulative Conjunctions, 160
Cylinder, 70, 71
Dangling Modifier, 158, 159
Dangling Modifiers, 158, 159
Dash, 169
Data Table, 197, 198
Decay, 113
Decimal Point, 37, 40, 204, 205
Decimals, 13, 14, 27, 29, 30, 33, 35, 42, 43
Declaration of Independence, 215, 216, 218, 220, 221, 230, 234
Decompose, 178
Deduction, 229
Deference, 226
Definition, 119, 120, 136, 152, 182, 207
Degree, 84, 103, 119, 149, 175, 179, 192, 204
Delegated Powers, 299
Democratic Party, 221
Democratic-Republican Party, 220
Denominator, 14, 21, 23, 30, 31, 32, 33, 35, 37, 38, 39, 40, 42, 43, 44, 45, 47, 49, 51, 52, 53, 91, 92, 93, 114
Denotation, 133
Density, 179
Dependent, 62, 96, 98, 160, 162, 166, 183, 184, 195, 198, 208, 236, 314, 315, 316, 319
Dependent Clause, 316
Dependent Variable, 62, 183, 184, 195, 198, 208, 319
Dependent Variables, 184
Description, 72, 75, 93, 128, 136, 193
Descriptive, 72, 131, 138
Descriptive Writing, 131, 138
Diction, 133
Difference, 16, 26, 28, 33, 36, 37, 38, 47, 81, 82, 93, 95, 129, 137, 158, 167, 169, 193, 206, 238
Discontent, 225
Distributive Property, 18, 26, 82
Distributive Property States, 26, 82
Dividend, 21

Division, 24, 52, 89, 90, 92, 93, 112, 135, 197, 221
Divisor, 21, 92
Domain, 120, 121, 122, 228
Dot Plot, 63
Dred Scott, 216
Duel, 225
Effect, 73, 126, 133, 135, 136, 138, 139, 141, 151, 152, 154, 180, 229, 230, 231, 232, 233, 236
Egalitarian, 225
Electoral College, 225
Electromagnetic Spectrum, 179, 181
Electron, 178
Electrons, 287, 327
Element, 287, 327
Elitism, 226
Ellipsis, 166
Emancipation Proclamation, 216, 223, 224
Energy, 178, 179, 233
Entertain, 131
Equator, 177
Ethos, 131, 132
Eurocentrism, 224
Evaluate, 40, 82, 83, 122, 142, 144, 149, 180, 181
Even Numbers, 13
Evidence, 128, 129, 131, 139, 141, 142, 143, 144, 145, 146, 147, 148, 149, 175, 180, 185, 188, 193, 194, 214, 228, 233, 236
Exemplification, 136
Experiment, 126, 180, 181, 182, 183, 184, 187, 188, 193, 195, 196, 197, 198, 206, 236
Exploitation, 224
Exponent, 51, 52, 53, 80, 83, 84, 85, 113, 204, 205
Exponential Function, 113, 116
Exponents, 51, 52, 81, 90, 94
Exposition, 137
Fact, 3, 24, 79, 127, 135, 137, 145, 146, 148, 158, 179, 180, 185, 194, 206, 207, 228, 230, 233
Factionalism, 308
Factor Tree, 25
Factors, 18, 24, 25, 26, 32, 39, 86, 88, 94, 105, 146, 148, 162, 164, 187, 188, 230, 232, 236
Fahrenheit, 42
Farewell Address, 308
Federalists, 220
Figurative, 132, 134, 135, 214
Finding, 24, 38, 39, 69, 86, 96, 99, 105, 113, 175, 181, 187
First, 287, 314, 315
First Continental Congress, 220
First Quartile, 61, 73
Five Civilized Tribes, 219
Flashback, 141
Fourth Quartile, 73
Fractional Exponents, 51
French and Indian War, 218, 232
Frequency, 63, 65, 72, 75, 179, 181
Friction, 179
Fugitive Slave Act, 223
Function, 53, 77, 84, 92, 102, 103, 109, 110, 112, 113, 114, 115, 116, 117, 118, 119, 120, 121, 122, 144, 163, 194
Function Notation, 120
Gadsden Purchase, 223
Gap, 75
Gas, 178, 179
General Andrew Jackson, 216
General Robert E. Lee, 216
Generalization, 143, 145, 180, 234
Genocidal, 224
George Washington, 308
Gerunds, 159
Gettysburg Address, 223
Gravity, 179, 193, 194
Great Compromise, 218
Great Lakes Region, 216
Greatest Common Factor, 32
Growth, 113, 183, 184, 185, 188, 190, 193, 195, 196, 197, 198, 230
Hasty Generalization, 145
Hemisphere, 177
Hierarchical, 226
Histogram, 60, 75
Histograms, 60
Historical Narrative, 224, 229
Historically Accurate, 224
Hole, 92
Hyperbole, 135
Hyphen, 168, 169
Hypotenuse, 60

Hypothesis, 180, 182, 183, 184, 185, 186, 188, 192, 197, 206
Identity Property of Addition, 26
Identity Property of Multiplication, 26
Illustrative Diagram, 199
Immigration, 226, 231
Implication, 180
Implied Powers, 299
Improper Fractions, 31
Inca, 219
Independent, 62, 78, 79, 98, 113, 146, 162, 166, 167, 168, 183, 184, 195, 196, 198, 208, 217, 218, 236, 315, 316, 319
Independent Clause, 316
Independent Variable, 62, 113, 183, 184, 185, 195, 198, 208, 236, 319
Independent Variables, 184
Index, 53, 106
Indian Removal Act, 223
Indigenous People, 224
Industrial Revolution, 221, 225
Industrialization, 225, 226
Inequality, 36, 37, 100, 101, 121
Inference, 126, 127, 128, 143, 151, 180, 183, 188, 229
Infinitive, 159
Infographics, 149, 150, 236
Informative, 129, 131, 138, 151, 152
Inherent Powers, 299
Insurgency, 226
Integers, 13, 14, 16, 17
Intersecting Lines, 98, 118
Intertextual Analysis, 140, 176
Intolerable Acts, 222
Introductions, 139
Inverse Operations, 93
Inverse Property of Addition, 26
Inverse Property of Multiplication, 26
Ion, 178
Ionic Bond, 178
Iroquois, 219
Irrational Numbers, 14
Jacksonian Democracy, 221
James K. Polk, 216
James Madison, 216, 220
James River, 217
Jamestown, 215, 217, 218
Jeffersonian Republicans, 220
Jim Crow Laws, 223
John Smith, 215
Joint-Stock Company, 224
King James I of England, 215
King Philip's War, 218
Kurtosis, 75
Law, 45, 46, 154, 155, 159, 183, 193, 222, 223
Law of Conservation of Mass, 287
Least Common Denominator, 33
Least Common Denominator (LCD), 91
Least Common Multiple, 24
Lexington and Concord, 218
Liberty Boys, 220
Like Terms, 80, 81, 82, 85, 91
Line Graph, 62, 189, 190, 202, 236
Line Graphs, 150, 202, 236
Line Plot, 63
Liquid, 177, 178, 179, 203
Logical Sequencing, 139
Logos, 131
Louisiana Purchase, 216, 219, 221
Louisiana Territory, 217
Main, 171, 172, 173, 314
Main Idea, 129, 130, 137, 139, 140, 142, 143, 171, 172, 173, 181, 185, 214, 232
Manufacturing, 221, 225, 226
Market Revolution, 221
Mass, 287, 327
Massachusetts Bay Colony, 217
Maya, 219
Mayflower, 215, 217, 221, 224
Mayflower Compact, 215, 221
Mean, 72, 73, 74, 75, 76, 133, 152, 154, 163, 175, 187, 237
Median, 61, 72, 73, 74, 75, 237
Mesoamerica, 216
Message, 131, 137, 140, 162, 229
Metaphor, 134
Metric System, 26, 42
Mexican-American War, 216, 219, 223, 233
Middle Colonies, 217
Minutemen, 220
Misplaced, 158
Misplaced Modifier, 158
Mississippi River, 216, 217
Mixed Numbers, 31, 33

Mode, 72, 73, 74, 75, 237, 238
Model, 37, 53, 80, 113, 122, 183, 193, 194
Modernism, 223
Modifiers, 155, 158, 159
Mohegan, 220
Momentum, 179, 225
Monomial, 80, 84, 86
Motive, 128
Multiples, 24
Multiplication, 24, 25, 52, 76, 83, 85, 90, 91, 92, 93, 103, 197
Multiplication Rule, 76
Mystic River Valley, 217
Narragansett, 220
Narration, 136, 137
Negating, 148, 149
Negative Correlation, 62, 196
Negative Exponents, 52, 90
New England Colonies, 217
New Left, 223, 233
Normal Distribution, 75
Nuanced, 224
Numerator, 21, 22, 23, 30, 31, 32, 33, 35, 37, 38, 39, 42, 44, 45, 49, 51, 52, 53, 90, 91, 92, 93, 114
Observation, 145, 182, 183, 197
Odd Numbers, 13
Olmec, 219
Ones, 66, 103, 132, 134, 162, 197, 232
Orbit, 177, 179
Ordered Pair, 62, 97, 107, 108, 115, 117, 118, 120, 319
Ordering, 36, 37, 39
Outlier, 61, 73, 75
Outliers, 61, 72, 73, 74, 75
Oxidation, 178
Parabola, 102, 104, 113, 115, 116, 121
Paradigm Shifting, 224
Paragraph, 315
Parallel Postulate, 118, 119
Parallel Structure, 159
Paraphrasing, 141
Parentheses, 14, 18, 81, 82, 168, 169
Parliament, 220
Participles, 315
Past, 315
Pathos, 131, 132
Patriots, 218, 220
PEMDAS, 52
Pequot Indians, 218, 220
Pequot War, 218, 220
Percentage, 35, 42, 43, 44
Percentiles, 74
Perfect Square, 53
Perimeter, 54, 55, 56, 57, 59, 71, 89
Perpendicular, 56, 118
Personification, 134, 135
Persuasive, 129, 131, 135, 229
Pie, 38, 65, 150, 161, 203, 236
Pie Chart, 38, 65, 150
Pie Charts, 150
Place Value, 27, 35
Plane, 67, 104, 106, 107, 108, 112, 113, 121, 195
Plantations, 226
Plebeian, 226
Plymouth, 215, 217, 219, 221, 224
Plymouth Harbor, 217
Pocahontas, 215
Point-Slope Form, 117, 118
Polynomial, 40, 84, 85, 86, 88, 89, 90, 92, 94, 113
Polynomial Function, 84, 113
Popular Media, 205
Populism, 221
Position, 107, 130, 131, 135, 149, 158, 228
Positive Correlation, 62, 188, 196
Postmodernism, 223
Powhatan, 215
Precise, 185, 186, 205
Prefix, 27
Prefixes, 26
Premises, 144, 146, 147, 149
President, 308
Primary Sources, 227, 234, 235
Prime Factorization, 25
Prime Meridian, 177
Prime Numbers, 13
Probability Distribution, 77
Problem, 2, 24, 45, 46, 48, 49, 50, 51, 53, 54, 55, 70, 71, 81, 88, 89, 92, 94, 95, 100, 121, 122, 123, 136, 137, 138, 142, 144, 156, 164, 182, 183, 318
Problem-Solution Structure, 138

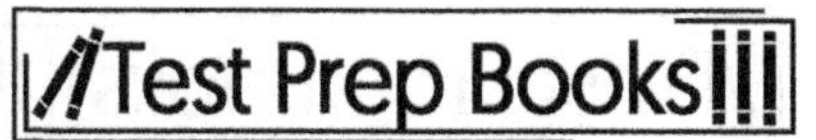

Proclamation of 1763, 222
Product, 18, 24, 25, 26, 32, 79, 81, 86, 89, 93, 105, 118, 162, 196, 204, 224, 226
Products, 287
Progressivism, 223
Pronoun, 253, 256, 314, 315, 316
Pronoun Person, 157
Pronoun Reference, 162
Pronoun-Antecedent Agreement, 162
Proper Fractions, 31
Proselytizing, 224
Protesting, 224
Purpose, 130, 131, 133, 135, 138, 140, 141, 142, 181, 185, 197, 205, 227, 233
Quadratic Equation, 102, 103, 104, 105, 113
Qualitative, 182, 188, 197
Qualitative Observation, 182
Quantitative, 182, 188, 189, 191, 192, 197, 215
Quantitative Observations, 182
Quebec Act, 222
Quotient, 21, 24, 93
Racial Exclusivity, 226
Racist, 226
Radical, 53, 106, 219
Radioactivity, 178
Radius, 49, 59, 60, 70, 72, 266
Random Errors, 187
Range, 5, 60, 66, 72, 75, 76, 77, 120, 121, 122, 186, 203, 217, 237, 238
Rate, 45, 46, 47, 72, 89, 109, 110, 112, 114, 117, 118, 163, 164, 179, 186
Rate of Change, 109, 110, 114, 117, 118
Rates, 40, 41
Rational Expressions, 90, 91, 92, 94
Rational Numbers, 14
Ratios, 31, 40, 41, 47, 48, 49
Reactant
Reactants, 287
Real Numbers, 14
Reasonableness, 146
Reciprocal, 26, 53, 92, 118
Reciprocal Numbers, 26
Reconstruction, 221, 223
Rectangular Prism, 67, 68
Rectangular Pyramid, 68
Reductive, 223
Region Graph, 203
Regular, 29
Relation, 106, 119, 120, 184, 186, 236
Relationship, 36, 40, 41, 47, 48, 62, 89, 94, 95, 103, 108, 111, 112, 119, 122, 129, 138, 139, 141, 142, 179, 183, 188, 194, 195, 196, 201, 206, 229, 231, 232, 316
Remainder, 13, 21, 22, 23, 34
Repeating, 237
Republic, 217, 225, 228
Republic of Texas, 217, 225
Republican Party, 220
Research, 3, 131, 132, 175, 180, 185, 188, 197, 205, 206, 207, 228, 235
Reservations, 217
Reserved Powers, 299
Resistance, 179, 232
Resolution, 137
Revisionism, 225
Revolve, 177
Rhetoric, 226
Rhetorical Device, 136
Rhetorical Mode, 135
Rhetorical Questions, 132
Rhetorical Strategy, 135
Rio Grande River, 217, 231
Rising Action, 137
Roanoke Island, 217
Root, 39, 51, 52, 53, 106, 180
Roots, 51, 53, 90, 94
Run-on Sentence, 162, 164
Salt, 179
Sample, 75, 184, 192, 197, 204, 237
Sanitize, 225
Savage, 224
Scale Factor, 41, 48, 53
Scatter Diagram, 191
Scatter Plot, 62, 191, 192, 201, 202
Scatter Plots, 201, 202
Scientific Journals, 205
Scientific Method, 138, 180
Scientist, 176, 180, 181, 182, 183, 184, 185, 187, 206, 207
Second, 314
Second Continental Congress, 220
Second Quartile, 61, 73
Secondary Sources, 227, 232, 233, 234, 235
Sectional Crisis, 221

Seismic, 177
Self-Sufficiency, 225
Semicolon, 167, 315
Sentence, 173, 254, 256, 314, 315, 316
Sentence Fragment, 163, 164
Separatists, 217, 219, 221
Sequence, 126, 137, 139, 141, 232
Sequence of Events, 126, 141
Sequence Structure, 137
Sequential Order, 126
Simile, 134
Simple Event, 79, 196
Simplified, 52, 54, 70, 71, 81, 82, 83, 90, 91, 92, 94, 96, 106
Skewed Left, 75
Skewed Right, 75
Slavery, 216, 219, 224, 226, 227, 230, 231
Slope, 62, 95, 97, 101, 102, 109, 110, 112, 114, 117, 118, 263, 321
Slope-Intercept Form, 95, 97, 110, 112, 114, 117
Solar System, 177
Solution, 19, 20, 22, 23, 26, 30, 34, 35, 41, 42, 45, 49, 83, 95, 96, 97, 98, 99, 100, 101, 118, 136, 138, 158, 179, 233
Southern Colonies, 217
Sphere, 70, 177
Spurious, 226
Square Root, 39, 51, 53, 74, 104, 106
Stamp Act Controversy, 218
Stamp Act of 1765, 218, 222
Stance, 130, 131, 142, 233
Standard Deviation of X, 74
Star-Spangled Banner, 219, 222
Starving Time, 218
Stem-and-Leaf Plot, 66
Sub-Conclusion, 144
Subject, 3, 4, 89, 129, 131, 132, 133, 140, 142, 147, 155, 156, 157, 160, 161, 162, 163, 185, 186, 197, 223, 225, 233, 235, 256, 314, 315, 316
Subjugation, 225
Subordinate, 164, 166
Subordinating, 160
Subscript, 287, 327
Subscripts, 287
Substitution, 96
Subtraction, 23, 24, 52, 55, 76, 80, 81, 83, 85, 89, 90, 93, 197
Suffrage, 221, 226
Sum, 14, 15, 16, 23, 25, 26, 32, 54, 58, 60, 71, 72, 74, 79, 80, 81, 82, 84, 93, 95, 100, 119, 187, 196, 203, 237
Summarizing, 140, 141, 232
Summation Notation, 72
Supporting Details, 129, 130, 142, 214
Surface Area, 67, 68, 69, 70, 71, 72
System, 327
System of Equations, 96, 97, 98, 99, 118
Systematic Errors, 187
Tables, 60, 95, 108, 112, 121, 149, 150, 175, 176, 177, 181, 197, 206, 208, 227, 234, 235, 236
Tally Chart, 67
Tea Act of 1773, 222
Tectonic, 177
Tenths, 37, 319
Terminological, 225
Terms, 39, 50, 75, 80, 81, 82, 84, 85, 89, 91, 103, 121, 122, 133, 135, 141, 156, 176, 177, 178, 179, 180, 181, 182, 187, 188, 193, 214, 215, 223, 224, 229, 230, 236, 266
Textual Evidence, 143, 149, 214
the Quartering Act, 222
Theory, 180, 183, 185, 193, 194, 199
Thesis Statement, 142
Third Quartile, 61, 73
Thomas Jefferson, 216, 219, 220, 225
Thomas Paine, 216, 222
Three-Fifths Compromise, 219
Tone, 126, 127, 132, 133, 140, 141, 172
Topic, 129, 130, 132, 135, 142, 143, 146, 169, 188, 191, 192, 206, 214, 230, 233
Tories, 220
Townsend Acts, 222
Trans-Appalachia, 218
Transitions, 139, 164
Treaty of Ghent, 222
Treaty of Guadalupe Hidalgo, 223
Treaty of Paris, 222
Treaty of Paris (1783), 222
Tyranny, 226, 233
Ulysses S. Grant, 216
Uniform Probability Distribution, 77, 78

Unit Fraction, 38
Unit Rates, 40, 47
Urbanization, 226
US Constitution, 222
Variance of X, 74
Venn Diagrams, 138
Verb, 256, 316
Vertex, 68, 102, 107, 115, 116
Vertical Asymptote, 92
Virtue, 225
Voltage, 179
Volume, 49, 67, 68, 70, 71, 72, 179
War of 1812, 216, 219, 222
Water, 72, 177, 178, 184, 186, 207, 217, 228
Weather, 177
White Supremacy, 216, 225
Whole, 2, 24, 25, 36, 37, 38, 39, 51, 53, 65, 90, 96, 118, 122, 140, 141, 148, 150, 156, 164, 230, 260, 318
Whole Numbers, 13, 32, 33
William Bradford, 215, 221
Wind, 177, 233
Working Class, 221, 225
Zero Correlation, 196
Zeros of Polynomial Functions, 113

Dear GED Test Taker,

Thank you again for purchasing this study guide for your ASWB Bachelors exam. We hope that we exceeded your expectations.

Our goal in creating this study guide was to cover all of the topics that you will see on the test. We also strove to make our practice questions as similar as possible to what you will encounter on test day. With that being said, if you found something that you feel was not up to your standards, please send us an email and let us know.

We would also like to let you know about other books in our catalog that may interest you.

HiSET

This can be found on Amazon: amazon.com/dp/1637753357

SAT

This can be found on Amazon: amazon.com/dp/1637759878

ACT

This can be found on Amazon: amazon.com/dp/163775583X

ACCUPLACER

This can be found on Amazon: amazon.com/dp/1637750250

We have study guides in a wide variety of fields. If the one you are looking for isn't listed above, then try searching for it on Amazon or send us an email.

Thanks Again and Happy Testing!
Product Development Team
info@studyguideteam.com

FREE Test Taking Tips Video/DVD Offer

To better serve you, we created videos covering test taking tips that we want to give you for FREE. **These videos cover world-class tips that will help you succeed on your test.**

We just ask that you send us feedback about this product. Please let us know what you thought about it—whether good, bad, or indifferent.

To get your **FREE videos**, you can use the QR code below or email freevideos@studyguideteam.com with "Free Videos" in the subject line and the following information in the body of the email:

a. The title of your product

b. Your product rating on a scale of 1-5, with 5 being the highest

c. Your feedback about the product

If you have any questions or concerns, please don't hesitate to contact us at info@studyguideteam.com.

Thank you!

Made in United States
North Haven, CT
15 July 2023